To John and Mabel and to the memory of Don and Mary

Special Populations in College Counseling

A Handbook for Mental Health Professionals

edited by

Joseph A. Lippincott
Ruth B. Lippincott

AMERICAN COUNSELING ASSOCIATION
5999 Stevenson Avenue • Alexandria, VA 22304
www.counseling.org

Special Populations in College Counseling
A Handbook for Mental Health Professionals

10   9   8   7   6   5   4   3   2

American Counseling Association
5999 Stevenson Avenue
Alexandria, VA 22304

Director of Publications • Carolyn C. Baker

Production Manager • Bonny E. Gaston

Editorial Assistant • Catherine Brumley

Copy Editor • Sharon Sites

Cover photo by Garry Walz.
Cover and text design by Bonny E. Gaston.

Library of Congress Cataloging-in-Publication Data
Lippincott, Joseph A., and Lippincott, Ruth B.
Special populations in college counseling: a handbook for mental health professionals/edited by Joseph A. Lippincott and Ruth B. Lippincott
    p. cm.
Includes bibliographical references and index.
ISBN-13: 978-1-55620-258-2 (alk. paper)
ISBN-10: 1-55620-258-X (alk. paper)
1. College students—Counseling of—Handbooks, manuals, etc. 2. College students—Mental health services—Handbooks, manuals, etc. 3. Counseling in higher education—Handbooks, manuals, etc. I. Lippincott, Ruth, A. II. American Counseling Association. III. Title.
RC451.4.S7L57 2006
616.89'00711—dc22   2006009501

Table of Contents

Section 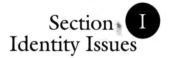 I
Identity Issues

Section II
Culture, Ethnicity, Class, and Age Issues

Section III
Developmental and Situational Issues

Section Ⅳ
Medical, Physical, and
Severe Psychological Issues

Preface

Joseph A. Lippincott

College Counseling: Changes and Challenges

College counseling in the 21st century is a profession experiencing changes on multiple fronts. The steady increase in numbers of matriculated college students (U.S. Department of Education, 2004) brings with it a concomitant growth among the numbers of students seeking counseling services. As numbers of counseling center clients continue to rise, many institutions are finding that the human and financial resources needed to provide a robust standard of care are not increasing accordingly, and, at some institutions, resources are actually decreasing (Keeling & Heitzmann, 2003). In addition, there are often concerns about administrative decisions to outsource counseling services, along with the specter of managed care (Williams & Edwardson, 2000). Counseling center staff members are continually challenged to find creative ways not only to manage finite resources but also, more important, to continue to be effective allies for their clients.

In addition to basic resource restrictions, college counselors are working with a population of students who are presenting with increasingly complicated and serious counseling issues (Benton, Robertson, Tseng, Newton, & Benton, 2003; Pledge, Lapan, Heppner, Kivlighan, & Roehlke, 1998). The severity of psychological problems is such that one writer made the overt comparison between college counseling centers and community mental health clinics (Rudd, 2004).

Witness as well the warm reception to a popular press book about the topic entitled *College of the Overwhelmed: The Campus Mental Health Crisis and What You Can Do About It* (Kadison & DiGeronimo, 2004). The book is intended not only for students and their parents but also for administrators and counselors. In the book, the authors asserted that "there is a crisis on our campuses. Depression, sleep disorders, substance abuse, anxiety disorders, eating disorders, impulsive behaviors (including sexual promiscuity and self-mutilation), and even suicide are no longer rare anomalies. They are part of college life" (p. 153).

It should be noted that increases in the numbers of persons seeking mental health services, particularly for severe disorders, are also occurring in the non-collegiate, general adult population. A special article in *The New England Journal of Medicine* (Kessler et al., 2005) presented research suggesting that the past decade has seen significant increases in adults seeking treatment, even though the prevalence rates of mental health disorders among the same group have not increased significantly. The fact that more adults are choosing to seek these services is indicative of an increasing appreciation among the general population of the value of counseling and other mental health services.

The increase in the numbers and the seriousness of problems among college students is paralleled by "momentous changes in the demographics of today's college student population" (Kitzrow, 2003, p. 167). The result of these changes is an increase not only in the diversity of the students themselves but also in the variety and complexity of the issues, concerns, and conflicts they present. The guidance-oriented, developmental approach in college counseling of past generations has evolved into an era in which college counselors must be confident, comfortable, and competent in their work among a rich mosaic of students.

There are select counselors on college campuses whose work is population-specific (e.g., alcohol and other drug specialists). However, the vast majority of college counselors are more integrative regarding their clinical skills and techniques, and especially regarding their client caseloads. College counselors, by virtue of the changing nature of their client populations, are becoming generalists who must be able to work effectively with a vast variety of clients, presenting an equally vast variety of issues and concerns. As Kitzrow (2003) stated,

> Just as the demographics of the current generation of college students have changed considerably from the past, so have their needs, including their mental health needs. The need to provide counseling for such a broad range of students and issues . . . is one of the major challenges facing college counseling centers. (p. 168)

The information contained in this book is intended to assist counselors in meeting these challenges.

Goals and Audience of This Book

The goals of this book are twofold. The first goal is to introduce counselors to historical, theoretical, and practical information about college student populations with whom they are unfamiliar. The second and foremost goal is to provide salient therapeutic, clinical knowledge and skills to enable clinicians to engage more effectively in their counseling work with clients, especially those clients described among the special populations in this book.

This book is intended for counselors, psychologists, and other mental health professionals who work with college students in a counseling environment either on- or off-campus, including private practitioners, community agency counselors, and inpatient setting clinicians. This book should also prove useful to college administrators and policymakers, faculty members (particularly those in graduate counseling, psychology, social work, and mental health nursing), and other professionals who are concerned about college students' mental health and well-being.

This book should be of particular interest and use, however, to college counselors. The increasing diversity of college students presents an on-going challenge to counselors to become familiar with the unique stressors and issues presented by each of the different populations. Education is the key element through which counselors maintain their effectiveness in this changing environment. Continued learning occurs through course work, workshops and seminars, conferences, and familiarity with current professional literature. This book is intended to provide a resource that will enhance the knowledge and effectiveness of individuals who provide counseling services to college students.

What Makes These Populations Special?

Counselors working with college students are fortunate to have available a body of professional literature that addresses many of the major life experiences and clinical issues that their clients are experiencing. College student depression and suicidal ideation, anxiety, and eating disorders are among the issues discussed in the literature (e.g., Kisch, Leino, & Silverman, 2005; Moo-Estrella, Perez-Benitez, Solis-Rodriguez, & Arankowsky-Sandoval, 2005; Thome & Espelage, 2004). Current literature also discusses issues in counseling female, gay and lesbian, and racial and ethnic minority students (Constantine, 2002; Ellis, Robb, & Burke, 2005; Lee, 2006; Lucas & Berkel, 2005; Palma & Stanley, 2002). In addition, texts discussing college counseling center issues such as programmatic and organizational approaches, scope of practice, and ethical concerns are represented (Archer & Cooper, 1998; Davis & Humphrey, 2000; Stanley & Manthorpe, 2002). Within the existing literature, however, there is an underrepresentation of a number of specific groups among college students. Each of the special populations discussed in this book was chosen for inclusion because of the scant information existing in the literature concerning that population, particularly information about the clinical skills, approaches, and techniques suggested in working with that population.

The reader is cautioned, however, to avoid thinking in overly generalized or stereotypical terms about any of the student populations described in this book. There are variations and idiosyncrasies within each special population that make assignation of each population into one of four sections of the book particularly challenging. Further, each student is unique and defies any singular categorization. Some students may not present any of the issues identified with their special population, and other students may be appropriately included in and present issues associated with several of the special populations.

The first section of this book describes students who are experiencing issues of identity on some level. These issues are similar to the age-specific maturational phenomena portrayed in Erikson's (1959) model of psychological development. These students, however, are simultaneously experiencing evolutions of self-identity ranging from temporary and situation-specific to life-long. Counselors working with these special populations often explore existential concerns, self-labeling, and peer acceptance issues.

The students discussed in the second section of this book find themselves facing stressors and biases that are related to age, culture and ethnicity, and class. Although much has been written regarding diversity and multiculturalism, there still remain groups of individuals who have been relatively invisible on campuses as well as in the literature. For many students in these special populations, counseling issues include a sense of heredity or personal and familial legacy that is intrinsic in their everyday lives and sense of selves.

Situational factors are a main feature among the special populations in the third section of this book. The students represented by these populations seek counseling to resolve the stressful or painful consequences of negative experiences or overt trauma. While treating an existing problem, counselors often simultaneously develop strategies with their clients for avoiding recurrences of that same problem. Present, immediate emotional distress is typically a focus in treatment, with concomitant exploration of ways and means to minimize future distress or occurrences. Many of the students who have experienced severe trauma require longer term follow-up interventions.

The final section of this book focuses on students whose issues are more protracted or intrinsic in nature. Many of these students experience lifelong conditions that include coping mechanisms and adaptation, rehabilitative technologies, and self-care issues. Some of these students experience vacillations between reduction and exacerbation of symptoms. These special populations are, fortunately, becoming more visible on campuses, but they present significant challenges for counselors who are unfamiliar with the students' unique stressors and lifestyle issues.

Increases in the number and diversity of college students and in the complexity and severity of their problems present an on-going challenge for the individuals who provide counseling services to these students. It can also be an ongoing struggle to find the resources needed to counsel students who represent populations that are unfamiliar to the counselor. It is hoped that this book will provide such a resource, contributing to the skills and knowledge base of its readers.

References

Archer, J., Jr., & Cooper, S. (1998). *Counseling and mental health services on campus: A handbook of contemporary practices and challenges.* San Francisco: Jossey-Bass.

Benton, S. A., Robertson, J. M., Tseng, W. C., Newton, F. B., & Benton, S. L. (2003). Changes in counseling center client problems across 13 years. *Professional Psychology: Research and Practice, 34,* 66–72.

Constantine, M. G. (2002). Predictors of satisfaction with counseling: Racial and ethnic minority clients' attitudes towards counseling and ratings of their counselor's general and multicultural counseling competence. *Journal of Counseling Psychology, 49,* 255–263.

Davis, D. C., & Humphrey, K. M. (Eds.). (2000). *College counseling: Issues and strategies for a new millennium*. Alexandria, VA: American Counseling Association.

Ellis, L., Robb, B., & Burke, D. (2005). Sexual orientation in United States and Canadian college students. *Archives of Sexual Behavior, 34,* 569–581.

Erikson, E. H. (1959). *Identity and the life cycle.* New York: International Universities Press.

Kadison, R., & DiGeronimo, T. F. (2004). *College of the overwhelmed: The campus mental health crisis and what you can do about it.* San Francisco: Jossey-Bass.

Keeling, R. P., & Heitzmann, D. (2003). Financing health and counseling services. *New Directions for Student Services, 103,* 39–58.

Kessler, R. C., Demler, O., Frank, R. G., Olfson, M., Pincus, H. A., Walters, E. E., et al. (2005). Prevalence and treatment of mental disorders, 1990 to 2003. *The New England Journal of Medicine, 352,* 2515–2523.

Kisch, J., Leino, V. T., & Silverman, M. M. (2005). Aspects of suicidal behavior, depression, and treatment in college students: Results from the Spring 2000 National College Health Assessment Survey. *Suicide & Life-Threatening Behavior, 35,* 3–13.

Kitzrow, M. A. (2003). The mental health needs of today's college students: Challenges and recommendations. *National Association of Student Personnel Administrators, 41,* 167–181.

Lee, C. C. (Ed.). (2006). *Multicultural issues in counseling: New approaches to diversity* (3rd ed.). Alexandria, VA: American Counseling Association.

Lucas, M. S., & Berkel, L. A. (2005). Counseling needs of students who seek help at a university counseling center: A closer look at gender and multicultural issues. *Journal of College Student Development, 46,* 251–266.

Moo-Estrella, J., Perez-Benitez, H., Solis-Rodriguez, F., & Arankowsky-Sandoval, G. (2005). Evaluations of depressive symptoms and sleep alterations in college students. *Archives of Medical Research, 36,* 393–398.

Palma, T. V., & Stanley, J. L. (2002). Effective counseling with lesbian, gay, and bisexual clients. *Journal of College Counseling, 5,* 74–90.

Pledge, D. S., Lapan, R. T., Heppner, P. P., Kivlighan, D., & Roehlke, H. J. (1998). Stability and severity of presenting problems at a university counseling center: A 6-year analysis. *Professional Psychology: Research and Practice, 29,* 386–389.

Rudd, M. D. (2004). University counseling centers: Looking more and more like community clinics. *Professional Psychology: Research and Practice, 35,* 316–317.

Stanley, N., & Manthorpe, J. (2002). *Students' mental health needs: Problems and responses.* London: Jessica Kingsley.

Thome, J., & Espelage, D. L. (2004). Relations among exercise, coping, disordered eating, and psychological health among college students. *Eating Behaviors, 5,* 337–351.

U.S. Department of Education. (2004). *Digest of education statistics 2003.* Washington, DC: Author.

Williams, E. N., & Edwardson, T. L. (2000). Managed care and counseling centers: Training issues for the new millennium. *Journal of College Student Psychotherapy, 14,* 39–58.

About the Editors

Joseph A. Lippincott, Ph.D., is a Professor and Director of Intern Training at Kutztown University Counseling Services in Kutztown, Pennsylvania. He is a certified clinical specialist in adult psychiatric/mental health nursing, with an M.S. (Psychiatric Nursing) from Rutgers University and a Ph.D. (Counseling Psychology) from Lehigh University. Dr. Lippincott has more than 20 years of experience in the college counseling field. In addition to numerous articles in various journals, including those of the American Medical Association and the American Psychological Association, he has authored book chapters on counseling expatriates and on cross-cultural treatment issues among Asian sojourners and international students. He has also presented papers at international conferences throughout the United States and Canada as well as in Argentina, Australia, China, Italy, Scotland, and Turkey.

Ruth B. Lippincott, Esq., is a corporate in-house commercial attorney at Air Products and Chemicals, Inc., a company with operations in more than 30 countries and 20,000 employees around the globe, headquartered in Allentown, Pennsylvania. Through her drafting and negotiation of contracts and other legal instruments and her review and revision of memoranda, letters, press releases, and corporate documents, Ms. Lippincott has the opportunity to hone her editing skills on a daily basis. She is also the author of a publication issued by the U.S. Department of Commerce, coauthor of a book chapter published by the American Counseling Association, copresenter on acculturation issues at various international conferences, and a recurrent presenter of training throughout her company on topics such as proper drafting of contracts, memoranda, and other documentation.

Contributors

Cheryl Blalock Aspy, Ph.D.
University of Oklahoma College of
Medicine

Mark E. Beecher, Ph.D.
Brigham Young University

James J. Bergin, Ed.D.
Georgia Southern University

Joyce Williams Bergin, Ed.D.
Armstrong Atlantic State University

Ian Birky, Ph.D.
Lehigh University

Timothy Black, Ph.D., CCC
University of Victoria, Victoria,
British Columbia, Canada

Scott Browning, Ph.D.
Chestnut Hill College

Lynne Carroll, Ph.D.
University of North Florida

Laura Hensley Choate, Ed.D.
Louisiana State University

Juneau Mahan Gary, Psy.D.
Kean University

Kevin F. Gaw, Ph.D.
University of Nevada, Reno

Neil German, M.A.
Webster University, Geneva,
Switzerland

Gary G. Gintner, Ph.D.
Louisiana State University

Kathleen Hartman, Ed.D.
Kutztown University

Shannon Hodges, Ph.D.
Niagara University

Rachel Hoffman, M.A.
Youngstown State University

Stacey Ilko-Hancock, Psy.D.
Youngstown State University

Kelley Kenney, Ed.D.
Kutztown University

Donna Knox, M.Ed., L.P.C.
Kutztown University

D. Shane Koch, Rh.D., CRC
Southern Illinois University,
Carbondale

Victoria E. Kress, Ph.D.
Youngstown State University

Joseph A. Lippincott, Ph.D.
Kutztown University

Laurane S. McGlynn, M.S.
Chestnut Hill College

Patricia Miron, MCAT, LPC
Chestnut Hill College

Tiffany O'Shaughnessy, B.A.
Lehigh University

Aaron Petuch, B.A.
Youngstown State University

Julie E. Preece, Ph.D.
Brigham Young University

Norman L. Roberts, Ph.D.
Brigham Young University

Lauri L. Rush, Psy.D.
Gallaudet University

Bruce S. Sharkin, Ph.D.
Kutztown University

Kendra L. Smith, M.A., LPC
Gallaudet University

Michael N. Sorsdal, M.A.
Private Practice, Victoria, British
    Columbia, Canada

Heather Trepal, Ph.D.
University of Texas, San Antonio

Marvin J. Westwood, Ph.D.
University of British Columbia,
    Vancouver, British Columbia,
    Canada

Robyn L. Williams, Ph.D.
Troy University, Montgomery
    Campus

Brian Wlazelek, Ph.D.
Kutztown University

Section I

Identity Issues

From the Front Line to the Front of the Class: Counseling Students Who Are Military Veterans

Timothy Black, Marvin J. Westwood,
and Michael N. Sorsdal

Introduction

"Our nation's veterans represent a pool of highly talented individuals who can greatly benefit our economy and society through further education and training in a postsecondary setting" (Pierce, 1995, p. 3). This statement, made by David R. Pierce, the president of the American Association of Community Colleges, to the U.S. House of Representatives Subcommittee on Education, Training, Employment and Housing on Veterans' Affairs, underscores the collective feeling about the military members who attend America's colleges. Many students with military backgrounds go on to successful postsecondary experiences. However, students with military backgrounds can also face multiple challenges after leaving the military and attempting to navigate the transition into civilian life (Covert, 2002), which may include postsecondary education at the college level.

Transition of the military veteran into civilian life is not a modern-day issue. However, following the Vietnam War, it became painfully apparent that transition from the military to civilian life is not unproblematic (Caron & Knight, 1974). Former military members may face challenges, including physical and psychological injuries (MacDonald, Chamberlain, Long, Pereira-Laird, & Mirfin, 1998; Rosebush, 1998; Westwood, Black, & McLean, 2002) resulting

---

We dedicate this chapter to the men and women of the armed forces who struggle to find their way in civilian life.

from combat and noncombat situations; health issues (Spaulding, Eddy, & Chandras, 1997); learning how to function in a nonstructured environment (Mares & Rosenheck, 2004); family discord (Dekel, Goldblatt, & Keidar, 2005; Galovski & Lyons, 2004; Hendrix, Erdmann, & Briggs, 1998); difficulties with authority (Lubin & Johnson, 2000); issues of perceived support (Greenberg et al., 2003); and identity issues, both as a result of military service (Herman, 1997) and as a result of leaving the military (Clewell, 1987).

Part of making a successful transition from the military into civilian life may involve the choice to pursue postsecondary education after discharge. However, institutes of higher education are often far removed, culturally speaking, from the realities of military life both in combat and during peacetime. Students with military backgrounds may struggle to find their way in these bastions of the civilian world. These students represent an invisible minority in campus classrooms and in campus counseling centers, especially if they do not self-identify as former military members. Transition from the military into civilian life is inevitable for the majority of military members; successful transition is not.

Physical injuries can be visible or unseen, whereas psychological injuries such as posttraumatic stress disorder (PTSD; American Psychiatric Association [APA], 2000) and posttraumatic stress reactions (PTSR; APA, 2000) are largely invisible to the casual observer. Students who are military veterans may experience intrusive memories and flashbacks, outbursts of anger, distrust of authority, inability to concentrate, inability to sleep, hypervigilance, and psychological numbing, all of which may negatively affect their ability to succeed in a postsecondary setting. Counseling issues often include substance abuse, posttraumatic symptomatology, physical pain, problems with intimate relationships, existential issues, grief/loss, disability, and identity issues. A team-based approach is often indicated, including medicine, social work, psychiatry, counseling, the Veterans Administration, and learning assistance.

Assessment Issues

To understand the transition from military life to civilian life, it can be helpful to think of it as a cross-cultural transition. It is a transition that requires, for some, the attainment of a new set of cultural competencies and awarenesses for success. Much like new immigrants to a country who need to learn the social–cultural nuances of their new culture (Ishiyama & Westwood, 1992; Mak, Westwood, & Ishiyama, 1999; Westwood & Ishiyama, 1990, 1991; Westwood, Mak, & Barker, 2000), military members, depending on how long they have been in the military and depending on their rank and status when leaving the military and their experiences in the war theater (see Grossman, 1996), may experience a kind of culture shock when leaving the military and entering the civilian world. They are leaving a world in which authority is absolute; responsibility for their actions lies in the hands of superiors; trust is based on life and death; and their day-to-day living, learning, and promotion are prescribed by the military organization.

Structure is at the heart of military life, and it is what makes the military work. The rules are clear, absolute, and understood by all. In many ways, the military culture is the antithesis of the individualistic, materialistic, litigious culture that pervades much of modern North American society. Our clients from the military often view modern civilian society as one in which the only rule is that there are no rules; the "anything I want I get" type of attitude prevails; and concepts such as duty, honor, and respect are seen as quaint ideas from a "time gone by."

The military can be thought of as a one-way door to a different way of being in the world. Once you go in, you can never go back to the way you were before. To borrow from psychology, behavioral conditioning and reinforcement are just a few of the tools the modern military has been able to use effectively to create the soldier that they require. The basic formula for creating soldiers is to strip them of their individual identities; push them to their limits physically, mentally, and emotionally; and build them up with a new identity based on obedience to authority and loyalty to their fellow soldiers. Following that, the military uses behavioral reinforcement methods to teach the newly formed soldiers how to overcome the natural human aversion to killing (Grossman, 1996). During their training and time in the military, the soldiers are taught that they are different from civilians as part of their induction into the military culture.

The cultural difference between military and civilian life can have deleterious consequences to a counseling relationship for the uninformed counselor. Because of military training, it is unlikely that a student with a military background will offer what he or she really thinks about counseling, and so it may be up to the counselor to elicit information from the client with direct questions. Use of action-oriented language by the counselor may be helpful because it demonstrates the counselor's sensitivity to the kind of language that is valued in military culture: a language of doing and accomplishing.

Some aspects of students' background experiences in the military assist them in college and in everyday life, and other aspects hinder them. No two students with military backgrounds are exactly the same. They come with different premilitary and military experiences; different lengths of service, rank, and training; and different sets of resources that can influence how well they navigate the cross-cultural transition from the military to civilian life.

Time and Rank in the Military

The amount and type of time spent in the military is a good place for the counselor to begin a dialogue with students who have military backgrounds. When we speak of amount of time, we are literally speaking about the time between when they entered the military and when they left. By type of time, we mean to discover whether they were full-time regular forces, reserve forces, militia, National Guard, or other.

It is particularly important for the counselor to learn the student's rank in the military. A student's issues with authority, for example, may be linked with rank and with the student's impressions, both positive and negative, of leaders in his or her military past. Generally speaking, rank can be considered in terms of two broad categories—enlisted personnel and officers—that can be further divided into the four categories of officers, senior noncommissioned officers (senior NCOs), noncommissioned officers (NCOs), and "other ranks." The senior NCOs, NCOs, and other ranks are all enlisted personnel, but the senior NCOs and NCOs have higher levels of responsibility and more authority, including what is termed warrant status (i.e., a warrant to command). "Other ranks" are relied on to follow orders, given to them by their superiors, who include NCOs, senior NCOs, and officers. In addition, NCOs, senior NCOs, and officers are required to follow orders given to them by their superiors. This means that when a superior gives an order, it is expected to be carried out without regard for personal safety or injury.

The ability to follow orders is especially important in situations in which there is a lack of certainty about the potential outcome. Superiors are expected to avoid putting their charges in unnecessary danger, and "other ranks" personnel are expected to follow orders, regardless of whether they trust their superiors. This hierarchical norm of following orders, and of superiors holding responsibility for their subordinates, is uniform through all four levels of rank.

Once the counselor knows the rank and type of time the student spent in the military, it is useful to ask what trade or occupation the student was trained in and in what branch of the military the student served. Was the student in the infantry or in communications? Was the student a mechanic, an engineer, or perhaps a medic? Was the student in the Army, Navy, Air Force, or Marines?

There are many different trades (i.e., jobs) in the armed forces, and the counselor should avoid making the assumption that all students with military backgrounds served in a combat role. In addition, the counselor should not assume that, because the individual was not in a combat role, the individual was not exposed to combat situations or postcombat traumas (e.g., body-bagging military casualties or civilian victims). Often combat support teams (e.g., transport) find themselves in the thick of battle, forced to contend with enemy attacks.

The counselor also wants to know how much, if any, combat experience the student did encounter. At this point, knowing the trade or occupation of the individual can be helpful. In our experience, most former military members with combat experience are unlikely to voluntarily divulge information about their tours of duty. This is often due to the perception that people really do not want to hear about it or that, in some way, it will be misunderstood. There is also the fear of being labeled or of being thought of as different. In the military, sameness to others is very important. Being unique or standing out can get a person into a great deal of trouble, or even killed. As a result, "blending in" is a learned skill with associated survival benefits.

One veteran we worked with, who served in a combat role, was forced to kill the enemy after receiving "effective fire" (i.e., gunshots close enough to pose an actual threat of being injured). After his return, people would ask him if he had to kill anyone when he was overseas, and he would avoid the question, not wanting it to become a sensationalized story in their minds. In our collective experience, relatively safe initial questions to ask regarding the type of combat experienced include the following:

1. I know that different people have different experiences when they are in a war zone. What was your experience like?
2. What was your role when in combat?
3. How bad did it get where you were?

Safe questions reflect both the counselor's willingness to talk about the client's war experiences and the counselor's respect for the boundaries of clients who may not know whether the civilian counselor is a person to whom they want to tell their story. In the initial assessment stages, it is usually not productive to go into detail regarding combat traumas, and this may result in the client unnecessarily experiencing the negative effects of traumatic memories.

Family Issues

Family issues are often interwoven into the transition process for students with military backgrounds. Family members can be a source of stability, contributing to resiliency in the students, and they can also be a source of incredible destruction and depletion of resources for the students. If family members are unsupportive of the students' transition out of the military or pursuit of a college education, this can represent a significant barrier to a successful transition.

It is important to learn about the family life of the students, including the structure of their current family situation. To get a quick read on the family climate, the counselor may wish to ask the client's spouse or partner, "In what ways has your partner changed since he or she returned?" If a student is not married or partnered, the counselor might ask the same question of a parent or a sibling. As an alternative, the counselor might ask the student, "What are your friends and family noticing since your return? Has anyone told you that you have changed?" This inquiry can be a valuable source of information for the counselor.

The family of students with military backgrounds may represent a resource for a student, for example, who is dealing with severe symptoms of PTSD. However, because the family members are at risk of developing secondary traumatic symptoms, other resources for the entire family may be helpful. Research has demonstrated that the experiences of military members can have deleterious effects on their family life, including lowered self-esteem in their children, increased levels of stress symptomatology, and decreased family functioning (Galovski & Lyons, 2004; Mellor & Davidson, 2001).

Many military personnel come from generations of family members who also served in the military. It may be prudent for the counselor to ask the student if anyone else in the family has a military background. The following are some helpful questions to ask:

1. Who else in the family served? What does the client know about his or her relatives' war or military experiences?
2. Is the family promilitary, neutral, or opposed?
3. Is there anyone in the family who understands what it is like for the client to leave the military and try to make it in the civilian world? How did that family member make the transition?

On the basis of qualitative research conducted at the University of British Columbia (Westwood, 1998), it became apparent that most veterans of World Wars I and II, Korea, and Vietnam disclosed very little to their family members about their wartime experiences. When asked, veterans stated that they did not want to burden their families with what happened or be perceived as weak or unable to keep the role prescribed in their family dynamic. However, when asked to tell their stories in a respectful and caring environment, veterans experienced a sense of relief at having told even a piece of their wartime story. Therefore, the student may know very little about the military experience of a family member but may find that discussing transition issues with that family member proves to be beneficial for both of them.

The Impact of Trauma

> We can count the dead. We can see physical injuries. But in soldiers returning home, it's hard to see the psychological damage among those who have witnessed the blood, heard the screaming, felt the shattering blast and smelled the burning flesh. (Shalev & Miller, 2004, p. 70)

Students with military backgrounds may have been exposed to large-scale trauma on a daily basis for months at a time. Further, they may have been exposed to a kind of trauma that very few civilians will ever experience: the trauma of killing another human being. The act of killing itself, or simply the realization that one may be required to kill another human being, can result in clients dissociating from their natural feelings of repulsion (Grossman, 1996). It is for these reasons that the impact of trauma on students with military backgrounds must be acknowledged as qualitatively different from most civilian traumas.

The literature on traumatic stress tends to make a distinction between PTSD and combat-related PTSD (e.g., Chemtob, Hamada, Roitblat, & Muraoka, 1994; Forbes, Hawthorne, & Elliott, 2004; Keane, Caddell, & Taylor, 1988; King & King, 1994; Kubany, 1994; Turner, Beidel, & Frueh, 2005). Although the diagnostic criteria for PTSD are not meant to discriminate between causes of PTSD, there are some essential features of combat-related PTSD that are helpful to consider.

Frueh, Turner, and Beidel (2001) stated that although broad-based assessment strategies are needed to fully capture the severity and complexity of combat-related PTSD, perhaps more so than for other psychiatric disorders, several key characteristics of social functioning in individuals with combat-related PTSD have been acknowledged. Frueh et al. reported that social anxiety, guilt, anger, sexual dysfunction, unemployment, impulsive or violent behavior, and family discord are a few of the challenges that individuals experiencing combat-related PTSD may find themselves dealing with on return from overseas duty or release from the military.

The main symptom criteria for PTSD (APA, 2000) focus on three clusters of symptoms: reexperiencing, avoidance/numbing, and hyperarousal. Each of these symptom clusters potentially affects a student's ability to deal with the inherent stresses of a college education. Reexperiencing symptoms, for example, may include recurrent and intrusive distressing recollections of the event or intense psychological distress at exposure to internal or external cues that symbolize or resemble an aspect of the traumatic event.

Imagine a student in an economics class who has trouble concentrating because an image of a dead body he or she found in a war zone keeps popping into his or her head during the course lectures. Perhaps the student is taking a political science class in which the instructor is recounting the details of a recent event in a war-torn country in which the student served, and part of the lecture includes photographs of war-torn villages or mass executions like those seen in Rwanda. These kinds of images may become triggers that cause significant psychological distress in the student. The impact of these kinds of intrusive symptoms on student learning, attention, concentration, and memory is obvious.

Avoidance/numbing is the second set of symptoms required for a diagnosis of PTSD. Examples of symptoms in this category include efforts to avoid thoughts, feelings, or conversations associated with the trauma; a feeling of detachment or estrangement from others; restricted range of affect; and a sense of a foreshortened future. Individuals must have at least three symptoms in this category to receive a diagnosis of PTSD.

Again, let us consider the student in the political science class. If the class focuses on conflict areas that are similar to where the student served, efforts to avoid thoughts, feelings, or conversations associated with the trauma may result in decisions not to attend lectures or tutorials, which would have an impact on the student's success. Understanding the student's motivation to avoid the class may assist the counselor in helping the student avoid these problems.

Hyperarousal is the last of the symptom clusters related to PTSD. Symptoms include difficulty falling or staying asleep, irritability or outbursts of anger, difficulty concentrating, hypervigilance, and an exaggerated startle response. A student's inability to fall asleep or stay asleep and the resultant difficulty in concentrating inevitably affect the student's learning and retention. Likewise, an instructor's position of authority may be a trigger for a student, resulting in the student's inappropriate outburst of anger during class or in consultation with the instructor. The outburst may be falsely interpreted as aggression or an intimidation tactic on the part of the student, when in fact it may be the result of heightened general arousal in the nervous system of the student with PTSD.

Understanding the symptom clusters involved in PTSD can help counselors with clients from military backgrounds to reframe and work with some of the struggles these clients may have related to their school work. Naturally, the counselor will want to take the time to distinguish between those barriers to success that are related to PTSD symptoms and those that are related to poor study habits, partying all night, and simply not attending class.

Alcohol and Drugs

Research has shown that combat exposure increases the risk for both alcohol and drug dependence (Koenen, Lyons, & Goldberg, 2003). Alcohol dependence in individuals with PTSD has been linked to increases in both verbal and physical aggression (Zoricic, Buljan, & Thaller, 2003), and alcohol use has been linked to decreases in health-related quality of life and other psychiatric disorders in veteran populations (Kalman et al., 2004). Alcohol and drug use can represent one of the most significant barriers to a successful transition to civilian life. Alcohol and drugs are used during military service to help alleviate not only the realities of death and destruction in war but also the boredom of military service. It is important to be aware of the student's pattern of alcohol and drug use—how the student uses alcohol and drugs, what they do for the student, and when the student uses them—to determine whether they represent a means of self-medicating the effects of PTSD or PTSR.

Much has been written about the treatment of alcohol and drug dependence, and we do not wish to reproduce those materials here. However, because alcohol and drugs are frequently used to medicate the negative impact of traumatic memories and symptoms, it is essential that counselors who work with clients with military backgrounds have an addictions referral source to work with in collaboration with their own counseling goals.

Physical Injuries

Much of the focus today is on the psychological impact of war on individuals in the modern-day military. The literature on combat-related PTSD is extensive, and, unfortunately, some veterans who are experiencing PTSD make the headlines because of the explosive nature of their actions. It is important to realize, however, that a significant number of students with military backgrounds may have experienced physical injuries as part of their time in the military. Physical injuries might include visible injuries like the loss of a limb or limbs, disfigurement, scars, or damage to limbs, resulting in an impairment of functioning such as walking, sitting, or even writing. However, other injuries may not be as readily apparent to the naked eye, including mild brain damage, hearing impairment, visual impairment, back injuries, and environmental injuries such as Gulf War syndrome.

The impact of these kinds of physical injuries on students with military backgrounds may go unnoticed or unacknowledged for a variety of reasons. Let us look at an example of a student with a hearing impairment following a tour of duty in the Gulf War. The student, who was in the infantry as a machine gunner, has experienced loss of hearing in his right ear due to repeated exposure to muzzle blasts and now has tinnitus, or ringing in the ear. The student may not realize that his hearing impairment affects his ability to pay attention or even hear in a large lecture hall or that the tinnitus negatively affects his ability to concentrate. Military personnel are not used to being given special accommodation for their injuries, as indicated by the familiar phrase "soldier on." The student may not want to acknowledge the hearing loss or discuss it with an instructor for fear of being judged negatively by an instructor.

The student may also minimize the actual impact of the injury in discussions with the counselor, feeling that asking for help is acknowledging weakness and vulnerability. The student may not want to be perceived as different. Being different from others, especially as it relates to the inability to accomplish a particular task in the military, is functionally equivalent to being obsolete. Although there may be less of a stigma surrounding physical injuries than psychological injuries, physical injuries can be a source of shame or embarrassment for soldiers, who are valued for what they can do on the battlefield, not for what they used to be able to do and now cannot. In our collective experience, open, honest, and frank discussions about these kinds of issues with military personnel have been appreciated and are normally responded to favorably. The counselor should encourage the student to use college resources for students with disabilities and to consult with a trusted physician for ongoing consultation regarding the injuries.

Many veterans, however, may have had negative experiences with physicians due to lengthy and frustrating pension claim processes designed to determine the cause of injury. The counselor should inquire about the client's experience with physicians and not assume that the client will view physicians as allies. The client may have been discharged from active duty against his or her will because of inability to perform physical duties. Further, negative experiences with medical doctors within the military system may have influenced the client's trust and reliance on any medical system. For example, confidentiality by health practitioners in the military has not been the norm, and, as a result, the client may have difficulty believing that confidentiality in the civilian world exists. Experiences with medical services in the military may represent a fruitful avenue to discuss with clients prior to, or at the same time as, discussing possible referrals to health care providers.

Finally, it is important to note two things when the psychological and physical injuries that may constitute barriers to students' successes are being considered. First, the issue of PTSD diagnosis, outcome research, and the like is not uncomplicated (Black, 2004). Diagnosis of PTSD itself is problematic in that it represents a binary distinction of diagnosis/nondiagnosis. However, the absence of only one symptom criterion could mean that an individual would not be given a diagnosis of PTSD. This might lead to an assumption that those individuals who have PTSD suffer more than those who do not, which would be misleading. Likewise, the diagnostic criteria do not allow for a gradation of intensity of the symptoms but simply indicate the presence or absence of the symptoms. Individuals with PTSD have wide and varied experiences, and they all fall under the one diagnostic umbrella called PTSD. We recommend that the counselor not focus too narrowly on whether the individual has been formally diagnosed but rather view PTSR as being on a continuum that may or may not include a formal diagnosis of PTSD.

Second, it is important to acknowledge that PTSR and physical injuries may coexist. In fact, the event that caused the physical injury may be the traumatic event that precipitated the PTSR. Hence, the individual may have a constant reminder of the trauma in the physical injury. Knowing this can help counselors to develop an appreciation for the complex interweaving of the physical and psychological injuries that students with military backgrounds may have experienced.

Counseling Implications

Military Identity: You Don't Know and You Will Never Understand

The bonding that soldiers experience in the military should not be underestimated and can often explain the common desire in former military members to return to the "good times" of their military days. This phenomenon especially plays out in group counseling situations in which participants believe that only other soldiers can truly understand them.

It is important that counselors who do not have military experience be upfront about their lack of knowledge in that area. "Honesty is the best policy" holds true herein, and transparency can be an effective technique for building the respect of the client and for demonstrating competence. At the same time, however, counselors should emphasize their knowledge and training in helping people. This can be dealt with in a simple and straightforward manner. When working with military clients, the counselor should acknowledge that there are two experts present. The client is the expert on what it means to be in the military, and the counselor is the expert on doing counseling. A frank and honest declaration of mutual expertise can help to balance the scales of power while instilling confidence in clients that the counselor can help them with their presenting issues. This speaks to the notion of competence and leadership in working with military clients.

Competence is an important quality in leadership in the military, and the lack of competence (perceived or actual) in military leadership has been the focus of much of our work with former military personnel. A counselor's perceived competencies and the military student's respect for the counselor are not given but must be painstakingly earned and can be quickly lost. Enlisted personnel often make the differentiation between following orders by an officer or a senior person and respecting them. Respect is the highest privilege an officer can receive from a subordinate, because it is the only thing over which enlisted men and women have control.

In our group work with military veterans, we have learned that the perception of responsibility in the counseling relationship can become a therapeutic issue. When a leader (e.g., the counselor) suggests that something might be helpful or therapeutic, there can be a perception by the individual of the suggestion as a direct order that must be followed. This may then lead to the perception that the counselor is responsible for everything that happens and is, therefore, responsible for any distress the individual might feel. This is a very important cross-cultural point to consider.

If a counselor in the civilian world states explicitly that the client has the choice to participate or not participate in an exercise, most clients will take the counselor's statement at face value. It is important to realize that the same client with a military background as an enlisted "other rank" may perceive the offer of personal choice as an order given by the counselor. Personal choice is the issue, and for some clients with military experience, there is no personal choice and therefore no personal responsibility, which can lead to unwarranted blame or praise being placed on the counselor.

There is also the possibility that no matter what rank the client is, the counselor may be looked at as a superior. This would mean that even for officers, NCOs, or senior NCOs, the counselor may still be viewed as the authority. Engaging in a candid discussion about the differences between military and counseling culture with clients can help to avoid this kind of cross-cultural confusion and can help the clients begin to take personal responsibility for the choices they make in their own counseling experience.

Loss of Identity, Role, Purpose, and Mission

To understand the student with a background as an enlisted member of the armed forces, it is important to understand issues related to identity, role, purpose, and mission. Each member of the military has an identity that is intimately linked to a clearly defined role, a definite purpose, and a mission. These issues become increasingly important in war zones, where the lives of fellow soldiers and innocent civilians depend on each individual knowing his or her role, purpose, and mission. Once removed from the military, many members feel a sense of being "rudderless" or without direction, in part due to the relative ambiguity of life outside of the military compared with the highly structured environment of the military. It may also be due to the loss of a clear role, purpose, and/or mission as a civilian. In war zones, these are often clearly defined. For example, a member's role might be that of machine gunner in the infantry, his or her purpose might be to bring up the rear of the section and protect the back of the section as they move through enemy territory, and finally his or her mission might include advancing on and securing a particular location. Once removed from such high-stress, high-feedback environments with such clearly defined roles and missions, many soldiers may find themselves at a loss for the purpose or meaning in their lives.

We have found that for some clients, thinking of transition out of the military as a new mission with new objectives and new expected outcomes can be helpful. Approaching college education, metaphorically, as a new mission can help both the counselor and the client feel grounded in familiar territory, using military terms and language. Engaging in conversations that address questions directed at the student client's role in college, the student's purpose for being there, and his or her mission in college can help to put the college experience into language that engenders feelings of competency and accomplishment in the client. As with all of these recommendations, one must never assume that the use of the "new mission" metaphor will resonate with everyone who has a military background. However, we have found it useful for certain clients who have spent a long period of time in the full-time regular forces and have limited experience in living outside of a military culture.

Campus Considerations

Authority, Trust, and Safety Issues

Issues with authority are not experienced exclusively in the military, but there are few organizations in which authority carries so much weight. In civilian society, only the quasi-military organizations, such as police departments, fire departments, or emergency medical response services, approach the type of relationship to authority that is present in the military. The separation of the ranks in the military (i.e., officer or enlisted) means that the entire social order is predicated on authority relationships. Exploring with clients their experiences of authority in the military can provide insight into some of the issues the clients may have related to college instructors, teaching assistants, and fellow students.

Most military people with whom we have worked report many difficult experiences with authority as well as some very positive experiences with authority. It is important to note that within the enlisted ranks it is part of the culture to privately criticize authority figures and attempt to undermine the authority of leaders deemed to be unworthy of following. Officer ranks, in contrast, share a culture of complaining about unruly or noncompliant enlisted ranks. There is much hostility that exists between these two rank divisions, and this hostility can then be transferred onto any authority relationship in which there is a perception of "us versus them." The classic example is of the student/instructor relationship paralleling the enlisted/officer relationship.

Clients who have negative experiences with authority in the military may find themselves reacting to their instructors, counselors, administrators, or administrative assistants in much the same way that they would have done with their superiors in the military. Discussing with clients their experiences (both positive and negative) with authority in the military can provide the counselor with insight as to problems that the student may encounter while attending college. Perceived breaches of trust on the part of instructors, fellow students, or even counselors, and the impact of those perceptions, can be better understood when one considers what occurs in the military, in which breaches of trust can result in serious injury or death.

Military members are trained to trust in the military organization for their safety, health, and success. Members are taught to trust the organization with no less than their very lives. This is an especially important point when thinking about former military members, who may feel that they have been let down or betrayed by the organization that was supposed to provide for and protect them. There is often a love–hate relationship with the military when members are discharged. They love the fact that they are military but hate what they often perceive is a betrayal by the military organization after release.

The structure of the military is such that the focus is on people within the organization. Once the individual is released from service, the military no longer accepts responsibility for the individual's well-being or safety. The responsibility is then shifted to the Veterans Administration, which adjudicates pension claims, provides health benefits, and generally cares for military veterans. This shift in responsibility is often not experienced as a positive one but rather as a feeling of being abandoned and betrayed, accompanied by feelings of intense anger and frustration, which can be overwhelming at times. It is as though a break in attachment has occurred, one that may have as much of an impact as the break from the parent after childhood, with negative effects on the client and his or her overall functioning.

Anger and Resentment

This kind of reaction to an organization can, at times, be transferred onto the college that the student attends. If a military client is experiencing anger or resentment toward the college administration, the counselor should explore the student's experience in being discharged from the military. A counselor who understands that a military member feels a sense of resentment toward the military will understand when such reactions toward the college organization seem to be out of proportion to the client's experience. Having the conversation with the student about his or her feelings toward the military can provide some much-needed insight into the client's response to college bureaucracy.

In the military, perceived bureaucratic incompetence or interference may have resulted in the loss of lives or serious injury. Thus, perceived bureaucratic incompetence or interference may be met with vociferous reactions from clients that, although unlikely to pose an actual threat to the students, represent a cross-cultural effect of having served in the military. Our recommendation is to speak with the students about their views on the military and how their views inform their experience of being in a college setting.

Some students with military backgrounds believe that the way to get ahead in college is to be as direct and as purposeful as they were in the military. In certain academic settings, this kind of approach may not be valued, and it may even be discouraged. The students may be frustrated because they perceive the college setting as one in which no one will make a decision, but no one wants anyone else to make a decision either, at the risk of being considered to be bullying or bulldozing. This underscores the fact that, although college counselors will benefit from gaining knowledge about the military culture, they can also serve as "cultural informants" who are able to assist the military member in succeeding in the culture of higher education.

Both academic venues and how courses are taught are very different in a college setting as compared with the way that courses are taught in the military.

The military puts their members through a rigorous academic study to quickly prepare them for combat, including how to live, how to act, how to socialize, how to trust, and how to follow directions precisely. The key thing to consider here is that it happens very quickly. Ambiguity in the college culture can be a challenge for students with military backgrounds because they have been taught the value of certainty and efficiency. A course that lasts for 3–4 months in a college setting might last only a month in the military, causing students with military backgrounds to question the efficiency and competency of the college organization. Theory that relates directly to practical ability is the focus in the military, and so dealing only with abstract theoretical concepts, devoid of real-world application, is a different experience for students with military backgrounds and can be challenging.

Military Minorities on Campus

It is important to consider all of what has been discussed in this chapter as it relates to the issues of military minorities, including racial, ethnic, sexual, and other minorities. We have purposefully discussed work with military clients as a general population, which is helpful but also limiting. Minority status itself does little to inform the counselor about what a particular person may be experiencing and struggling with in the military. Institutional and interpersonal racism, sexism, and sexual prejudice (Herek, 2000), whether overt or covert, have an impact both during military service and on campus. However, although racism, sexism, and sexual prejudice are real, it cannot be assumed that there is a single representative experience of these forces on individual minority clients (military or civilian) living in a dominant society.

The complexities of understanding minority experience in a majority culture have been addressed over the years by developmental models of identity formation proposed for minorities in general (Atkinson, Morten, & Sue, 1998), for African American clients (Vandiver, Cross, Worrell, & Fhagen-Smith, 2002), and for individuals who are homosexual (Johns & Probst, 2004). In addition, Berry (2005) discussed the role of acculturation in understanding the experience of minority individuals and their families, focusing on the interaction of two dimensions of experience: minority culture retention and majority culture maintenance. It is beyond the scope of this chapter to address the many complexities that accompany minority experience in general.

Military minorities may be faced with other challenges in terms of identity that civilian minorities do not face. As mentioned, the military attempts to strip individuals of their identity in order to "rebuild" them as military members, willing to sacrifice their very lives in the service of their country and in support of their comrades. It has been our experience that military members in general struggle with identity issues after release into civilian society, captured in the phrase "once military, always military." When counselors transpose the challenges of military transition onto the realities of minority experience in a majority culture, they should try to honor the distinction between military and civilian clients. We have found that the military identity can be deeply ingrained, even when not readily apparent in interpersonal transactions. We recommend that counselors consider the possibility that a student veteran who is also a member of a minority group may not identify with the experiences of a civilian student who is a minority. It has been our experience that, when the military identity is acknowledged alongside of any issues related to being a racial, ethnic, or other type of minority, defensive reactions can be reduced.

The military experience and identity are not widely understood by civilians, which often decreases the ability of students with military backgrounds to relate to other students as well as teachers and administrators. Counselors can serve as an important resource to the campus community to help communicate and explain the issues with which these students struggle and the challenges that they face as they navigate the transition into the civilian world in general and the college setting in particular.

Future Trends

It does not seem likely that there will be any decline in returning military personnel in the near future. Although the nature of the world has changed, and it is unlikely that we will ever see another international war on the same scale as World War I, World War II, or the Korean Conflict, it seems as though regional conflict, terrorist warfare, and multiple-front deployments will continue to be the norm in the global village. As such, the future of counseling students with military backgrounds will continue to become more and more complex as the political issues associated with each new conflict become more and more contentious. The recent war in Iraq caused division not only on a national but also on an international scale. In the end, the men and women who served their countries often do not return to ticker-tape parades but, much like after Vietnam, return to countries that are not unanimous in their support of the governments' decision to deploy troops.

One of the factors contributing to the development of PTSD in veterans of the Vietnam War was the societal reaction after their return (Grossman, 1996). Many veterans can come to terms with what they are asked to do during war, provided that they have support and acknowledgment as valuable members of society on their return home. The support of a nation on returning from war can create a positive buffer for the veteran, and a climate of misunderstanding or outright disapproval of a country's involvement in conflict can contribute to the development of psychological injuries after a soldier's return. Counselors working with these students have an important role to play, especially because campuses have the potential to be "hotbeds" of political demonstration, which has often been antiwar and antimilitary. We are encouraged by the recent societal trend of supporting the troops but not the war and feel this kind of social support of the men and women serving their country cannot be anything but helpful.

Another future trend will be an increase in issues faced by female combat veterans. Although women have played an integral role in military conflicts throughout history, it is only recently that women have been formally accepted in combat roles. Despite the increasing numbers of women serving in combat roles, the literature on the impact of combat on women is sparse, and research on the impact of combat on men and women is contradictory. Schnurr, Lunney, Sengupta, and Waelde (2003) reported that gender differences exist, whereas Unwin et al. (2002) reported no differences between male and female veterans in terms of health and PTSD symptoms. Pereira (2002) stated that female veterans, as compared with their male counterparts, may be underdiagnosed as having PTSD.

The issue of women in combat roles is a current and future issue to be aware of in the treatment of students with military backgrounds and in the treatment of military veterans in general. We cannot take for granted that female combat veterans will respond in ways that are either similar or dissimilar to their male counterparts. Counselors can take the lead role in this kind of research simply by asking female veterans about their experiences and listening to their stories with acceptance and openness.

Counseling students who are military veterans requires a cross-cultural sensitivity on the part of counselors in higher education. Awareness of the issues that these students may face can serve to ease their transition from the military into higher education institutions and into the rest of their civilian lives.

References

American Psychiatric Association. (2000). *Diagnostic and statistical manual of mental disorders* (4th ed., text rev.). Washington, DC: Author.

Atkinson, D. R., Morten, G., & Sue, D. W. (1998). *Counseling American minorities.* New York: McGraw-Hill.

Berry, J. W. (2005). Acculturation: Living successfully in two cultures. *International Journal of Intercultural Relations, 29,* 697–712.

Black, T. G. (2004). Psychotherapy and outcome research in PTSD: Understanding the challenges and complexities in the literature. *Canadian Journal of Counseling, 38,* 277–288.

Caron, H. S., & Knight, V. B. (1974). An outreach approach to facilitating the transition from military to civilian life: A critical choice point for the drug dependent. *Journal of Drug Issues, 4,* 52–60.

Chemtob, C. M., Hamada, R. S., Roitblat, H. L., & Muraoka, M. Y. (1994). Anger, impulsivity, and anger control in combat-related posttraumatic stress disorder. *Journal of Consulting and Clinical Psychology, 62,* 827–832.

Clewell, R. D. (1987). Moral dimensions in treating combat veterans with posttraumatic stress disorder. *Bulletin of the Menninger Clinic, 51,* 114–130.

Covert, C. M. (2002). *Counseling adult learners for new careers: The motivations and barriers associated with postsecondary educational participation of soldiers in transition.* Washington, DC: U.S. Department of Education. (ERIC Document Reproduction Service No. ED471458)

Dekel, R., Goldblatt, H., & Keidar, M. (2005). Being a wife of a veteran with posttraumatic stress disorder. *Family Relations: Interdisciplinary Journal of Applied Family Studies, 54,* 24–36.

Forbes, D., Hawthorne, G., & Elliott, P. (2004). A concise measure of anger in combat-related posttraumatic stress disorder. *Journal of Traumatic Stress, 17,* 249–256.

Frueh, B. C., Turner, S. M., & Beidel, D. C. (2001). Assessment of social functioning in combat veterans with PTSD. *Aggression & Violent Behavior, 6,* 79–90.

Galovski, T., & Lyons, J. A. (2004). Psychological sequelae of combat violence: A review of the impact of PTSD on the veteran's family and possible interventions. *Aggression & Violent Behavior, 9,* 477–501.

Greenberg, N., Thomas, S. L., Iversen, A., Unwin, C., Hull, L., & Wessely, S. (2003). Do military peacekeepers want to talk about their experiences? Perceived psychological support of UK military peacekeepers on return from deployment. *Journal of Mental Health, 12,* 565–574.

Grossman, D. (1996). *On killing: The psychological cost of learning to kill in war and society.* New York: Little, Brown.

Hendrix, C. C., Erdmann, M. A., & Briggs, K. (1998). Impact of Vietnam veterans' arousal and avoidance on spouses' perceptions of family life. *American Journal of Family Therapy, 26,* 115–128.

Herek, G. M. (2000). The psychology of sexual prejudice. *Current Directions in Psychological Science, 9,* 19–22.

Herman, J. (1997). *Trauma and recovery: The aftermath of violence—from domestic abuse to political terror.* New York: Basic Books.

Ishiyama, F. I., & Westwood, M. J. (1992). Enhancing client-validating communication: Helping discouraged clients in cross-cultural adjustment. *Journal of Multicultural Counseling and Development, 20,* 50–64.

Johns, D. J., & Probst, T. M. (2004). Sexual minority identity formation in an adult population. *Journal of Homosexuality, 47,* 81–90.

Kalman, D., Lee, A., Chan, E., Miller, D. R., Spiro, A., II, Ren, X. S., et al. (2004). Alcohol dependence, other psychiatric disorders, and health-related quality of life: A replication study in a large random sample of enrollees in the Veterans Health Administration. *American Journal of Drug & Alcohol Abuse, 30,* 473–488.

Keane, T. M., Caddell, J. M., & Taylor, K. L. (1988). Mississippi Scale for Combat-Related Posttraumatic Stress Disorder: Three studies in reliability and validity. *Journal of Consulting and Clinical Psychology, 56,* 85–90.

King, L., & King, D. (1994). Latent structure of the Mississippi Scale for Combat-Related Posttraumatic Stress Disorder: Exploratory and higher order confirmatory factor analyses. *Assessment, 1,* 275–291.

Koenen, K. C., Lyons, M. J., & Goldberg, J. (2003). Co-twin control study of relationships among combat exposure, combat-related PTSD, and other mental disorders. *Journal of Traumatic Stress, 16,* 433–438.

Kubany, E. S. (1994). A cognitive model of guilt typology in combat-related PTSD. *Journal of Traumatic Stress, 7,* 3–19.

Lubin, H., & Johnson, D. R. (2000). Interactive psychoeducational group therapy in the treatment of authority problems in combat-related posttraumatic stress disorder. *International Journal of Group Psychotherapy, 50,* 277–296.

MacDonald, C., Chamberlain, K., Long, N., Pereira-Laird, J., & Mirfin, K. (1998). Mental health, physical health, and stressors reported by New Zealand defense force peacekeepers: A longitudinal study. *Military Medicine, 163,* 477–481.

Mak, A. S., Westwood, M. J., & Ishiyama, F. I. (1999). Optimising conditions for learning sociocultural competencies for success. *International Journal of Intercultural Relations, 23,* 77–90.

Mares, A. S., & Rosenheck, R.A. (2004). Perceived relationship between military service and homelessness among homeless veterans with mental illness. *Journal of Nervous & Mental Disease, 192,* 715–719.

Mellor, D. J., & Davidson, A. C. (2001). The adjustment of children of Australian Vietnam veterans: Is there evidence for the transgenerational transmission of the effects of war-related trauma? *Australian & New Zealand Journal of Psychiatry, 35,* 345–351.

Pereira, A. (2002). Combat trauma and the diagnosis of post-traumatic stress disorder in female and male veterans. *Military Medicine, 167,* 23–27.

Pierce, D. R. (1995). *Statement by the President of the American Association of Community Colleges to the U.S. House of Representatives Subcommittee on Education, Training, Employment and Housing on Veterans' Affairs.* Washington, DC: American Association of Community Colleges.

Rosebush, P. A. (1998). Psychological intervention with military personnel in Rwanda. *Military Medicine, 163,* 559–563.

Schnurr, P. P., Lunney, C. A., Sengupta, A., & Waelde, L. C. (2003). A descriptive analysis of PTSD chronicity in Vietnam veterans. *Journal of Traumatic Stress, 16,* 545–554.

Shalev, A. Y., & Miller, M. C. (2004, December 6). To heal a shattered soul. *Newsweek, 144,* 70.

Spaulding, D. J., Eddy, J. P., & Chandras, K. V. (1997). Gulf War syndrome: Are campus health officials prepared to cope with Persian Gulf veterans? *College Student Journal, 31,* 317–322.

Turner, S. M., Beidel, D. C., & Frueh, B. C. (2005). Multicomponent behavioral treatment for chronic combat-related posttraumatic stress disorder. *Behavior Modification, 29,* 39–70.

Unwin, C., Hotopf, M., Hull, L., Ismail, K., David, A., & Wessely, S. (2002). Women in the Persian Gulf: Lack of gender differences in long-term health effects of service in United Kingdom Armed Forces in the 1991 Persian Gulf War. *Military Medicine, 167,* 406–413.

Vandiver, B. J., Cross, W. E., Worrell, F. C., & Fhagen-Smith, P. E. (2002). Validating the Cross Racial Identity Scale. *Journal of Counseling Psychology, 49,* 71–85.

Westwood, M. J. (1998). *Group life review program for Canadian veterans. Report prepared for Veterans Affairs Canada and the Royal Canadian Legion.* Unpublished manuscript, University of British Columbia, Vancouver, British Columbia, Canada.

Westwood, M. J., Black, T. G., & McLean, H. (2002). A re-entry program for peacekeeping soldiers: Promoting personal and professional transition. *Canadian Journal of Counseling, 36,* 221–232.

Westwood, M. J., & Ishiyama, F. I. (1990). The communication process as a critical intervention for client change in cross-cultural counseling. *Journal of Multicultural Counseling and Development, 18,* 163–172.

Westwood, M. J., & Ishiyama, F. I. (1991). Challenges in counseling immigrant clients: Understanding intercultural barriers to career adjustment. *Journal of Employment Counseling, 28,* 130–143.

Westwood, M. J., Mak, A., & Barker, M. (2000). Group procedures and applications for developing sociocultural competencies among immigrants. *International Journal for the Advancement of Counseling, 22,* 317–330.

Zoricic, Z., Buljan, D., & Thaller, V. (2003). Aggression in posttraumatic stress disorder comorbid with alcohol dependence. *European Journal of Psychiatry, 17,* 243–247.

Counseling Student Athletes: Sport Psychology as a Specialization

Ian Birky

Introduction

Athletics and sport are so often a part of collegiate life, it is not unusual to hear accounts of high school students selecting a college home based primarily on the promise or hope of playing on, or cheering for, a particular athletic team. When television cameras follow the action or pan the student crowds at athletic events, members of the academic community are often aware that, for prospective students, identification with the members of that crowd or the players in that athletic venue is as important as attaining any particular academic goal. Although perhaps unlikely to be in the forefront of their minds, counseling center staff members realize that such scenes are populated with the many students who will make use of, and eventually benefit from, the services provided by the counseling center.

Student athletes are often perceived as overindulged and pampered, but many of these students, stressed by the lifestyle; the alternating fame and scrutiny; and the multitasking required in managing, studying, and playing a sport, can benefit from counseling. College counselors, however, often have little opportunity to work with student athletes. Social pressures to be self-reliant and strong influence many of these students to avoid counseling, that is, unless counseling staff members have shown their commitment to the athletic domain, developed connections with the coaches and teams, and gained their trust.

This chapter seeks to identify key issues faced by student athletes and primary pathways to effective involvement by the counselor with this particular clientele. Although there may be little difference in how counselors treat the presenting problems of depression, heartbreak, career selection anxiety, or learning disabilities of athlete and nonathlete students following initial intake, college counselors may maximize their effectiveness with student athletes by developing specialized competency in sport psychology. The assessment and counseling of student athletes are most effective when provided by a counselor who has connections with and sensitivity to the athletic domain.

Assessment Issues

Clientele

On many college campuses, student athletes comprise a relatively large and often very visible subpopulation of potential clients who tend to be hesitant about seeking counseling center assistance. This reluctance to use services is often the natural outcome of social pressures to be self-reliant, to avoid showing weakness, and to resist the associated stigma of seeing a "shrink" (Davies et al., 2000; Kahn & Williams, 2003). With a counseling center's mandate to make itself accessible to the full student body, and recognizing that familiarity breeds use, association with athletes and athletic department personnel is likely to increase student athletes' use of a counseling center.

Presenting Issues

Certain types of issues arise regularly among student athletes and are of major concern. For example, confidence and self-esteem issues related to body image, along with concomitant disordered eating problems, can be critical areas for intervention with athletes, coaches, and teams (Hopkinson & Lock, 2004; Johnson et al., 2004). Student athletes are often working to exhaustion on a regular basis while being subjected to implicit and explicit demands by coaches and teammates to exhibit an ideal physical presentation. The National Collegiate Athletic Association (2005) gave special attention to disordered eating, amenorrhea, and osteoporosis in the female athlete triad, specifically identifying messages from coaches as a primary potential risk factor that must be understood when treatment interventions are being planned. The counselor who has expertise in working with athletes and has the trust of coaches is in a position to recognize and treat disordered eating before it leads to tragic outcomes. An amenorrheic athlete, for example, can lose 5% of her bone mass in 1 year (National Collegiate Athletic Association, 2005).

Student athletes may also experience self-esteem issues stemming from lower socioeconomic or poorer academic backgrounds than the majority of their academic peers. These issues may affect performance, cause feelings of isolation and alienation on the broader campus, and create additional stress arising from efforts to gain parity with their peers.

Student athletes often face constant stress because they are expected to maintain eligibility with full academic course loads while daily working to physical exhaustion on the practice fields under constant judgmental scrutiny. This stress is exacerbated when they fail tests, when they are in performance slumps, or when they are breaking up with a significant other.

Student athletes also face stress when serving in spokesperson roles or when becoming newsworthy icons for the college. They frequent the headlines both when they perform admirably and when they fail miserably. Whereas athletic departments may be quite intentional with regard to which athletes are seen on the front pages of their media guides, and those athletes typically are natured to thrive in that limelight, external news agencies select and choose their own newsmakers, and not all student athletes desire the limelight. Fame can sometimes be lonely as well as stressful, and intimate contact with a counselor can ameliorate some of the consequences during periods of failure or negative scrutiny.

Another common issue within the athletic world is substance abuse. Many athletes have difficulty assessing personal substance use when they perceive themselves as not dissimilar from their teammates, despite evidence of significant problems. Other substance-abusing athletes struggle with how to make sense of why they "got caught." In addition to working with individual athletes, counselors may be extremely helpful in giving teams insights into the perceived adaptive and actual effects of alcohol, steroids, and other drugs (Birky, 2004; Petipas & Van Raalte, 1992).

Sexual identity discrimination and homophobia are also prevalent issues within the athletic environment (Wolf-Wendel, Toma, & Morphew, 2001). Athletics can be daunting for athletes who are homosexual on heterosexist teams or who have to deal with homophobic coaches who fear their teams might become homosexual identified. On some teams, closeted or openly gay and lesbian athletes may be subjected to denigrating or insensitive comments and behaviors from coaches and athletic peers. Athletics can also provide a haven for homosexual athletes who are members of teams identified as predominantly homosexual, but heterosexual athletes on such teams may experiences tensions due to their minority status. Counselors not only may be of assistance to the individual athletes but also may be instrumental in sensitizing athletic department personnel to sexual identity and sexual abuse issues (Brackenridge, 2003) and in facilitating the creation of goals to maintain humane and respectful standards on teams and within the department. Counselors sensitive to (a) the in-group and often conservative cultural norms in athletics, (b) the power that coaches have to affect the lives and performance of team members, and (c) the effects of discriminatory stigma can be wise and proactive advocates for their student athlete clientele (Cogan & Petrie, 2002).

Students recovering from athletic injuries may present issues such as postinjury depression, fear of reinjury, postconcussion symptoms, and loss of confidence, which may be best recognized by the sport psychology counselor. Counseling affiliations with sports medicine personnel can provide connections with and referrals for athletes with postconcussion depression and confusion (Mainwaring et al., 2004) as well as for orthopedically injured and physically ill athletes struggling with associated emotional stress (Perna, Antoni, Baum, Gordon, & Schneiderman, 2003; Williams, Rotella, & Scherzer, 2001).

Advantages of a Proactive Approach

Although nearly all student athletes know where to obtain sports medicine assistance for strained muscles or concussions, they may be less likely to know where the counseling center is, or to use it, unless staff members from the counseling center interact closely within their culture or are readily available within their environment. Because a proactive approach may be necessary if one is to enter this territory, strategic planning may be important if a center is to foster the intentionality necessary for developing interpersonal friendship and consultation relationships with coaches, athletic directors, team captains, and anyone else who has the leadership authority to grant access or membership status to outsiders such as counseling center staff.

Once "part of the team," sport psychology counselors may very well find themselves with the opportunity to assist with team building (Weinberg & Gould, 2003); offer stress management (Kerr, 2001); address and provide alcohol, steroid, and other drug interventions (Carr & Murphy, 1995); comment on pain control and injury rehabilitation (Petipas & Danish, 1995); address sexual orientation issues (Cogan & Petrie, 2002); offer communication assistance (Yukelson, 2001); provide anger management (Hackfort, 1999); and develop performance enhancement programs (Moran, 1996). In addition, counselors may be contacted to provide the full range of crisis and psychotherapy services offered by counseling centers (Brewer & Petrie, 1996).

If the counselor develops a reputation in athletic circles grounded in "positive psychology," it is likely that student athlete clients will seek contact for peak performance or "sport psychology" assistance. Goals for treatment are likely to include management of preperformance anxiety; increased concentration, focus, and motivation; energy arousal management; how to get and maintain being "in the zone"; overcoming fear of reinjury; and management of critical or clutch moments during competition (Murphy, 2005).

Finally, students of color are another population who tend to underuse counseling center assistance (Davidson, Yakusha, & Sanford-Martens, 2004). Counselors are likely to find, however, that a primary way to develop significant relationships with students of color is through contacts via athletics. Thus, the sport psychology connections can potentially provide the opportunity to reach students of color on college campuses (Brinson & Kottler, 1995). These connections may also provide an opportunity to reach other students, such as those from lower socioeconomic and poorer educational backgrounds, who may not be aware of, or who may shy away from, counseling services or other such resources available to them on campus.

Counseling Implications

Practicing Within One's Area of Competency

When formulating strategic plans for fulfilling or extending the counseling center's central mandate to the athletic domain, directors of counseling centers and the professional staff working there may explore questions pertaining to commitment to target populations, outreach focus, and whether the athletic domain is being adequately served. Such questions might arise in the context of whether current services meet national best practice standards and whether the staff consists of personnel capable of fulfilling goals to reach out to student athletes if such a decision is made.

Once an individual counselor or staff member of a counseling center decides to assume responsibility for the college subgroup composed of student athletes, consideration must be given to American Psychological Association (APA; 2002) ethical Principles 2.01 and 2.04 and American Counseling Association (ACA; 2005) *Code of Ethics* 17 and 21 listing ethical Standards C.2 and C.4, which limit, mandate, and require psychologists and counselors to practice within their areas of competency. Questions arise as to when it is appropriate to profile oneself as a *sport psychologist* and how one best gains experience and begins working with athletes without ethical infraction (Bleiberg & Baron, 2004).

It seems that the simplest route to donning the mantle or title of sport psychologist would be to matriculate and graduate from a doctoral degree program in sport psychology. Without matriculation in or completion of such a doctoral specialty, the second means would be participation in supervised practicum work, an internship, or a postgraduate education program specializing in sport psychology.

In the absence of formal training, personal efforts to seek out professionals who are working as sport psychologists or in related areas, or intentional personal study and use of consultation in order to acquire specialty proficiency, should meet the APA (2002) ethical guidelines listed under Principle 2.01 c and e and the ACA (2005) Standards listed under C.2.a and b, which require the taking of reasonable steps to learn.

Perusal of and immersion into the research and applied literature of sport can be an effective way to begin gradually familiarizing oneself with the language and culture of the athletic domain. Excellent and comprehensive texts abound, such as *Exploring Sport and Exercise Psychology,* by Van Raalte and Brewer (1996); *Applied Sport Psychology: Personal Growth to Peak Performance,* by Williams (2001); *Handbook of Sport Psychology,* by Singer, Hausenblas, and Janelle (2001); and *Foundations of Sport and Exercise Psychology,* by Weinberg and Gould (2003). These texts easily supplement the many specific sport self-help books and journal articles that ably introduce the would-be sport psychologist to the field. Reading the literature, while working closely with a supervisor willing to help think through the various applications of general psychology to sport psychology, attending sport-oriented research and application sessions at regional or national conferences, and becoming directly involved in the open sessions at specific sport annual conventions, can be a helpful way of gaining familiarity and competency.

Practically speaking, however, many counselors are likely to develop expertise in the specialty by simply extending the traditional work they do in the college setting. Through these means, a counselor might begin working with teams and athletes, often relying on the universal core skills used by most counselors on college campuses. Through the years, many counselors have succeeded in doing excellent individual and group psychotherapy work with depressed or anxious students who also happened to be varsity athletes. Because of the group bonds within the fraternity of athletes, some of these athletes are likely to refer their friends when the opportunity arises, and these friends may be athletic peers. Other counselors may have noted, when offering outreach programs on study skills or management of test anxiety, the occasional student athlete who mentioned using or planning to use those same strategies in preparation for the "big game."

Such discoveries can be clues to the observant counselor that much of what therapists provide to their college clientele is based on common therapeutic factors and generally applicable even in the absence of specific references to sport or athletic competition. Counselors talking about eating disorders with members of a sorority chapter almost invariably have student athletes in the meeting room. They might suddenly find themselves responding to a request from one of these members, now representing her athletic team, to provide a similar workshop to her athletic team.

Counselors performing research on self-esteem, motivation, or alcohol use among college students may extend the literature review and designate one of the demographic variables as varsity sport-related, methodologically including student athletes as part of the subject pool and perhaps adding steroid use as one of the factors. Setting up the research protocol might necessitate significant contact with athletic directors, coaches, and student athletes, during both the design (e.g., getting permission) phase and the intervention phase. If the topic or focus of the research is potentially applicable to peak performance, the research contact may very well lead to requests for further involvement in the growing expertise areas of the counselor.

Ethical Challenges Concerning Dual Relationships and Boundary Management

Once training and competency issues have been resolved, the aspiring sport psychology counselor might soon be chewing his or her mouth guard, primed to begin taking the steps leading to riding the team plane or bus and sitting courtside. Before boarding a plane or bus, however, counseling center staff would do well to reflect on the ethical issues likely to arise in working with this population.

Matters related to dual relationships, for example, can become complex simply because the work with members of the team is constantly taking place at virtually all the myriad points of contact. Although it may be possible to refer an athlete to a colleague if one feels the need to engage in intense and prolonged work, an athlete's use of the counselor's expertise may occur specifically because the student athlete (a) will tolerate or use only pool- or courtside interventions, (b) trusts the counselor on the basis of familiarity, and (c) needs to prove that there is nothing so wrong or problematic that it cannot be resolved in the public arena, especially outside the stigmatized confines of the counseling center. ACA Standard A.5.c (ACA, 2005) recognizes the possibility of such occurrences and challenges the counselor to enter the therapeutic relationship only after noting the acknowledged benefit to the client. APA Principle 3.05 (APA, 2002) similarly calls for a careful scrutiny of the multiple relationships and places the responsibility on the counselor to determine whether treatment might be negatively affected.

Confidentiality and Privileged Communication

Counselors would also do well to anticipate potential breaches of confidentiality given that untrained coaches may make inquiries about an athlete after observing a courtside therapy session, sometimes involving tears, frustration, or self-flagellation. Whereas many athletes may readily offer permission to "tell my coach anything you wish," counselors may soon discover that some athletes share intimate personal material in direct proportion to their gradual recognition of the confidentiality granted by the counselor. At the same time, opportunities for continued in-depth work with the team may also be directly correlated with how open and helpful the counselors are in responding to the inquiries of the coaches, team captains, or even teammates. Whereas most counselors rely on their well-developed clinical skills, enabling them to suggest to the coach that he or she make the inquiry directly to the player, some wisdom is required in knowing when it is best to use the permission of the athlete to divulge information and when it is most advantageous to facilitate interaction between coach and player. Above all, ACA Standards B.1.c and B.2.d (ACA, 2005) and APA Principles 4.01 and 4.04 (APA, 2002) set standards of confidentiality for the sharing of only pertinent and necessary information when consent is granted.

Regardless of the circumstance, most counselors quickly learn that early discussions with coaches about the unique nature of privileged communication will pay dividends during those moments when communications must be protected. If discussed early on, most coaches are likely to assist in protecting the communication of the athlete, especially if there is some sense that, by doing so, the athlete's performance might improve. If discussed early on, most coaches are likely to exhibit a deep respect for the rules of the profession, given their intimate understanding and belief that the structure of the sport they coach is literally dependent on the rules governing it.

Finally, because of an appreciation of the reality that every game is different and one does well to be prepared for the unexpected, the novice, as well as the longtime sport psychologist, recognizes that survival in the specialty may depend on one's capacity for experimentation and flexibility. Some counselors are effective because of their strict and perhaps conservative adherence to the rules and ethical standards of their profession. These counselors, however, may find the work of a sport psychologist, given the constant demands for negotiating the complex interfaces between team, athlete, coach, parent, and counselor, too stressful and one they prefer to avoid. They may also find themselves "off the team" if unable to be flexible when managing the seemingly dual and multiple relationships. In contrast, if the counselor (a) maintains a curiosity about how best to negotiate the complexity; (b) is capable of full disclosure regarding ambivalence, uncertainty, confusion, and doubt when with a supervisor or colleague; and (c) discovers the powerful benefits of seeking insights from the full contingent of persons involved (i.e., players, coaches, and colleagues), the counselor is likely to offer helpful and effective assistance directly proportional to his or her curiosity, openness, and desire to best represent all treatment and ethical guidelines of the profession.

Moving One's Sport Psychology Interest Into the Action Phase

One question frequently heard at counseling center conferences in which sport psychology is being discussed is "I have strong interest, in-depth book knowledge, supervisory arrangements set up, and programs designed and ready to present to varsity athletes, but I'm not sure how to get the big break leading to meeting a team in the locker room or on the field. How do I get to the action phase?" The answer to this question may be one of the "make or break" issues for many counselors with aspiring sport psychology interests. Although some counselors may be fated by good fortune to acquire that opportunity via a series of events that thrust them suddenly onto the field/arena with their favorite sport and team, most counselors make it to the action phase by successfully marketing their credentials up front or through a very gradual process of prolonged effort.

In the first case, it may be that a degree and credentialing in sport psychology and previous good relationships between the counseling center and the athletic department may lead to a designed contract with an athletic team. This especially may occur if the center's director is supportive of the work being offered without expectation of monetary compensation, an athletic director is committed to such adjunctive assistance, and a coach is specifically looking for aid. The counselor or counseling center is likely to fall into such good fortune when the athletic department or coach is willing to try out the counselor's proposed product and when there is no indication that there will be a cost that accrues to the athletic budget. However, unless there is a precedent and money is specifically budgeted for such work, demands for financial compensation may limit the early development of a relationship.

In reality, the actual answer to the question for most counselors is likely to be one entailing a gradual process of contiguity and integration with the athletic domain. Involvement as a sport psychology counselor typically involves going through five stages: selection (scouting), introductions (recruitment), reconnaissance (signing), intentional contact (warm-up), and action (playing the game).

The first stage involves scouting, or attempting to select or choose a sport to play or be involved with. Scouting entails the counselor identifying a sport or two of primary personal or professional interest. For example, if the counseling staff decides to market its eating disorder expertise to the campus, the sport-oriented counselor might select the cross-country team, the women's swim team, or the men's wrestling team. Before even making initial contact with the coach or players, the aspiring sport psychology counselor may commit to attend the meets, learn players' names and performance statistics, and check out related Web sites. Familiarity with the venue, the fans, the team record, the different uniforms, and the game announcers all help when moving to the next stage. Mentally signing up with a team also helps focus the effort and enables better time management because much of the work involves time outside of the office.

The second stage is similar to the sometimes lengthy recruitment process, involving personal introductions and expressions of interest. Work during this stage involves meeting some of the players and coaches and engaging in positive commentary or expressions of interest or empathy regarding individual or team performance outcomes. Introductions at this point might simply include the counselor exchanging names and identifying him- or herself as personnel at the college and an interested fan. Equally important is the counselor becoming a familiar face, manifesting a personal profile of commitment to and interest in the sport. Coaches and players are likely to notice an increasingly familiar face and gradually become convinced of, and begin to value, the commitment and interest exhibited.

The third stage is reconnaissance and preparation to sign up with a team, having learned the critical elements of the sport. It is during this stage that the counselor, if it has not already been completed, does some reconnoitering. Knowing where the practice fields are located, which locker room the team uses, the name of the team's trainer, where the coaches' offices are, the names of the assistant coaches, and when the coaches are likely to be sitting in their offices can be highly beneficial. Knowing the turf and feeling confident negotiating one's way around in it help immeasurably when approaching key players in contract negotiation. Frequency of dropping by the coaches' offices with a quick hello and "good game" increases familiarity with both the rhythm of the athletic department and the character of the coaches.

It generally pays to realize that good coaches are often effective at recruiting. This means most are quite good at sizing up a person, including a counselor, not only in terms of expertise in the sport but also on how well that person fits into the personality of the organization and team. Counselors who can recognize fit or misfit may save themselves much time in pursuit of team involvement. When the fit is good, things may move quickly. When the fit is uncomfortable, for whatever reason, there may be some real advantages to looking for another team. When the fit is right and the relational work has been done properly, the sport psychology counselor may be ready to sign up and prepare to move to the next step.

The fourth stage is the stretching and warm-up period and involves intentional contact with some of the key players. In working with teams, rather than individual athletes coming to the counseling center, it may be important to recognize that head coaches, and occasionally assistant coaches and team captains, are typically the gatekeepers to the team. If Stages 2 and 3 have been successfully managed, the counselor may be in a strategic position to converse with the coach, mentioning a fascination with the game and specifically making comments about recognizing the importance of the mental part of it on the basis of having worked individually with student athletes and having watched games during the past season or two. Specifically mentioning the names of students taught in summer or regular semester courses can be advantageous to easy conversation and help facilitate a sense of familiarity.

When talking to the coach, the counselor may want to make an inquiry about gaining permission to watch some of the team's practices. An expression of interest in order to observe the dynamics of sport involvement for the purpose of better helping student athletes in general might result in the coach saying, "Sure, we practice between 4:00 and 7:00 p.m." A quick follow-up to the invitation will help indicate real interest. Once on site, the counselor is advised to begin watching team practices from a nonintrusive distance and to avoid pressuring the coach through too intense pursuit. Most counselors, should they decide to pursue more aggressively, will intuitively make contact if and only when it entails no disruption of the practice. Such opportunities may occur during practice breaks or at the end of practice, although there are occasionally times when coaches themselves are observing and reflecting and might enjoy reflecting aloud on what is being observed.

The fifth and final stage is one of action, or playing the game. It involves scoring. If a counselor has done the homework, put in the hours, sensed a successful match with the personality of the coach, and persisted with interest despite bad weather, odd hours, and times of defeat, there will ideally come a time when the coach asks if there is anything the counselor thinks might help the team, or the coach responds affirmatively to the counselor's expression of willingness to provide the team with the latest on preperformance anxiety, pain management, or peak performance training.

Some well-prepared counselors might have a designed intervention ready at all times. Other highly confident counselors, well versed in the basics of the profession and familiar with interventions such as relaxation strategies to reduce stress, may exhibit easy confidence in discussing or demonstrating the fundamentals of counseling outreach by accepting a spontaneous invitation to do a quick intervention with the team. That intervention might consist of facilitating a brief discussion about athletes' ideas of optimal responses to stress and a brief demonstration of deep muscle relaxation or calming breaths to lower anxiety. Demonstrating that a meaningful intervention can occur in 10 minutes may assure some coaches that counselors are not necessarily long-winded psychobabblers but can be compatriots capable of positive impact without threat of taking over the team. After the first intervention, the counselor needs to "review the game," perhaps talk it over with the coaches or team leaders, and begin settling in for a long season.

Campus Considerations

The range of services provided to athletic departments and teams by counseling center staff members is as varied as the subcultures and personalities of the athletic directors, coaches, players, and counselors themselves. Given this variability, a number of suggestions might be helpful to the novice counselor who has developed the requisite relationships with coaches and players and is faced with the decision of where to begin when invited to introduce the team to the potential benefits and power of sport psychology.

One strategy for getting started, similar to the warm-up phase of athletic activity, is for the counselor to begin working within an area of comfort and personal expertise, delivering a program already presented in other contexts. The counselor could request the opportunity to meet with the team a week or two before midterms in order to introduce stress-reducing strategies involving deep breathing or muscle relaxation exercises as preliminary aides to concentration and test preparation. The focus could be primarily on the anticipated midterms, although the student athletes could be additionally informed about how the exercises can be adapted to the big game or used for peak performance.

Another warm-up presentation could be on body image, eating disorders, and healthy diet, with the latter topic practically tied in with management of alcohol, steroid, and other drug use. Because many coaches have concerns about alcohol and drug use but hesitate to put themselves on the line given the high probability of players using regardless of the coaches' pleas, the coaches might be happy to have the sport counselor do the unenviable work of addressing alcohol and drug use. When such opportunities arise, the counselor is able to benefit from beginning his or her work in an area of confidence and familiarity.

Following the warm-up phase of involvement, the "frosh" sport psychology counselor hopefully will be in a position to extend the work, trying out suggestions from the literature or evolved from self-generated ideas. Because most college student athletes have not yet been inundated with the messages of sport psychologists, many are likely to try out usable techniques that hold promise for giving them the edge on the competition. Others, because of their competitiveness, at least want access to the same information that their competition has.

Many of the players may have heard of mental imagery or energy regulation but have never been given guided assistance in actually practicing it. Coaches as well as players may manifest a willingness to learn self-hypnosis if the sport psychology counselor points out that some players may find intentional strategies helpful during pregame focusing time. For some, this may be preferable to sitting in an unstructured situation, possibly trying to guess how other players are using the time, or wondering whether the personal strategies being used are as effective as those used by teammates or by elite athletes.

Some players are likely to be open to practicing strategies supported by empirical research or at least those taught to and used by elite and professional athletes. Although not all players are natured in such a way as to believe energy and arousal management is necessary for them, others will value input on how to manage adrenalin surges, how to progress quickly from anger or frustration to focus, and how to calm themselves or raise their energy level.

Finally, pain management is a constant challenge for athletes. If a counselor openly discusses such a topic with the team, individual players may well remember the counselor's willingness to address this issue and request specific assistance during rehab following injury or surgery.

Another area of consultation for sport psychology counselors involves work with teams around matters of team dynamics. Some coaches prefer teams consisting of members who are close and like each other. These coaches may want help creating even greater team cohesion than already exists, or they may exhibit some distress if cliques form or team chemistry seems poor. The counselor may want to introduce research suggesting that cohesion does not necessarily correlate positively with winning (Melnick & Chemers, 1974) and help determine with the coach whether a focus on team cohesion is the best use of time. Also, the group counseling skills of college counselors may be of significant aid to facilitate open discussions about the nature of the team's dynamics and the factors that either enhance or detract from the team's peak performance. Although counselors are urged to be very cautious about prematurely introducing athletes to group activities that threaten the "macho" or unemotional culture of the team, athletes are used to being pushed and to taking risks.

The counselor who has done appropriate homework—consulted with the coach regarding proposed interventions, spent time with team captains getting their "buy in" before taking ideas directly to the team, and found ways to encourage the team itself to experiment with what it is capable of doing—may experience success in helping teams better realize the predicted outcomes acquired by exercising psychological principles. These can include discovering that sharing fears aloud can sometimes normalize and thus diminish fear, that mentally imaging fearful situations can increase self-efficacy, and that group risk taking and cooperative goal attainment can increase group cohesion.

Finally, counselors may receive requests to do team or individual assessments. Profile, personality, and psychological skills evaluation may be perceived as helpful for coaches and for players, with this focus varying on a continuum from team cohesion to motivation, psychological vigor, and repressive tendencies, to anger management and capacity for concentration. Texts, such as *Advances in Sport and Exercise Psychology Measurement* (Duda, 1998) and *Directory of Psychological Tests in the Sport and Exercise Sciences* (Ostrow, 1996), can be helpful in identifying tests, making determinations about empirical support, and conducting such assessments.

Future Trends

Given the recent and ongoing discussions within the psychology profession regarding criteria for competence in designated specialties, a focus on sport psychology is likely to be one component of that discussion. Competency-based credentials eventually may lead to counselors being certified as sport psychology consultants by the Association for the Advancement of Applied Sport Psychology (AAASP) governing body. Members of the AAASP and members of Division 47 of APA have been dealing with this issue for more than a decade (Murphy, 1995) and still await answers concerning the degree to which the larger profession will embrace their criteria for credentialing. In 2005, the National Institute of Sports, moving ahead independently and in association with the National Register, began registering sport psychology with its own certification criteria. Questions remain unanswered as to what benefits might accrue on the basis of this certification and whether the professional community and, perhaps more important, members of athletic departments will value the certification.

Another associated question that may arise is how often credentialed sport psychologists will choose to work in college counseling centers or how competitive they will be in the counseling center applicant pool. Although the answer is unknown, it is probable that such candidates will be competitive only if they have spent a significant number of training hours working in a counseling center and understand well the culture and work in college-based centers.

In addition, counselors trained in sport psychology, and the professional communities that stand behind them, will be faced with questions regarding evidence for empirically supported interventions in sport psychology. Although these counselors will be able to reference evidence specific to work with anxiety or eating disorders, much future research will most likely be guided by efforts to show direct application to student athletes. Regardless of the outcome, members of counseling centers who develop services for student athletes on campus may find themselves enjoying and being energized by this new dimension of application and outreach and be encouraged by the generous appreciation extended by this clientele.

References

American Counseling Association. (2005). *ACA code of ethics*. Alexandria, VA: Author.

American Psychological Association. (2002). Ethical principles of psychologists and code of conduct. *American Psychologist, 57,* 1060–1073.

Birky, I. (2004, July–August). *Peak performance intervention effects on the drinking associated behaviors of intercollegiate athletes.* Poster session presented at the 112th Annual Convention of the American Psychological Association, Honolulu, HI.

Bleiberg, J., & Baron, J. (2004). Entanglement in dual relationships in a university counseling center. *Journal of College Student Psychotherapy, 19,* 21–34.

Brackenridge, C. (2003). Dangerous sports? Risk, responsibility, and sex offending in sport. *Journal of Sexual Aggression, 9,* 3–12.

Brewer, B. W., & Petrie, T. A. (1996). Psychopathology in sport and exercise. In J. L. Van Raalte & B. W. Brewer (Eds.), *Exploring sport and exercise psychology* (2nd ed., pp. 257–274). Washington, DC: American Psychological Association.

Brinson, J. A., & Kottler, J. A. (1995). Minorities' underutilization of counseling centers' mental health services: A case for outreach and consultation. *Journal of Mental Health Counseling, 17,* 371–385.

Carr, C. M., & Murphy, S. M. (1995). Alcohol and drugs in sport. In S. M. Murphy (Ed.), *Sport psychology interventions* (pp. 283–306). Champaign, IL: Human Kinetics.

Cogan, K. D., & Petrie, T. A. (2002). Diversity in sport. In J. L. Van Raalte & B. W. Brewer (Eds.), *Exploring sport and exercise psychology* (3rd ed., pp. 417–436). Washington, DC: American Psychological Association.

Davidson, M. M., Yakusha, O. F., & Sanford-Martens, T. C. (2004). Racial and ethnic minority clients' utilization of a university counseling center: An archival study. *Journal of Multicultural Counseling and Development, 32,* 259–271.

Davies, J., McCrae, B., Frank, J., Dochnahl, A., Pickering, T., Harrison, B., et al. (2000). Identifying male college students' perceived health needs, barriers to seeking help, and recommendations to help men adopt healthier lifestyles. *Journal of American College Health, 48,* 259–267.

Duda, J. L. (Ed.). (1998). *Advances in sport and exercise psychology measurement.* Morgantown, WV: Fitness Information Technology.

Hackfort, D. (1999). The presentation and modulation of emotions. In R. Lidor & M. Bar-Eli (Eds.), *Sport psychology: Linking theory and practice* (pp. 231–244). Morgantown, WV: Fitness Information Technology.

Hopkinson, R. A., & Lock, J. (2004). Athletics, perfectionism, and disordered eating. *Eating and Weight Disorders, 9,* 99–106.

Johnson, C., Crosby, R., Engel, S., Mitchell, J., Powers, P., Wittrock, D., et al. (2004). Gender, ethnicity, self-esteem and disordered eating among college athletes. *Eating Behaviors, 5,* 147–156.

Kahn, J. H., & Williams, M. N. (2003). The impact of prior counseling on predictors of college counseling center use. *Journal of College Counseling, 6,* 144–154.

Kerr, J. H. (2001). *Counseling athletes: Applying reversal theory.* New York: Routledge.

Mainwaring, L., Bisschop, S., Green, R., Antoniazzi, M., Comper, P., Kristman, V., et al. (2004). Emotional reaction of varsity athletes to sport-related concussion. *Journal of Sport and Exercise Psychology, 26,* 119–135.

Melnick, M. J., & Chemers, M. M. (1974). Effects of group structure on the success of basketball teams. *Research Quarterly, 45,* 1–8.

Moran, A. P. (1996). *The psychology of concentration in sport performers: A cognitive analysis.* East Sussex, England: Psychology Press.

Murphy, S. M. (1995). Introduction to sport psychology interventions. In S. M. Murphy (Ed.), *Sport psychology interventions* (pp. 1–15). Champaign, IL: Human Kinetics.

Murphy, S. M. (Ed.). (2005). *The sport psych handbook: A complete guide to today's best mental training techniques.* Champaign, IL: Human Kinetics.

National Collegiate Athletic Association. (2005). *NCAA coaches handbook: Managing the female athlete triad.* Indianapolis, IN: Author.

Ostrow, A. C. (Ed.). (1996). *Directory of psychological tests in the sport and exercise sciences* (2nd ed.). Morgantown, WV: Fitness Information Technology.

Perna, F., Antoni, M., Baum, A., Gordon, P., & Schneiderman, N. (2003). Cognitive behavioral stress management effects on injury and illness among competitive athletes: A randomized clinical trial. *Annals of Behavioral Medicine, 25,* 66–73.

Petipas, A. J., & Danish, S. J. (1995). Caring for injured athletes. In S. M. Murphy (Ed.), *Sport psychology interventions* (pp. 255–282). Champaign, IL: Human Kinetics.

Petipas, A. J., & Van Raalte, J. L. (1992). Planning alcohol education programs for intercollegiate student-athletes. *The Academic Athletic Journal, 9,* 12–25.

Singer, R., Hausenblas, H., & Janelle, C. (2001). *Handbook of sport psychology* (2nd ed.). New York: Wiley.

Van Raalte, J. L., & Brewer, B. W. (Eds.). (1996). *Exploring sport and exercise psychology* (2nd ed.). Washington, DC: American Psychological Association.

Weinberg, R. S., & Gould, D. (2003). *Foundations of sport and exercise psychology* (3rd ed.). Champaign, IL: Human Kinetics.

Williams, J. M. (Ed.). (2001). *Applied sport psychology: Personal growth to peak performance* (4th ed.). Mountain View, CA: Mayfield Publishing.

Williams, J., Rotella, R., & Scherzer, C. (2001). Injury risk and rehabilitation: Psychological considerations. In J. M. Williams (Ed.), *Applied sport psychology: Personal growth to peak performance* (4th ed., pp. 456–479). Mountain View, CA: Mayfield Publishing.

Wolf-Wendel, L., Toma, J., & Morphew, C. (2001). How much difference is too much difference? Perceptions of gay men and lesbians in intercollegiate athletics. *Journal of College Student Development, 42*, 465–479.

Yukelson, D. P. (2001). Communicating effectively. In J. M. Williams (Ed.), *Applied sport psychology: Personal growth to peak performance* (4th ed., pp. 135–149). Mountain View, CA: Mayfield Publishing.

Counseling Religious Students: Embracing Spiritual Diversity

3

Shannon Hodges

Introduction

Since the mid-1990s, numerous articles addressing the specialized needs of 21st-century students have proliferated student affairs literature. It is perhaps surprising that spirituality and religiosity have emerged as significant areas of inquiry for colleges (Fish, 2005) and college counseling professionals (Gorsuch & Miller, 1999). Spiritual–religious importance within U.S. culture is clear; reportedly, 96% of persons in the United States believe in God, more than 90% of them pray, and 69% of them regularly attend a church, synagogue, or mosque (Princeton Religion Research Center, 2000). What seems to have been lost in the literature, however, is the dramatic shift that has occurred in recent decades from students with predominantly Protestant backgrounds to growing numbers of students from Jewish, Muslim, Buddhist, charismatic Christian, and other spiritual orientations.

Despite much evidence affirming that a religious or spiritual orientation seems to be positively correlated with lower rates of addiction, depression, and anxiety (Pargament et al., 1990; Seligman, 1997), spirituality and religious concepts are often divorced from college counseling centers. Counseling centers seldom engage in any organized outreach to religious organizations, gear any programming toward religious or spiritual students, or maintain any formal lines of communication with campus ministers. Although a formal separation of the institution from religious organizations is important for institutional autonomy, alienation from campus religious and spiritual groups is not desirable for the counseling center because it disenfranchises large numbers of students who could benefit from counseling services.

Although the terms *religion* and *spirituality* are often used interchangeably, they are distinct from one another. For this chapter, religion is defined as an organized system of faith, worship, cumulative traditions, and prescribed rituals (Worthington, 1989). Religion by definition means "to bind together or express concern" (from the Latin root *religare*; Fukuyama & Sevig, 1999, p. 6). According to the Association of Spiritual, Ethical, and Religious Values in Counseling, spirituality refers to

> the animating force in life, represented by such images as breath, wind, vigor and courage. . . . It is an active and passive process. It is an innate capacity and tendency to move towards knowledge, love, meaning, hope, transcendence, connectedness and compassion. ("Summit Results," 1995, p. 30)

There is much overlap between the terms *religion* and *spirituality,* although religion is more institutionally defined, and spirituality is less attached to specific dogmatic regulations.

Assessment Issues

Many people find peace, solace, and community in their spiritual beliefs and community. Richards and Bergin (as cited in Gregory, 2004) offered several compelling arguments in favor of clinicians' assessment of the spiritual dimension:

1. Increase empathy by helping therapists to better understand the worldview of their clients.
2. Identify and assess the impact of healthy and unhealthy religious–spiritual orientations in clients.
3. Determine whether religious and spiritual beliefs and community can provide support to help clients.
4. Identify possible spiritual interventions that can be used in therapy to help clients.
5. Determine whether clients possess unresolved spiritual doubts or concerns that need to be addressed. (p. 476)

Richards and Bergin (as cited in Gregory, 2004) argued that clinicians need to address the whole person in order to provide a best practices model for counseling and assessment. Because most clients possess a religious–spiritual belief system, and college students are no exception, clinicians who address these dimensions of the human experience may be more prepared to provide effective counseling.

No counselor can be an expert in all religious or spiritual pathways, any more than a counselor can be an expert in all other clinical issues. In the best case scenario, the counselor who engages in an active learning process in multicultural counseling will be sensitive to religion and spirituality in the cultural context of counseling. The recommendation is not that counselors support tenets of faith but that counselors understand that religious and/or spiritual issues may be very important for the client.

A short projective-type assessment is the Spiritual Quest Form (SQF) developed by Nino (1997). The SQF is a brief 10-item screening questionnaire designed to explore spiritual attitudes. The SQF consists of 10 sentence fragments:

1. I see myself now . . .
2 I think the spiritual . . .
3 The people I have met . . .
4. Thinking about my past . . .
5. When I feel fragmented . . .
6. My relation to God . . .
7. The world around me . . .
8. A meaningful life . . .
9. The best I have ever done . . .
10. What I really would like to do . . . (p. 207)

Nino (1997) emphasized that the counselor should administer the SQF in a fashion similar to other projective techniques (e.g., the Rotter Incomplete Sentences Blank; Rotter, Lah, & Rafferty, 1992). Counselor–client exploration of the SQF can serve as a catalyst for clarification and exploration of deeper spiritual and personality issues. The counselor can assist the client in addressing particular spiritual themes and can readminister the SQF at a later stage of treatment to assess attitudinal changes. Nino advocated that spiritual assessments such as the SQF can serve as a base for exploration, and further inquiry regarding the client's answers results in more useful and therapeutic assessment.

Quantitative assessments differ from qualitative assessments in that they tend to have more focused functions and are scored more objectively. A common instrument for assessing spiritual health is the Spiritual Health Inventory (SHI; Veach & Chappel, 1992). The SHI is an 18-item self-report instrument that measures four factors of spirituality: personal experience, spiritual well-being, sense of harmony, and personal helplessness. Answers range from *strongly disagree* to *strongly agree*. The assessment is based on the hypothesis that spirituality includes contributions from the biological, psychological, social, and spiritual dimensions. The SHI highlights the spiritual aspects of these dimensions and is meant to be used, along with personal counseling, for deeper exploration. The SHI has the advantage of brevity (Kelley, 1994) and has been used frequently for research purposes (Standard, Sandhu, & Painter, 2000). The counselor should note, however, that the Judeo-Christian language of the SHI may not be appropriate for clients of other religious orientations.

Other instruments include the Index of Core Spiritual Experiences (Kass, Friedman, Zuttermeister, & Benson, 1991), which is a 7-item instrument designed to measure spiritual events and personal relationships with a spiritual presence. The Spirituality Assessment Scale (Howden, 1992), in contrast, is designed to measure unifying interconnectedness, purpose and meaning in life, innerness, and transcendence. This instrument is composed of general, nonreligious language and may be applicable to diverse populations. Finally, the Wellness Evaluation of Lifestyle (Hattie, Myers, & Sweeney, 2004) is designed to assess 19 dimensions of wellness. The model places spirituality at the center of a wheel of wellness. Spirituality is one of the subscales of the instrument.

Counseling Implications

Historically, religion and psychotherapy were connected because individuals providing what passed for counseling were ministers, rabbis, shaman, and numerous holy people in a variety of spiritual and religious traditions (Campbell, 1983). The word *psychology* comes from the Greek root words of *psyche,* meaning soul, and *ology,* meaning the study of a particular subject (Vande Camp, 1982).

The emergence of Charles Darwin's studies in the 19th century displaced the era of faith and led to the original split between faith and reason. Pioneers in psychology such as Freud, Watson, Skinner, Ellis, and others aligned themselves with the scientific worldview. As a result, religion and spirituality were divorced from psychology by all but a few, notably Jung, Frankl, and Allport.

These are the historical roots of the conflict between mental health professionals and spiritual health professionals (Hood, Spilka, Hunsburger, & Gorsuch, 1996). Freud (1938/1961) compared religion with a "childhood neurosis" (p. 53), and this view was supported by the widespread portrayal of religion as mental illness in psychological texts. The American Psychiatric Association's (1980) *Diagnostic and Statistical Manual of Mental Disorders (DSM–III)* seemed to suggest that religious experiences were evidence of mental illness in the same way as hallucinations. In response, Kilbourne and Richardson (1984) claimed that *DSM–III* had "an implicit and sometimes explicit tendency to devalue experiences common to many religions and to cast them into the pale of psychopathology" (as quoted in Hood et al., 1996, p. 407).

Many leaders in the religious community have also borne animosity to the field of counseling. At the same time, they have been providing individual and marital counseling in addition to spiritual guidance (Campbell, 1983). Unfortunately, many, if not most, religious leaders have little formal counseling training. Thus, although students may receive appropriate spiritual guidance from their religious leader, they may receive inadequate counseling. Conversely, some religious students may be hesitant to seek counseling from a secular counselor because they fear the professional may not respect their religious worldview (Constantine, Lewis, Conner, & Sanchez, 2000).

The divorce between psychological and spiritual matters has been nowhere more evident than on college campuses, where rationality and the scientific method are held in highest esteem. Although some researchers picked up on the scientific study of religion as a distinct field (Frankl, 1978; Hood et al., 1996), spirituality has only recently become a popular topic of study in higher education. Religion as an academic subject, taught in departments of psychology, philosophy, religious studies, and sociology, may have helped pave the way for the broader psychotherapeutic field to embrace the legitimacy of the spiritual domain (Cashwell & Young, 2005).

Yet, although nonspecific spiritual movements may be popular with members in the counseling movement, there remain challenges with regard to dispensing services to conservative Christian, Islamic, and other religious students. The best starting place for a model of understanding for religious–spiritual students and counseling is the spiritual competencies established by the Association of Spiritual, Ethical, and Religious Values in Counseling ("Summit Results," 1995):

1. The professional counselor can explain the relationship between religion and spirituality, including similarities and differences.
2. The professional counselor can describe religious and spiritual beliefs and practices in a cultural context.
3. The professional counselor engages in self-exploration of religious and spiritual beliefs in order to increase sensitivity, understanding, and acceptance of diverse belief systems.
4. The professional counselor can describe his or her religious and/or spiritual belief system and explain various models of religious or spiritual development across the life span.
5. The professional counselor can demonstrate sensitivity to and acceptance of a variety of religious and/or spiritual expressions in client communication.
6. The professional counselor can identify limits of his or her understanding of a client's religious or spiritual expression, demonstrate appropriate referral skills, and generate possible referral sources.
7. The professional counselor can assess the relevance of the religious and/or spiritual domains in the client's therapeutic issues.
8. The professional counselor is sensitive to and receptive of religious and/or spiritual themes in the counseling process as befits the expressed preference of each student.
9. The professional counselor uses a client's religious and/or spiritual beliefs in the pursuit of the client's therapeutic goals as befits the client's expressed preference. (p. 30)

The above competencies likely stretch the boundaries of counselor comfort regarding client religious–spiritual issues. Clinicians may well insist that spiritual and religious issues should not be addressed in public college centers because of separation of church and state. College counselors, however, grapple with many personal issues that are inappropriate outside of the counseling domain. Counselors should respect and remain open to assisting students to explore their religious–spiritual path, just as counselors help students with other areas of their lives: sexuality, anxiety, addictions, and so forth. Imagine a counselor saying to a client interested in exploring his or her spirituality in counseling,

"Sorry, I'm not allowed to discuss that." Simply referring a student back to his or her minister, priest, or rabbi may not be wise: first, because the student chose to see a counselor, not a cleric, and second, as previously stated, because religious leaders seldom are trained counselors, social workers, or psychologists.

Projective assessments, such as the Rotter Incomplete Sentences Blank (Rotter et al., 1992), may provide a counselor with a creative format to assist clients in spiritual self-exploration:

"My spiritual beliefs help by _____."
"What I find most fulfilling about my religious/spiritual life is _____."
"The most difficult aspect of being religious is _____."
"My spiritual community _____."
"My image of Higher Power (or God, or whatever is meaningful) is _____."

Bullis (1996) suggested that counselors delve into a client's spiritual background and use that background in counseling, such as exploring spiritual elements in the client's dreams, using spiritual language or metaphors in sessions, using or recommending spiritual books, or recommending participation in meditation groups, 12-step programs, and other spiritual programs.

For some clients, it may be helpful to incorporate a meditation of compassion into the counseling process, as taught by the Buddhist monk Thich Nhat Hahn (1997). When an individual is emotionally ready, the individual is instructed to meditate by sending an image of loving kindness to individuals who have hurt him or her. Hahn taught that compassion toward an offender does not imply consent to abuse or oppression. Rather, it means there is a deeper understanding of the root causes of injustice, oppression, fear, and so forth. Hahn also recommended compassion toward perpetrators as a means of empowerment.

The Gestalt empty chair technique (Perls, 1969) may prove useful in sessions with some religious or spiritual students. Using this technique, the counselor instructs the client to bring an absent person of concern into the room and pretend that the person is sitting in a nearby empty chair. The client is then instructed to address the chair, as if the person of concern were actually present. In some instances, the counselor may choose to take on the role of the person in the empty chair.

Some clients may find journaling their spiritual experience to be worthwhile. Christ (1995), for example, encouraged women to use journal writing as a guide for internal exploration or facilitative expression. With instructions to complete a sentence stem like "If God were a She," the journaling process allows women to validate their own religious experiences and claim them through their own words, without being restricted to patriarchal language imposed on them.

Some college students may find inspiration in spiritual expressions, such as gospel music or drumming (Fukuyama & Sevig, 1999). Other students, particularly international students, may find comfort through religious or spiritual practices that are connected to cultural traditions, such as worship of gods and goddesses (e.g., the orishas of West Africa) or the voudou movements of the Caribbean. The term *voudou* (or *voodoo*), which literally means "life principle" or "spirit," is a spiritual practice that includes imagining healing energy in nature, music, meditation, and so forth and is unrelated to the distortions and myths that Hollywood has created. For many students, particularly international students, religious practices may be as much about cultural connection as about religiosity.

It is recommended that counselors tread carefully with clients when dealing with religious and spiritual issues but essentially approach these issues as they would any other personal concerns. Cook and Wiley (2000) argued that instead of viewing religiosity or spirituality as competing forces against the counseling process, counselors can use these beliefs to enhance therapeutic effectiveness. Further, it is not necessary for the counselor to agree or disagree with the client's belief system to be clinically effective; the counselor must simply understand that individual belief systems are important to the client. What is important is for the counselor to craft a trusting, accepting, and nonjudgmental relationship with the client.

A final set of possible suggestions for incorporating spirituality into college counseling involve self-reflecting questions. For example, think of a way in which you have personally experienced suffering (emotional, physical, spiritual, etc.).

1. To what extent do you attribute the causes of this suffering?
2. What has helped you relieve your pain?
3. How have your spiritual–religious practices helped or hindered your healing?
4. What have others done that has helped or hindered your healing?
5. What is the next step for you in the healing process?

Campus Considerations

With ever increasing psychopathology on college campuses (Gallagher, 2004), and the fact that there is a strong link between the use of counseling services and student academic success (Turner & Berry, 2000; Wilson, Mason, & Ewing, 1997), it is vital that all students view counseling services as available. It is likely, however, that conservative religious organizations may feel threatened by college counseling professionals because they fear that counseling may drive students from their religious organizations.

Although I have yet to see any research on the topic, my experience as a counselor in several college counseling centers has been that campus ministers often have a mistrust of counseling services. Further, from my own experience, college counseling centers frequently do not see religious organizations as an important resource for college students. This chasm of misunderstanding and hostility on both sides can serve only to further alienate college students from seeking needed services to address sexual assaults, depression, anxiety, and so forth. In an era in which religion and spirituality are understood as important components to the client's framework, the counseling center and campus ministries would seem to have a real opportunity to work together and dispel long-held prejudices.

Many counseling centers sport rainbow signs to emphasize that the center is a "safe zone" for gay and lesbian students. Such displays are appropriate vehicles to convey to a segment of the population that the counseling center respects and values their (e.g., gay and lesbian students') presence. Likewise, counseling centers should make it clear in their informed-consent literature that they respect a student's religious and spiritual orientation. Many counseling centers, following their professional association (e.g., American Counseling Association, American Psychological Association, or National Association of Social Workers), have nondiscrimination statements that include religion or spirituality. The recommendation here is to do away with the notion of a nondiscrimination statement and replace it with an affirmation statement. The rationale for such a change goes much further than standard academic political correctness; instead, it conveys the message that spirituality, like sexuality, is a natural human expression. In addition, terms such as *tolerance* imply the bare minimum of collegiality and should be avoided.

College counselors must also take the first step in cultivating a relationship with campus religious and spiritual groups. Holding open-house gatherings that target campus religious leaders, offering in-services for campus ministers, and distributing counseling center literature are simple vehicles to establish rapport. Additional strategies include meeting with student leaders of religious–spiritual organizations to explain the services of the counseling center. Proactive outreach steps on the counseling center's part might help promote more understanding among campus religious organizations and greater counseling usage by their student members.

It is natural for humans to gravitate toward spiritual belief systems and religious organizations that are culturally familiar, make sense for them, or present what is perceived as a healthier way of life. College counselors must first take personal inventory and understand their own values and then move to understanding the values of the college students whom they serve. At this chapter's conclusion, several Web sites are listed to assist college counselors (see the Appendix).

Future Trends

The counseling profession has paid little attention to religious and spiritual issues in counseling until very recently (Cashwell & Young, 2005). Since the late 1980s, however, an interest in religious and spiritual themes in counseling has emerged. In a survey of 343 graduate students in counseling, 90% of those surveyed rated religious–spiritual issues as very important, important, or somewhat important in counselor education (Kelley, 1994). Most of the counselor education programs now require that human growth and development be included as an integral part of counseling programs. The Council for Accreditation of Counseling and Related Educational Programs (CACREP; 2001) has even developed spiritual competencies for CACREP-accredited programs, and the American Psychological Association has a division (Division 36) for the study of spiritual and religious themes in psychology. Nevertheless, regardless of this interest shown within professional associations, it is my experience that religious and spiritual students continue to be a relatively forgotten population in college counseling centers.

In the late 1980s, the mental health profession began to address multicultural issues as a new force in the profession (Arrendondo, 2002; Sue & Sue, 1999). *Multiculturalism* is a broad term that often covers ethnicity, gender, sexual orientation, veterans' status, disabilities, geography, and religion and spirituality. College counseling centers now target much of their outreach effort on addressing multicultural issues (Gallagher, 2004), but relatively little information exists in the literature regarding outreach to campus religious organizations.

In an ever increasing, pluralistic college population, college counseling will be challenged to address psychological needs from students of a variety of spiritual orientations. Wherever counselors find themselves on the continuum, they need to be as open as possible when engaging clients who represent a wide range of religious, spiritual, and cultural perspectives. In an era of increasing international, multicultural, and spiritually pluralistic student populations, counselors are being asked to stretch their skills even more. If college counseling centers are unwilling to dialogue across the secular–spiritual divide, not only will needy students go untreated, but counseling centers run the risk of becoming yet another anachronism.

References

American Psychiatric Association. (1980). *Diagnostic and statistical manual of mental disorders* (3rd ed.). Washington, DC: Author.

Arrendondo, P. (2002). Counseling individuals from marginalized and underserved groups. In P. B. Pedersen, J. B. Draguns, W. L. Lonner, & J. E. Trimble (Eds.), *Counseling across cultures* (5th ed., pp. 233–249). Thousand Oaks, CA: Sage.

Bullis, R. K. (1996). *Spirituality in a social work practice*. Washington, DC: Taylor & Francis.

Campbell, J. (1983). *Myths to live by*. New York: Penguin.

Cashwell, C. S., & Young, J. S. (Eds.). (2005). *Integrating spirituality and religion into counseling: A guide to competent practice*. Alexandria, VA: American Counseling Association.

Christ, C. P. (1995). *Diving deep and surfacing: Women writers on a spiritual quest* (3rd ed.). Boston: Beacon Press.

Constantine, M. G., Lewis, E. L., Conner, L. C., & Sanchez, D. (2000). Addressing spiritual and religious issues in counseling African Americans: Implications for counselor training and practice. *Counseling & Values, 45*, 28–38.

Cook, D. A., & Wiley, C. Y. (2000). African American churches and Afrocentric spiritual traditions. In S. P. Richards & A. E. Bergin (Eds.), *Psychotherapy and religious diversity: A guide to mental health professionals* (pp. 412–432). Washington, DC: American Psychological Association.

Council for Accreditation of Counseling and Related Educational Programs. (2001). *CACREP accreditation manual: 2001 standards*. Alexandria, VA: Author.

Fish, S. (2005, January 7). One university under God? *The Chronicle of Higher Education, Chronicle Careers,* 1.

Frankl, V. E. (1978). *The unheard cry for meaning.* New York: Simon & Schuster.

Freud, S. (1961). *The future of an illusion.* New York: Norton. (Original work published 1938)

Fukuyama, M. A., & Sevig, T. D. (1999). *Integrating spirituality into multicultural counseling.* Thousand Oaks, CA: Sage.

Gallagher, R. P. (2004). *National survey of counseling center directors.* Alexandria, VA: International Association of Counseling Services.

Gorsuch, R. L., & Miller, W. R. (1999). *Assessing spirituality.* In W. R. Miller (Ed.), *Integrating spirituality into treatment* (pp. 47–64). Washington, DC: American Psychological Association.

Gregory, R. J. (2004). *Psychological testing: History, principles, and applications* (4th ed.). New York: Pearson.

Hahn, T. N. (1997). *To be, to be free, to be happy. Thursday dharma talk* (Cassette Recording No. 5A-B). Longmont, CO: Backcountry Publications.

Hattie, J. A., Myers, J. E., & Sweeney, T. J. (2004). A factor structure of wellness: Theory, assessment, analysis, and practice. *Journal of Counseling & Development, 82,* 357–364.

Hood, R. W., Spilka, B., Hunsburger, B., & Gorsuch, R. (1996). *The psychology of religion: An empirical approach.* New York: Guilford Press.

Howden, J. W. (1992). Development and psychometric characteristics of the Spirituality Assessment Scale. *Dissertation Abstracts International, 54*(01), 166B. (UMI No. 9312917)

Kass, J. D., Friedman, J., Zuttermeister, P. C., & Benson, H. (1991). Healthy outcomes and a new index of spiritual experience. *Journal for the Scientific Study of Religion, 30,* 203–211.

Kelley, E. W. (1994). The role of spirituality and religion in counselor education: A national survey. *Counselor Education and Supervision, 33,* 227–237.

Nino, A. G. (1997). Assessment of spiritual quests in clinical practice. *International Journal of Psychotherapy, 2,* 192–212.

Pargament, K. I., Ensing, D. S., Falgout, K., Olsen, H., Reilly, B., Van Haitsma, K., et al. (1990). God help me: Coping effects as predictors of the outcomes to significant negative life events. *American Journal of Community Psychology, 18,* 793–824.

Perls, F. (1969). *Gestalt therapy verbatim.* Moab, UT: Real People Press.

Princeton Religion Research Center. (2000). Americans remain very religious, but not necessarily in conventional ways. *Emerging Trends, 22*(1), 2–3.

Rotter, J. B., Lah, M. I., & Rafferty, J. E. (1992). *Rotter Incomplete Sentences Blank second edition manual.* New York: Psychological Corporation.

Seligman, M. E. P. (1997, October). *Learned optimism.* Keynote address at the annual national convention of the Association of University and College Counseling Center Directors, Williamsburg, VA.

Standard, R. P., Sandhu, D. S., & Painter, L. C. (2000). Assessment of spirituality in counseling. *Journal of Counseling & Development, 78,* 204–210.

Sue, D. W., & Sue, D. (1999). *Counseling the culturally different: Theory and practice* (3rd ed.). New York: Wiley.

Summit results. (1995, December). *Counseling Today,* 30.

Turner, A. L., & Berry, T. R. (2000). Counseling center contributions to student retention and graduation: A longitudinal assessment. *Journal of College Student Development, 41,* 627–636.

Vande Camp, H. (1982). The tension between psychology and theology: The etymological roots. *Journal of Psychology and Theology, 10,* 105–112.

Veach, T. L., & Chappel, J. N. (1992). Measuring spiritual health: A preliminary study. *Substance Abuse, 13,* 139–147.

Wilson, S. B., Mason, T. W., & Ewing, M. J. (1997). Evaluating the impact of receiving university-based counseling services on student retention. *Journal of Counseling Psychology, 44,* 316–320.

Worthington, E. L. (1989). Religious faith across the life span: Implications for counseling and research. *Counseling Psychologist, 17,* 555–612.

Appendix

Web Sites of Interest

(not a comprehensive list but a beginning)

American Association for Pastoral Counselors (AAPC): www.aapc.org

American Psychological Association (APA), Division 36: Psychology of Religion: www.apa.org

Association for Humanistic Psychology (AHP): www.ahpweb.org/index.html

Association of Spiritual, Ethical, and Religious Values in Counseling (ASERVIC): www.aservic.org

Association for Transpersonal Psychology (ATP): www.igc.apc.org/atp

Buddhism: www.tricycle.com

Center for Spirituality and Health: www.spiritualityandhealth.ufl.edu/purpose/

Council for Secular Humanism: www.secularhumanism

Hinduism: www.indiadivine.com

Islam: www.islamworld.net

Judaism: www.zipple.com

The Pluralism Project (Harvard University): www.pluralism.org/about/mission.tolerance

Psychotherapy and Spirituality Institute: www.mindspirit.org

Religious Tolerance Organization: www.religioustolerance.org

World Religions Index: wri.leaderu.com

4

Coming to Terms With Gender Identity: Counseling Transgender Students

Tiffany O'Shaughnessy and Lynne Carroll

Introduction

The counseling field has been making progress in the quest to become more multiculturally competent (e.g., American Psychological Association [APA], 2003; Sue, Arredondo, & McDavis, 1992). The number of publications regarding ethnic (Atkinson, 2004), racial (Sue & Sue, 2003), and sexual diversity issues (Perez, DeBord, & Bieschke, 2000) has been increasing. However, the counseling field has remained relatively silent on the topic of gender diversity. Although transgender issues have been largely ignored in the professional literature (APA, 2000; Carroll, Gilroy, & Ryan, 2002; Fontaine, 2002), transgender persons themselves have become increasingly visible in our culture.

This chapter explores ways in which clinicians in college counseling centers can become more competent in working from a transpositive framework, that is, a framework in which clinicians affirm and advocate for their transgender clients (Carroll et al., 2002; Raj, 2002). The traditional knowledge, awareness, and skills approach to increasing multicultural competencies (Sue et al., 1992; Sue & Sue, 2003) was expanded and clarified by Constantine and Ladany (2001), whose recommendations for counselors included (a) acquiring a general knowledge of multicultural issues as well as a specific understanding of individual client variables, (b) increasing self-awareness and developing greater self-efficacy as a multicultural counselor, (c) developing a strong working alliance with the client, and (d) acquiring specific multicultural counseling skills.

Coming to Terms With Gender Diversity

Establishing a general knowledge about the transgender community must start with an understanding of the language and definitions used within the community. Language and labels are immensely important in the trans community. According to transgender activist Leslie Feinberg (1996), "It is forged collectively, in the fiery heat of struggle" (p. ix), and, as such, respecting the client's self-definition and language is crucial to the counseling process. We have included a glossary of terms in the Appendix to familiarize the reader with the language of the trans community. For the purposes of this chapter, the term *transgender* is used to refer to a diverse mix of individuals encompassing the full spectrum of nontraditional gender identities (e.g., cross-dressers, transvestites, transsexuals [pre- and postoperative], transgender persons, and gender queers).

Traditional approaches to labeling gender provide only two categories, male and female, which clearly exclude transgender individuals. Eyler and Wright's (1997) "nine-point gender continuum" (p. 6), ranging from "female-based" to "male-based" and including bigendered, can be extremely useful to the counselor in expanding his or her own conceptualization of gender. Counselors may use this continuum as a tool to understand and converse with transgender clients about the highly differentiated ways that they come to define their sense of gender identity.

According to Ettner (1999), attempts at estimating the size of the transgender community at large have been troublesome because most counts include only persons requesting sexual reassignment surgery. Ettner argued that persons with *gender dysphoria,* defined as a psychological discomfort with one's biological sex, composed 3%–10% of the general population. Attempts to estimate the prevalence of transgender persons on college campuses are even more problematic on the basis of Eyermann and Sanlo's (2002) observation that many college students are unwilling to share their sexual or gender identities either verbally or on forms. However, given the 3%–10% estimate, it is likely that there are transgender students on every college campus.

Culture Wars and the Transgender Community

Although the history of gender "transgressors" is vast and far-reaching (Feinberg, 1996), the current political movement grew dramatically during the 1990s. Parlee (1998) and Denny (1992) referred to many events that have shaped the transgender community, including the First Annual International Conference on Transgender Law and Employment Policy in 1992; the formation of the first transgender political action committee, Gender PAC, in 1995; the formation of Transgendered Officers Protect and Serve (TOPS) in 1995; and the First International Conference on Gender, Cross-Dressing, and Sex Issues in 1992.

The proliferation of conferences and committees is striking, but it pales in comparison to the amount of activism and networking that has taken place online (Denny, 1997). According to Shapiro (2004), the anonymity and accessibility of the Internet have made it an appealing place for the transgender community to communicate and offer support. It is likely that transgender clients will find much of their support through this medium.

In addition to increased institutional organizing, several highly publicized tragedies have further galvanized the community to speak out against transphobia and hate crimes and demand equal rights. These tragedies include the 1993 rape and murder of Brandon Teena, a female-to-male transgenderist depicted in the award-winning film *The Brandon Teena Story* (Muska & Olafsdottir, 1998).

Assessment Issues

Psychiatry and the Transgender Community

The standards of care developed by the Harry Benjamin International Gender Dysphoria Association (HBSOC; Meyer et al., 2001) outline several areas of focus for mental health professionals when working with transgender individuals who are seeking hormonal therapies or sex reassignment surgeries. These standards require that counseling professionals accurately diagnose gender identity disorder and provide letters of recommendation in order for clients to proceed with medical treatment. These standards have been extremely controversial in the transgender community for several reasons, including casting mental health professionals in the role of gatekeepers who either deny or recommend medical intervention. The requirement to live as the desired gender identity for a period of time before beginning medical treatment is also problematic for many transgender persons who are less able to "pass" and are therefore more vulnerable to detection and subsequent verbal and physical harassment (Fontaine, 2002).

At the Second Annual International Conference on Transgender Law and Employment Policy, the transgender bill of rights was drafted, a document that, among other concerns, asserts that all transgender individuals have the right to "freedom from psychiatric diagnosis or treatment as mentally disordered solely on the basis of a self-defined gender identity" (Feinberg, 1996, p. 174). This asserted right is in stark contrast to the reality of the HBSOC. Since the 1950s, individuals seeking sex reassignment surgery or hormonal treatment have been required to seek therapy and receive a diagnosis such as gender dysphoria, transvestic fetish, or gender identity disorder (see American Psychiatric Association, 1994, for detailed diagnosis information).

Although many transgender individuals are able to successfully pass as their desired gender without being detected, others are less successful in doing so. For some, the cost of medical treatment is too expensive or painful, and others struggle with a body that does not easily pass as their desired gender (Carroll et al., 2002). The HBSOC presents an additional challenge for the traditional-age (18- to 22-year-old) college student who is seeking hormonal or surgical interventions in order to pass. The HBSOC requires anyone under the age of 18 to wait at least

2 years after seeking consultation before beginning treatments, making it very likely that the person has been unable to access the medical interventions desired. Feinberg (1998) advocated for transsexual persons to come out as transgender and fight the oppressive gender norms instead of attempting to pass. Bockting (1997) noted that by asserting a transgender identity, persons with nontraditional gender identities could lessen the negative feelings of shame and isolation that often accompany attempts to pass as a desired gender.

Counseling Implications

Attitudinal Shifts

Treatment with transgender individuals historically focused on helping gender dysphoric persons adjust to their new gender identity. Bockting (1997) noted, however, that the focus had begun shifting and now included the opportunity to affirm a unique gender identity. In order for this paradigm shift to proceed, clinicians need to rethink their assumptions about gender, sexuality, and sexual orientation (Carroll et al., 2002).

There are several stereotypes and misconceptions about the transgender community that must be addressed. For example, there are still counselors who believe that transsexual people are ego-dystonic homosexuals or "fundamentally homophilic but unable to consciously accept their sexual orientation" (Fagan, Schmidt, & Wise, 1994, p. 7). Ettner (1999) noted that many counselors have communicated unnecessary "either or" messages, including counseling clients out of sex reassignment on the basis of their body type or pressuring clients into coming out to their families and communities without first exploring the possible repercussions if they are not emotionally, financially, and psychologically prepared for the transition. In addition, there is often a faulty assumption that transgender individuals are gay or lesbian. The literature (Denny & Green, 1996) has indicated that many transsexuals are, in fact, bisexual. Challenging assumptions and changing attitudes about the transgender community are critical steps toward working effectively with transgender clients.

Transpositive counseling is grounded in a social constructionist and client-centered approach (Bockting, 1997; Ettner, 1999). The clinical skills most necessary for working with transgender clients are active listening, empathy, and provision of a safe zone (Carroll & Gilroy, 2002). Building a strong working alliance with the client requires the ability to form an empathic bond (Bordin, 1979), but it may be difficult for counselors to empathize with their clients if they have not explored their own gender identity. Increasing self-awareness is essential. Bornstein's (1998) *My Gender Workbook* can be used as a resource to facilitate this process and help increase not only self-awareness but also self-efficacy.

Key Therapeutic Issues

According to Keeling (1998), the most important specific health issues for gay, lesbian, bisexual, and transgender (GLBT) students are (a) the psychological, emotional, spiritual, and physical consequences of homophobia and transphobia; (b) coming out; and (c) the challenge of developing healthy, empathic, and caring relationships. In addition, Keeling reported that isolation from self, others, and community; concerns about and consequences of unprotected, unwanted, or unvalued sexual behavior (including sexually transmitted disease and HIV infection); alcohol and other drug use and their negative impact on personal health and relationships; and reproductive health concerns are all critical issues for GLBT students.

Transpositive counseling creates a balance between facilitating client self-discourse and incorporating more directive interventions (Carroll et al., 2002). The societal discrimination that transgender individuals routinely confront further intensifies the need for trust within the counseling working relationship. Using constructivist therapies that include an analysis of the impact of social discrimination on mental health is very useful. Effective therapy with the transgender community requires that the counselor possess effective clinical, consultation, case management, and referral skills. Ettner (1999) suggested that mental health professionals should possess cognitive flexibility and work toward adapting a more directive and holistic style of therapy. Case studies (Carroll et al., 2002; Miller, 1996) have illustrated the benefits of taking a client-centered social constructionist approach.

Expanding Knowledge Bases

It is important to be aware that not every transgender client is at the same stage of identity development. Using an identity development model to assist in conceptualizing the client's interpersonal functioning can be useful in targeting interventions. There are few identity models that address gender diversity. However, Ancis and Ladany (2000) and Nuttbrock, Rosenblum, and Blumenstein (2002) proposed identity models that seem useful with transgender clients.

Ancis and Ladany (2000) proposed an interpersonal identity development model rooted in the idea of socially privileged groups and socially oppressed groups. It is believed that on the basis of demographic variables such as gender, race, and socioeconomic status, clients progress through different means of interpersonal functioning. This model is unique in that it allows for people to be members of seemingly disparate groups. Being transgender, for example, would place a portion of the identity in a socially oppressed category. However, it is possible that the client is simultaneously a member of a socially privileged group (e.g., middle-upper class, European-American). Individuals progress through four stages (adaptation, incongruence, exploration, and integration) of means of interpersonal functioning for each of their identity variables. Understanding the stage that the clients are in will assist the counselor in working with them.

In the adaptation phase, individuals generally conform or align with the socially oppressive environment, perhaps not noticing disparities or believing that the dominant culture is correct and that individual characteristics, rather than societal systems, perpetuate oppression. Clients in this phase might exhibit depressive symptoms, feeling that there is something wrong with them because they do not fit societal gender expectations.

The incongruence stage is characterized by dissonance and confusion. Typically an event will be witnessed or experienced by the client that highlights the disparities between socially privileged and socially oppressed individuals, leaving the client to question the dominant culture. Clients in this stage may present with agitated or frustrated views about society but generally still try to find ways to believe that the dominant culture is correct.

The exploration phase is typically characterized by anger and activism. The individual has recognized the extent of societal oppression and is actively working against it. Clients in this phase tend to immerse themselves in their culture to the exclusion of others. Transgender clients in this phase may be searching for ways to get involved, and the role of the counselor may be more of an advocate or consultant.

In the final stage, integration, individuals understand the implications of societal oppression and work toward equality. They are, however, more comfortable in their identity, able to navigate through the different environments and to integrate the seemingly disparate aspects of their entire identity. Nuttbrock et al. (2002) identified four stages through which transgender persons navigate while developing their identity: identity awareness, identity performance, identity congruence, and identity support. Each of these stages is characterized by a different task or struggle. The role of the therapist is to provide a space to help facilitate growth and development through these stages.

In the first stage, identity awareness, the issue is whether to keep the secret or begin to disclose that secret. Keeping the secret usually seems to be the safest option, but it is hypothesized that sharing this information with trusted sources would contribute to mental health. Nuttbrock et al. (2002) noted, however, that in the second stage, identity performance, "even if a transgender identity is revealed to others, a failure to act upon it in the context of the relationship may negatively affect mental health."

The third stage, identity congruence, focuses mainly on the concept of reciprocity from others. In explaining this stage, Nuttbrock et al. (2002) stated that "even if others are aware of transgender identity (identity awareness), and this identity is acted upon in the context of the relationship (identity performance), a failure of relationship partners to respond in terms of this identity may be disconcerting." Issues for exploration during this stage may include fear of rejection and communication concerns.

In the fourth and final stage, identity support, transgender clients have successfully navigated the previous three stages and are now in a relationship characterized by acceptance and reciprocity. The focus of sessions in this stage will likely be on maintenance of healthy relationships and will eventually move toward beginning the process again in a new situation or with a new individual.

Counselors and student affairs professionals on college campuses encounter students at various phases of transgender identity formation. They are likely, therefore, to find the models proposed by Ancis and Ladany (2000) and Nuttbrock et al. (2002) to be especially useful tools in their work with these students.

Campus Considerations

Transgender students on college campuses face the possibility of being "outed" on a daily basis. Society so clearly adheres to the binary conceptualization of gender that simple tasks such as using the restroom or a gym locker room can be frustrating and potentially dangerous for transgender students. Winters (2002) discussed the importance and power of a systemwide organization that addresses GLBT concerns. The report indicated that systemwide policies against discrimination and mistreatment help establish safer campuses for GLBT students.

Systemic Supports

Nakamura (1998) presented several case studies demonstrating some of the struggles of transgender students, including accessing bathrooms, fearing for their safety if their gender identity were known by their roommates, dealing with harassment and taunting after transitioning, and dealing with professors and administrators who continue to refer to the students on the basis of prior gender identity expression.

Student support services, such as the academic or tutoring center, career center, health center, women's center, and multicultural center, need to be aware of the specific needs and concerns of transgender students (Nakamura, 1998). Several researchers (Himbeault-Taylor, McQuaid-Borland, & Vaughters, 1998; Worthington, McCrary, & Howard, 1998) have noted the relative absence, yet extreme importance, of GLBT affirmative career advising in college settings. When necessary, the counselor must be willing to be an advocate for transgender clients with these centers. If counselors do not share their knowledge and work to educate the administrators in these positions, they essentially support continued discrimination.

Future Trends

Until very recently, research on transgender issues focused on curing or fixing transsexuals (Fontaine, 2002). Largely because of an increasingly vocal and visible transgender community, the counseling field has been gradually moving toward a transpositive approach to treatment and research. Because young people have begun to negotiate issues of sexual and gender identities at earlier ages (Ryan, 2001), it is likely that college campuses will witness the increasingly visible and active presence of GLBT students. Colleges need to provide a safe climate and services necessary to meet the needs of their transgender students. The reliance on case studies and anecdotal evidence and the lack of outcome research on the effectiveness of treatment strategies necessitate further empirical research.

References

American Psychiatric Association. (1994). *Diagnostic and statistical manual of mental disorders* (4th ed.). Washington, DC: Author.

American Psychological Association. (2000). Guidelines for psychotherapy with lesbian, gay, and bisexual clients. *American Psychologist, 55,* 1440–1451.

American Psychological Association. (2003). Guidelines for multicultural education, training, research, practice, and organizational change for psychologists. *American Psychologist, 58,* 377–402.

Ancis, J. R., & Ladany, N. (2000). A multicultural framework for counselor supervision. In L. Bradley & N. Ladany (Eds.), *Counselor supervision: Principles, process, and practice* (pp. 63–86). Philadelphia: Brunner-Routledge.

Atkinson, D. R. (2004). *Counseling American minorities* (3rd ed.). New York: McGraw-Hill.

Bockting, W. O. (1997). Transgender coming out: Implications for the clinical management of gender dysphoria. In B. Bullough, V. L. Bullough, & J. Elias (Eds.), *Gender blending* (pp. 48–52). Amherst, NY: Prometheus Books.

Bordin, E. (1979). The generalizability of the psychoanalytic concept of the working alliance. *Psychotherapy: Theory, Research and Practice, 16,* 252–260.

Bornstein, K. (1998). *My gender workbook.* New York: Routledge.

Carroll, L., & Gilroy, P. J. (2002). Transgender issues in counselor preparation. *Counselor Education and Supervision, 41,* 233–242.

Carroll, L., Gilroy, P. J., & Ryan, J. (2002). Counseling transgendered, transsexual, and gender-variant clients. *Journal of Counseling & Development, 80,* 131–139.

Constantine, M. G., & Ladany, N. (2001). New visions for defining and assessing multicultural counseling competence. In J. G. Ponterotto, J. M. Casas, L. A. Suzuki, & C. M. Alexander (Eds.), *Handbook of multicultural counseling* (2nd ed., pp. 482–498). Thousand Oaks, CA: Sage.

Denny, D. (1992). The politics of diagnosis and a diagnosis of politics. *Chrysalis Quarterly, 1,* 9–20.

Denny, D. (1997). Transgender: Some historical, cross-cultural, and contemporary methods of coping and treatment. In B. Bullough, V. L. Bullough, & J. Elias (Eds.), *Gender blending* (pp. 33–47). Amherst, NY: Prometheus Books.

Denny, D., & Green, J. (1996). Gender identity and bisexuality. In B. Firestein (Ed.), *Bisexuality: The psychology and politics of an invisible minority* (pp. 84–102). Thousand Oaks, CA: Sage.

Ettner, R. (1999). *Gender loving care: A guide to counseling gender-variant clients.* New York: Norton.

Eyermann, T., & Sanlo, R. (2002). Documenting their existence: Lesbian, gay, bisexual, and transgender students on campus. In R. Sanlo, S. Rankin, & R. Schoenberg (Eds.), *Our place on campus: Lesbian, gay, bisexual, transgender services and programs in higher education* (pp. 33–40). Westport, CT: Greenwood Press.

Eyler, A. E., & Wright, K. (1997). Gender identification and sexual orientation among genetic females with gender-blended self-perception in childhood and adolescence. *The International Journal of Transgenderism, 1.* Retrieved March 8, 2005, from http://www.symposion.com/ijt/ijtc0102.htm

Fagan, P. J., Schmidt, C. W., & Wise, T. N. (1994, August 22 & 29). Born to the wrong sex [Letter to the editor]. *The New Yorker, 7,* 15.

Feinberg, L. (1996). *Transgender warriors: Making history from Joan of Arc to Dennis Rodman.* Boston: Beacon Press.

Feinberg, L. (1998). *Trans liberation: Beyond pink or blue.* Boston: Beacon Press.

Fontaine, J. H. (2002). Transgender issues in counseling. In L. Burlew & D. Capuzzi (Eds.), *Sexuality counseling* (pp. 177–194). Hauppauge, NY: NOVA Science Publishers.

Himbeault-Taylor, S., McQuaid-Borland, K., & Vaughters, S. D. (1998). Addressing the career needs of lesbian, gay, bisexual, and transgender college students. In R. Sanlo (Ed.), *Working with lesbian, gay, bisexual, and transgender college students: A handbook for faculty and administrators* (pp. 123–133). Westport, CT: Greenwood Press.

Keeling, R. P. (1998). Effective and humane campus health and counseling services. In R. Sanlo (Ed.), *Working with lesbian, gay, bisexual, and transgender college students: A handbook for faculty and administrators* (pp. 147–157). Westport, CT: Greenwood Press.

Meyer, W., Bockting, W., Cohen-Kettenis, P., Coleman, E., Dicegli, D., Devor, H., et al. (2001, January–March). *The Harry Benjamin International Gender Dysphoria Association's standards of care for gender identity disorders* (6th ed.). Retrieved March 8, 2005, from http://www.hbigda.org/pdf/socv6.pdf

Miller, N. (1996). *Counseling in genderland: A guide for you and your transgendered client.* Boston: Different Path Press.

Muska, S., & Olafsdottir, G. (Directors). (1998). *The Brandon Teena story* [Motion picture]. United States: Zeitgeist Films.

Nakamura, K. (1998). Transitioning on campus: A case studies approach. In R. Sanlo (Ed.), *Working with lesbian, gay, bisexual, and transgender college students: A handbook for faculty and administrators* (pp. 179–186). Westport, CT: Greenwood Press.

Nuttbrock, L., Rosenblum, A., & Blumenstein, R. (2002). Transgender identity affirmation and mental health. *The International Journal of Transgenderism, 6.* Retrieved March 8, 2005, from http://www.symposion.com/ijt/ijtvo06no04_03.htm

Parlee, M. B. (1998). Situated knowledge of personal embodiment: Transgender activists' and psychological theorists' perspectives on "sex" and "gender." In H. J. Stern (Ed.), *The body and psychology* (pp. 120–140). Thousand Oaks, CA: Sage.

Perez, R. M., DeBord, K. A., & Bieschke, K. J. (2000). *Handbook of counseling and psychotherapy with lesbian, gay, and bisexual clients.* Washington, DC: American Psychological Association.

Raj, R. (2002). Towards a transpositive therapeutic model: Developing clinical sensitivity and cultural competence in the effective support of transsexual and transgendered clients. *The International Journal of Transgenderism, 6.* Retrieved March 8, 2005, from http://www.symposion.com/ijt/ijtvo06no02_04.htm

Ryan, C. (2001). Counseling lesbian, gay, and bisexual youths. In A. R. D'Augelli & C. J. Patterson (Eds.), *Lesbian, gay, and bisexual identities and youth* (pp. 224–250). New York: Oxford University Press.

Shapiro, E. (2004). "Trans"cending barriers: Transgender organizing on the Internet. *Journal of Gay and Lesbian Social Services, 16,* 165–179.

Sue, D. W., Arredondo, P., & McDavis, R. J. (1992). Multicultural counseling competencies and standards: A call to the profession. *Journal of Counseling & Development, 70,* 484–486.

Sue, D. W., & Sue, D. (2003). *Counseling the culturally diverse: Theory and practice* (4th ed.). New York: Wiley.

Winters, J. (2002). The power of a system-wide organization: The University of California LGBTI Association. In R. Sanlo, S. Rankin, & R. Schoenberg (Eds.), *Our place on campus: Lesbian, gay, bisexual, transgender services and programs in higher education* (pp. 121–130). Westport, CT: Greenwood Press.

Worthington, R. L., McCrary, S. I., & Howard, K. A. (1998). Becoming an LGBT affirmative career adviser: Guidelines for faculty, staff, and administrators. In R. Sanlo (Ed.), *Working with lesbian, gay, bisexual, and transgender college students: A handbook for faculty and administrators* (pp. 136–143). Westport, CT: Greenwood Press.

Appendix

Glossary of Terms

Please note that the following terms and their definitions are not necessarily universally accepted. Variations exist both within and outside the trans communities in the usage and interpretation of these terms.

Cross-Dresser: An individual who dresses in clothing that is culturally associated with members of the "other" sex. Most cross-dressers are heterosexual and conduct their cross-dressing on a part-time basis. Cross-dressers cross-dress for a variety of reasons, including pleasure, a relief from stress, and a desire to express "opposite" sex feelings to the larger society.

Drag King: A term usually reserved for individuals who identify themselves as lesbians and who cross-dress for entertainment purposes in lesbian and gay bars.

Drag Queen: A term usually reserved for individuals who identify themselves as gay men and who cross-dress for entertainment purposes in lesbian and gay bars.

Gender: A complicated set of sociocultural practices whereby human bodies are transformed into "men" and "women." Gender refers to that which a society deems "masculine" or "feminine." Gender identity refers to an individual's self-identification as a man, woman, transgendered, or other identity category.

Gender Bender: An individual who brazenly and flamboyantly flaunts society's gender conventions by mixing elements of "masculinity" and "femininity." The gender bender is often an enigma to the uninitiated viewer, who struggles to comprehend sartorial codes that challenge gender bipolarity. Boy George, a popular culture icon, was often referred to as a "gender bender" by the press.

Gender Dysphoria: A term used by the psychiatric establishment to refer to a radical incongruence between an individual's birth sex and gender identity. An individual who is "gender dysphoric" feels an irrevocable disconnect between his or her physical body and his or her mental sense of gender. Many in the transgender community find this term offensive or insulting because it often pathologizes the transgendered individuals due to its association with the *DSM–IV*.

Gender Identity: See Gender.

Gender Outlaw: A term popularized by trans activists such as Kate Bornstein and Leslie Feinberg, a gender outlaw refers to an individual who transgresses or violates the "law" of gender (i.e., one who challenges the rigidly enforced gender roles) in a transphobic, heterosexist, and patriarchal society.

Gender Queer: A term that refers to individuals who "queer" the notions of gender in a given society. It may also refer to a person who identifies as both transgendered and queer (i.e., individuals who challenge both gender and sexuality regimes and see gender identity and sexual orientation as overlapping and interconnected).

Gender Trash: A term that calls attention to the way that differently gendered individuals are often treated like "trash" in a transphobic culture.

Gender Variant: A term that refers to individuals who stray from socially accepted gender roles in a given culture. This word may be used in tandem with other group labels, such as gender-variant gay men and lesbians.

Intersex: Formerly termed *hermaphrodites,* individuals termed *intersex* are born with some combination of ambiguous genitalia. The Intersex movement seeks to halt pediatric surgery and hormone treatments that attempt to normalize infants into the dominant "male" and "female" roles.

Queer: *Queer* is a term that has been reclaimed by members of the gay, lesbian, bisexual, and transgender communities to refer to people who transgress culturally imposed norms of heterosexuality and gender traditionalism. Although it is still often an abusive epithet when used by heterosexuals, many queer-identified people have taken back the word to use it as a symbol of pride and affirmation of difference and diversity.

Queer Theorist: An individual, usually an academic, who uses feminism, psychoanalysis, poststructuralism, and other theoretical schools to critically analyze the position of gay, lesbian, and transgendered individuals in cultural texts.

Sex: Separate from gender, this term refers to the cluster of biological, chromosomal, and anatomical features associated with maleness and femaleness in the human body. Sexual dimorphism is often thought to be a concrete reality, whereas in reality the existence of the intersex points to a multiplicity of sexes in the human population.

Sexual Orientation: This term refers to the gender(s) that a person is emotionally, physically, romantically, and erotically attracted to. Examples of sexual orientation include homosexual, bisexual, heterosexual, and asexual. Transgendered and gender-variant people may identify with any sexual orientation, and their sexual orientation may or may not change during or after gender transition.

Sexuality: An imprecise word that is often used in tandem with other social categories, as in race, gender, and sexuality. *Sexuality* is a broad term that refers to a cluster of behaviors, practices, and identities in the social world.

Trans: An umbrella term that refers to cross-dressers, transgenderists, transsexuals, and others who permanently or periodically disidentify with the sex they were assigned at birth. Trans is preferable to "transgender" to some in the community because it does not minimize the specifics of transsexuals.

Transgender: A range of behaviors, expressions, and identifications that challenge the pervasive bipolar gender system in a given culture. This, like *trans,* is an umbrella term that includes a vast array of differing identity categories such as transsexual, drag queen, drag king, cross-dresser, transgenderist, bigendered, and a myriad of other identities.

Transgendered Lesbian: An individual, regardless of biological sex, who identifies as both transgendered and lesbian. This could include male-to-female transgenders who are sexually attracted to women or biological females who identify as lesbians and who often "pass" as men or who identify to some degree with masculinity or with "butch."

Transgenderist: Coined by Virginia Prince, this category refers to an individual who disidentifies with his or her assigned birth sex and lives full-time in congruence with his or her gender identity. This may include a regimen of hormone therapy, but transgenderists usually do not seek or want sex reassignment surgery.

Transphobia: The irrational fear and hatred of all those individuals who transgress, violate, or blur the dominant gender categories in a given society. Transphobic attitudes lead to massive discrimination and oppression against trans, drag, and intersex communities.

Transsexual: An individual who strongly disidentifies with his or her birth sex and wishes to use hormones and sex reassignment surgery (or gender confirmation surgery) as a way to align his or her physical body with his or her internal gender identity.

Transvestite: An older term, synonymous with the more politically correct term *cross-dresser*, that refers to individuals who have an internal drive to wear clothing associated with a gender other than the one that they were assigned at birth. The term *transvestite* has fallen out of favor because of its psychiatric, clinical, and fetishistic connotations.

From Carroll, L., Gilroy, P. J., & Ryan, J. (2002). Counseling transgendered, transsexual, and gender-variant clients. *Journal of Counseling & Development, 80,* 131–139.

Section II
Culture, Ethnicity, Class, and Age Issues

Mobility, Multiculturalism, and Marginality: Counseling Third-Culture Students

5

Kevin F. Gaw

Introduction

Karen, a first-semester, first-year 17-year-old American student at a midwest university, stumbles over the ever-asked question, yet again: "Where are you from, Karen?" Her mind reels with the many possible answers, and she tries to assess the other person's world-mindedness by dress, accent, body language, and expressed affiliation. She tries to know whether her response, normal for Karen and students like her, will sound snobby and pompous or, worse, condescending. Her roommates all discuss their recent work experiences, interests, and social lives—jobs, breakups, friends, shopping, sports, boyfriends, and family at home. They question whether they will go home at all during the upcoming Thanksgiving break, they discuss the expected reunion parties and the football rivalries, and they talk about working at chain stores to make money during the holidays. She opts for the chronology approach to the question, hoping that a list of cities, a list of the many places in which she has lived overseas, sounds normal and explanatory. With no true American hometown roots other than a birth city and no clearly identifiable lineage, cultural or social, Karen knows she can't sound as American as the young women with whom she's interacting. Karen feels like a fish out of water, like a foreigner in her own country.

The third-culture kid (TCK) is not defined by an affluent lifestyle overseas, as is often the stereotypic assumption by those with little or no out-of-country living experience. The TCK is also not an imaginary definition of a population trying to gain a foothold in the multicultural mosaic of American society. TCKs are an immensely diverse multinational population and are passport holders of many different countries. Culturally, however, they share unique attributes that allow the third-culture identity to emerge as a defining feature.

Pollock and Van Reken (1999) defined the TCK as

> a person who has spent a significant part of his or her developmental years outside the parents' culture. The TCK builds relationships to all of the cultures, while not having full ownership in any. Although elements from each culture are assimilated into the TCK's life experience, the sense of belonging is in relationship to others of a similar background. (p. 19)

The *third culture* is the intersection between the parents' culture, the student's passport culture if not the same as the parents', and the intercultural environment in which the student develops. The result is a dynamic sense of cultural space, marked by mobility, multiculturalism, and marginality—an interstitial cultural milieu. Being in between cultures is an experience shared by the TCKs, and, thus, the community of the third culture emerges.

The TCKs' parents are usually expatriates, or "expats," living for an extensive number of years "abroad," outside of their passport country. They are also frequently "global nomads," moving from one job assignment to another, from one country to another. The TCK constituency therefore includes the children of missionaries, relief agency workers, educators, Fulbrighters, corporate and entrepreneurial business professionals, and government personnel (civilian, military, and diplomatic corps). The TCK community is represented by nearly every nationality. Together, these TCKs share an experience that binds them as a multiethnic, multiracial, and multireligious group—the experience of growing up outside their passport countries in an ever-fluid multicultural and international community.

This chapter discusses TCKs from the United States, although what is stated within this chapter is applicable to Singaporean TCKs, Dutch TCKs, Indian TCKs, Japanese TCKs, or Moroccan TCKs, within the contexts of their experiences. In addition, this chapter focuses on the college student population of TCKs and, more specifically, the mental health issues related to this experience.

The TCK college student population is special for several important clinical as well as humanistic reasons. TCKs often return to a home culture with which they never have truly affiliated despite looking like they should fit in. This "out of placeness" can be deeply troubling for returnees and for the nonreturnees around them. Reentry, or reverse, culture shock is actually more challenging and disruptive than initial culture shock, affecting the returnee's academic, social, and personal functioning. Identity and social development issues are significant because the TCK's role models are no longer immediately available.

Social support is limited for most TCKs because campuses have often failed to recognize TCKs as a uniquely defined student population and have therefore provided little to no systemic support. The mental health professional has often conceptualized reentry culture shock as a clinical syndrome rather than a developmental experience and, as such, has identified deficits rather than strengths and opportunities. Finally, some 37,000 TCKs return to the United States every year for college (Gaw, 2000). This is not a small group of entering students but a very real multicultural population. In fact, some institutions, such as Lewis &

Clark College in Portland, Oregon, specifically recruit TCKs, seeing them as valuable contributors to the campus community.

Assessment Issues

The TCK experience is not a pathology or disorder, and there are no subcategories of the TCK for deviance or clinical risk. However, assessment is as valid an activity with the TCK client as any other client. In general, the TCK expresses clinical issues in much the same way as domestic students, although the clinician needs to be aware that cultural definitions and experiences of issues may be different. For example, a European-American TCK raised primarily in Indonesia may liken a broken heart from a relationship breakup to a sick liver *(sakit hati)*, a Javanese concept. This reference may seem strange, or even attention getting, to domestic clinicians. A TCK who has experienced many transitions and endings in friendships because of parental contract changes, and therefore frequent moves, may feel little regret over relationship changes because they are perceived as normal. In these situations, the counselor needs to ask for more information to learn whether there is a deeper experience that is not spoken about.

Practitioners must be cognizant of possible misdiagnoses, or incorrect clinical pictures, that may result from (a) not understanding this population, (b) not accepting and validating this population as real, (c) assuming the TCK experience is transitory and something a client will grow out of, or (d) assuming that majority-normed assessment tools and constructs will be applicable. For example, a TCK's lack of experience with the American way may cause a TCK to literally interpret "twenty-one-hundred" as "20-1-100," rather than "2100," which is the common meaning within the United States. Another example is that a TCK may have learned interpersonal behaviors that are completely different from the U.S. norm and that, on reentry, are viewed as deviant or alternative (e.g., two men holding hands in public who are friends and not a gay couple). Such examples of difference can be found in values, behavior, language, formalities, relationships, academic skills and identity, thought, and emotion, to name a few dimensions.

Cultural identity development is a key assessment dimension for TCKs, because much of what brings them into counseling is related to the difficult question, "Who am I?" M. J. Bennett's (1993, 1998) model is particularly useful in assessing intercultural sensitivity development, a cornerstone to TCK identity. One might also explore the TCK literature on identity formation (e.g., Jordan, 2002; Pollock & Van Reken, 1999), attachment theory (Schaetti, 2002), and vocational maturation factors (Cottrell, 2002). In addition, the identity development models commonly used in counseling nonmajority clients may be helpful in structuring the TCK's identity experience (e.g., stages of development from no recognition of difference to resolution and integration of differences).

Reentry culture shock is an essential developmental experience and requires careful attention. One of the more obvious signs of adjustment challenges is

TCKs' uncomfortable, yet frustrated, efforts to fit in with their home country. Assimilation is not a reasonable goal, although, through assimilation, many TCKs feel they might be able to resolve their struggles to affiliate. Acculturation and multicultural development are the key goals (Adler, 1975).

Counseling Implications

TCKs bring to the counseling session not only many of the same clinical and developmental concerns that traditional students present but also some unique issues: reentry culture shock, or reverse culture shock; cultural identity confusion; and cultural affiliation challenges.

Culture Shock and Reentry Culture Shock

Psychologically adjusting to a new cultural environment is the essence of both culture shock and reentry culture shock. The initial *U-curve hypothesis*, first proposed in 1955 by Lysgaard, and then the *W-curve hypothesis*, proposed by Gullahorn and Gullahorn (1963), remain the cornerstones for describing the adjustment challenges of the person experiencing the transition stresses of intercultural engagement and change. All of the literature to date presents descriptive models that have essentially the same stages of adjustment, with minor variations (see Gaw, 2000, for a detailed discussion), as depicted in Figure 5.1.

Typically, all of the models have an initial contact phase with the new cultural environment, commonly described as seeking and experiencing similarities, en-

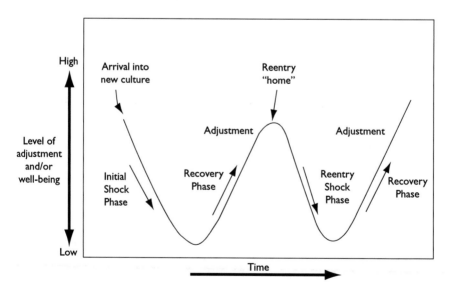

Figure 5.1

Culture Shock and Reentry Culture Shock

joyment, excitement, and euphoria in being someplace culturally new. Then the person encounters difficulties related to culture shock, specifically, issues associated with cultural differences between the individual and the culturally different "others": worldviews, values, behaviors, beliefs, attitudes, and so forth. The cultural schism for some individuals is quite dramatic, and they may experience considerable distress. Other individuals, depending on their resilience, resources, and preparedness, may find the experience deeply intriguing, although also challenging. As individuals learn to manage and resolve these differences and experience them as contextually normal and acceptable, they recover into a more resolved phase, eventually leading to a level of competent intercultural functioning, which connotes adjustment.

Reentry culture shock is somewhat similar in stages yet is often significantly more difficult to manage. According to Gullahorn and Gullahorn (1963), the main difference between reentry culture shock and culture shock is the expectations of the individual. TCKs usually expect, and thus are more or less cognitively prepared for, cultural differences when entering a new culture, thereby potentially minimizing the effects of culture shock (Gullahorn & Gullahorn, 1963; Searle & Ward, 1990; Weissman & Furnham, 1987). They often expect, however, that coming home will be easier (Blake & Gaw, 2004; Gaw, 2000, 2004). They may expect, for example, to return to an unchanged home as unchanged individuals, which is not the case. Although many TCKs may have been to the United States on "home leave" with their parents, their stay was probably more akin to a tourist vacation, disconnected from deep-rooted American cultural features that are typical of students of comparable age. For returnees who have spent most of their lives abroad, the expectations are probably based on what they think home is supposed to be as communicated by parents, peers, media, and so forth (Stelling, 1991).

There is no time frame for either culture shock or reentry culture shock. Some individuals quickly work their way through these developmental stages, within a few weeks to several months, whereas others may need much longer to resolve the issues (Gaw, 2000). Support, validation, encouragement, intercultural competency development, and intercultural knowledge development are all interventions that assist the "shocked."

Although both culture shock and reentry culture shock are now conceptualized as normal developmental experiences when one is adjusting to a cultural environment (e.g., Adler, 1975; Harris, Moran, & Moran, 2004), they were originally perceived differently. For example, culture shock was seen as ranging from psychologically distressing to pathological (Lysgaard, 1955; Oberg, 1960), whereas reentry culture shock was seen as an affluent experience of no social, clinical, or professional concern or interest. Current literature (e.g., Blake & Gaw, 2004; Gaw, 2004; Harris et al., 2004; Pollock & Van Reken, 1999) regards both experiences as developmental, although clinicians also recognize that the adjustment stress may bring to the forefront already existing disorders or clinical issues, such as anxiety, depression, or eating disorders (e.g., Befus, 1988; Blake & Gaw, 2004; Gaw, 2004; Searle & Ward, 1990; Thomas & Althen, 1989).

Common psychological correlates of cultural adjustment, such as loneliness, disorientation, homesickness for the overseas home or lifestyle, impatience, or irritability (Thomas & Althen, 1989), are frequently transitory and are resolved once the returning TCKs begin to develop the intercultural awareness and skills applicable to their new cultural environment—their passport country and culture. In fact, one of the more useful interventions with TCKs reporting reentry difficulties is to promote the perspective that the home country, in this case, the United States, is a new country and culture and for TCKs to deploy their skills as interculturally adept, global citizens. Validating the skills and the cultural identity of the TCKs can promote acculturation.

The reentry culture shock concerns in Table 5.1 are provided to further illustrate the psychologically challenging nature of the experience. Reentry culture shock is clinically serious and also developmental when managed well. Clinical interventions used with domestic majority college students are applicable with the TCK population but so too are interventions supported by established multicultural counseling practices: knowledge and acceptance of the client's experience, support for identity development, validation of experiences and self, promotion of skills development (e.g., coping, cultural empathy, perspective, ethnorelativity, and acculturation—not assimilation), values exploration, social advocacy, justice work, and so forth.

Marginality: The Good and the Bad for Identity Development

The term *third culture* implies a state of cultural marginality, but there are two types: encapsulated and constructive. The former has negative implications, and the latter has favorable outcomes. Typically, cultural marginality has been characterized as a negative experience because the individual is on the edge of his or her cultural foundation.

Encapsulated marginality is profoundly detrimental to any individual (J. M. Bennett, 1993). J. M. Bennett, who has extensively explored the intercultural experience, noted that when an individual is encapsulated, he or she is stuck between cultures and experiences conflicting cultural loyalties. The results can be devastating: (a) alienation; (b) self-absorption; (c) the loss of reference to one's group; (d) the disintegration of self because of shifting cultural lines; (e) loose boundaries and low self-control; (f) poor decision making; (g) low tolerance for ambiguity; (h) a general sense of unease and never feeling at home; and (i) on a postmodern tone, a feeling of being culturally fractured (J. M. Bennett, 1993).

Conversely, when TCKs have developed their cultural identity so as to experience a strong identification with their TCK roots, they often express a highly functional constructive marginality, which J. M. Bennett (1993) described as feeling comfortable with and able to function between cultural groups, feeling authentic with self, having a reference group (i.e., other TCKs and interculturally experienced peers), having well-developed boundaries and a sense of control, having the ability to make decisions and evaluate those decisions, feeling at home with ambiguity and the complexity of multiple cultural environments, and

Table 5.1

Common Reentry Culture Shock Concerns

Behavioral	Emotional
Acting out	Anger
Arguing	Frustration
Reversal (a form of ethnocentrism)	Irritability
Rejectionism	Defensiveness
Overly critical of others	Feeling invalidated
Refusal to participate	
Compulsive behaviors	Obsessive fears
Tension	Nervousness
Stress responses	Anxiety
Restlessness	Excessive worrying
Judgmental	Confusion
Stereotyping	
Overly critical of others	
Communication problems	
Lack of direction, activity	
Mood swings	
Identity concerns	
Career indecision or lack of direction	
Losses	
Communication problems	Disorientation
Identity concerns	
Isolation	Anomie
Withdrawal	
Boredom	
Regressive behaviors	Apathy
Low energy, drive	
Withdrawal	
Sleep disturbances	Depression
Substance abuse	
Weight changes	
Withdrawal	
Isolation	
Self-injury	
Suicidal ideation	
Mood swings	
Crying spells	
Identity concerns	
Career indecision or lack of focus	
Grief	

being committed to ethnorelativism. It is important to note, however, that a TCK must resolve his or her reentry culture shock experience before the constructive marginality frame of reference can become a strength that allows the TCK to successfully navigate between and within multiple cultures.

The Strengths of the TCK

The preceding sections have conveyed some of the strengths of the TCKs resulting from their intercultural experiences. It is, in fact, the international and intercultural milieu of the TCK that creates the opportunity for a unique and inherent form of development that domestic students and programs strive for as a supplemental process: intercultural sensitivity development (M. J. Bennett, 1993, 1998). M. J. Bennett's model emphasized the movement from ethnocentrism to ethnorelativity. Similarly, Figure 5.2 depicts a personal developmental process in which the individual progresses through six stages. Recognizing cultural differences, accepting differences, and then valuing and integrating differences characterize the developmental process of the individual.

When a person only applies his or her worldview to analyze phenomena, events, or culture, that person is said to be ethnocentric. Ethnocentrism is vital and natural with regard to establishing identity and a sense of self; humans and cultures need the reference point to define themselves and their culture. Yet, re-

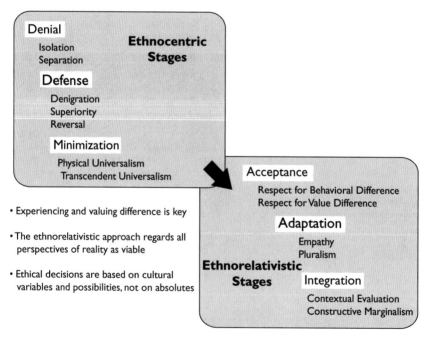

Figure 5.2

Intercultural Sensitivity Development Model

Note. Adapted with permission of the author from "Towards Ethnorelativism: A Developmental Model of Intercultural Sensitivity" by M. J. Bennett, 1993, in R. M. Paige (Ed.), *Education for the Intercultural Experience,* pp. 21–71.

maining within an ethnocentric worldview is also what generates intercultural conflicts. Denial is marked by the assumption and belief that cultural differences do not exist. When an individual is in the defense stage, differences are seen as threats to oneself and one's culture. Minimizing individuals trivialize cultural differences and focus on similarities, thus negating real differences. Across these three stages, one's own cultural perspective is always the primary lens, and all differences are viewed through this one lens.

Ideally, the TCK is defined by *ethnorelativity*—the ability to (a) accept, acknowledge, and value differences (acceptance); (b) empathize with culturally different people and also recognize that there are multiple valid cultural perspectives (adaptation); and (c) express an identity that is not rigid but instead flexible and contextually responsive to cultural differences (integration). Granted, many TCKs are at many different places on this developmental continuum, but the interstitial cultural milieu of the third-culture community is itself the environment in which such development can occur naturally. As such, TCKs are potential campus leaders and followers with regard to campus diversity initiatives (Luebke & Gaw, 2000).

As a result of growing up in an intercultural environment, TCKs may possess strong intercultural skill sets. Tokuhama-Espinosa (2003) noted how TCKs often learn multiple languages and have a desire to acquire language because they understand the relevance of language and culture, although Pollock and Van Reken (1999) also observed that TCKs are not necessarily fully proficient in any one foreign language, sometimes including their home language.

In addition to language skills, TCKs may also be able to, and like to, interact effectively with culturally different people because this is the norm in their TCK communities. On college campuses, TCKs frequently find their peer groups through other TCK networks, international student offices, study abroad offices, and nonmajority domestic students. The sharpened and broad global perspectives that TCKs may bring to the campus are yet another strength, although this characteristic is often received with a degree of suspicion and xenophobia by domestic counterparts and campus officials.

Closure skills are yet another possible strength because TCKs are usually accustomed to transition, change, and endings. Part of this naturally derives from the work contracts of parents, which normally entail moving every few years as contracts are completed and new ones are entered. TCKs learn to say goodbye to friends, home, and communities, and they typically establish new TCK friendships with ease.

Challenges for TCKs

Although there are clear strengths that the TCK experience may afford these students, as the above discussion briefly outlines, there are also obvious challenges. For example, the high level of mobility that TCKs experience tends to result in a sense of rootlessness, geographically and culturally (Cottrell, 2002; Pollock & Van Reken, 1999). A sense of place is critical for mental health.

TCKs may feel alienated and isolated from home-country peers (Gaw, 2000). They may feel misunderstood, undervalued, and culturally out of place. This cultural disability is troubling because TCKs typically look similar to their domestic peers, but they often think, behave, and feel considerably different. Furthermore, TCKs frequently do not really know their home culture as is assumed by domestic peers. Although TCKs befriend other TCKs, as well as overseas-experienced domestic students, minorities, and international students, they often have such a small community that they feel limited with regard to social support.

As noted in the reentry culture shock discussion above, TCKs do experience many psychological challenges, most of which are directly associated with the dissonance of being home and reentry culture shock. Grief and loss, however, are two primary challenges that TCKs encounter (Gaw, 2000; Jordan, 2002; Pollock & Van Reken, 1999) that arise from moving away from their host-country home. The losses include the loss of a lifestyle and status, friends and relationships, support systems, foods and music, role models, and what was known and familiar. With loss and grief come disbelief, numbness, and anger, and also resolution.

Academic concerns may arise based on reentry culture shock, such as the inability of the TCK student to focus or concentrate on his or her studies or confusion about career opportunities and the realities of those opportunities. Yet, as Cottrell (2002) and Pollock and Van Reken (1999) observed, TCKs tend to be more academically achieving than their domestic peers, partly, the authors reasoned, due to the cultural capital of the TCKs' parents and the environments in which they developed.

Where is home for the TCK? Often the TCK will make the campus home if his or her parents remain overseas. Because international travel is costly and time-consuming, holidays are often celebrated alone or with distant relatives or, commonly, on campus with other such "homeless" students. This chapter began with Karen's dilemma of identifying where she comes from. The question "Where are you from?" is about home and roots for domestic Americans, which they can definitively answer. For the TCK, it is nearly impossible to answer and generates internal questions and dilemmas.

Role shock is yet another challenge for some TCKs who may have grown up with servants and with a privileged social status. Returning to their passport country for college may induce role shock because the privileges associated with living in the international and expatriate community are no longer in place. The TCK is just another new kid on campus and, often, one who blends in with the majority with no driver, no servant, and no special status, assumed or real.

Another unique challenge for TCKs is related to their career development. It is extremely common for TCKs to have not worked as teenagers while abroad because host countries require work permits that are issued to the working parent(s), much like in the United States. As a result, TCKs generally have little or no work experience. This lack of work experience, although not detrimental, requires them to obtain it on their return, and they are competing with their domestic counterparts who already know the system and the rules and have many of the jobs.

In addition, TCKs have often been exposed to higher level executives and decision makers than have their domestic counterparts in the world of work. It is not uncommon to discover that a TCK knows an ambassador in the diplomatic corps, a United Nations area director, a high-level multinational corporation executive, or an important host-country official. It is also not uncommon for a TCK to possess in-depth knowledge about the political workings of several countries and government agencies as well as religious systems and cultures. Such exposure is, in part, due to privilege, discussed previously, but may also be due to the small and extremely interactive community in which TCKs have lived. As such, TCKs' career aspirations may be somewhat naive and/or distorted because of the lack of actual work experience yet very focused and high level because of the role models that they have had.

Cottrell (2002) observed that TCKs often seek and obtain careers that are characterized by expertise, leadership, and independence. Cottrell's research revealed that a significant proportion of TCKs go into the human services/helping professions, and another significant proportion end up in professional, executive, and administrative careers. As has been observed by researchers and TCKs alike, one significant career decision for TCKs is whether to go abroad again after college and continue the mobile lifestyle or stay in one location and develop a sense of connectedness. Cottrell found that most TCKs in her study desired an internationally oriented career path, although many struggled to decide whether to put down roots for their children's development.

Campus Considerations

One might assume that because of the intercultural skills and life experiences of the TCK, this population does not need much support. This assumption is incorrect. TCKs experience the same maturational and developmental challenges and the same relationship woes and personal worries as any other college student. The discussion below highlights several key areas in which to provide support for TCKs so that they may achieve their personal and professional goals.

Although counseling for TCKs may take the form of outreach programs, support groups, and individual therapy, residence hall personnel and other campus professionals can also offer support. The housing department, for example, can help TCKs to establish enough roots to be able to call the campus their home. Housing departments may be able to offer international/multicultural housing options to TCKs or assign roommates who are international students. TCKs may also be good candidates to be residence assistants, and in that position they may be able to model to domestic students the kind of intercultural competencies that most campuses now desire and promote for their students.

Involving TCKs on and off campus is perhaps one of the most effective interventions. For example, TCKs can be involved through new student orientation programs and campus leadership opportunities, as mentors for incoming

TCKs and other students and as diversity peer trainers. Off-campus involvement might include service-learning and volunteering projects, activities with which many TCKs are already familiar.

Many TCKs have experience and skills already in place to be dynamic campus leaders in training in the residence halls, in student government and student activities, and in the classroom. Moreover, having grown up in cultural milieus in which differences are the norm, rather than a barrier, TCKs have the potential to demonstrate to other students what it means to be multicultural and multilingual and to value diversity.

Appropriately trained and interculturally sensitive student affairs practitioners and academic faculty will make a significant difference in the quality of experience the TCK has on campus, as an individual and as a campus community member. It can start with admissions, engaging the TCKs in facilitative predeparture activities and preparing them for a new community, country, and culture (Pollock & Van Reken, 1999). Once on campus, academic departments can encourage TCKs to explore their heritages through assignments and projects, legitimizing their identities and histories.

For the same reasons that nonmajority students need culture clubs, TCKs need a community of peers from whom they can obtain peer-level support. Their cultural identity is as real as, though perhaps more elusive than, most and therefore deserves the same campus recognition and endorsement as any other cultural group on campus. This requires acceptance, advocacy, and promotion on the part of the administration and the college counseling center, as well as guidance.

Future Trends

TCKs may be adept and achieving college students, but often there are issues hidden just under the surface. TCKs, like other traditional college students, have personal and professional challenges that go with the territory of young adulthood on a college campus. They also bring to the table unique issues, such as reentry culture shock and all of its various attending concerns; an intercultural identity that is in need of support and encouragement for further development; responses and internalizations to xenophobia and cultural misunderstandings; and interpersonal and intercultural competencies that, without support, might whither.

TCK students, however, are in a unique position as interculturally experienced young adults who are frequently multilingual and open to diversity in the broadest sense. TCKs are typically not boxed in by domestic political definitions of diversity or politics, because, as TCKs, they have lived diversity and politics as both outsiders and insiders. These students are potentially competitive candidates for entering the globalizing workforce (private and public sectors, nongovernmental organizations, and governments). In today's evolving cultural, social, and political connectedness, such a prepared student is paramount, and TCKs can serve as leaders.

References

Adler, P. S. (1975). The transitional experience: An alternative view of culture shock. *Journal of Humanistic Psychology, 15,* 13–23.

Befus, C. P. (1988). A multilevel treatment approach for culture shock experienced by sojourners. *International Journal of Intercultural Relations, 12,* 381–400.

Bennett, J. M. (1993). Cultural marginality: Identity issues in intercultural training. In R. M. Paige (Ed.), *Education for the intercultural experience* (2nd ed., pp. 109–135). Yarmouth, ME: Intercultural Press.

Bennett, M. J. (1993). Towards ethnorelativism: A developmental model of intercultural sensitivity. In R. M. Paige (Ed.), *Education for the intercultural experience* (2nd ed., pp. 21–71). Yarmouth, ME: Intercultural Press.

Bennett, M. J. (Ed.). (1998). *Basic concepts of intercultural communication: Selected readings.* Yarmouth, ME: Intercultural Press.

Blake, E., & Gaw, K. F. (2004). Reentry and reverse culture shock: Helping the study abroad student transition back home. In W. Settle (Ed.), *Mental health and crisis management: Assisting University of Notre Dame study abroad students: A handbook for international educators* (2nd ed., pp. 34–39). (Available from the University of Notre Dame Counseling Center, P.O. Box 564, Notre Dame, IN 46556)

Cottrell, A. B. (2002). Educational and occupational choices of American adult third culture kids. In M. G. Ender (Ed.), *Military brats and other global nomads: Growing up in organization families* (pp. 229–253). Westport, CT: Praeger Publishers.

Gaw, K. F. (2000). Reverse culture shock in students returning from overseas. *International Journal of Intercultural Relations, 24,* 83–104.

Gaw, K. F. (2004). The study abroad student and culture shock. In W. Settle (Ed.), *Mental health and crisis management: Assisting University of Notre Dame study abroad students: A handbook for international educators* (2nd ed., pp. 2–5). (Available from the University of Notre Dame Counseling Center, P.O. Box 564, Notre Dame, IN 46556)

Gullahorn, J. T., & Gullahorn, J. E. (1963). An extension of the U-curve hypothesis. *Journal of Social Issues, 19,* 33–47.

Harris, P. R., Moran, R. T., & Moran, S. V. (2004). *Managing cultural differences: Global leadership strategies for the 21st century* (6th ed.). Amsterdam: Elsevier.

Jordan, K. A. F. (2002). Identity formation and the adult third culture kid. In M. G. Ender (Ed.), *Military brats and other global nomads: Growing up in organization families* (pp. 211–228). Westport, CT: Praeger Publishers.

Luebke, P. T., & Gaw, K. G. (2000). Intercultural sensitivity and culture shock. In R. J. Simpson & C. R. Duke (Eds.), *American schools overseas* (pp. 51–91). Bloomington, IN: Phi Delta Kappa.

Lysgaard, S. (1955). Adjustment in a foreign society: Norwegian Fulbright grantees visiting the United States. *International Social Science Bulletin, 7,* 45–51.

Oberg, K. (1960). Culture shock: Adjustment to new cultural environments. *Practical Anthropology, 7,* 177–182.

Pollock, D. C., & Van Reken, R. E. (1999). *The third culture kid experience.* Yarmouth, ME: Intercultural Press.

Schaetti, B. F. (2002). Attachment theory: A view into the global nomad experience. In M. G. Ender (Ed.), *Military brats and other global nomads: Growing up in organization families* (pp. 103–120). Westport, CT: Praeger Publishers.

Searle, W., & Ward, C. (1990). The prediction of psychological and sociocultural adjustment during cross-cultural transitions. *International Journal of Intercultural Relations, 14,* 449–464.

Stelling, J. L. (1991). Reverse culture shock and children of Lutheran missionaries. *Dissertation Abstracts International, 52/12B,* 6671. (UMI No. 9211075)

Thomas, K., & Althen, G. (1989). Counseling foreign students. In P. Pedersen, J. G. Draguns, W. J. Lonner, & J. E. Trimble (Eds.), *Counseling across cultures* (3rd ed., pp. 205–241). Honolulu: University of Hawaii Press.

Tokuhama-Espinosa, T. (2003). Third culture kids: A special case for foreign language learning. In T. Tokuhama-Espinosa (Ed.), *The multilingual mind: Issues discussed by, for, and about people living with many languages* (pp. 165–169). Westport, CT: Praeger Publishers.

Weissman, D., & Furnham, A. (1987). The expectations and experiences of a sojourning temporary resident abroad: A preliminary study. *Human Relations, 40,* 313–326.

6

Strategies and Counselor Competencies in Counseling Multiracial Students

Kelley Kenney

Introduction

This chapter discusses multiracial college students, defined as students whose biological parents are of two or more different racial backgrounds or heritages (Root, 1992). The repeal of laws in the United States that opposed mixed-race coupling or marriages, brought about by the *Loving et ux. v. Virginia* (1967) Supreme Court decision, has resulted in a dramatic increase in interracial unions. Subsequently, there has also been a dramatic increase in the births of persons of mixed-race heritage. For the first time in its history, the 2000 Census provided persons of mixed-race heritages and backgrounds with the opportunity to describe how they identify racially by selecting more than one racial category (Root & Kelley, 2003). According to data from the 2000 Census, 6.8 million people were identified as being of more than one racial category, or multiracial (Jones & Smith, 2001).

The multiracial population is young. Jones and Smith (2003) indicated that approximately 42% of the population is under 18 years of age and close to 70% is under 35 years of age. At the time of the 2000 Census, only 5.4% of the multiracial population was between the ages of 18 and 20; however, a dramatic increase is expected in the near future. Although all children do not aspire to attend college, these figures suggest that the number of multiracial individuals who will be attending college could also show a dramatic increase (Paladino, 2004).

Assessment Issues

Entrance into college marks a significant developmental period in an individual's life, and it represents the start of the transition from adolescence to young adulthood (Paladino, 2004; Wehrly, Kenney, & Kenney, 1999). A myriad of factors are associated with this transition, and success, particularly for first-year students, is often defined by the ability to differentiate from family and become independent; navigate personal growth and development issues, including those involving interpersonal relationships; and balance academic and social demands (Newman & Newman, 1999; Von Steen, 2000). As indicated by Palmer and Shuford (1996), "college students have many ties that bind them to their families and home communities" (p. 214). Hence, for the many students who are leaving home for the first time, the acclimation and successful transition to the new environment may also depend on their ability to find commonalities between their college and precollege lives. This includes finding individuals who share their cultural views and contexts.

Today's college campuses are becoming increasingly diverse with regard to age, gender, race, ethnicity, religion, socioeconomics, physical and mental ability, and sexual orientation (Von Steen, 2000). Palmer and Shuford (1996) discussed the extent to which institutions are challenged in their efforts to promote welcoming environments for their increasingly diverse student populations, particularly students of diverse racial and ethnic backgrounds. For students of color, entering a predominantly White campus environment can be an uncomfortable experience. This is especially true for those whose home communities and previous educational experiences offered either a match to their cultural context or a more culturally diverse environment.

The point at which multiracial students enter college is often the first time they experience challenges around their multiracial heritage. These challenges may be manifested in the experiences they have related to completing admissions applications, establishing friendships and intimate relationships, separating from family, and pursuing their academic and career endeavors (Gasser, 2002; Sands & Schuh, 2004). Multiracial students in many campus environments also encounter issues that are further complicated by the unrest and unresolved issues brought about by the increase of multiculturalism on college campuses (Levine & Cureton, 1998). In addition, interracial and interethnic group interactions often stir up and are met with heightened sensitivity (Hurtado, Milem, Clayton-Pederson, & Allen, 1998).

According to Paladino (2004), colleges have typically provided social and other support services, networks, and cultural activities focused on mono-racial-minority group identification. However, even multiracial students who strongly identify with a particular mono-racial-minority aspect of their heritage may not feel accepted in these networks (Paladino, 2004; Sands & Schuh, 2004; Wallace, 2003). Often, this lack of acceptance is based on the reactions of others to multiracial individuals' physical appearance (Sands & Schuh, 2004; Wallace, 2003). Physical appearance plays a major role in how multiracial individuals are perceived by others and often results in a socially imposed racial identity or pressure to choose one aspect of one's racial identity over another (Sands & Schuh, 2004; Wallace, 2003; Wijeyesinghe, 2001). Thus, despite how multiracial students choose to identify, they may experience bias, loss, cultural conflict, and confusion, as well as challenges about their cultural legitimacy, as a result of campus social politics that often direct levels of belonging and participation (Sands & Schuh, 2004; Wallace, 2003). Root's (1998, 2002) ecological framework for understanding identity, discussed later in this chapter, provides evidence of the powerful influence of physical appearance and is a useful tool for assessing presenting issues and concerns of multiracial college students that may be related to their racial identity and to the challenges they encounter regarding physical appearance.

Counseling Implications

Multicultural Framework

Multiracial individuals are a part of our ever-growing multicultural society, and a multicultural counseling competency framework should be applied when one is counseling this population (Kenney, 2002; Wehrly et al., 1999; Wright, 2000). The first domain of the multicultural counseling competencies requires counselors to be aware of their own assumptions, values, and biases (Sue, Arredondo, & McDavis, 1992). Stereotypes abound and continue to cloud perceptions of multiracial individuals as tainted or doomed to troubled existences (Wehrly et al., 1999). These perceptions influence reactions and responses to mixed-race individuals and, when made apparent, could deter a mixed-race college student from seeking help or assistance when needed, particularly if the services sought are viewed as culturally insensitive or inappropriate (Constantine & Gainor, 2004; Sands & Schuh, 2004; Wijeyesinghe, 2001).

College counselors should take the responsibility to become aware of multiracial college students and their needs and concerns and examine their own personal attitudes and beliefs about race and racial mixing (Kenney, 2002; Wehrly et al., 1999; Wright, 2000). Counselors and other campus staff are important role models for students and can significantly influence their thinking. Failure to examine their own assumptions about race may perpetuate biases and stereotypes and reinforce typical thinking about race, thus negatively affecting and alienating many students (Root, 2003a).

The second domain of the multicultural counseling competencies requires counselors to have knowledge of the worldview experiences of their clients (Sue et al., 1992). Counselors working with multiracial individuals must have knowledge of the various groups that are part of the individual's heritage. They must also be aware of the sociopolitical history of interactions between these groups, the impact of that history on current interactions, and the significance of all of this for the individual and his or her identity (Wehrly et al., 1999).

Identity Development Models

Counselors working with multiracial college students must have an understanding of the salience of identity development for multiracial individuals. Chickering (1978) provided a college student development model that outlines several developmental tasks that college students undergo while navigating the college experience. Included in Chickering's "seven vectors" is the task of establishing identity. The search for and establishment of a solid identity and self-concept is a process that continues throughout, and long after, one's college years (Wehrly et al., 1999).

For multiracial individuals, identity and self-concept are particularly significant because they both affect and are affected by many other aspects of development. Root (1994) outlined six themes around which issues and concerns may arise for multiracial individuals: uniqueness, acceptance and belonging, physical appearance, sexuality, self-esteem, and identity. Self-esteem, according to Root (1994), is related to and affected by the other five themes, and identity, which is closely related to one's sense of connectedness and belonging, encompasses all aspects of a person's being. The establishment of a positive racial identity is critical to successfully negotiating one's multiracial existence (Root, 1990, 1992, 1996).

The following is a summation of racial identity development models that provides a paradigm through which counselors can begin to understand the racial identity development of multiracial college students.

Poston. Poston (1990) developed a five-stage model of biracial identity that describes the stages that biracial individuals experience in moving toward an integrated racial identity:

1. *Stage 1:* Personal identity. The individual's sense of self is independent of racial/ethnic identity.
2. *Stage 2:* Choice of group categorization. The individual feels pressured to choose one racial/ethnic identity, often making a choice based on the influence of parents, peers, and other social forces.
3. *Stage 3:* Enmeshment/denial. The individual experiences confusion as a result of the pressures to choose experienced in Stage 2, and successful movement to the next stage largely depends on the individual's ability to resolve this confusion.
4. *Stage 4:* Appreciation. The individual may continue to identify solely with the group chosen in Stage 2 but has moved toward developing knowledge of and value for both racial/ethnic heritages.
5. *Stage 5:* Integration. The individual has knowledge of, values, and appreciates his or her multiple heritages and has acquired a sense of security and wholeness, along with an integrated identity.

Phinney. Phinney (1993) developed a three-stage model of adolescent ethnic identity development based on several years of research on various aspects of ethnic identity development. This model has been applied to persons of monoracial and multiracial identity:

1. *Stage 1:* Unexamined ethnic identity. Individuals are either diffused, having no interest in their ethnic identity, or foreclosed, basing their perceptions of self and identities on the views of significant others in their lives.

2. *Stage 2:* Ethnic identity search moratorium. Individuals engage in active exploration of the various aspects of their ethnic identities in order to determine their meaning and significance in their lives.
3. *Stage 3:* Achieved ethnic identity. Individuals have developed a solid and secure sense of their ethnic identities.

Kich. Kich (1992) presented a three-stage model of biracial identity development based on his dissertation study of the influences of family, peers, and social variables on the racial and ethnic identity development of 15 Japanese-White individuals ages 17 to 50:

1. *Stage 1:* Awareness and dissonance (ages 3 to 10). Individuals feel that they are different and are affected by experiences that occur with peers outside of the home. Positive self-concept and a complete multiracial identity at this stage are dependent on parental and family support and involvement.
2. *Stage 2:* Struggle for acceptance (age 8 to late adolescence). Individuals see themselves and their families as unique and different in contrast to their peers, other families, and the larger community. Conflicts around identification with one parent over the other are common during this stage.
3. *Stage 3:* Self-acceptance and assertion of an interracial identity (postadolescence). Individuals develop a definition of self that is no longer based on the perceptions and influences of others, become interested in all aspects of their multiple heritages, and are open to questions regarding their multiple racial identities.

Kerwin and Ponterotto. Kerwin and Ponterotto (1995) addressed the identity development of biracial college students and young adults in the fifth stage of their biracial identity development model. This model suggests that, although biracial college students and adults may continue to identify with one aspect of their multiple heritages over the other, they may, with maturity, be less likely to do so as a result of the expectations they feel from others, and they may develop greater awareness and acceptance of themselves as biracial and bicultural. The successful completion of all five stages of the Kerwin–Ponterotto model is dependent on the extent to which the individual is able to conceptualize from multiple perspectives and acknowledge the advantages and disadvantages of being biracial.

Root. A final model is Root's (1998) ecological framework for understanding racial identity (see Figure 6.1). Although not developed specifically with college students in mind, it is useful from the perspective of college students' navigation of the microclimate of the college environment. This model was initially designed to illustrate the various elements influencing the identity development of multiracial Asian Americans at given times in their lives; however, it has also been applied to the experiences of other multiracial individuals. The model has

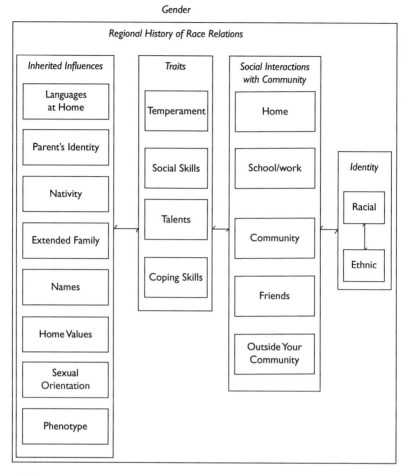

Figure 6.1

Ecological Identity Model

Note. From Root, M. P. P. (1998). Multiracial Americans: Changing the face of Asian America. In L. C. Lee & N. W. Zane (Eds.), *Handbook of Asian American psychology* (pp. 261–287). Thousand Oaks, CA: Sage.

its theoretical basis in symbolic interactionism and includes the following variables: (a) gender; (b) regional history of race relations; (c) inherited influences, including languages at home, parent's identity, nativity, extended family, names, home values, sexual orientation, and phenotype; (d) traits, including temperament, social skills, talents, and coping skills; (e) social interactions with community, including home, school or work, community, friends, and foreign communities; and (f) identity, including race and ethnicity (Root, 1998, 2003a).

The revised version of Root's (1998) model takes into account common and presumed influences on identity while also specifying the influence of invisible factors (Root, 2003b; see Figure 6.2). In understanding Root's (2002)

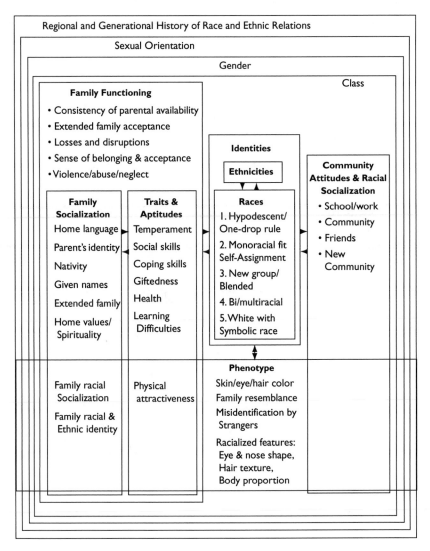

Figure 6.2

Ecological Framework for Understanding Multiracial Identity Development

Note. © Maria P. P. Root, Ph.D., 2002.

ecological framework, it is important to look at the influencing variables as lenses through which the experiences of multiracial individuals can be viewed and discerned. The meaning and significance of these experiences for identity development differ depending on the generation into which the individual was born. Hence, generational history is a salient factor in this model (Root, 2003a). Identities, as included in the ecological model, consist of ethnicities and races (Root, 1998, 2002).

The research on mixed-race individuals suggests that there are five specific identity possibilities that seem to be based on and affected by the generation of birth (Root, 1999, 2003a, 2003b). The first identity is hypodescent/one-drop rule, which is a monoracial identity status assigned by society, indicative of the racial status perceived as having lesser value. The second identity is monoracial fit/self-assignment and is indicative of a decision made by mixed-race individuals to identify with a specific monoracial aspect of their heritage based on how it fits with their experiences. These first two identities were often the only identity possibilities afforded to many older generation mixed-race individuals.

The next two identities have become common identity possibilities for younger generation mixed-race individuals. The third identity is new group/blended identity, in which mixed-race individuals are free to identify equally with both aspects of their heritages. Similarly, in the fourth identity, bi/multiracial identity, individuals are free to identify with their multiple heritages; however, they do so without quantification or limits. The multiracial identity is viewed as the most radical and illustrates the fluidity of identity. White with symbolic race is the final and newest identity, in which mixed-race individuals with White ancestry, while not denigrating or rejecting their other racial heritages, identify more with the worldview values and lifestyle afforded to them by their White ancestry (Root, 1999, 2003a, 2003b).

Regional and generational history of race and ethnic relations, gender, and class are referred to as the macro lenses of the model. They are the foundational influences of identity development and the central contexts through which multiracial individuals learn social norms and rules regarding their racial and ethnic identities. According to Root (2003b), in the context of sexual orientation, the politics associated with race are often minimized or sexualized. Although sexual identity development can be viewed as a process of family socialization, sexual orientation may also be a macro lens identity depending on stage of life, circumstances, and how other influencing experiences are viewed (Allman, 1996; Kich, 1996; Root, 2003a).

Patterns of family functioning are included in the revised model and comprise consistency of parental availability; extended family acceptance; losses and disruptions; sense of belonging and acceptance; and extent of violence, abuse, and neglect (Root, 2002). How the family functions is critical to all aspects of a child's development, most specifically his or her identity development. The family-functioning variables are therefore significantly related to the inherited influences, or family socialization variables, as well as to the trait and aptitude variables (Root, 2003a, 2003b).

According to Root (2003a), the middle lenses of the model encompass specific inherited influences, traits, and social interactions with community, phenotype, and identity. Inherited influences in this version of the model are not biological; rather, they are family socialization factors such as language, nativity, given names, parental identity, family identity, existence of extended family, home values, customs, spirituality, family racial socialization, and family racial and ethnic identity (Root, 1999, 2003a). Traits, according to Root (1999,

2003a), consist of tendencies and environmental influences, including temperament, social skills, coping skills, giftedness, health, learning difficulties, and physical attractiveness. Community attitudes and racial socialization combine personal and group relationships and interactions that exist in the categories of home, school or work, community, friends and peers, and foreign communities. The extent to which an individual experiences acceptance, belonging, or oppression in each category determines its significance (Root, 1999, 2003a).

Phenotype, or physical appearance, which was listed under inherited influences in Root's (1998) model, plays a major role in one's experience and existence as a multiracial individual (Wijeyesinghe, 2001). Phenotype is a magnifying lens that cuts across and interacts with all three middle lenses: family socialization, traits, and community (Root, 2003a). Although phenotype may not determine how multiracial individuals choose to identify, it is a constant fixture in their life experiences and interactions (Root, 2003b).

Root (1998, 2002) provided evidence of the importance of understanding that the worldview experience of multiracial college students may entail navigating multiple identities. Wijeyesinghe (2001) further substantiated this, indicating that individuals may incorporate the identities of ethnicity, gender, spirituality, social class, sexual orientation, and others into their racial identity. It is important, however, for counselors to note that, although identity may be at the core of the issues and concerns presented by some multiracial students in counseling, it may not be for all such students. Multiracial students may present with critical issues not related to their racial heritages or identity (Wehrly et al., 1999; Wijeyesinghe, 2001).

Intervention Strategies

The third domain of the multicultural counseling competencies requires that counselors develop culturally appropriate intervention strategies for working with all clients (Sue et al., 1992). The factors of campus environment, students' sense of fit and belonging, and issues related to identity and self-concept discussed earlier in this chapter are well documented as areas in which multiracial students, similar to mono-racial-minority students, need support. Hence, in doing initial assessments and in providing ongoing support for multiracial students, counselors must inquire about the extent to which these factors play a part in the students' presenting concerns. Students struggling with feelings of alienation and rejection may be set at ease by the counselor who raises these factors as potential areas of concern (Paladino, 2004).

Root's (1998, 2002) ecological model for understanding racial identity not only is a useful assessment tool but also can be used to explore issues in both individual and group counseling. The strategies of focused discussions, bibliotherapy, homework assignments, role-playing, journaling, storytelling, and behavioral goal setting can be helpful when one is counseling multiracial college students (Gibbs & Moskowitz-Sweet, 1991; Pinderhughes, 1995).

Nishimura (1998) cited the benefits of support groups for multiracial college students, indicating that such groups can provide a much-needed sense of community as well as serve as a source of empowerment and affirmation for multiracial students as they attempt to negotiate campus environments and systems. The term *support* is often negatively associated with deficits. Wehrly et al. (1999) emphasized the importance of assisting multiracial individuals in recognizing and acknowledging the inherent strengths associated with having multiple heritages. Hence, many campuses have established social groups or clubs geared toward promoting these strengths and presenting positive images of what it means to be multiracial (Root & Kelley, 2003).

Campus Considerations

Advocacy has become an integral part of the role and responsibility of counselors (American Counseling Association, 2005). As advocates, college counselors have the duty to make college administrators, faculty, staff, and student leaders aware of the issues and concerns of multiracial college students, particularly those that affect their academic persistence and retention. College counselors must also be the forerunners in the establishment of outreach strategies and services, including professional development training and educational workshops, lecture series, cultural events and forums, mentoring programs, learning communities, support groups, and social clubs, depending on the assessed needs of the multiracial student population and the campus (Kenney, 2000; Nishimura, 1998; Sands & Schuh, 2004; Wehrly et al., 1999).

The MAVIN Foundation, a national grassroots advocacy organization for multiracial families, is an excellent resource with which all college counselors should be familiar. *Mavin* is a word that has its roots in the Yiddish language and means "one who understands." The MAVIN Foundation was founded in 1998 by a man of multiracial heritage while he was a student at Wesleyan College. In addition to being a primary source of information on this population through its Web site (www.mavinfoundation.org), magazine, and other publications, the MAVIN Foundation can be and has been an excellent resource to college campuses across the country on effective ways to advocate for multiracial students, including how to provide opportunities to enhance their leadership skills and abilities and how to establish clubs, organizations, and services for multiracial students.

Future Trends

As indicated by Root and Kelley (2003), the increase in multiracial individuals "provides both challenges and opportunities to educators and other professionals" (p. x). As interracial unions continue to increase and the United States continues to experience a mixed-race baby boom, colleges can expect to see an increasing number of students of mixed race. Multiracial college students are extremely diverse, and campus administrators, faculty, and staff should take the time to understand their experiences. In addition, in acknowledging their responsibilities as critical role models, campus administrators, faculty, and staff must make efforts to create climates that are supportive and conducive to the positive learning experiences of these and all students (Wallace, 2003). In fulfilling their roles as advocates, college counselors must take the lead in this process.

References

Allman, K. M. (1996). (Un)natural boundaries: Mixed race, gender, and sexuality. In M. P. P. Root (Ed.), *The multiracial experience: Racial borders as the new frontier* (pp. 277–291). Thousand Oaks, CA: Sage.

American Counseling Association. (2005). *ACA code of ethics.* Alexandria, VA: Author.

Chickering, A.W. (1978). *Education and identity.* San Francisco: Jossey-Bass.

Constantine, M. G., & Gainor, K. A. (2004). Depressive symptoms and attitudes toward counseling as predictors of biracial college women's psychological help-seeking behavior. In A. R. Gillem & C. A. Thompson (Eds.), *Biracial women in therapy: Between the rock of gender and the hard place of race* (pp. 147–158). New York: Haworth Press.

Gasser, H. S. (2002). Portraits of individuality: A qualitative study of multiracial college students. *Colorado State University Journal of Student Affairs, 11,* 42–53. Retrieved March 16, 2005, from http://www.colostate.edu/Depts/DSA/SAHE/JOURNAL/2002/gasser.htm

Gibbs, J. T., & Moskowitz-Sweet, G. (1991). Clinical and cultural issues in the treatment of biracial and bicultural adolescents. *The Journal of Contemporary Human Services, 72,* 579–591.

Hurtado, S., Milem, J., Clayton-Pederson, A., & Allen, W. (1998). Enhancing campus climates for racial/ethnic diversity: Educational policy and practice. *The Review of Higher Education, 21,* 279–302.

Jones, N. A., & Smith, A. S. (2001). *The two or more races population: 2000* (Census 2000 Brief Series C2KBR/01-6). Washington, DC: U.S. Census Bureau.

Jones, N. A., & Smith, A. S. (2003). A statistical portrait of children of two or more races in Census 2000. In M. P. P. Root & M. Kelley (Eds.), *Multiracial child resource book: Living complex identities* (pp. 3–10). Seattle, WA: MAVIN Foundation.

Kenney, K. (2000). Multiracial families. In J. Lewis & L. Bradley (Eds.), *Advocacy in counseling: Counselors, clients, community* (pp. 55–70). Greensboro, NC: ERIC/CASS.

Kenney, K. (2002). Counseling interracial couples and multiracial individuals: Applying a multicultural counseling competency framework. *Counseling and Human Development, 35,* 1–12.

Kerwin, C., & Ponterotto, J. G. (1995). Biracial identity development: Theory and research. In J. G. Ponterotto, J. M. Casas, L. A. Suzaki, & C. M. Alexander (Eds.), *Handbook of multicultural counseling* (pp. 199–217). Newbury Park, CA: Sage.

Kich, G. K. (1992). The developmental process of asserting a biracial, bicultural identity. In M. P. P. Root (Ed.), *Racially mixed people in America* (pp. 304–317). Newbury Park, CA: Sage.

Kich, G. K. (1996). In the margins of sex and race: Difference, marginality, and flexibility. In M. P. P. Root (Ed.), *The multiracial experience: Racial borders as the new frontier* (pp. 263–276). Thousand Oaks, CA: Sage.

Levine, A., & Cureton, J. S. (1998). *When hope and fear collide: A portrait of today's college student.* San Francisco: Jossey-Bass–Wiley.

Loving et ux. v. Virginia, 18 U.S.S.C. R. Ann. 1010 (1967).

Newman, P. R., & Newman, B. M. (1999). What does it take to have a positive impact on minority students' college retention? *Adolescence, 34,* 483–492.

Nishimura, N. J. (1998). Assessing the issues of multiracial students on college campuses. *Journal of College Counseling, 1,* 45–53.

Paladino, D. A. (2004). *The effects of cultural congruity, university alienation, and self-concept upon multiracial students' adjustment to college.* Unpublished doctoral dissertation, University of Arkansas, Fayetteville.

Palmer, C. J., & Shuford, B. C. (1996). Multicultural affairs. In A. L. Rentz (Ed.), *Student affairs practice in higher education* (pp. 214–237). Springfield, IL: Charles C Thomas.

Phinney, J. S. (1993). A three-stage model of ethnic identity in adolescence. In M. E. Bernal & G. P. Knight (Eds.), *Ethnic identity: Formation and transmission among Hispanics and other minorities* (pp. 61–79). Albany: State University of New York Press.

Pinderhughes, E. (1995). Biracial identity—Asset or handicap? In H. W. Harris, H. C. Blue, & E. E. H. Griffith (Eds.), *Racial and ethnic identity: Psychological development and creative expression* (pp. 73–93). New York: Routledge.

Poston, W. S. C. (1990). The biracial identity development model: A needed addition. *Journal of Counseling & Development, 69,* 152–155.

Root, M. P. P. (1990). Resolving "other" status: Identity development of biracial individuals. In L. S. Brown & M. P. P. Root (Eds.), *Diversity and complexity in feminist therapy* (pp. 185–205). New York: Haworth Press.

Root, M. P. P. (Ed.). (1992). *Racially mixed people in America.* Newbury Park, CA: Sage.

Root, M. P. P. (1994). Mixed-race women. In L. Comas-Diaz & B. Greene (Eds.), *Women of color: Integrating ethnic and gender identities in psychotherapy* (pp. 455–478). New York: Guilford Press.

Root, M. P. P. (Ed.). (1996). *The multiracial experience: Racial borders as the new frontier.* Thousand Oaks, CA: Sage.

Root, M. P. P. (1998). Multiracial Americans: Changing the face of Asian America. In L. C. Lee & N. W. Zane (Eds.), *Handbook of Asian American psychology* (pp. 261–287). Thousand Oaks, CA: Sage.

Root, M. P. P. (1999). The biracial baby boom: Understanding ecological constructions of racial identity in the 21st century. In R. H. Sheets, R. Hernandez, & E. R. Hollins (Eds.), *Racial and ethnic identity in school practices: Aspects of human development* (pp. 67–89). Mahwah, NJ: Erlbaum.

Root, M. P. P. (2002). Methodological issues in multiracial research. In G. C. Nagayama-Hall & S. Okazaki (Eds.), *Asian American psychology: The science of lives in context* (pp. 171–193). Washington, DC: American Psychological Association.

Root, M. P. P. (2003a). Multiracial families and children: Implications for educational research and practice. In J. A. Banks & C. A. McGee Banks (Eds.), *Handbook of research on multicultural education* (2nd ed., pp. 110–124). San Francisco: Jossey-Bass.

Root, M. P. P. (2003b). Racial identity development and persons of mixed race heritage. In M. P. P. Root & M. Kelley (Eds.), *Multiracial child resource book: Living complex identities* (pp. 34–41). Seattle, WA: MAVIN Foundation.

Root, M. P. P., & Kelley, M. (Eds.). (2003). *Multiracial child resource book: Living complex identities.* Seattle, WA: MAVIN Foundation.

Sands, N., & Schuh, J. H. (2004). Identifying interventions to improve the retention of biracial students: A case study. *Journal of College Student Retention, 5,* 349–363.

Sue, D. W., Arredondo, P., & McDavis, R. J. (1992). Multicultural counseling competencies and standards: A call to the profession. *Journal of Multicultural Counseling and Development, 20,* 64–88.

Von Steen, P.G. (2000). Traditional-age college students. In D. C. Davis & K. M. Humphrey (Eds.), *College counseling: Issues and strategies for a new millennium* (pp. 111–132). Alexandria, VA: American Counseling Association.

Wallace, K. R. (2003). Contextual factors affecting identity among mixed heritage college students. In M. P. P. Root & M. Kelley (Eds.), *Multiracial child resource book: Living complex identities* (pp. 87–93). Seattle, WA: MAVIN Foundation.

Wehrly, B., Kenney, K. R., & Kenney, M. E. (1999). *Counseling multiracial families.* Thousand Oaks, CA: Sage.

Wijeyesinghe, C. L. (2001). Racial identity in multiracial people: An alternative paradigm. In C. L. Wijeyesinghe & B. W. Jackson III (Eds.), *New perspectives on racial identity development: A theoretical and practical anthology* (pp. 129–152). New York: New York University Press.

Wright, D. J. (2000). College counseling and the needs of multicultural students. In D. C. Davis & K. M. Humphrey (Eds.), *College counseling: Issues and strategies for a new millennium* (pp. 153–168). Alexandria, VA: American Counseling Association.

From Blue Collar to Ivory Tower: Counseling First-Generation, Working-Class Students

Joseph A. Lippincott and Neil German

Introduction

College can be a strange new world for first-generation college students, students who come from families in which neither parent attained any level of postsecondary education. These students are often the first member within their entire extended families to attend college. Although these students may come from virtually any socioeconomic class, the majority are from what have been traditionally described as blue-collar or working-class backgrounds (Bui, 2002; Hertel, 2002).

First-generation students represented 22% of students who entered postsecondary education between 1992 and 2000, according to a report published by the National Center for Education Statistics (Chen, 2005). Only 24% of these first-generation students, however, completed a bachelor's degree, compared with 68% of students whose parents were college graduates. The report stated that first-generation students were at a "distinct disadvantage" (Chen, 2005) compared with students whose parents were college graduates, including being more likely to (a) come from low-income families, (b) be Black or Hispanic, (c) be less prepared academically for college, (d) delay entry into college, (e) begin college at a 2-year institution, and (f) attend college part-time and discontinuously. According to the report, the disadvantage continued after the first-generation students entered college on the basis of evidence that these students "completed fewer credits, took fewer academic courses, earned lower grades, needed more remedial assistance, and were more likely to withdraw from or repeat courses they attempted" (Chen, 2005, p. ix) than students whose parents were college graduates.

First-generation students are often not adequately prepared for college, not only academically but also emotionally, particularly if they are coming from a working-class background. When exposed to the middle- and upper-class values and aspirations of the typical college campus, students question whether they belong there. They struggle with issues of identity, social acceptance, and self-esteem as they aspire to transcend the traditional blue-collar values and occupations of their parents and enter the white-collar world.

First-generation students are also frequently faced with the difficulty of trying to adapt to the college environment while at the same time having limited time to devote to campus activities or studies. Financial constraints and financial dependents often dictate that these students must live at home and/or work part-time.

Thus, first-generation students face challenges that can at times seem insurmountable. College counselors, however, can play an important role in helping first-generation students cope with these challenges.

Assessment Issues

In working with a first-generation student, the counselor should assess the student's academic functioning, adjustment to college life, and family-of-origin issues. In assessing the client's ability to adjust, the counselor should explore the client's sense of identity and values, self-esteem and confidence, and ability and desire to become engaged both academically and socially in the college environment.

Academic Functioning

Studies have indicated that first-generation students tend to enter college with lower SAT scores and lower high school grade point averages than other college students (Gibbons & Shoffner, 2004). Once in college, they tend to be less committed to their studies, receive lower grades, and have a higher dropout rate than other students (Orbe, 2004). The counselor should therefore assess the first-generation student's preparedness for college and risk of academic failure. These students often express a fear of failing and feel that they have to study harder than their peers (Bui, 2002).

The counselor should also explore the value the client places on education. For example, many first-generation, working-class students have been brought up believing that knowledge for knowledge's sake is a waste of time, in contrast to many middle-class students. As Lubrano (2004) noted,

> middle-class kids are groomed for another life. They understand . . . why reading *Macbeth* in high school could be important years down the road. Working-class kids see no such connection, understand no future life for which digesting Shakespeare might be of value. Very much in the now, working-class people are concerned with immediate needs. (p. 55)

Even after entering college, first-generation students may not fully appreciate the value of intellectual pursuits and the educational experience. These students may view higher education as merely a means to an end—a way to get a good job. The counselor should ask these students why they are in college and what they hope will be the result. The counselor should explore the extent to which limitations as to the student's interest in education may pose a barrier to the student's success in college and ultimate career aspirations.

The counselor should also assess the level of financial hardship affecting the client. First-generation students typically work many more hours per week than do other students (Pascarella, Pierson, Wolniak, & Terenzini, 2004). The long hours and additional stress associated with working while going to school may significantly interfere with class attendance, ability to concentrate, and the time and energy these students have to study. Working is also likely to reduce the possibility for extracurricular and social activities, thereby hindering adjustment by first-generation students to college life.

Adjustment to College Life

A central issue to explore with first-generation students is their ability to adjust to college life. Without the benefit of parental experience, many first-generation students do not know what to expect when they arrive at college. Moreover, the transition tends to be more problematic depending on the degree to which the college environment differs from the home environment. Thus, colleges dominated by middle-class students, and particularly elite colleges dominated by upper-class students, may pose a significant challenge to first-generation students from working-class families. Further, the degree of differences in other aspects of the college culture, such as the dominant racial, ethnic, and religious backgrounds of the students, may add to the transitional dilemma.

Counselors should ask their clients how they are adjusting to campus life and what impact being first-generation students has on their ability to adjust. Many first-generation students are very conscious of being different from other students, and many feel disadvantaged in comparison with middle- and upper-class students, who have been privileged to have educated and wealthy parents. It is not unusual for first-generation, working-class students, particularly in elite colleges, to feel intimidated by other students and to feel resentful and inadequate. One of the authors (Joseph A. Lippincott) recalls, for example, working with a working-class student who felt a stinging sense of rejection from her roommates, all of whom were traveling to a Caribbean island for spring break and refused to believe that the student's parents could not afford such a luxury.

The students from working-class families often experience a crisis of identity on entering college—a type of culture shock. These students identify with a set of core values they grew up with, such as reliance on common sense and intuition and focus on loyalty to the group—family, friends, union, and country. These values may seem to be in conflict with the values they see on campus, such as reliance on cultivated, logical thinking and focus on the individual and personal achievement (Lubrano, 2004).

The college experience may challenge the realities of first-generation, working-class students. For example, many students whose parents are laborers or hourly wage earners may have developed a sense of an external locus of control. The cultural reality faced by their parents of having little autonomy in the workplace, of having to closely report to a boss or manager (in addition to other classism effects), may predispose working-class offspring to expect their roles and life options to be proscribed. Working-class students are typically not as exposed to the array of choices and options afforded their middle- and upper-class counterparts. As an illustration, one of the authors (Joseph A. Lippincott) is familiar with a large manufacturing facility near a local university that closes for maintenance for 1 week every July. Although managers may choose to work during this week, the rank-and-file employees in the plant must use their allotted vacation days during this mandatory shutdown. Such disparity between blue- and white-collar reality may predispose first-generation students to expect rigidity and minimal autonomy in life, including the college setting.

When compared with other students, first-generation students are more likely to live off-campus and to have less time to spend on campus and in extracurricular activities because of their work schedules (Pascarella et al., 2004). This limited ability to engage in campus life compounds the problems associated with adjusting to college.

It is not surprising that many first-generation students report that they do not feel like they fit in or belong on college campuses. They have difficulty establishing meaningful social relationships, which are crucial for an overall sense of well-being, in college as in life itself. In their study of depression among students, Ndoh and Scales (2002) found an inverse relationship between level of socialization and scores on the Beck Depression Inventory.

The results of culture shock and inability to find social acceptance may cause first-generation students to feel isolated, anxious, and depressed. These students often experience low self-esteem and a lack of confidence in their ability to succeed in college. These feelings are likely to discourage their engagement, both in the classroom and in social and extracurricular activities, and often lead these students to drop out of college.

Family-of-Origin Issues

Family-of-origin issues are an important assessment area for first-generation students. Counselors should ask the students to describe their overall parental and family involvement and support in the students' application to and matriculation at college. For some of these students, their consciousness of living out the hopes and dreams of their family as the first member in college weighs heavily on them. Some of these students, however, have to deal with the jealousy of members of the family who are less fortunate. Other students have to contend with parents or other family members who are highly critical of or feel threatened by the students' accomplishments (Orbe, 2004; Piorkowski, 1983). Still other students have to deal with their own "survivor guilt" caused by their knowledge that, by going to college, they may be the only member of their families to escape poverty, unemployment, or other problems that plague their families (Piorkowski, 1983).

Adjustment to college life does not solve all problems for first-generation students. The counselor should assess the impact of the changes inherent in the adjustment process on the student's relationship with his or her family. Many students become disconnected from their families in the process of adjustment, finding they have progressively less in common with family and friends back home (Christopher, 2003). As Lubrano (2004) described the process, "one world opens and widens; another shrinks" (p. 41).

For some students, the adjustment to college life creates even greater internal conflicts, particularly for those students who grew up facing racial or ethnic prejudice in addition to being poor. Merullo (2002) noted that those students who were raised to believe that there was "an oppressor just on the other side of some invisible border" have to contend with "guilt, doubt, and anger" as they "find themselves on the other side of that invisible border consorting with the enemy" and as they question whether they have "become the very people their parents and peers despised" (p. B11).

Counseling Implications

First-generation students who have the desire to succeed in college but do not have the necessary academic skill sets to do so may be good candidates for referral to remedial support programs on campus (see chapter 13 in this book, "Counseling for Success: Assisting Students in Academic Jeopardy"). The most beneficial referrals and liaisons, however, may be with specific faculty members.

Those students who are focused on college as simply the means to a job may benefit from the counselor's insight into the "big picture" of education. Helping students to find a level of excitement in the journey that is the learning process affords counselors the opportunity to invite these students to a deeper and, we hope, more meaningful college experience.

Those students who are at risk of academic failure because they are trying to juggle work and college may need assistance in finding alternative forms of financial aid and guidance in choosing a reasonable course load. It is also important for counselors to be aware of possible stigma or a negative sense of self among financial aid recipients. Merullo (2002) described having to wait on faculty tables as a "scholarship boy" and lamented that he and fellow aid recipients were referred to as "wombats."

Adjustment to college life may be a formidable task for first-generation students. Many of these students have chosen to attend college because they hope to transcend the socioeconomic level of their families. These students therefore have an incentive to adjust to college life and the new culture it presents. The adjustment process itself, however, is not easy because it leaves many students questioning their identity. Lubrano (2004) described the people going through this process as "straddlers" because "they straddle two worlds, many of them not feeling at home in either" (p. 2).

The conflicts that these students experience have been described as identity continuity versus identity transformation (Wentworth & Peterson, 2001). The challenge of navigating between cultures can also be conceptualized as occurring on an ego syntonic/dystonic continuum. As new relationships, ideas, and experiences become assimilated, the first-generation student moves toward a more grounded sense of self.

In assisting these students through this transitional process, the counselor should also reassure the students that they are deserving and capable of a college education and a career. In a study comparing overall adjustment of first- and second-generation students, self-esteem was found to be one of the primary predictors of college adjustment (Hertel, 2002). In addition, the students should be encouraged to become actively engaged not only in the classroom but also in social and extracurricular activities on campus. Counselors can simultaneously acknowledge the need of these students to hold jobs while exploring creative ways in which they can establish and maintain campus connections. Studies have indicated that involvement in campus activities and interaction with other students play positive roles in the intellectual and personal adjustment of first-generation college students (Pascarella et al., 2004).

The task of integrating dual worlds is often complicated for first-generation students by issues regarding their families of origin. This task can at times be facilitated, however, by the counselor's incorporation of one or more family sessions into the individual treatment plan. A family approach may be warranted for a number of reasons and may be practical particularly for first-generation students who attend college close to home or who live at home and commute to classes. The inclusion of parents in a few sessions allows all present to explore experiences, expectations, and likely incongruities regarding the student's college encounter. A short-term family approach also allows parents to ask questions about and gain insight into college life and culture.

Although individual and family counseling can be effective, group work with first-generation students can be particularly potent. The Freshmen Empowerment Program at Central Michigan University was designed to support first-generation freshmen students who are "at risk" because of difficulties in coping with the academic and social transition into college (Folger, Carter, & Chase, 2004). The program calls for weekly group meetings that focus on students' adjustment concerns and issues such as academics, relationships, and college resources.

The ABle model of group intervention was developed to support working-class and minority students (Farley, 2002). It was so named by the program developers because they wanted the involved students to get As and Bs and believed they would be "able" to do so. This model includes weekly group sessions that emphasize group problem solving concerning personal and academic issues and, in addition, includes mentoring and regular, intensive individual advising.

First-generation graduate students face similar stressors. Granfield's (1991) study of first-generation law students revealed a common theme of insecurity as well as a sense of having to "fake it" among second-generation, non-working-class peers. The very concept of continuing educationally after the baccalaureate is confounding for many parents, friends, and family members (Langston, 1993; Luttrell, 1997). Counselors at universities with graduate programs may wish to consider initiating outreach programs to reach this underserved population.

Campus Considerations

The most salient factor regarding first-generation students' sense of comfort and identity maintenance seems to be the type of institution they choose to attend (Christopher, 2003; Granfield, 1991; Ostrove, 2003). The differences in overall experiences among students attending 2-year community colleges, 4-year state/regional colleges, and 4-year elite/upper-tier colleges are vast. First-generation students attending community colleges seem to have the least transition stress, in part because such schools "offer a less threatening, and perhaps more accommodating, environment" (Pascarella, Wolniak, Pierson, & Terenzini, 2003, p. 429). Social class homogeneity within the student body composition is an important determinant for first-generation students' comfort and sense of fit (Orbe, 2004). Students at 2-year and regional 4-year colleges tend to find others like themselves. This is not to suggest, however, that all students at these institutions experience a seamless transition. The large numbers of first-generation students at these schools predispose counseling centers to use early identification and intervention strategies, perhaps by targeting students in orientation groups.

On-campus student support, from a variety of sources, has proven to be a potent predictor of first-generation students' adjustment (Hertel, 2002). There are a number of campus offices, departments, and organizations with which counseling centers can liaison to serve first-generation students. The admissions office, for example, can provide first-generation status information for each incoming freshman class, thereby allowing counseling centers to strategize programming and other direct services. As is true with so many other professional liaisons and consultations, collaborating closely with a particular person from each department affords an affiliative, reciprocal relationship.

As has been noted, counselors should consider making referrals to offices on campus that provide academically related assistance. The availability of academic advising, tutoring, study skills, and other academic success strategies can be crucial for the retention and academic success of first-generation students.

Offices of student affairs and activities can help first-generation students integrate into the campus community. Involvement in campus activities and interaction with other students are key to the adjustment process. First-generation students, particularly those who have sparse connections with the campus because they live and/or work off-campus, can benefit from creative programs and personal guidance that help them become engaged in the campus community.

The office of housing and residence life is often the first college contact for students choosing to live on campus. For students who have concerns about the dormitories or who are commuters but may wish to consider on-campus life, an informal meeting with a housing staff liaison can answer questions and allay concerns. Hertel (2002) suggested enlisting junior and senior first-generation students to provide mentoring and to lead panel discussions in residence halls.

Financial aid offices often provide the "make or break" difference that allows first-generation students to remain matriculated. As noted previously, economic needs are often primary concerns for these students, who are more likely than second-generation students to worry about paying for college, to come from lower socioeconomic backgrounds, and to feel the need to financially help out their families (Bui, 2002). In addition, Pike and Kuh (2005) encouraged those colleges that are committed to improving the success rates of first-generation students to develop innovative financial assistance programs that permit first-generation students to live on campus for at least the first year.

Future Trends

An undergraduate degree in the 21st century is the currency needed to obtain many personal and professional goals. It is akin to a high school diploma of one or two generations ago. For these and many other reasons, the influx of college students from families with no postsecondary educational backgrounds will continue to rise. College counselors need to be prepared to meet the unique needs of these students. Research, particularly treatment and outcome studies, is scant for this population, and efforts should be increased.

On a broader scale, the issue of class itself is often overlooked, or at least given a muted status, in academia in general and counseling in particular. Issues of race, gender, and ethnicity (but not class) have traditionally been granted the focus in academic discourse and research (Orbe, 2004; Piper, 1995). Further research is warranted on the impact of being a first-generation, working-class student, and that research should be expanded to the intersection of this status with other aspects of a person's identity, particularly those based on race, gender, ethnicity, and age.

Within this class domain, other underexamined issues exist regarding first-generation and working-class college students. The differences between first-generation students attending elite, first-tier, selective enrollment colleges and those attending regional, second- and third-tier, open registration colleges deserve closer attention. Christopher (2003) asserted that first-generation students at elite colleges often experience class prejudice and discrimination but that regional universities, although often a more comfortable environment for these students, fail to provide them with the skills and exposure necessary to flourish in many professional milieus. It is clear that the need exists for more knowledge and research about the inequities among institutions but, more important, about the needs of first-generation students attending them.

College and university professionals—from admissions recruiters to research faculty to counselors—need to examine collaboratively the effects of individual institutional variables on first-generation students. More important, the concept of class needs to be recognized and included as a variable in the diversity equation. The opening of the Center for Working-Class Studies at Youngstown State

University (Borrego, 2001) is an excellent step in this direction. This is the first center of its kind in the country, "providing a space for scholars and practitioners to come together to explore class issues from a host of perspectives" (Borrego, 2001, p. 32).

References

Borrego, S. (2001). Social class in the academy. *About Campus, 6*, 31–32.

Bui, K. V. (2002). First generation college students at a four-year university: Background, characteristics, reasons for pursuing higher education, and first year experiences. *College Student Journal, 36*, 3–12.

Chen, X. (2005). *First generation students in postsecondary education: A look at their college transcripts* (NCES Rep. No. 2005-171). Washington, DC: U.S. Department of Education, National Center for Education Statistics.

Christopher, R. (2003). Damned if you do, damned if you don't. *Academe, 89*, 37–41.

Farley, J. E. (2002). Contesting our everyday work lives: The retention of minority and working-class sociology undergraduates. *Sociological Quarterly, 43*, 1–25.

Folger, W. A., Carter, J. A., & Chase, P. B. (2004). Supporting first-generation college freshmen with small group intervention. *College Student Journal, 38*, 472–477.

Gibbons, M. M., & Shoffner, M. F. (2004). Prospective first-generation college students: Meeting their needs through social cognitive career theory. *Professional School Counseling, 8*, 91–98.

Granfield, R. (1991). Making it by faking it: Working-class students in an elite academic environment. *Journal of Contemporary Ethnography, 20*, 331–351.

Hertel, J. B. (2002). College student generational status: Similarities, differences, and factors in college adjustment. *The Psychological Record, 52*, 3–18.

Langston, D. (1993). Who am I now? The politics of class identity. In M. M. Tokarczyk & E. A. Fay (Eds.), *Working-class women in the academy: Laborers in the knowledge factory* (pp. 60–72). Amherst: University of Massachusetts Press.

Lubrano, A. (2004). *Limbo: Blue-collar roots, white-collar identity.* Hoboken, NJ: Wiley.

Luttrell, W. (1997). *School-smart and mother-wise: Working-class women's identity and schooling.* New York: Routledge.

Merullo, R. (2002, June 14). The challenge of first-generation college students. *Chronicle of Higher Education, 48*, B10–B11.

Ndoh, S., & Scales, J. (2002). *The effects of social economic status, social support, gender, ethnicity, and grade point average on depression among college students* (Report No. ED 477 960). Washington, DC: U.S. Department of Education, Office of Educational Research and Improvement.

Orbe, M. P. (2004). Negotiating multiple identities within multiple frames: An analysis of first-generation college students. *Communication Education, 53*, 131–149.

Ostrove, J. M. (2003). Belonging and wanting: Meanings of social class background for women's constructions of their college experience. *Journal of Social Issues, 59*, 771–784.

Pascarella, E. T., Pierson, C. T., Wolniak, G. C., & Terenzini, P. T. (2004). First-generation college students: Additional evidence on college experiences and outcomes. *The Journal of Higher Education, 75*, 249–284.

Pascarella, E. T., Wolniak, G. C., Pierson, C. T., & Terenzini, P. T. (2003). Experiences and outcomes of first-generation students in community colleges. *Journal of College Student Development, 44*, 420–429.

Pike, G. R., & Kuh, G. D. (2005). First- and second-generation college students: A comparison of their engagement and intellectual development. *The Journal of Higher Education, 76*, 276–300.

Piorkowski, G. K. (1983). Survival guilt in the university setting. *Personnel & Guidance Journal, 61*, 620–623.

Piper, D. (1995). Psychology's class blindness: Investment in the status quo. In C. L. B. Dews & C. L. Law (Eds.), *This fine place so far from home: Voices of academics in the working class* (pp. 286–296). Philadelphia: Temple University Press.

Wentworth, P. A., & Peterson, B. E. (2001). Crossing the line: Case studies of identity development in first generation college women. *Journal of Adult Development, 8,* 9–21.

8

Counseling Adult Learners: Individual Interventions, Group Interventions, and Campus Resources

Juneau Mahan Gary

Introduction

Student demographics on the average American college campus increasingly reflect diversity, including adult learners (Bishop, Lacour, Nutt, Yamada, & Lee, 2004), defined as students 25 years of age or older (Carney-Crompton & Tan, 2002). Over half of adult learners pursue an academic degree for career-related reasons, such as promotions. They are often geographically limited by their family and employment responsibilities and, consequently, enroll in colleges near their residence or employer, making local colleges or online colleges their primary educational options.

The developmental concerns and tasks of adult learners differ from those of traditional-age college students (i.e., 18 to 24 years old; Gary, Kling, & Dodd, 2004). Some of the differences may include age, family demands, life experiences, work responsibilities, personal interests, and military experience (Hansen, 1999). Further, adult learners may not have attended a college recently, if at all, and may experience significant anxiety and doubt about their ability to achieve, insecurity about their computer skills, and concern about how or whether college will fit into their already busy schedules (Carney-Crompton & Tan, 2002).

Historically, colleges recruited traditional-age students and established campus services, such as college counseling centers, to meet the needs of traditional-age students. Thus, one may ask, "How do campus counselors ad-

Special thanks are extended to Melvin L. Gary and Beverly Kling for their editorial comments on drafts of this chapter.

equately help adult learners seeking counseling when services were not designed to meet their specific needs and developmental concerns?" It is critical that college counselors be familiar with the needs and issues of this growing population of students. This chapter addresses effective group and individual counseling interventions and campus support services for adult learners.

Assessment Issues

Although all college students encounter stressors associated with transition and adjustment to college life, each adult learner faces added stressors compared with the traditional-age student. When working with adult learners, in addition to using standard counseling assessment procedures, counselors are advised to assess for the adverse impact of stressors common to adult experiences, to evaluate the efficacy of coping strategies, and to gauge the adequacy of support systems.

Adult learners may encounter significant stress in resolving conflicts among their multiple roles, which, in addition to their new role as student, may already include spouse, partner, caregiver of aging parents, employee, and religious or civic leader (Swanson, 2002). Zamarripa, Wampold, and Gregory (2003) found that conflict between family and work responsibilities is one major predictor of depression and anxiety in male and female adult learners. Unsuccessful resolution of multiple stressors such as these may result in emotional distress, burnout, missed classes, premature withdrawal from school, and absenteeism at work (Burns, 1997). If stressors such as these become barriers to graduation, they may thwart career-related opportunities and personal satisfaction.

Subgroups of adult learners, such as American minority students, international students, female students, and male students, encounter specific stressors in addition to the general stressors experienced by adult learners. Each subgroup's stressors may act as additional barriers to retention if not addressed in counseling.

American minority adult learners, sometimes referred to as adult students of color, may experience cultural messages that reflect the impact of family, community, political, and historical influences on their particular ethnic or racial group. Culturally ingrained messages, such as "keep your problems and dirty linens within the family," may influence students' reactions to stressors and their choice of coping strategies (Jenkins, 1999). For instance, if they feel or believe the campus to be hostile or indifferent to their needs or issues, their social support system may consist of ethnocentric student and community organizations.

International and first-generation immigrant adult learners may experience language limitations, homesickness, lack of appropriate assertiveness, and financial or immigration problems (Poyrazli, Arbona, Nora, McPherson, & Pisecco, 2002). The adjustment and acculturation issues of a spouse or partner and children, who may also experience language limitations, immigration problems, and homesickness, may further stress married immigrant or international learners. These learners and their relatives may suffer in silence because of a cultural stigma or barrier to requesting help in general or seeking counseling in particular. Nilsson, Berkel, Flores, and Lucas (2004) found that only about 2% of international students sought counseling, and about one third of them dropped out after the initial intake session. Seeking counseling may compete with internalized cultural messages such as "you're in school to learn so don't focus on problems." Moreover, campus services will most likely not be available for the learner's relatives.

Female adult learners are often encumbered with a disproportional burden of household tasks and caregiver responsibilities for children and aging parents and may struggle with reproductive crises (e.g., pregnancy or menopause), gynecologic illnesses (e.g., ovarian cancer), relationship issues, and family conflicts while managing multiple role responsibilities (Carney-Crompton & Tan, 2002). In addition to parenting, self-care, and nurturing issues, 40%–90% of working women report being sexually harassed, one quarter are typically burdened by sexual trauma, and many continue to be clustered in low-paying and low-status jobs (Prochaska & Norcross, 2003).

Finally, a man may desire to return to college full-time to complete a degree or change career paths but may be confronted by male gender role conflict (Zamarripa et al., 2003). For instance, the employer may shun him when a leave of absence is requested, or his spouse or partner, children, or parents may dissuade him if he is a significant wage earner. The male adult learner may feel unsupported by most of the support systems in his life.

Counseling Implications

College counselors assist students to overcome perceived or actual barriers, envision academic and personal success, resolve personal issues affecting academic achievement, and accomplish the ultimate academic goal of graduation. In counseling, students become aware of personal strengths and support systems to use as a foundation for change. They also become aware that a problem exists and that effective problem-solving skills are available. In this section, support groups and five individual counseling orientations are reviewed as effective interventions to use with adult learners to reduce their stressors and promote change involving feelings, thoughts, and behaviors.

Support Groups

Counselors may facilitate support groups designed exclusively for adult learners that stress effective transition and adjustment to academic life and the expectations of higher education. Research on the efficacy of support groups has indicated that members benefit from group participation and a combination of therapeutic factors (Corey & Corey, 2005; Schwartz & Waldo, 1999; Yalom, 2005). Support groups facilitate adult learners in leaning on others who understand and live their plight. Through dialogue and self-disclosure, mutual support is offered and received, aiding members in adjusting to significant changes and major stressors by learning from the experiences of others. Participation unites adult learners as they share similar thoughts, feelings, anxieties, and emotional reactions. Bonding with other adult learners reduces the sense of isolation and increases the realization that other learners also struggle. Members also experience validation and a sense of identity and purpose on campus (Mills-Novoa, 1999).

Counselors are advised to facilitate support groups in the late afternoons or evenings (after the learner's workday) and on weekends. Prepared topics for group discussion could focus on pragmatic academic and personal issues and be designed to build or strengthen coping behaviors and skill development (Gazda, Ginter, & Horne, 2001). Topics may include coping with multiple role conflicts; establishing priorities; setting realistic expectations; coping with guilt about missed family activities; handling family, work, and personal crises that occur without warning (e.g., divorce, serious illness, or downsizing); incorporating stress management skills into a busy schedule; and handling conflict resolution. Group members may engage in experiential exercises and role-plays to practice these skills and apply them in daily living situations. At times, though, members' needs may differ from a counselor's prepared topic, and the counselor must be flexible in order to meet the group's immediate needs. Counselors who were former adult learners in college may choose to self-disclose and become models of academic success, thereby communicating nonverbally, "This too can be accomplished."

Adult learners may need attention to bonding and communication issues in support groups. Members bring a wide range of life experiences, coping mechanisms, personal attitudes, biases, beliefs, and knowledge that influence their ability to seek help. Their experiences affect what is perceived to be appropriate to discuss in front of strangers and beyond family boundaries, as well as how and when to seek help (Caldera, Robitschek, Frame, & Pannell, 2003; Wu & Carter, 1999). Allowing each member to establish individual communication patterns involving what and how much to self-disclose will facilitate individual comfort levels and foster a sense of personal control.

Another basic communication issue for adult learners involves English language limitations when English is not the primary language. This type of adult learner may be challenged in clearly communicating feelings and thoughts to other group members. Conversely, others may be challenged to respond in a supportive and helpful manner if they are unable to grasp the adult learner's needs. If the counselor suspects that an adult learner is struggling with English language limitations, the counselor may role model a different level of vocabulary and periodically check with the adult learner to ensure comprehension and accurate expression. The adult learner may also benefit from individual counseling with a bilingual counselor.

Individual Counseling Services

Individual counseling may be the most effective mode of intervention for specific issues or for certain adult learners. Many theories and models of individual counseling may be effective with the lifestyle and developmental issues of the adult learner. An eclectic counselor, using integrative counseling (Corey,

2001), is in a position to select the most effective theories and corresponding techniques of individual counseling that match the specific characteristics and needs of each adult learner.

The counseling models of cognitive–behavior therapy, solution-focused brief counseling, family/systems counseling, gender-based counseling, and multicultural counseling are described briefly and applied to adult learners. Each model of counseling is discussed separately; however, in actuality, these models, as is true of most models of counseling, overlap regarding target populations and techniques.

Cognitive–Behavior Therapy Counseling

Cognitive–behavior therapy is a general category of theories with a cognitive–behavioral belief system as the foundation (Capuzzi & Gross, 2003). Counselors help clients to alter faulty cognitions and change how they think, feel, and behave. Interventions are goal- or problem-oriented, structured, directive, and time-limited and focus on problem-solving skills. This theory works best with adult learners who have a strong belief system and is less effective with adult learners who seek insight or are very emotive.

The counselor uses a variety of behavioral assessments and strategies. Typically, the counselor may focus on catastrophic thinking and self-defeating beliefs (also called cognitive distortions). An example of a self-defeating thought for an adult learner may be "Do I really belong in college when my family needs me?" Typical assessments and strategies of cognitive–behavior therapy include the following:

1. Self-monitor the frequency of self-defeating intrusions into the adult learner's daily living routine. For example, ask the adult learner to do a frequency count on the number of times a day he or she feels badly about time away from home or work to attend college.
2. Help the adult learner objectively examine self-defeating thoughts. These may consist of all-or-nothing thinking and catastrophizing. In all-or-nothing thinking, things must be either perfect or terrible. This dichotomous thinking may result in depression because the adult learner ruminates on the "nothing" or terrible side of the pendulum. Catastrophizing is exaggerating negative events in which the impact is perceived to be severely adverse. For instance, a grade of B may be catastrophized to failing the course and concluding the need to withdraw from college.
3. Use interventions that target cognitive and behavioral excesses and deficits. Cognitive interventions, such as thought stopping, positive self-statements, and cognitive restructuring, are effective in identifying faulty underlying assumptions and changing cognitions. Other common interventions are reframing, shaping, role-playing, modeling, bibliotherapy, relapse prevention, systematic desensitization, risk-taking, and positive and negative reinforcement. Homework assignments between

sessions, called skills practice, assist in reinforcing and maintaining new behavior in the adult learner's daily living routine.

Solution-Focused Brief Therapy

Solution-focused brief therapy is useful with adult learners in college counseling centers. Counseling objectives are specific, limited, and realistic. Counseling is partially defined by the time limit established from the onset, with the average number of sessions ranging between three and five (Capuzzi & Gross, 2003). Sessions may be scheduled flexibly and strategically to maximize therapeutic gains.

The therapeutic relationship focuses on solutions, with the assumption that the client already has resources and capabilities to effect change and solutions. By capitalizing on what is already working and focusing on the adult learner's strengths, both known and unrecognized (rather than on deficits), the therapeutic relationship concentrates on behaviors and goals that result in and maintain solutions. In sessions, the counselor and adult learner engage in collaborative dialogues to create a positive alliance. The adult learner is perceived as an expert in his or her life and is responsible for establishing specific goals based on his or her unique qualities and circumstances. This collaborative relationship contributes to a shared solution with established and specific goals within a brief interval.

Therapeutic goals assist the client to develop a self-perception of competence, see possibilities for creating success and solutions, and create the capability of change in the present or future. The intentional use of strategies guides interventions in a purposeful and optimistic way to help the adult learner achieve competence. Techniques, such as solution talk (a series of future-oriented questions), precounseling self-improvements (helping the adult learner appreciate his or her own power to change), and assignments to observe oneself and one's environment, enable the adult learner to quickly implement action, rather than focus on past experiences and events (Capuzzi & Gross, 2003). Solution-focused brief therapy is effective with adult learners who have limited time and seek an intervention that is quick, focused, efficient, and optimistic. Most multitasking adult learners find these aspects to be empowering and consistent with the adult learner lifestyle.

Meeting the therapeutic goals of adult learners results in successful termination. The relationship lasts only as long as needed to create effective solutions. Thus, solution-focused brief counseling is designed to start, not finish, the solution process as quickly as possible. Following termination, the empowered adult learner continues implementing solutions independently.

The briefest form of solution-focused brief therapy is single-session counseling (Talmon, 1990, 1994). This model is specifically designed to occur in a planned single session with very modest and focused goals. A single session, for example, might be scheduled to evaluate graduate school options and opportunities. Single sessions are not appropriate for all or most people. The model works optimally when the adult learner is highly motivated, has severe time constraints, has very specific issues, is able to focus, perceives himself or herself to be in charge of the changes, and has cognitive and emotional strengths. The counselor must decide the type of adult learner and the type of issues that would benefit from limited therapeutic contact. Follow-up sessions may be scheduled, if needed, by telephone or online. Audiotaping the session for the adult learner to revisit periodically is advisable. Single-session counseling may also be used as a follow-up session after solution-focused brief therapy is terminated.

Family/Systems Counseling

Family/systems theorists assert that one can best understand individuals by considering the social context in which they exist. Thus, systems theory expands the counselor's perspective from a narrow focus on the individual to inclusion of the impact of family and society on the individual (Caldera et al., 2003; Hall, 2003; Lawson & Brossart, 2004). Counselors are advised to consider the familial and sociocultural dynamics that contribute positively and negatively to the individual's outlook on life, including the family's implicit and explicit rules governing individual family members (Lawson & Brossart, 2004; Whiston & Keller, 2004). Therefore, issues in counseling are influenced by factors external to the client and are not based solely on individual traits or personality constructs.

In systems theory, the adult learner may be affected by two family constellations: the family of origin, in which the adult learner is the child/sibling, and the current nuclear family, in which the adult learner is the spouse/partner and/or parent. Family dynamics of the family of origin often have far-reaching effects on the adult learner and on current family dynamics through the internalization of ingrained family messages learned early in life. Messages, either spoken or inferred, may influence self-confidence or self-empowerment in adulthood. That is, internalized injunctions such as "don't ask for help" or "be a martyr and sacrifice your needs for the family's welfare" become emotional baggage and may adversely influence decisions made as an adult in general and an adult learner in particular.

To understand the family cycle and break its negative effects, the counselor is advised to gather information about the adult learner's strengths and challenges from both family constellations in order to understand the adult learner's current issues. The counselor may inquire about how the rules of the family of origin affected family and cultural roles, identity, and styles of communication for the adult learner as a child or sibling (Caldera et al., 2003; Hall, 2003; Lawson & Brossart, 2004). For instance, if the learner played the family role of rescuer in the family of origin and the role continued into adulthood, the adult learner may feel conflicted if the next family crisis occurred simultaneously with a term-paper deadline. The adult learner might feel pressured to select between being the traditional rescuer and completing a term paper by the deadline.

In sessions with adult learners, counselors should listen for guilt about not focusing on other adult priorities, such as family, career, or civic or religious responsibilities, as revered older relatives from the family of origin may have done. Counselors should help the adult learners to evaluate the worth or value of the internalized family messages in adult terms. They should also assist the adult learners in gaining new insight and seeking other options to resolve family crises and guilt in healthy, empowering, and mature adult terms.

Gender-Based Counseling

Theorists of gender-based counseling believe that a person's identity is influenced by environmental and cultural factors such as family dynamics, the media, religious institutions, and societal norms (Caldera et al., 2003; Lawson & Brossart, 2004). From birth, both sexes are bombarded with messages of gender expectations, gender role stereotypes, role strain, and gender-related economics. By adulthood, these messages become deeply ingrained (Prochaska & Norcross, 2003; Zamarripa et al., 2003).

Gender-based counseling, also called feminist counseling, may be used successfully to assist female, and male, adult learners struggling with gender-based personal issues and with career counseling issues (Caldera et al., 2003; Whiston & Keller, 2004; Zamarripa et al., 2003). Gender-based counseling frees women, and men, from the bondage of predetermined and assigned responsibilities and career paths based on gender and cultural roles. In this section, female gender-based issues are discussed first, followed by male gender-based issues.

Typically, women encounter a disproportionate burden of household tasks and caregiver responsibilities for children and aging parents. When some women express a desire to enroll in college, they may face family resistance to changes in household responsibilities. Moreover, a woman may encounter family resistance in gender role expectations, by a reluctant husband or partner or children unwilling to accept additional household responsibilities or by disapproving parents or grandparents who believe she will ignore the children (Lawson & Brossart, 2004). The challenge to balance career, school, and traditional household responsibilities may result in role overload or role strain, and gender-based counseling may be effective. The goals of counseling, using feminist or gender-based theories, include the following: (a) equality (i.e., freedom from traditional gender roles, pursuit of economic self-sufficiency, and equity in work and personal relationships), (b) empowerment (i.e., control over outcomes and ability to advocate for oneself and others), and (c) self-care (i.e., increase in self-esteem, self-confidence, and self-awareness of personal needs and goals).

In sessions, therapeutic content may consist of discrimination issues, responsibility concerns, intimacy/sexuality/reproductive issues, power inequity, low self-esteem, and communication difficulties. The counselor may start with examining socialization messages ingrained by society, the female adult learner's culture and family, and the media (Caldera et al., 2003). The counselor may evaluate the client's personal problems within contextual roots based on social and political oppression, stereotyping, cultural influences, and subordination. The counselor is advised to recognize oppression and its socially restrictive effects and to use reframing to shift the etiology of the problem from the client to society. This shift will most likely help the client to confront internal conflicts about identity by searching beyond traditionally defined female gender roles.

To complete the shift, the client may benefit from differentiating between what she was raised to believe to be socially acceptable and what is now considered psychologically healthy. Then, attention may focus on making choices that will positively change the client's life and facilitate making self-directed choices.

As an adjunct to counseling, the client may benefit from participation in a women's support group or online support group (e.g., www.tapestrycounseling.org) offering education, information giving, and support to experience self-direction, autonomy, empowerment, and self-confidence. Finally, female counselors may use the technique of self-disclosure to share their own struggles and coping strategies with similar issues.

Gender-based counseling has sparked the realization that men may also be negatively affected by gender role expectations and may experience role strain (Zamarripa et al., 2003). That is, men are expected to be continuously successful in a career. They are not expected to stop midcareer to attend college in order to make a major career change or experience self-satisfaction. The desire to return to college full-time to complete a degree or change career paths is often discouraged by the employer. The client's spouse or partner, children, and parents may not support his desire to leave employment for financial and social status reasons. In counseling, the male adult learner may recognize unmet emotional needs, identify and change culturally ingrained and unhealthy beliefs, and receive the support to continue education if this is the best, reasoned decision for him and his aspirations. As an adjunct to counseling, the client may benefit from participation in a men's support group or online support group (e.g., www.themenscenter.com/National/national11.htm#COUNCILS_/ _SUPPORT_GROUPS).

Multicultural/Cultural Competence Counseling

Counseling students from diverse backgrounds signals the need for cultural competence in the counseling process. Multicultural counseling is not a single or discrete treatment modality, but it is most effective when used with and across all counseling modalities (Prochaska & Norcross, 2003). Pedersen (1991) called multicultural counseling the fourth force in counseling, with psychodynamic, behavioral, and humanism as the other three forces.

The concepts of diversity and multicultural counseling are used in their most inclusive forms in this chapter. The traditional definition of multicultural counseling focuses mainly on racial, ethnic, class, and cultural differences. Yet, clients have other physical and psychological aspects that shape them as human beings. When one takes a broad perspective to diversity and includes other human differences such as age, religion, physical disability, and sexual orientation, among others, each human difference becomes its own "culture" within a broad multicultural perspective.

The terms *multicultural counseling* and *cultural competence* are used interchangeably in this chapter. Cultural competence does not require familiarity with all cultural rituals, values, resources, or worldviews; this would be an impossible task. It does, however, require a respect for and understanding of cultural and societal influences and their impact on clients living a bicultural lifestyle. Moreover, cultural competence requires the counselor to incorporate a broad perspective when assessing and counseling clients from different backgrounds, including the acknowledgment of societal forces of marginalization, oppression, identity, alienation, powerlessness, and rejection.

Counselors must transcend communication and cultural barriers of differences and maintain open relationships, as well as offer appropriate support and interventions based on an adult learner's cultural background and cultural supports. Specifically, the counselor is advised to incorporate a worldview and a communication style that enable a counselor from one background to interact effectively with a client from a different background in order to promote the client's emotional, cognitive, and spiritual development by using the client's value system (D'Andrea & Daniels, 1995). In doing so, the counselor will begin to appreciate differences (rather than perceive weaknesses), recognize cultural similarities, and value each client's individual strengths.

Attention to cultural factors can enhance the counselor's engagement of adult learners in counseling and maintain healthy therapeutic relationships. When one is counseling from a multicultural counseling perspective, some of the following issues may be addressed in sessions:

1. *Identity.* An adult learner's personal and cultural identity and worldview are usually connected to self-referent labeling (e.g., calling oneself "deaf" versus "hearing-impaired"). The counselor is advised to use the adult learner's self-referent labels when addressing members of the adult learner's group.

2. *Family and social relations.* Many members of cultural groups perceive family loyalty and responsibilities to the extended family as superseding individual needs (Hall, 2003; Lawson & Brossart, 2004). Although such prioritization may affect academic performance, if the counselor overemphasizes the Western value of one's individual needs as paramount over the needs of others without understanding influences of culture and family dynamics, the adult learner may feel additional stress and prematurely terminate counseling.

3. *Language.* The counselor must consider language content and context as well as assess the adult learner's language proficiency when English is not the native language. Although an adult learner may be proficient in English, emotional words may have a different affective meaning from the language of origin because affect is usually first learned in the language of origin and may not translate accurately (Capuzzi & Gross, 2003). Thus, some adult learners may have difficulty in self-expression of emotional content in English when it is a second language acquisition.

4. *Acculturation.* Acculturation refers to the transformation of one's behaviors, social and work activities, thinking patterns, values, attitudes, feelings, and self-identity that leads to a successful and effective adjustment in a new culture and environment (Coelho & Stein, 1980), either

in the United States or on a college campus. Acculturation is a complex, personal, and individual process of transformation and is unique for each person. People acculturate at different rates based on their personal experiences on campus or in a new country. Moreover, variables such as age, language proficiency, socioeconomic status, academic and career history of older relatives, family structure, and social support may impede or facilitate transition through the acculturation process (Hall, 2003; Kenney, Blustein, Chaves, Grossman, & Gallagher, 2003; Whiston & Keller, 2004). Therefore, adult learners new to the campus environment must grasp new social normative behaviors as they acculturate to a new lifestyle and new experiences. Finding their place on campus may require significant adjustment, change, adaptation, and support.

5. *Cultural customs.* Cultural customs may affect communication style, family roles, and family harmony (Caldera et al., 2003; Lawson & Brossart, 2004). In many cultures, sibling lineage or gender may prescribe specific family roles or responsibilities (e.g., eldest child, youngest child, or male child may have specific roles; Lawson & Brossart, 2004). Communication between parent and child may be directive or one-way (e.g., "Do as you're told to do") rather than two-way (e.g., "Do you have an opinion?"). Directive communication tends to limit a child's language skills, including self-expression of needs that may go unmet (Espinosa, 1995). A family's well-ingrained directive communication style may thwart the adult learner's ability to communicate a need for tutoring services in college, for example, if the family of origin's communication style discouraged communicating, or even identifying, personal needs. Therefore, being told what to do for an assignment or told to seek tutoring, rather than initiating tutoring assistance, may be culturally based and may not be a sign of laziness or incompetence.

6. *Religious traditions.* Spiritual or religious practices are usually rooted deeply in many racial and ethnic groups. Religion offers social cohesion as well as support, guidance, and physical or emotional shelter in adverse situations. One cultural support intervention is collaboration with members of the adult learner's natural support system (with the adult learner's consent), which may include civic and spiritual or religious leaders.

Online Resources as Adjuncts to Counseling

Counselors may recommend some adjuncts to counseling interventions for adult learners who require more support or more frequency than individual or group counseling provides and who possess strong computer skills. Counselors can make referrals to online support groups (e.g., www.psychcafe.net) and suggest Internet links to mental health Web sites (e.g., www.psychcentral.com), culture-based Web sites (e.g., www.nativeweb.com), and gender-based counseling Web sites (e.g., www.tapestrycounseling.org). Because adult learners experience significant constraints of time, online resources such as these may be accessed 24 hours a day when the learner has available time, perhaps at nontraditional times. Counselors will find Grohol's (2003) book helpful for referrals to mental health Web sites.

Campus Considerations

Each adult learner will face a unique combination of issues, problems, and barriers during enrollment in college. Beyond the confines of the counseling center, counselors and other campus helpers may advocate for meeting the needs of adult learners and eliminating barriers to graduation. Some additional campus resources, however, are also recommended as adjuncts to counseling.

Traditional Campus Services

For adult learners, traditional professional counseling, support groups, and referrals to online resources are not sufficient or appropriate. Some adult learners may need additional academic, medical, social, and financial services. Campus services that are responsive to the adult learner require programmatic interventions that modify traditional assistance to reflect meeting the needs of all students, including adult learners.

Counselors are one group of campus helpers with first-hand information about how to assist adult learners. Counselors may advocate for campus services that are convenient, flexible, and responsive to the scheduling needs of adult learners. Counselors may collaborate with other campus service providers and helpers to meet the full complement of needs of adult learners, including: (a) academic support services (e.g., for tutoring); (b) new student services (e.g., for orientation programs); (c) child care services; (d) health services; (e) academic programs and departments that attract female, ethnic minority, and international or immigrant adult learners (e.g., for women's studies, Holocaust studies, and Asian studies); (f) financial aid office (e.g., for grants and scholarships designed for adult learners); and (g) career services.

Office for Adult Learners

The college should establish an Office for Adult Learners, if one does not already exist, preferably staffed by a coordinator who was a former adult learner. The coordinator would evaluate the campus climate to identify actual and perceived barriers that thwart academic success (Hayes & Lin, 1994; Kenney et al., 2003) and would advocate for services and supports to meet adult learners' needs.

The coordinator of the Office for Adult Learners should sponsor an orientation program for new and transfer adult learners, in addition to the college's general orientation programs. Adult learners would benefit from the early support and not feel isolated. The office should also (a) provide a quiet study lounge specifically for adult learners that is open during the times that adult learners are primarily on campus, (b) post information about events and services specific to adult learners on a bulletin board in the study lounge, (c) sponsor a campus Web page to disseminate information electronically, and (d) publish a handbook describing campus services relevant to the adult learner.

Computer Workshops

The college should offer computer workshops exclusively for adult learners, who may feel intimidated by the computer skills of traditional-age students. Many adult learners were not raised with access to computers. The exclusion of traditional-age students may help the adult learner feel less overwhelmed or inadequate and more likely to admit computer inadequacies among peers. The pace of sessions should be tailored to the learning needs of adult learners, and the sessions should confront computer phobia by discussing its emotional aspects of anxiety, fear, and inadequacy. Word processing, e-mail, statistical analysis, literature search strategies, and the like should be included.

Study Skills Workshops

The college should offer study skills workshops exclusively for adult learners. Adult learners returning to college after several years in the workplace or at home raising children may benefit from a refresher workshop.

Cultural Support Interventions

The counselor may incorporate cultural support interventions by collaborating with members of the adult learner's natural support systems, with the adult learner's consent. Cultural support may consist of (a) relational support from relatives, partners, and close friends who empower the adult learner; (b) social networks that offer cultural nurturance (e.g., ethnocentric student organizations such as the National Association for the Advancement of Colored People [NAACP], fraternities, and sororities such as Lambda Theta Phi/Alpha); (c) institutions that give information and spiritual support (e.g., church, synagogue, or mosque and campus religious organizations); and (d) other campus groups that provide safe havens (e.g., students with disabilities and gay, lesbian, bisexual, and transgendered student alliance). Counselors may provide information about these support networks and facilitate adult learners' involvement through referral, distribution of literature, and personal contacts.

Family Support

In contemplating how to retain and graduate adult learners, college administrators should consider incorporating family support into campus activities (Kenney et al., 2003). Inadequate family support is often based on a relative's misunderstanding of the adult learner's academic requirements and priorities. To strengthen family support, a family newsletter should be disseminated to apprise relatives about important events, accomplishments of learners, and special programs of interest to the whole family. Relatives should be encouraged to participate in campus activities, such as "Family Day," or to attend campus performances as a family. Family support and understanding of the adult learner's commitment to career development and personal satisfaction reduce some of the adult learner's guilt and empower the adult learner to graduate.

Future Trends

Adult learners on American campuses represent a growing campus constituency. They warrant counseling and campus services that meet their specific needs and reduce the effects of their developmental stressors. As colleges attract an increasingly diverse group of students, administrators must offer specific interventions to support them.

The college community must communicate to the adult learner that "we want you to succeed." Thus, counseling and campus support services must be responsive to the needs and experiences of adult learners. In addition to professional counseling, adult learners may benefit from comprehensive campus supports that facilitate retention and graduation. Attention to the emotional, cognitive, and developmental needs of this growing campus constituency can result in a win–win situation for the adult learner, the college, the family, and the employer.

References

Bishop, J., Lacour, M. A., Nutt, N., Yamada, V., & Lee, J. (2004). Reviewing a decade of change in the student culture. *Journal of College Student Psychotherapy, 18,* 3–30.

Burns, S. (1997). Assistance programs: A timely solution for the adult education setting. *Adult Learning, 9,* 26–28.

Caldera, Y., Robitschek, C., Frame, M., & Pannell, M. (2003). Intrapersonal, familial, and cultural factors in the commitment to a career choice of Mexican and non-Hispanic White college women. *Journal of Counseling Psychology, 50,* 309–323.

Capuzzi, D., & Gross, D. (2003). *Counseling and psychotherapy: Theories and interventions* (3rd ed.). Upper Saddle River, NJ: Merrill/Prentice Hall.

Carney-Crompton, S., & Tan, J. (2002). Support systems, psychological functioning, and academic performance of nontraditional female students. *Adult Education Quarterly, 52,* 140–154.

Coelho, G. V., & Stein, J. J. (1980). *Change, vulnerability, and coping: Stresses of uprooting and overcrowding.* New York: Plenum.

Corey, G. (2001). *The art of integrative counseling.* Belmont, CA: Wadsworth.

Corey, G., & Corey, M. (2005). *Groups: Process and practice* (7th ed.). Belmont, CA: Thomson Brooks/Cole.

D'Andrea, A., & Daniels, J. (1995). Promoting multiculturalism and organizational change in the counseling profession: A case study. In J. Ponterotto, J. M. Casas, L. Suzuki, & C. Alexander (Eds.), *Handbook of multicultural counseling* (pp. 17–33). Thousand Oaks, CA: Sage.

Espinosa, L. M. (1995). Hispanic parent involvement in early childhood programs. *ERIC Digest,* 1–3. Retrieved July 9, 2006, from http://www.eric.ed.gov/ERICWebPortal/Home. portal?_nfpb=true&ERICExtSearch_SearchValue_0=Hispanic+parent+involvement+in+early+childhood+programs&ERICExtSearch_SearchType_0=ti&+_pageLabel=RecordDetails&objectID=0900000b801b4c72&accno=ED382412

Gary, J., Kling, B., & Dodd, B. (2004). A program for counseling and campus support services for African American and Latino adult learners. *Journal of College Counseling, 7,* 18–23.

Gazda, G. M., Ginter, E. J., & Horne, A. M. (2001). *Group counseling and group psychotherapy: Theory and application.* Needham Heights, MA: Allyn & Bacon.

Grohol, J. (2003). *The insider's guide to mental health resources online* (rev. ed.). New York: Guilford Press.

Hall, A. (2003). Expanding academic and career self-efficacy: A family systems framework. *Journal of Counseling & Development, 81,* 33–39.

Hansen, D. (1999). Key factors that differentiate nontraditional from traditional students. In Y. Jenkins (Ed.), *Diversity in college settings: Directives for helping professionals* (pp. 191–199). New York: Routledge.

Hayes, R., & Lin, H. (1994). Coming to America: Developing social support systems for international students. *Journal of Multicultural Counseling and Development, 22,* 7–17.

Jenkins, Y. (Ed.). (1999). *Diversity in college settings: Directives for helping professionals.* New York: Routledge.

Kenney, M., Blustein, D., Chaves, A., Grossman, J., & Gallagher, L. (2003). The role of perceived barriers and relational support in the educational and vocational lives of urban high school students. *Journal of Counseling Psychology, 50,* 142–155.

Lawson, D., & Brossart, D. (2004). The association between current intergenerational family relationships and sibling structure. *Journal of Counseling & Development, 82,* 472–482.

Mills-Novoa, A. (1999). Potential roles a college counselor can play in promoting the academic success of students of color. *Journal of College Counseling, 2,* 92–96.

Nilsson, J., Berkel, L., Flores, L., & Lucas, M. (2004). Utilization rate and presenting concerns of international students at a university counseling center: Implications for outreach programming. *Journal of College Student Psychotherapy, 19,* 49–59.

Pedersen, P. B. (Ed.). (1991). Multiculturalism as a fourth force in counseling. *Journal of Counseling and Development, 70,* 6–12.

Poyrazli, S., Arbona, C., Nora, A., McPherson, R., & Pisecco, S. (2002). Relation between assertiveness, academic self-efficacy, and psychosocial adjustment among international graduate students. *Journal of College Student Development, 43,* 632–642.

Prochaska, J., & Norcross, J. (2003). *Systems of psychotherapy: A transtheoretical analysis* (5th ed.). Pacific Grove, CA: Brooks/Cole.

Schwartz, J., & Waldo, M. (1999). Therapeutic factors in spouse-abuse group treatment. *The Journal for Specialists in Group Work, 24,* 197–207.

Swanson, J. (2002). Understanding the complexity of clients' lives: Infusing a truly integrative career–personal perspective into graduate training. *The Counseling Psychologist, 30,* 815–832.

Talmon, M. (1990). *Single session therapy: Maximizing the effect of the first (and often only) therapeutic encounter.* Hoboken, NJ: Jossey-Bass.

Talmon, M. (1994). *Single-session solutions: A guide to practical, effective, and affordable therapy.* Reading, MA: Addison-Wesley.

Whiston, S., & Keller, B. (2004). The influences of the family of origin on career development: A review and analysis. *The Counseling Psychologist, 32,* 493–568.

Wu, Y., & Carter, K. (1999). Volunteer voices: A model for the professional development of volunteer teachers. *Adult Learning, 11,* 16–19.

Yalom, I. (2005). *The theory and practice of group psychotherapy* (5th ed.). New York: Basic Books.

Zamarripa, M., Wampold, B., & Gregory, E. (2003). Male gender role conflict, depression, and anxiety: Clarification and generalizability to women. *Journal of Counseling Psychology, 50,* 333–338.

Section III

Developmental and Situational Issues

9

When Dating Relationships Go Bad: Counseling Students Involved in Relationship Violence

Cheryl Blalock Aspy

Introduction

There is widespread agreement that violence between intimate partners in dating relationships is a substantial public health problem. It has been labeled as *intimate partner violence, courtship violence, dating violence, domestic violence, battering,* and *spouse abuse.* Each of these terms has specific definitions and restrictions that may limit comparisons across studies and prevent a complete description of the magnitude of the total problem (Berkel, Vandiver, & Bahner, 2004; National Center for Injury Prevention and Control, 2003). This lack of agreement regarding the definition of relationship violence has been a limiting factor in the accumulation of evidence regarding its etiology and in the development of effective treatments for both victims and perpetrators.

In general, the definitions of relationship violence center on descriptors of physical violence or the combination of physical and psychological violence. The term most often used by various criminal justice and public health groups has been *intimate partner violence* (IPV). The definition of IPV includes "those murders, rapes, robberies, or assaults committed by spouses, ex-spouses, boyfriends, or girlfriends" (Zawitz, 1994, p. 1). The National Violence Against Women Study defined IPV against women as "rape, physical assault, and stalking perpetrated by a current or former date, boyfriend, husband or cohabiting partner with cohabiting meaning living together as a couple" (National Center for Injury Prevention and Control, 2003, p. 8).

Although such definitions may be helpful for crime statistics, they have less appeal for dating violence because, from an epidemiological perspective, these events are rare when compared with the host of behaviors that emerge when a broader view of violence as a continuum is considered. In addition to acts of physical aggression, these behaviors could include such acts as threatening communication and verbal abuse (Lewis & Fremouw, 2001). Previous research has suggested that psychological aggression may be a predictor of physical aggression and, therefore, must be considered in the causal pathway defining relationship violence (Leonard & Senchak, 1996; Stets & Henderson, 2001).

A more comprehensive definition of IPV was provided by the American Academy of Obstetricians and Gynecologists (1995) in describing domestic violence:

> Violent acts between partners have been categorized as verbally abusing the partner, threatening violence, throwing an object at someone, pushing, slapping, kicking, hitting, beating up, threatening with a weapon and using a weapon. Definitions of intimate partner violence may also include sexual assault, stalking, psychological abuse, enforced social isolation, intimidation and the deprivation of key resources such as food, clothing, money, transportation or health care. (p. 9)

Perhaps the most appropriate term for dating violence, however, is *relationship violence,* and the best definition is "any harmful, unwanted physical, sexual, verbal, or emotional act inflicted by a casual or intimate dating partner with the intention, either real or perceived, of causing pain or injury to another person" (Wisner, Gilmer, Saltzman, & Zink, 1999, p. 439). This definition can apply equally well to partners in heterosexual and same-sex relationships. The cautionary note is that regardless of the term used, specifics regarding prevalence and costs associated with dating violence can be determined only from available data, and, most often, those data concern only the incidence and prevalence of physical violence.

Frequency of Dating Violence

Makepeace (1981), one of the first to study dating violence, found that about 20% of college students were involved in a violent dating relationship and that about 60% of college students knew someone who was a participant in such a relationship. Sugarman and Hotaling (1989) reported that 33% of male college students and 36% of female college students had been victims of at least one physically violent act in a dating relationship and that 33% of male college students and 39% of female college students had perpetrated at least one violent act within a dating relationship.

In 1997, Magdol et al. reported that 37.2% of women and 21.8% of men in a study of 21-year-olds had been perpetrators of violence. Another study showed that about 25% of heterosexual college men had battered a current or previous female partner and that 20% of these men reported using severe violence such as kicking or punching (Silverman & Williamson, 1997).

More recently, a longitudinal study of female adolescents in college showed that 88% of these women had experienced at least one incident of physical or sexual victimization and that 64% of them had experienced both from a romantic partner (Smith, White, & Holland, 2003). In another study, Howard and Wang (2003a) found that 12% of 18-year-old men reported experiencing dating violence. Finally, it seems that the prevalence of dating violence in same-sex partners is about the same as for heterosexual couples (Halpern, Young, Waller, Martin, & Kupper, 2004).

In the period 1993–1999, the rate of intimate partner physical violence against women ages 16–24, the primary age of college students, was the highest rate for any age group of women and was significantly higher than for all other age groups of women (Rennison, 2001). Some estimates have suggested that women ages 16–24 are four times more likely to be sexually assaulted than women in all other age groups (Rickert & Wiemann, 1998). The National Violence Against Women Survey (Tjaden & Thoennes, 2000), which was the basis for these estimates, included multiple items designed to assess the prevalence of intimidation and violence against women. The areas surveyed included sexual violence (attempts, threats, or acts of nonconsensual sexual contact), physical assault (pushing, grabbing, shoving, slapping, etc., including threats of harm), and stalking behaviors (being spied on or followed, destruction of personal property, or unsolicited communication in any form).

The enormity of the individual and societal burden for acts of violence toward women was translated into a dollar estimate for acts occurring in 1995, including costs attributed to health care, lost productivity, and present value of lifetime earnings. For that year, the estimated total cost of IPV against U.S. adult women over the age of 18 was $5.8 billion (National Center for Injury Prevention and Control, 2003).

These statistics are alarming. Yet, because their focus is entirely on physical acts of violence, they are an underestimate of actual abuse. Although several studies have shown that dating violence can also leave victims with negative psychological sequelae (Coffey, Leitenberg, Henning, Bennett, & Jankowski, 1996; Simonelli & Ingram, 1998; Weitzman, 2004), psychological violence is rarely the focus in the research literature (Jackson, 1999; Watson, 2005).

A disturbing trend is that women may be equally as likely as men to engage in physical violence with their partners (Poole, 2003; Stets & Henderson, 2001). However, women report low-level violence such as slapping or pushing, whereas men are more likely to engage in moderate levels of violence such as punching or hitting with objects (Poole, 2003).

Assessment Issues

The public health model focuses efforts at prevention of relationship violence at three levels. Primary prevention strategies are directed at the general population in order to prevent problems from emerging. Secondary prevention targets the at-risk population—those with characteristics that make them vulnerable for a particular problem—in order to prevent emergence of the problem. Finally, tertiary prevention focuses on treatment in order to prevent a reoccurrence of the problem.

Primary prevention strategies for relationship violence on most campuses involve awareness activities and educational interventions, as described later in this chapter. For secondary prevention, assessment is the key to determining those at risk for relationship violence and specifying the intervention. Identifying those at risk is a complex process because the phenomenon is multidimensional and not completely understood (Hickman, Jaycox, & Aronoff, 2004). However, once a victim of relationship violence has been identified, tertiary prevention is most likely to result from effective counseling interventions (Burke, 2002; Carlson, 1987; Schewe, 2002; Wexler, 1999).

Factors Predisposing to Relationship Violence

Sugarman and Hotaling (1989) grouped risk factors for relationship violence into five areas: (a) intrapsychic (acceptance of relationship violence, gender role identity, personality, and psychopathology), (b) familial (family history of divorce or dysfunction, experiencing/witnessing family-of-origin violence), (c) interpersonal (past dating experience, level of relationship commitment, jealousy, relationship problems, past violent behavior, power and control issues, and sexual aggression), (d) stress (environmental stress), and (e) sociodemographic (race, socioeconomic status, age, religion, place of origin, community violence, and alcohol and drug use). In all five areas, evidence was reported indicating that each of these factors had contributed to relationship violence.

The Centers for Disease Control and Prevention (2005) developed a fact sheet of vulnerability factors for IPV that can be found on their Web site. These factors include a history of physical abuse, prior injury from the same partner, having a verbally abusive partner, partner history of alcohol or drug abuse, childhood abuse, economic stress, and being under the age of 24.

A study under the auspices of the National Institute of Justice (Tjaden & Thoennes, 2000) also identified several factors predicting a greater likelihood of IPV: (a) having been physically assaulted as a child, (b) being an unmarried couple, (c) being African American, and (d) having a verbally abusive and controlling partner. The notion that witnessing or experiencing childhood abuse places one at risk for relationship violence has been broadly reported (Follingstad, Bradley, Laughlin, & Burke, 1999; Foshee, Benefield, Ennett, Bauman, & Suchindran, 2004; Gray & Foshee, 1997; N. K. O'Keefe, Brockopp, & Chew, 1986).

Another vulnerability factor for IPV is alcohol (Abbey, Clinton-Sherrod, McAuslan, Zawacki, & Buck, 2003; Luthra, 2004; Makepeace, 1981, 1988; N. K. O'Keefe et al., 1986; Stets & Henderson, 2001). Abbey et al. (2003) noted that about one half of college male assaults on women involved the consumption of alcohol by the perpetrator, the victim, or both, and Luthra (2004) found that men were more likely to perpetrate violence if they had used alcohol. Makepeace (1981) found a significant correlation between drinking and dating violence in college students but concluded that moderate drinking, rather than extreme intoxication, was more predictive of violence.

Jackson (1999) found support for both social learning theory and feminist theory as explanations of violent behavior. However, although support has been found for power and control issues as reasons for violence (Follingstad, Bradley, Helff, & Laughlin, 2002; Laner, 1989; Stets & Pirog-Good, 1989), the fact that these issues apply equally well to men and women lends support to the notion that interpersonal power, rather than structural power (i.e., power derived from a patriarchal society), might explain relationship violence (Stets, 1991).

Attitudes that support violence have also been a topic of study (Cauffman, Feldman, Arnett Jensen, & Jensen Arnett, 2000; Harrison & Abrishami, 2004; Malik, Sorenson, & Aneshensel, 1997). The presence of personal norms that justify violence and the notion that members of one's own group are less culpable in dating violence attribution are contributors to the greater likelihood that dating violence will occur. Gender role egalitarianism has been another attitudinal factor related to support for violence against women. Berkel et al. (2004) reported that men with lower egalitarian scores (i.e., traditional gender role attitudes) were much more supportive of the use of violence against women and had less sympathy for battered women.

Most studies have found that men and women differ in both their risks and their reasons for using violence (Berkel et al., 2004; Emanuele, 2002; Fiebert & Gonzalez, 1997; Finn, 1986; Luthra, 2004; M. O'Keefe, 1997; Poole, 2003; Riggs & O'Leary, 1996). For example, women more often reported that they used violence against their partners in order to engage them emotionally (Fiebert & Gonzalez, 1997). Men reported that they were more likely to use violence if their partners were violent against them, disrespected them in front of friends, or tried to make them jealous (Foshee, Linder, MacDougall, & Bangdiwala, 2001).

Assessing Warning Signs for Potential Abuse

Parrot and Bechhofer (1991) identified four behaviors that are likely to predict potential for violence in a dating relationship. These included (a) sexual entitlement (e.g., touching another person with no regard for his or her wishes), (b) power and control (e.g., being a bad loser), (c) hostility and anger (e.g., blaming others when things go wrong), and (d) acceptance of interpersonal violence (e.g., approving observed violence).

Levy (1993) also developed a checklist describing behaviors of abusers. Individuals, for example, can assess the quality of their relationships by honestly assessing their partners' anger and jealousy and the behaviors used to express these feelings. Also, it is important for young women to confront their emotions, especially fear, that may be aroused by their partners' behaviors. Finally, behavioral changes that are made to placate an intimate partner in order to reduce the likelihood of an angry response are warning signs that the relationship may be at risk for escalating physical violence. Helping clients define the problem in ways that are meaningful to them is much more effective than putting them on the defensive, and checklists can help in this process.

Potential sequelae from dating violence must also be assessed in order to provide preventive interventions. In a study of Black female adolescents, those experiencing psychological distress, which is often a sequela of dating violence, were much more likely to become pregnant, report high-risk sexual behaviors, and have attitudes supportive of participating in risky sexual behaviors (DiClemente et al., 2001). When the relationship between dating violence and high-risk behaviors was studied directly, researchers found that adolescents who reported dating violence within the previous 6 months were nearly three times more likely to have a sexually transmitted disease, almost three times more likely to have nonmonogamous partners, and half as likely to use condoms as other adolescents (Wingood, DiClemente, McCree, Harrington, & Davies, 2001). In addition, these women were almost three times more likely to see themselves as having very little control over their sexuality than women who had not been victims of dating violence, thus making them afraid to discuss condom use or pregnancy prevention with their partners and putting them at high risk for sexually transmitted diseases and pregnancy. Berenson, Wiemann, and McCombs (2001) also found that victims of violence were significantly more likely to report early initiation of sexual intercourse, have sex with strangers, have multiple partners, use alcohol or other drugs, or have a sexually transmitted disease.

Counseling Implications

Crisis Intervention

For victims of many forms of physical violence, the first responder is likely to be a health care provider in the emergency department. Depending on the location of the event, campus security and administrative officials may be aware of, and will of necessity respond to, media and parental concerns. For the victim, the health care system responses initially focus not only on the emergent health care needs but also on the collection of evidence for future judicial processes. Although most hospitals have trained personnel for rape crisis response, no specific response may be available for injuries inflicted within the context of a relationship, other than physical injuries, unless specifically requested by the victim. If the injuries occur on or near the campus, the counselor on call should be prepared to meet with the victim in the hospital, offer support and crisis care, and arrange for follow-up once the victim leaves the hospital.

Most often, campus counselors will discover that clients are involved in an abusive dating relationship while providing counseling for other reasons because most individuals involved in relationship violence will not seek help (Ashley & Foshee, 2005). This places a greater burden on the counselor to focus resources on prevention through raising campus awareness and educational interventions as well as to use screening tools discussed previously. Both victims and perpetrators are likely to first seek the counsel of friends (Ashley & Foshee, 2005; Emanuele, 2002), and, therefore, an educated student population can be of great help in encouraging students who may be victims or perpetrators of dating violence to seek out counseling services.

Individual Counseling

Because there are numerous negative sequelae from dating violence, the presenting problem may include weight problems (Silverman, Raj, Mucci, & Hathaway, 2001); low self-esteem (Aguilar & Nightingale, 1994; Emanuele,

2002; Follingstad et al., 1999; Foshee et al., 2004); depression, anxiety, and suicidal ideation (Callahan, Tolman, & Suanders, 2003; Ellis, 2001; Magdol et al., 1997; Roberts, Klein, & Fisher, 2003; Simonelli & Ingram, 1998; Weitzman, 2004); high-risk sexual behavior (Berenson et al., 2001; Howard & Wang, 2003b; Wingood et al., 2001); and alcohol use (Abbey et al., 2003; Katz & Arias, 2001; Luthra, 2004).

Therapy for any of these presenting problems may include any of the common techniques, such as Adlerian therapy, person-centered counseling, transactional analysis, rational emotive therapy, cognitive–behavior therapy, or family systems therapy. Educational interventions could address the cycle of violence, risk, and protective factors for interpersonal violence; general prevention strategies; or theoretical models of relationship violence. In addition, on the basis of the clinical assessment, skills training might address effective communication and relationship skills, self-care techniques, and stress management.

Rickert, Vaughan, and Wiemann (2002) suggested a four-step process to reduce dating violence and the negative sequelae that often follow: (a) use effective screening tools to measure victimization and attitudes that promote dating violence, (b) increase self-efficacy, (c) reduce drug/alcohol abuse, and (d) eliminate the influence of negative peer behavior. Hadley (2002) emphasized that once an individual victim's needs for a "safe place" and other immediate services are determined and responded to, the goal of the counselor should be to help the client "a) rediscover a sense of self, b) build hope and reduce isolation, c) develop strength and direction, and when ready d) take small steps" (p. 22).

Group Therapy

Rycroft (2001) evaluated the effectiveness of a short-term group therapy program for women who had been victims of partner violence. The intervention was a 12-session program that addressed personal "herstories," myths and facts, causes of battering, the decision to stay, alcohol and battering, anger and rage, passive and assertive behavior, self-care, and moving on. Women reported improvement in five areas—loneliness, depression, anxiety, disclosure shame, and self-blame—and were in agreement that group therapy was helpful in recovering from the impact of battering. However, participants also suggested that the combination of group therapy with individual therapy would be most helpful. When asked how therapy helped them, women responded that feelings of acceptance or belonging countered feelings of being alone, crazy, or different. They also noted that they experienced empowerment and inner strength and that sharing their abuse stories helped them achieve a new understanding of their experience. Problem solving also increased as a result of group participation.

Campus Considerations

Every college campus must recognize that dating violence, although unseen, is a significant problem that can have lifelong implications for both victims and perpetrators (Berkel et al., 2004). Appropriate programming can reduce beliefs that violence against women is an acceptable approach to relationship conflict (O'Neal & Dorn, 1998). Training for personnel involved in security, housing, Greek and other social and service organizations, and advising/mentoring can increase awareness of dating violence and campus referral resources, thereby improving the likelihood that appropriate referrals will increase (Burke, 2002; Puig, 1984; Schwartz, Magee, Griffin, & Dupuis, 2004). Training should include not only skills in identification but also specific strategies to ensure immediate safety of the victim. A coordinated campus effort can increase the likelihood that students in a violent relationship will seek help before the violence escalates.

A campuswide focus on dating violence, even if only for a day, can provide opportunities to make students aware of the signs of an abusive relationship, help them understand what to do if they or their friends are involved, and make them aware of services available through the counseling center. College and university counseling center Web sites and bulletin boards in college housing, student centers, and libraries are all opportunities to alert students to the problem and to the resources to help them confront and resolve the situation.

The University of South Carolina Office for Sexual Health & Violence Prevention (2005) offers a sound example of a campus plan of action. Components of the plan include (a) emergency room advocacy, (b) alternative housing to provide a safe place, (c) safety planning through individual risk assessment, (d) relationship violence support groups, (e) referrals to counseling, (f) academic assistance by providing letters of support to faculty regarding extenuating circumstances, and (g) assistance with the criminal justice system (e.g., setting up appointments with law enforcement, prosecution, and other judicial officers and helping to obtain orders of protection or restraining orders). In addition, the University of South Carolina's Office for Sexual Health & Violence Prevention (2005) provides a comprehensive educational program and training for members of the campus community, as described on the office's Web site:

> Another major role of the office is to raise campus awareness about relationship violence. The staff regularly provides workshops and training sessions for University faculty and staff, residential student staff, academic classes, and student organizations. Additionally, the Office for Sexual Health & Violence Prevention selects undergraduate and graduate students to serve as S.H.A.R.E. (Sexual Health Awareness & Rape Education) peer educators. The main focus of the S.H.A.R.E. peer educators is to provide workshops regarding the topics of sexual health, high-risk behaviors, STDs [sexually transmitted diseases], relationship violence, consensual sex, and sexual assault.

Future Trends

In the past, it was assumed that relationship violence was primarily targeted at women. More recently, research has shown that men and women are both perpetrators and victims (Hickman et al., 2004), although the type of violence perpetrated by women is likely to differ from that of men (Wolfe et al., 2001). Much remains to be learned about relationship violence and particularly the role of gender—that is, how men and women use violence in terms of purpose, nature, context, and effect (Foshee et al., 2001; Jackson, 1999; Wolfe et al., 2001). This research is essential for determining what constitutes effective treatment for men and women and whether programs should be gender-specific (Hickman et al., 2004).

Other areas of research that need more focus are basic incidence and prevalence and theory testing. A systematic approach to the problem of relationship violence will build the evidence required to inform theory building and program development, especially if different models are appropriate for men and women (Emanuele, 2002; Hickman et al., 2004; Jackson, 1999; Lewis & Fremouw, 2001).

References

Abbey, A., Clinton-Sherrod, A. M., McAuslan, P., Zawacki, T., & Buck, P. O. (2003). The relationship between the quantity of alcohol consumed and the severity of sexual assaults committed by college men. *Journal of Interpersonal Violence, 18,* 813–833.

Aguilar, R., & Nightingale, N. (1994). The impact of specific battering experiences on self-esteem of abused women. *Journal of Family Violence, 9,* 35–45.

American Academy of Obstetricians and Gynecologists. (1995). *Domestic violence* (ACOG Tech. Rep. No. 209). Washington, DC: Author.

Ashley, O. S., & Foshee, V. A. (2005). Adolescent help-seeking for dating violence: Prevalence, sociodemographic correlates, and sources of help. *Journal of Adolescent Health, 36,* 25–31.

Berenson, A. B., Wiemann, C. M., & McCombs, S. (2001). Exposure to violence and associated health-risk behaviors among adolescent girls. *Archives of Pediatrics & Adolescent Medicine, 155,* 1238–1242.

Berkel, L. A., Vandiver, B. J., & Bahner, A. D. (2004). Gender role attitudes, religion, and spirituality as predictors of domestic violence attitudes in White college students. *Journal of College Student Development, 45,* 119–133.

Burke, L. K. (2002). Effects of a dating violence intervention on college students' knowledge, attitudes, and behavior intentions. *Dissertation Abstracts International, 62*(07), 3417B. (UMI No. 3020999)

Callahan, M. R., Tolman, R. M., & Suanders, D. G. (2003). Adolescent dating violence victimization and psychological well-being. *Journal of Adolescent Research, 18,* 664–681.

Carlson, B. E. (1987). Dating violence: A research review and comparison with spouse abuse. *Social Casework, 68,* 16–23.

Cauffman, E., Feldman, S., Arnett Jensen, L., & Jensen Arnett, J. (2000). The (un)acceptability of violence against peers and dates. *Journal of Adolescent Research, 15,* 652–673.

Centers for Disease Control and Prevention. (2005). *Intimate partner violence factsheet.* Retrieved September 9, 2005, from http://www.cdc.gov/ncipc/factsheets/ipvfacts.htm

Coffey, P., Leitenberg, H., Henning, K., Bennett, R. T., & Jankowski, M. K. (1996). Dating violence: The association between methods of coping and women's psychological adjustment. *Violence & Victims, 11,* 227–238.

DiClemente, R. J., Wingood, G. M., Crosby, R. A., Sionean, C., Brown, L. K., Rothbaum, B., et al. (2001). A prospective study of psychological distress and sexual risk behavior among Black adolescent females. *Pediatrics, 108,* E85.

Ellis, G. M. (2001). College mental health provider's ability to identify dating violence as the etiology of depression in a battered college female. *Dissertation Abstracts International, 62*(04), 1333A. (UMI No. 3012564)

Emanuele, J. M. (2002). Protection against relationship violence? The role of risk and protective factors in a theoretical model. *Dissertation Abstracts International, 63*(01), 521B. (UMI No. 3040992)

Fiebert, M. S., & Gonzalez, D. M. (1997). College women who initiate assaults on their male partners and the reasons offered for such behavior. *Psychological Reports, 80,* 583–590.

Finn, J. (1986). The relationship between sex role attitudes and attitudes supporting marital violence. *Sex Roles, 14,* 235–244.

Follingstad, D. R., Bradley, R. G., Helff, C. M., & Laughlin, J. E. (2002). A model for predicting dating violence: Anxious attachment, angry temperament and need for relationship control. *Violence & Victims, 17,* 35–48.

Follingstad, D. R., Bradley, R. G., Laughlin, J. E., & Burke, L. (1999). Risk factors and correlates of dating violence: The relevance of examining frequency and severity levels in a college sample. *Violence & Victims, 14,* 365–380.

Foshee, V. A., Benefield, T. S., Ennett, S. T., Bauman, K. E., & Suchindran, C. (2004). Longitudinal predictors of serious physical and sexual dating violence victimization during adolescence. *Preventive Medicine: An International Journal Devoted to Practice & Theory, 39,* 1007–1016.

Foshee, V. A., Linder, G. F., MacDougall, J. E., & Bangdiwala, S. (2001). Gender differences in the longitudinal predictors of adolescent dating violence. *Preventive Medicine, 32,* 128–141.

Gray, H. M., & Foshee, V. (1997). Adolescent dating violence: Differences between one-sided and mutually violent profiles. *Journal of Interpersonal Violence, 12,* 126–141.

Hadley, S. M. (2002). Linking the orthopaedic patient with community family violence resources. *Orthopaedic Nursing, 21,* 19–23.

Halpern, C. T., Young, M. L., Waller, M. W., Martin, S. L., & Kupper, L. L. (2004). Prevalence of partner violence in same-sex romantic and sexual relationships in a national sample of adolescents. *Journal of Adolescent Health, 35,* 124–131.

Harrison, L. A., & Abrishami, G. (2004). Dating violence attributions: Do they differ for in-group and out-group members who have a history of dating violence? *Sex Roles, 51,* 543–550.

Hickman, L. J., Jaycox, L. H., & Aronoff, J. (2004). Dating violence among adolescents: Prevalence, gender distribution, and prevention program effectiveness. *Trauma Violence & Abuse, 5,* 123–142.

Howard, D. E., & Wang, M. Q. (2003a). Psychosocial factors associated with adolescent boys' reports of dating violence. *Adolescence, 38,* 519–533.

Howard, D. E., & Wang, M. Q. (2003b). Risk procedures of adolescent girls who were victims of dating violence. *Adolescence, 38,* 1–14.

Jackson, S. M. (1999). Issues in the dating violence research: A review of the literature. *Aggression & Violent Behavior, 4,* 233–247.

Katz, J., & Arias, I. (2001). Women's attributions for hypothetical dating violence: Effects of partner alcohol use and violence severity. *Journal of Applied Social Psychology, 31,* 1458–1473.

Laner, M. R. (1989). Competition and combativeness in courtship: Reports from women. *Journal of Family Violence, 4,* 181–195.

Leonard, K. E., & Senchak, M. (1996). Prospective prediction of husband marital aggression within newlywed couples. *Journal of Abnormal Psychology, 105,* 369–380.

Levy, B. (1993). *In love and in danger: A teen's guide to breaking free of abusive relationships.* Seattle, WA: Seal Press.

Lewis, S. F., & Fremouw, W. (2001). Dating violence: A critical review of the literature. *Clinical Psychology Review, 21,* 105–127.

Luthra, R. (2004). Physical dating violence among college men and women: Evaluation of a theoretical model. *Dissertation Abstracts International, 64*(12), 6333B. (UMI No. 3115083)

Magdol, L., Moffitt, T. E., Caspi, A., Newman, D. L., Fagan, J., & Silva, P. A. (1997). Gender differences in partner violence in a birth cohort of 21-year-olds: Bridging the gap between clinical and epidemiological approaches. *Journal of Consulting and Clinical Psychology, 65,* 68–78.

Makepeace, J. (1981). Courtship violence among college students. *Family Relations: Interdisciplinary Journal of Applied Family Studies, 32,* 97–102.

Makepeace, J. M. (1988). The severity of courtship violence and the effectiveness of individual precautions. In G. T. Hotaling (Ed.), *Family abuse and its consequences: New directions in research* (pp. 297–311). Thousand Oaks, CA: Sage.

Malik, S., Sorenson, S. B., & Aneshensel, C. S. (1997). Community and dating violence among adolescents: Perpetration and victimization. *Journal of Adolescent Health, 21,* 291–302.

National Center for Injury Prevention and Control. (2003). *Costs of intimate partner violence against women in the United States*. Atlanta, GA: Centers for Disease Control and Prevention.

O'Keefe, M. (1997). Predictors of dating violence among high school students. *Journal of Interpersonal Violence, 12,* 546–568.

O'Keefe, N. K., Brockopp, K., & Chew, E. (1986). Teen dating violence. *Social Work, 31,* 465–468.

O'Neal, M. D., & Dorn, P. W. (1998). Effects of time and an educational presentation on student attitudes toward wife beating. *Violence & Victims, 13,* 149–157.

Parrot, A., & Bechhofer, L. (1991). *Acquaintance rape: The hidden crime.* New York: Wiley.

Poole, B. E. (2003). Mutually violent dating relationships among college students. *Masters Abstracts International, 42*(03), 1077. (UMI No. 1417172)

Puig, A. (1984). Predomestic strife: A growing college counseling concern. *Journal of College Student Personnel, 25,* 268–269.

Rennison, C. M. (2001). *Intimate partner violence and age of victim, 1993–99* (NCJ Publication No. 178247). Washington, DC: U.S. Department of Justice, Office of Justice Programs.

Rickert, V. I., Vaughan, R. D., & Wiemann, C. M. (2002). Adolescent dating violence and date rape. *Current Opinion in Obstetrics & Gynecology, 14,* 495–500.

Rickert, V. I., & Wiemann, C. M. (1998). Date rape among adolescents and young adults. *Journal of Pediatric & Adolescent Gynecology, 11,* 167–175.

Riggs, D., & O'Leary, K. (1996). Aggression between heterosexual dating partners. *Journal of Interpersonal Violence, 8,* 18–35.

Roberts, T. A., Klein, J. D., & Fisher, S. (2003). Longitudinal effect of intimate partner abuse on high-risk behavior among adolescents. *Archives of Pediatrics & Adolescent Medicine, 157,* 875–881.

Rycroft, P. J. (2001). An evaluation of short-term group therapy for battered women. *Dissertation Abstracts International, 61*(7-B), 3861. (UMI No. NQ51664)

Schewe, P. A. (2002). *Preventing violence in relationships: Interventions across the life span.* Washington, DC: American Psychological Association.

Schwartz, J. P., Magee, M. M., Griffin, L. D., & Dupuis, C. W. (2004). Effects of a group preventive intervention on risk and protective factors related to dating violence. *Group Dynamics, 8,* 221–231.

Silverman, J. G., Raj, A., Mucci, L. A., & Hathaway, J. E. (2001). Dating violence against adolescent girls and associated substance use, unhealthy weight control, sexual risk behavior, pregnancy, and suicidality. *Journal of the American Medical Association, 286,* 572–579.

Silverman, J. G., & Williamson, G. M. (1997). Social ecology and entitlements involved in battering by heterosexual college males: Contributions of family and peers. *Violence & Victims, 12,* 147–164.

Simonelli, C. J., & Ingram, K. M. (1998). Psychological distress among men experiencing physical and emotional abuse in heterosexual dating relationships. *Journal of Interpersonal Violence, 13,* 667–681.

Smith, P. H., White, J. W., & Holland, L. J. (2003). A longitudinal perspective on dating violence among adolescent and college-age women. *American Journal of Public Health, 93,* 1104–1109.

Stets, J. E. (1991). Psychological aggression in dating relationships: The role of interpersonal control. *Journal of Family Violence, 6,* 97–114.

Stets, J. E., & Henderson, D. A. (2001). Contextual factors surrounding conflict resolution while dating: Results from a national study. *Family Relations: Interdisciplinary Journal of Applied Family Studies, 40,* 29–36.

Stets, J. E., & Pirog-Good, M. A. (1989). Sexual aggression and control in dating relationships. *Journal of Applied Social Psychology, 19,* 1392–1412.

Sugarman, D. B., & Hotaling, G. T. (1989). Dating violence: Prevalence, context and risk markers. In M. A. Pirog-Good & J. E. Stets (Eds.), *Violence in dating relationships* (pp. 3–32). New York: Praeger Publishers.

Tjaden, P., & Thoennes, N. (2000). *Extent, nature, and consequences of intimate partner violence* (NCJ Publication No. 181867). Washington, DC: U.S. Department of Justice, National Institute of Justice.

University of South Carolina, Office for Sexual Health & Violence Prevention. (2005). *Relationship violence services.* Retrieved April 7, 2005, from http://www.sa.sc.edu/wellness/rvservices.html

Watson, T. N. (2005). Issues of intent and injury: A comparative analysis of gender differences in African-American college students' perceptions of dating violence. *Dissertation Abstracts International, 65*(07), 3732B. (UMI No. 3137504)

Weitzman, E. R. (2004). Poor mental health, depression, and associations with alcohol consumption, harm, and abuse in a national sample of young adults in college. *Journal of Nervous & Mental Disease, 192,* 269–277.

Wexler, D. B. (1999). The broken mirror: A self psychological treatment perspective for relationship violence. *Journal of Psychotherapy Practice & Research, 8,* 129–141.

Wingood, G. M., DiClemente, R. J., McCree, D. H., Harrington, K., & Davies, S. L. (2001). Dating violence and the sexual health of Black adolescent females. *Pediatrics, 107,* E72.

Wisner, C. L., Gilmer, T. P.,. Saltzman, L. E., & Zink, T. M. (1999). Intimate partner violence against women: Do victims cost health plans more? *Journal of Family Practice, 48*(6), 439–443.

Wolfe, D. A., Scott, K., Reitzel-Jaffe, D., Wekerle, C., Grasley, C., & Straatman, A.-L. (2001). Development and validation of the Conflict in Adolescent Dating Relationships Inventory. *Psychological Assessment, 13,* 277–293.

Zawitz, M. W. (1994). *Violence between intimates* (NCJ Publication No. 149259). Washington, DC: U.S. Department of Justice, Office of Justice Programs.

Counseling College Students Who Have Been Sexually Assaulted

Victoria E. Kress, Robyn L. Williams,
and Rachel Hoffman

Introduction

Within a period of 1 year, over 300,000 women and 90,000 men in the United States reported being the victim of sexual assault, and estimates indicate that 1 in 6 women will experience an attempted or completed rape during her lifetime (Beebe, 1991; Tjaden & Thoennes, 2000). Moreover, Petter and Whitehill (1998) reported that a woman is four times more likely to be raped by someone she knows, making the problem of sexual assault particularly salient on college campuses across the country. According to Humphrey and White (2000), between 24% and 31% of female college students report sexual assault during each year of college. A study that analyzed data from a sampling of over 4,000 students representing 148 colleges across the country found that 1 in 5 undergraduate women had experienced forced sexual intercourse (Brener, McMahon, Warren, & Douglas, 1999). Considering the above statistics, it is likely that many college students will continue to be sexually assaulted and that many of these students will, thus, come into contact with college counseling centers.

Although there is much research and theoretical literature regarding the role of college counselors in sexual assault prevention (Frazier, Valtinson, & Candell, 1994), there is a limited theoretical basis and virtually no empirical research related to the most effective interventions to use when counseling college students who have been sexually assaulted. Despite this paucity of research, counselors

---

This chapter is largely based on the following article: White, V. E., Trippany, R. L., & Nolan, J. (2003). Responding to sexual assault victims: A primer for college counselors. *Journal of College Counseling, 6*, 124–133.

have an ethical obligation to apply best practices, and they must consider the efficacy of the interventions they choose to use with students who have been sexually assaulted (Hodges, 2001).

This chapter integrates research and theory from the general literature on working with sexual assault survivors and applies it to college counselors' work with sexually assaulted students. In addition, original research and experts' perceptions of the most efficacious practices to use when counseling trauma survivors are described and applied specifically to counseling college students. It is hoped that this review will provide college counselors with an understanding of what specific interventions they might use when counseling sexual assault survivors at different stages of their recovery process.

Assessment Issues: Clients' Reactions to Sexual Assault

Clients' reactions to sexual assault are typically intense fear, helplessness, or horror. As a result of such a traumatic event, the person often experiences severe anxiety or arousal that was not present prior to the trauma (American Psychiatric Association [APA], 2000; Shapiro, 1997). Other symptoms noted are a sense of anger and worthlessness, fear, depression (e.g., crying or suicidal ideation), and a decline in self-esteem and sexual self-esteem (Burkhart & Fromuth, 1996; Kilpatrick, Veronen, & Best, 1985; Shapiro, 1997). The psychological sequelae of sexual assault can be long-term, often resulting in what was originally called rape trauma syndrome (Burgess & Holstrom, 1974) and is currently referred to as posttraumatic stress disorder (PTSD; APA, 2000). It is important to note that the experience of a traumatic event (e.g., sexual assault) is a necessary but not sufficient condition for a diagnosis of PTSD. Thus, not all sexual assault victims experience full-blown PTSD reactions (Marotta, 2000). Although almost all sexual assault survivors have the aforementioned trauma-related symptoms, it is stated that between 30% and 50% of sexual assault survivors continue to have PTSD symptoms throughout their lives (Foa, Hearst-Ikeda, & Perry, 1995).

Research indicates that susceptibility to continued PTSD reactions is a function of many factors: (a) past life experiences (e.g., a history of prior assaults), (b) developmental level at onset of the trauma, (c) spiritual beliefs, (d) social support systems before and after the trauma (e.g., negative interactions with family, peers, or law enforcement systems), (e) content and intensity of the event (e.g., injury during the attack, threat of being hurt or killed), and (f) genetic predisposition (James & Gilliland, 2001; Regehr, Cadell, & Jansen, 1999). A multivariate analysis conducted by Ullman and Filipas (2001) indicated that young Caucasian women who perceived the assault to be life-threatening were more upset at the time of the assault and that the women who blamed themselves and others for the assault had more PTSD symptoms.

It is important for college counselors to be aware of the symptoms of PTSD and to be able to recognize PTSD symptoms in clients (Marotta, 2000).

Identifying and assessing the severity of responses to the sexual assault are critical in determining the most appropriate interventions to use with students at their presenting stage of recovery (Foa, Davidson, & Frances, 1999).

Individuals' reactions to sexual assault generally progress through two different phases, varying in degree of severity: Phase 1, representing the acute phase and initial reactions to the traumatic event, and Phase 2, representing the reorganization phase and involving the psychological adjustment, integration, and ultimate recovery from the traumatic event (Burgess & Holstrom, 1974; Petter & Whitehill, 1998). The acute phase lasts for several hours or several weeks, whereas the reorganization phase is a longer term stage associated with varying levels of recovery time.

During the acute phase, the victim experiences shock, numbing, and disbelief as well as physical symptoms of the trauma. All of the aforementioned symptoms occur secondary to the person losing his or her ability to cognitively control and organize the experience and effects of the assault (James & Gilliland, 2001). More specifically, when a traumatic event occurs, the person's mind is unable to effectively answer the questions of how and why the event happened and what meaning and implications the event has on the person's life. This disequilibrium causes the person to experience a sense of crisis that lasts as long as the person needs to organize and develop a coherent meaning system in relation to the assault.

In the reorganization phase, emotional reactions and sleep disturbances are common. Along with a sense of helplessness, depression, self-criticism, blame, and guilt, there are impairments in interpersonal relationships, intrusive thoughts and images, constrained activities, difficulties with concentration, avoidance, fear, phobias, sleep disturbances, and hyperalertness (APA, 2000; Burgess & Holstrom, 1974; Koss, Dinero, Seibel, & Cox, 1988). In general, as with the acute-phase symptoms, the aforementioned symptoms are believed to develop as the person continues to struggle to effectively organize the traumatic event.

In addition, psychobiological perspectives may explain some of the symptoms associated with the reorganization phase. For example, there is evidence that people who are exposed to traumatic events experience a dramatic change in the discharge of neurotransmitters such as endorphins as well as central and peripheral sympathetic nervous system changes and hypothalamic–pituitary–adrenocortical axis changes (James & Gilliland, 2001). These neurological changes may relate to and predict many of the reorganization-phase symptoms. In severe situations, degrading effects on emotions, behaviors, and cognitions may ensue and cause long-term impacts on the person's functioning (Burges-Watson, Hoffman, & Wilson, 1988; van der Kolk, 1996).

Long-term impacts of sexual assault may ensue if the person is not able to effectively integrate the assault into his or her conscious awareness and organize it as part of the past (James & Gilliland, 2001). As with the reorganization phase, long-term reactions to sexual assault include affective and psychophysiological reactions. Affective effects of sexual assault include depression, anger, anxiety, and problems with social and sexual intimacy, and psychophysiological effects involve a heightened startle response, increased arousal, and hyperresponsiveness (Foa & Rothbaum, 1998).

On the basis of the aforementioned reactions to sexual assault, college counselors must select interventions that are sensitive to students' individual reactions and their recovery developmental stage. College counselors' sensitivity to developmental levels melds well with a developmental approach to assessing students' trauma reactions (Hodges, 2001). The following sections describe counseling interventions that can be useful with students who are recent victims of an assault as well as students who present for counseling in the later stages of their assault recovery process.

Counseling Implications

Crisis Intervention With the Recent Sexual Assault Victim

Counselors must have expertise in providing interventions for the recent and nonrecent sexual assault survivor. Sexual assault survivors typically do not seek services in the year following the assault, and even fewer seek help immediately following the assault (Calhoun & Atkeson, 1991; Kimerling & Calhoun, 1994). However, early intervention is an important factor in preventing more severe reactions to the traumatic event (Marotta, 2000).

At the crisis stage of recovery, students are typically not ready to engage in counseling that requires sustained attention and intense involvement, and a crisis intervention approach in which the counselor is active, directive, and supportive may be most helpful (Calhoun & Atkeson, 1991). Generally, goals at this juncture in counseling may involve reducing emotional distress, enhancing positive coping skills, and preventing the development of intensified trauma reactions such as severe anxiety and depression (Calhoun & Atkeson, 1991). More specifically, goals related to crisis intervention include (a) establishing a therapeutic working alliance, (b) encouraging the expression of feelings, (c) providing education about immediate and possible sexual assault symptoms, (d) helping students adjust to role responsibilities (e.g., academic and social responsibilities), (e) mobilizing social support, and (f) providing support and education related to interfacing with the medical and legal systems (Calhoun & Atkeson, 1991; Wiehe & Richards, 1995).

Shortly after the sexual assault, education about the reactions the student may experience is essential. Kilpatrick, Veronen, and Resick (1982) found that educating survivors regarding the potential reactions to sexual assault during the first few weeks after the assault resulted in reduction of PTSD-related symptoms at a 3-month assessment. In addition, education regarding rape myths is important to the management of trauma reactions. Burkhart and Fromuth (1996) suggested that unchallenged rape myths perpetuate feelings of guilt, shame, and self-blame for victims. Existing rape myths provide a schema from which victims accommodate and attach meaning to their sexual assault. Challenging these rape myths may help the sexual assault victim "come to terms with the personal and interpersonal meaning of the trauma" (Burkhart & Fromuth, 1996, p. 164).

With regard to crisis intervention, Deblinger and Heflin (1994) discussed the counselor's role in the legal and medical process secondary to a sexual assault. They suggested that the counselor discuss with the client the procedures involved with the rape kit and the medical examination as well as the legal and court procedures. It is suggested that explaining these procedures will help the client understand what to expect and will minimize the client's anxiety (Deblinger & Heflin, 1994). Thus, counselors should educate themselves regarding their community and state policies, or at least know resource people to contact with questions and concerns (e.g., local rape crisis centers, sexual trauma specialists at police stations, and hospitals that have special service providers who assess for sexual assault). College counseling centers might also establish formal policies regarding support persons to whom students may be referred when they initially present following a sexual assault or if they would like to take legal action at a later date.

In addition to coordination of services between the victim and the legal and medical process, college counselors may also coordinate services on behalf of the client within the college structure. Because the recently assaulted victim is in crisis, attending classes, completing assignments, and participating in other college-related activities are not of primary concern. The college counselor may consider contacting the dean of students, with the victim's permission, to request a temporary excuse from these activities.

For the recent sexual assault victim, support systems play a particularly important role in the recovery process. Muran and DiGiuseppe (1994) stated that counselors should encourage victims to depend on their identified social network for confidence and emotional support. Armsworth (1989) discussed the impact of the initial responses of family and friends on students' recovery process. Armsworth reported that victims of sexual assault state that advocacy, empathic understanding, absence of negative response, and validation are the most effective responses to a sexual assault disclosure. The counselor, too, should become a valuable support for the victim. Burkhart and Fromuth (1996) stated that "validation and a nonjudgemental, supportive stance of the therapist cannot be overstated" (p. 156). Similarly, Frazier and Burnett (1994) found empirical evidence that indicates social support is the most helpful and frequently used coping mechanism for recent sexual assault victims.

When the recent sexual assault victim is being counseled, rape crisis centers are commonly recommended as a source of support. Rape crisis centers are typically based on a model in which clients receive crisis intervention and participate in psychotherapy groups (Koss & Harvey, 1987). However, there has been little research to assess the effectiveness of this model (Foa & Rothbaum, 1998).

One model that preliminarily has been shown to be helpful when working with sexual assault victims 2 weeks postassault is a brief prevention program (Foa et al., 1995). This model includes various techniques found to be helpful in treating chronic PTSD, such as exposure, relaxation training, and cognitive restructuring. Participants engage in four 2-hour psychoeducational sessions over a 4-week period. More specifically, the sessions incorporate education about reactions to assault, breathing and relaxation training, reliving the assault, in vivo exposure, and cognitive restructuring. Initial findings indicate this program to be generally successful, and this type of brief model would lend itself well to a college counseling center environment.

It is important to provide a word of caution to a college counselor working with a recently traumatized client. Lindy and Wilson (2001) noted that the current mental health trend seems to be encouraging the immediate expression of emotion as a universal goal in helping the recently traumatized client to talk about the event, how it happened, and the client's subjective feelings surrounding the event. However, the authors contended that trauma survivors may be using appropriate emergency defenses such as denial and disbelief and that by forcing the survivors to immediately discuss aspects of the assault, counselors are likely to harm clients by not understanding or respecting the role that defenses play in the process of healing. In working with traumatized survivors, college counselors must exercise patience and sensitivity and understand the crucial role of psychological defenses.

Modalities of Interventions With the Nonrecent Sexual Assault Victim

There are numerous theoretical models that have been applied to counseling sexual assault victims. Experts in the area of PTSD recommend anxiety management, cognitive therapy, exposure therapy, and psychoeducation when treating trauma survivors (Foa & Rothbaum, 1998; Marotta, 2000).

The following discussion of applicable theories is intended not to be exhaustive but to briefly indicate the most commonly discussed and empirically supported approaches in the theoretical and research literature. An emphasis is placed on approaches that are most aligned with developmental, strength-based, and brief theoretical approaches espoused by most college counseling centers (Davis & Humphrey, 2000; Komives & Woodard, 1996). The majority of the empirically supported interventions fall under the theoretical realm of cognitive–behavioral therapy (Gore-Felton, Arnow, Koopman, Thoreson, & Spiegel, 1999). Although there are many different types of cognitive–behavioral therapy, all of these approaches have in common an emphasis on helping clients change their cognitions and meanings related to the rape and on helping clients engage in adaptive behaviors.

A great deal of research has supported cognitive–behavioral therapy models as being effective in counseling traumatized clients and effective relative to other theoretical approaches. Research has also found cognitive therapy approaches to be superior to purely supportive approaches (Bryant, Harvey, Dang, Sackville, & Basten, 1998; Foa, Rothbaum, Riggs, & Murdock, 1991). For example, Bryant et al. (1998) conducted a study with sexual assault victims to determine the more effective treatment, cognitive–behavioral or supportive counseling. The authors found that the incidence of PTSD was 17% at follow-up after clients had received cognitive–behavioral therapy, compared with 67% after clients had received supportive counseling. Thus, a supportive approach to working with sexually traumatized college students is helpful and surely necessary, but it may not be sufficient. The literature indicates that a purely supportive approach may be negligent and may not help in preventing PTSD symptoms as effectively as a cognitive–behavioral approach.

In the experimental research literature, exposure therapy has consistently been shown to be effective in managing sexual assault reactions (Foa & Rothbaum, 1998). Exposure therapy involves the client confronting the traumatic stimuli and, thus, his or her fears. It is believed that the client—through remembering the trauma and reminders of the trauma—becomes less emotion-laden over time with repeated exposure. Through exposure therapy, the thoughts of the traumatic event and overwhelming feelings associated with the event become increasingly separated, precluding intrusive traumatic recollections and the need to use avoidant behaviors. How the client is exposed to the traumatic material is varied with regard to the dimension of the exposure type (imagining the trauma vs. in vivo exposure), the length of exposure (short vs. long), and the client's arousal level during the exposure (low vs. high; Foa & Rothbaum, 1998). For sexual trauma survivors, the stimuli typically represent specific aspects of the sexual assault.

Muran and DiGiuseppe (1994) developed a minimally intrusive exposure model of cognitive therapy specifically developed to manage sexual assault. The authors suggested that, for therapy to be effective, the counselor must focus on exposure, which in their model required clients to verbally recount the events of the trauma. They indicated that this verbalization plays a key role in helping clients organize their experiences and keep flashbacks, nightmares, and other intrusive thoughts to a minimum.

Some researchers and clinicians recommend using exposure techniques, such as having clients verbalize the sexual assault scenario in sessions. Some clinicians also recommend having clients audiotape their discussions of the rape and assigning them to listen to this tape as a homework assignment until they are able to listen to the tape without anxiety and discomfort. Journaling is another commonly used exposure technique in which the client writes about the details and emotions associated with the assault. Clients can either reread their journal as homework assignments or share their entries with the counselor in sessions (Resick & Schnicke, 1993). As clients repeat their story and become more comfortable, they may be asked to include increasing levels of detail and emotion.

Anxiety management therapy (AMT) is another promising therapy that has been shown, through controlled studies, to be helpful in working with sexually assaulted clients displaying PTSD reactions (Foa & Rothbaum, 1998). The most researched and effective form of AMT is stress inoculation training (Meichenbaum, 1974; see also Kilpatrick & Veronen, 1984; Kilpatrick et al., 1982). Although the aforementioned approaches seek to help alter the thought processes underlying trauma reactions and anxiety, AMT provides ways to manage anxiety when it occurs by having clients develop and apply various cognitive and behavioral skills to their experiences. Examples of coping skills that may help reduce anxiety are covert modeling, positive thinking and self-talk, assertiveness training, guided imagery, and thought stopping (Hensley, 2002). Research has indicated that controlled breathing and deep muscle relaxation are two particularly helpful behavioral methods that can be used in controlling anxiety and fear related to sexual assault (Muran & DiGiuseppe, 1994).

Cognitive restructuring is a specific form of cognitive therapy by which the counselor helps clients to name the rape, correct distortions that perpetuate self-blame, and find meaning in the experience (Burkhart & Fromuth, 1996; Koss & Burkhart, 1989). Cognitive processing therapy (CPT; Resick & Schnicke, 1993) is one of the only empirically supported models for treating rape victims. Resick and Schnicke (1993) suggested that CPT works by "identifying and modifying . . . conflicts between prior schemata and this new information (the rape)" (p. 750). Resick and Schnicke conducted a study that exposed rape victims to CPT and, in a majority of the cases, found significantly improved levels of depression and symptoms of PTSD at a 3-month follow-up.

In using cognitive restructuring, college counselors can have students challenge their beliefs as they arise in sessions. When these beliefs arise, the counselor can help a student to replace self-defeating and self-blaming beliefs with more logical self-statements that reflect the student's strengths and sense of power (Kubany, 1998). Students can also be given homework assignments in which they either write or cognitively practice challenging their self-blaming thoughts.

Related to cognitive restructuring, college counselors should be aware of the differences in self-blame experienced by sexual assault victims who encountered a stranger sexual assault versus an acquaintance sexual assault. Survivors of an acquaintance sexual assault tend to engage in more self-blame and are less likely to label their experiences as sexual assault when compared with victims of a stranger sexual assault (Koss & Kilpatrick, 2001; McEwan, de Man, & Simpson-Housley, 2002). Because most college students are sexually assaulted by acquaintances, college counselors can validate students' fears and reactions to the assault and assist them in challenging the specific self-blaming cognitions associated with an acquaintance assault. Because many students who were sexually assaulted by acquaintances were under the influence of alcohol, counselors can also educate students as to the college and legal systems' definitions of sexual assault as a means of helping them appropriately label their experience and combat defeating self-blame.

With regard to treating specific trauma reactions, many experts recommend (a) exposure therapy for treating intrusive thoughts, flashbacks, trauma-related factors and avoidance of trauma-related stimuli; (b) anxiety management for hyperarousal and sleep disturbances; and (c) general cognitive therapy for treating guilt and shame-related experiences (Marotta, 2000). However, exposure therapy may be out of the competency of some college counselors. Experts identify anxiety management, psychoeducation, and cognitive therapy as being the safest options as well as the options most preferred by clients (Marotta, 2000), and they may be particularly well-suited for college counselors, who are often not trained in exposure therapy procedures.

Counselor Issues

Vicarious Traumatization

All counselors are at risk for developing intense reactions to sexual assault and to survivors of sexual assault. Counselors who work with survivors may find their cognitive schemas and imagery system of memory (Pavio, 1986) altered or disrupted by long-term exposure to the traumatic experiences of survivor clients (McCann & Pearlman, 1989). Clinical work with trauma victims brings the counselor close to the "soul" of the pain and injury (Wilson & Lindy, 1999). The counselor is witness to the client's traumas through his or her vivid descriptions of traumatic events; reports of intentional cruelty or sadistic abuse; and experiences of reliving terror, grief, and yearning (Pearlman & Saakvitne, 1995). Given the extreme emotional content, it is not unusual for counselors to experience intense emotional reactions to survivors and their stories. This intense psychological reaction, referred to as *vicarious traumatization,* can be disruptive and painful for the helper and can persist for months or years after a counselor works with traumatized persons (McCann & Pearlman, 1989). Counselors treating survivors of sexual violence must be cognizant of their own reactions to trauma and engage in frequent self-care rituals as well as regular consultation and supervision.

Strength-Based Approach

The counseling profession's emphasis on strength-based and developmentally based interventions (Myers & Sweeney, 2005; Myers, Sweeney, & Witmer, 2001) can be particularly useful when one is working with sexually traumatized clients (Marotta, 2000). Because trust and identity (two important factors in normal development) are disrupted by sexual assault, college counselors are in a unique position to use their knowledge of these factors in helping clients recover from sexual assault. Also, the counseling profession's focus on the process and development of problems lends itself well to the developmental stages and shifts that sexually assaulted students may experience.

Another strength that college counselors have in working with sexually traumatized students is an emphasis on psychoeducation and outreach initiatives. Psychoeducation was mentioned as being important in counseling the recent sexual assault victim but is also important in counseling the nonrecent victim of sexual assault. Although psychoeducation alone is not enough to manage trauma reactions, research and expert opinions indicate it is an important component of intervention (Marotta, 2000). Psychoeducational information can be provided through outreach initiatives, the counseling center's Web site, and counseling center handouts (Davis & Humphrey, 2000; Komives & Woodard, 1996). Mental health bulletin boards, located in residence halls, can provide another source of information about common sexual assault reactions.

Campus Considerations

Secondary Victimization

Williams (1984) defined *secondary victimization* as a prolonged and compounded consequence of certain crimes that results from negative judgmental attitudes directed toward a survivor of crime and is manifested by a lack of support and perhaps even condemnation and alienation of the survivor. Secondary victimization commonly brings about feelings of blame and disbelief and is often encountered in the form of stigmatizing responses that others make to victims (Ullman & Filipas, 2001). Because of the high rate of blame that is often attributed to survivors of rape, secondary victimization tends to occur at rates higher than typically encountered with other, less blame-promoting crimes, such as robbery. Being treated differently or stigmatized by others after rape may cause survivors to feel as though the incident somehow permanently transformed them (Ullman & Filipas, 2001). In a multivariate analysis, Ullman and Filipas (2001) identified being treated differently (e.g., stigmatizing responses) as the most predictive factor of PTSD symptom severity.

The potential for secondary victimization is high on a college campus given the diverse opinions often raised in various college courses, such as an introductory psychology course or a course in women's studies. College counselors must be especially cognizant of the potential for stigmatizing comments arising in classes and social interactions. Stereotypes about rape victims include the notion that "she asked to be raped," "she secretly enjoyed the experience," or "she lied about it." These stereotypes are subsumed under what are referred to as rape myths (Buddie & Miller, 2001). Rape myths can be challenged through campus presentations, psychoeducation handouts, and roundtable discussions. Because the attitudes of the student body can be detrimental to the recovery of a sexual assault survivor, college counselors must take every opportunity to challenge these erroneous stereotypes and decrease the stigma associated with rape.

Impact of Sexual Assault on Educational Attainment

Although past neuropsychiatric manifestations of PTSD have focused largely on war veterans, impairments of learning and memory have been reported among survivors of sexual assault (Jenkins, Langlais, Delis, & Cohen, 2000). Specifically, sustained and focused attention is impaired, although selective attention seems to remain relatively unaffected (Jenkins et al., 2000). A study that assessed the classroom performance of sexually abused females between the ages of 6 and 16 demonstrated that sexual abuse had a deleterious effect on every component of academic performance with the exception of grades (Trickett, McBride-Chang, & Putnam, 1994).

Jenkins et al. (2000) proposed two explanations for the attentional dysfunction demonstrated by rape survivors. First, PTSD survivors may spend a considerable amount of energy trying to avoid intrusive thoughts, may sleep poorly, and may be easily startled by extraneous stimuli. Second, dissociation is a common symptom of PTSD, which can be manifested through daydreaming and can even include full-blown trancelike states. During a dissociative episode, one would expect the capacity to concentrate to diminish. A college counselor must work with the student to effectively assess the best possible solution to attentional problems within various courses. Options for successful completion of course work, such as tutoring and extended time to complete assignments, should be evaluated on the basis of personal need.

Future Trends

Because of the limited research on effective interventions with sexually assaulted students, there is much room for future research in this area. Although cognitive–behavioral approaches are generally shown to be most effective in counseling sexual assault victims, these findings may be due to the fact that many other approaches have not been subjected to controlled experimental studies (Foa & Rothbaum, 1998).

Almost all of the treatment efficacy research focuses on clients being seen in community contexts, and very few research investigations focus on college students. Future research using controlled studies in the context of a college counseling center would provide data that would be helpful to college counselors. Future research might also investigate students' treatment needs in the context of sociocultural variables such as ethnicity, socioeconomic status, and sexual orientation (Hensley, 2002). Specific to college counseling, future research might examine the effectiveness of various interventions such as individual and group counseling as well as specific therapeutic approaches beyond cognitive–behavioral interventions. In addition, more research is needed on the effectiveness of interventions with students presenting with differing levels of assault and varying levels of trauma reactions.

References

American Psychiatric Association. (2000). *Diagnostic and statistical manual of mental disorders* (4th ed., text rev.). Washington, DC: Author.

Armsworth, M. W. (1989). Therapy of incest survivors: Abuse or support. *Child Abuse & Neglect, 13,* 549–562.

Beebe, D. K. (1991). Emergency management of the adult female rape victim. *American Family Physician, 43,* 2041–2046.

Brener, N. D., McMahon, P. M., Warren, C. W., & Douglas, K. A. (1999). Forced sexual intercourse and associated health-risk behaviors among female college students in the United States. *Journal of Consulting and Clinical Psychology, 67,* 252–259.

Bryant, R. A., Harvey, A. G., Dang, S. T., Sackville, T., & Basten, C. (1998). Treatment of acute stress disorder: A comparison of cognitive–behavioral therapy and supportive counseling. *Journal of Consulting and Clinical Psychology, 66,* 862–866.

Buddie, A. M., & Miller A. G. (2001). Beyond rape myths: A more complex view of the perceptions of rape victims. *Sex Roles, 45,* 139–160.

Burgess, A. W., & Holstrom, L. L. (1974). Recovery from rape and prior life stress. *American Journal of Psychiatry, 131,* 981–986.

Burges-Watson, I. P., Hoffman, L., & Wilson, G. V. (1988). The neuropsychiatry of post-traumatic stress disorder. *British Journal of Psychiatry, 152,* 164–173.

Burkhart, B. R., & Fromuth, M. (1996). The victim: Issues in identification and treatment. In T. L. Jackson (Ed.), *Acquaintance rape: Assessment, treatment, and prevention* (pp. 145–176). Sarasota, FL: Professional Resource Press/Professional Resource Exchange.

Calhoun, K. S., & Atkeson, B. M. (1991). *Treatment of rape victims: Facilitating psychosocial adjustment.* New York: Pergamon Press.

Davis, D. C., & Humphrey, K. M. (Eds.). (2000). *College counseling: Issues and strategies for a new millennium.* Alexandria, VA: American Counseling Association.

Deblinger, E., & Heflin, A. H. (1994). Child sexual abuse. In F. M. Dattilio & A. M. Freeman (Eds.), *Cognitive–behavioral strategies in crisis intervention* (pp. 177–199). New York: Guilford Press.

Foa, E. B., Davidson, R. T., & Frances, A. (1999). Expert consensus guidelines series: Treatment of posttraumatic stress disorder. *The Journal of Clinical Psychiatry, 60*(Suppl. 16), 1–31.

Foa, E. B., Hearst-Ikeda, D., & Perry, K. J. (1995). Evaluation of a brief cognitive–behavioral program for the prevention of chronic PTSD in recent assault victims. *Journal of Consulting and Clinical Psychology, 63,* 948–955.

Foa, E. B., & Rothbaum, B. O. (1998). *Treating the trauma of rape: Cognitive behavioral therapy for PTSD.* New York: Guilford Press.

Foa, E. B., Rothbaum, B. O., Riggs, D. S., & Murdock, T. B. (1991). Treatment of posttraumatic stress in rape victims: Comparisons between cognitive–behavioral procedures and counseling. *Journal of Consulting and Clinical Psychology, 59,* 715–723.

Frazier, P., & Burnett, J. W. (1994). Immediate coping strategies among rape victims. *Journal of Counseling and Development, 72,* 633–639.

Frazier, P., Valtinson, G., & Candell, S. (1994). Evaluation of a coeducational interactive rape prevention program. *Journal of Counseling and Development, 73,* 153–157.

Gore-Felton, C., Arnow, B., Koopman, C., Thoreson, C., & Spiegel, D. (1999). Psychologists' beliefs about the prevalence of childhood sexual abuse. *Child Abuse & Neglect, 23,* 803–811.

Hensley, L. G. (2002). Treatment for survivors of rape: Issues and interventions. *Journal of Mental Health Counseling, 24,* 330–347.

Hodges, S. (2001). University counseling centers at the twenty-first century: Looking forward, looking back. *Journal of College Counseling, 4,* 161–174.

Humphrey, J. A., & White, J. W. (2000). Women's vulnerability to sexual assault from adolescence to young adulthood. *Journal of Adolescent Health, 27,* 419–424.

James, R. K., & Gilliland, B. E. (2001). *Crisis intervention strategies* (4th ed.). Belmont, CA: Brooks/Cole.

Jenkins, M. A., Langlais, P. J., Delis, D., & Cohen, R. A. (2000). Attentional dysfunction associated with posttraumatic stress disorder among rape survivors. *The Clinical Neuropsychologist, 14,* 7–12.

Kilpatrick, D. G., & Veronen, L. J. (1984). Treatment for rape related problems: Crisis intervention is not enough. In L. Cohen, W. Claiborn, & G. Specter (Eds.), *Crisis intervention* (pp. 165–185). New York: Human Sciences Press.

Kilpatrick, D. G., Veronen, L. J., & Best, C. L. (1985). Factors predicting psychological distress among rape victims. In C. R. Figley (Ed.), *Trauma and its wake* (pp. 113–141). New York: Brunner/Mazel.

Kilpatrick, D. G., Veronen, L. J., & Resick, P. A. (1982). Psychological sequelae to rape: Assessment and treatment strategies. In D. M. Dolyes, R. L. Meredith, & A. R. Ciminero (Eds.), *Behavioral medicine: Assessment and treatment strategies* (pp. 473–498). New York: Plenum Press.

Kimerling, R., & Calhoun, K. S. (1994). Somatic symptoms, social support, and treatment seeking among sexual assault victims. *Journal of Consulting and Clinical Psychology, 62,* 333–340.

Komives, S. R., & Woodard, D. B. (Eds.). (1996). *Student services: A handbook for the profession* (3rd ed.). San Francisco: Jossey-Bass.

Koss, M. P., & Burkhart, B. (1989). A conceptual analysis of rape victimization: Long term effects and implications for treatment. *Psychology of Women Quarterly, 13,* 27–39.

Koss, M. P., Dinero, T. E., Seibel, C. A., & Cox, S. L. (1988). Stranger and acquaintance rape: Are there differences in the victim's experiences? *Psychology of Women Quarterly, 12,* 1–24.

Koss, M. P., & Harvey, M. (1987). *The rape victim: Clinical and community approaches to treatment.* Lexington, MA: Stephen Greene Press.

Koss, M. P., & Kilpatrick, D. G. (2001). Rape and sexual assault. In E. Gerrity, T. Keane, & F. Tuma (Eds.), *Mental health consequences of torture* (pp. 177–193). New York: Plenum Press.

Kubany, E. S. (1998). Cognitive therapy for trauma related guilt. In V. Foltte, I. Ruzek, & F. Abug (Eds.), *Cognitive–behavioral therapies for trauma* (pp. 124–161). New York: Guilford Press.

Lindy, J. D., & Wilson, J. P. (2001). Respecting the trauma membrane: Above all, do no harm. In J. P. Wilson, M. J. Friedman, & J. D. Lindy (Eds.), *Treating psychological trauma and PTSD* (pp. 432–445). New York: Guilford Press.

Marotta, S. A. (2000). Best practices for counselors who treat posttraumatic stress disorder. *Journal of Counseling and Development, 78,* 492–495.

McCann, L., & Pearlman, L. A. (1989). Vicarious traumatization: A framework for understanding the psychological effects of working with victims. *Journal of Traumatic Stress, 3,* 131–149.

McEwan, S. L., de Man, A. F., & Simpson-Housley, P. (2002). Ego identity achievement and perception of risk in intimacy in survivors of stranger and acquaintance rape. *Sex Roles, 47,* 281–287.

Meichenbaum, D. (1974). *Cognitive behavioral modification.* Morristown, NJ: General Learning Press.

Muran, E. M., & DiGiuseppe, R. (1994). Rape. In F. M. Dattilio & A. M. Freeman (Eds.), *Cognitive–behavioral strategies in crisis intervention* (pp. 161–176). New York: Guilford Press.

Myers, J. E., & Sweeney, T. J. (Eds.). (2005). *Counseling for wellness: Theory, research, and practice.* Alexandria, VA: American Counseling Association.

Myers, J. E., Sweeney, T. J., & Witmer, J. M. (2001). Optimization of behavior: Promotion of wellness. In D. C. Locke, J. E. Myers, & E. L. Herr (Eds.), *The handbook of counseling* (pp. 641–652). Thousand Oaks, CA: Sage.

Pavio, A. (1986). *Mental representations: A dual coding approach.* New York: Oxford University Press.

Pearlman, L. A., & Saakvitne, K. W. (1995). *Trauma and the therapist: Countertransference and vicarious traumatization in psychotherapy with incest survivors.* New York: Norton.

Petter, L. M., & Whitehill, D. L. (1998). Management of female sexual assault. *American Family Physician, 58,* 920–929.

Regehr, C., Cadell, S., & Jansen, K. (1999). Perceptions of control and long term recovery from rape. *American Journal of Orthopsychiatry, 69,* 110–114.

Resick, P. A., & Schnicke, M. K. (1993). Cognitive processing therapy for sexual assault victims. *Journal of Consulting and Clinical Psychology, 60,* 748–756.

Shapiro, B. L. (1997). Date rape: Its relationship to trauma symptoms and sexual self-esteem. *Journal of Interpersonal Violence, 12,* 407–420.

Tjaden, P., & Thoennes, N. (2000). *Full report of the prevalence, incidence, and consequences of violence against women: Findings from the National Violence Against Women Survey.* Washington, DC: National Institute of Justice.

Trickett, P. K., McBride-Chang, C., & Putnam, F. W. (1994). The classroom performance and behavior of sexually abused females. *Development and Psychopathology, 6,* 183–194.

Ullman, S. E., & Filipas, H. E. (2001). Predictors of PTSD symptoms severity and social reactions in sexual assault victims. *Journal of Traumatic Stress, 14,* 369–389.

van der Kolk, B. A. (1996). The body keeps the score: Approaches to the psychobiology of posttraumatic stress disorder. In B. A. van der Kolk, A. C. McFarlane, & L. Weisaeth (Eds.), *Traumatic stress* (pp. 214–241). New York: Guilford Press.

Wiehe, V. R., & Richards, A. L. (1995). *Intimate betrayal: Understanding and responding to the trauma of acquaintance rape.* London: Sage.

Williams, J. E. (1984). Secondary victimization: Confronting public attitudes about rape. *Victimology: An International Journal, 9,* 66–81.

Wilson, J. P., & Lindy, J. D. (1999). Empathic strain and countertransference. In M. J. Horowitz (Ed.), *Essential papers on posttraumatic stress disorder* (pp. 518–543). New York: New York University Press.

11

Against Their Will? Counseling Mandated Students

Bruce S. Sharkin

Introduction

Mandated counseling has long been practiced in nonacademic settings such as the judicial system. For example, individuals often receive sentences that require their participation in drug rehabilitation or other counseling programs. Mandated counseling has also been used in the context of work settings, whereby employees may be required to undergo counseling as a condition of continued employment. Thus, it is not surprising that colleges would similarly apply the practice of mandating or coercing students to enter into psychological counseling as a condition of returning to school or remaining enrolled. Mandated counseling is likely to be increasingly relied on as a way for college administrators to deal with growing numbers of disruptive and emotionally disturbed students on campus (Kitzrow, 2003).

There are many reasons why students may be coerced or required to use counseling. Some of the more common reasons include alcohol abuse and policy violations, illicit drug use, violent behavior, sexual harassment, racial harassment, vandalism, severe eating disorders, suicidal threats and behavior, and other forms of self-harming behavior (Dannells & Consolvo, 2000). Mandated counseling is usually required by judicial affairs or student conduct officers, deans, and other administrative personnel whose role is to impose sanctions on students for violations of student conduct or problematic behavior on campus. Hence, mandated counseling tends to be used for disciplinary infractions, which is why it is sometimes referred to as *disciplinary counseling* (Dannells & Consolvo, 2000; Stone & Lucas, 1994).

The author thanks Lisa P. Coulter for her thoughtful comments and suggestions on an earlier draft of this chapter.

It is understandable that campus administrators would want students in counseling if they display any form of emotional disturbance that either places them at risk (e.g., self-harming or suicidal behavior) or contributes to misconduct. However, the rationale for requiring counseling for disciplinary infractions when there is no evidence of emotional disturbance is not as clear. It may be that underlying emotional or psychological issues are presumed to be involved in the problematic behavior, such as impulse control, stress, or depression (Dannells & Consolvo, 2000). Also, there may be an assumption on the part of administrators that being in counseling will somehow lessen or eliminate a student's problematic or disruptive behavior (Dannells & Consolvo, 2000).

The practice of mandating counseling for college students has persisted despite protests from some campus clinicians who view it as inadvisable. Several persuasive arguments have been made against the use of mandated counseling. Perhaps the most compelling argument is that counseling is unlikely to be effective with involuntary clients who are not ready or motivated for it (Dannells & Consolvo, 2000; Gilbert, 1989; Kiracofe, 1993). Some believe that mandated counseling can actually be counterproductive and potentially harmful to students, particularly if they feel resentful about having to do it against their wishes (Gilbert, 1989; Gilbert & Sheiman, 1995; Hernandez & Fister, 2001). The practice of mandating counseling has also been deemed questionable on ethical grounds (Gilbert & Sheiman, 1995; Kiracofe, 1993; Stone & Lucas, 1994). Other arguments against its use claim that it is a misuse of limited resources, stigmatizes emotional disturbance, inappropriately places campus clinicians in a disciplinary role with students, and confuses counseling with punishment.

Less commonly, there have been some who advocate for the use of mandated counseling under certain conditions. Indeed, at least for students identified as academically at risk, brief mandatory counseling was found to have positive effects, for example, in terms of improving overall grade point average and increasing the probability of subsequent help-seeking behavior (Schwitzer, Grogan, Kaddoura, & Ochoa, 1993). Mandated counseling is believed by some to have a potentially positive influence on students who might not otherwise seek professional help. It has also been suggested that campus clinicians need to show openness to doing mandated counseling in order to be responsive to the needs of administrators and to work within the "system" to ensure the safety and well-being of students (Francis, 2000, 2003). For example, Pollard (1995) considered the use of involuntary treatment appropriate for students who pose a risk of harm or danger to others. A willingness to do mandated counseling might also help foster stronger relationships between campus clinicians and specific departments such as athletics and judicial affairs.

Unlike some of the other special populations included in this book, mandated clients do not necessarily share many commonalities other than the requirement to be in counseling. Mandated clients are indeed a diverse student group, encompassing all demographics and characteristics. However, the forced nature of their entry into counseling does set them apart from the more common voluntary clients seen in most college counseling centers. This means that they will likely present with a certain set of attitudes and expectations different from the average (voluntary) client and even different from those clients who seek counseling at the urging of others. For example, they may be much more inclined than the average client to be reluctant, guarded, and mistrustful. Because of the circumstances that typically bring mandated students into counseling, they may be prone to withhold information or be dishonest. In general, there may be a greater probability of encountering antisocial or sociopathic behavior among students in this population, which can pose unique challenges for clinicians.

Assessment Issues

When seeing a mandated client, a counselor needs to consider the circumstances that precipitated the coerced referral and the expectations of both the mandate source and the mandated client. The nature of the circumstances resulting in the mandate can influence how the student presents, the degree of reluctance, and other aspects of the counseling process. Depending on the circumstances, administrative officials may be explicit in their expectations for the duration of counseling (e.g., that the student is in counseling for the period of time in which he or she is on disciplinary probation). In some cases, referral sources mandate the student to counseling without specifying the duration and leave that to the discretion of the counselor.

When asked to do mandated counseling with students, college counselors should be prepared to see students in one or more of the following conditions: (a) disciplinary or conduct infractions with no evidence of mental health disturbance, (b) disciplinary or conduct infractions with evidence of mental health disturbance, (c) suicide risk, and (d) risk of harm to others.

Disciplinary Infractions Not Associated With Emotional Disturbance

When students are charged with a disciplinary infraction not associated with emotional disturbance, it is often a first-time charge and/or for something not too serious or unusual. This condition is perhaps the most straightforward and easy to handle. Alcohol policy violations, particularly for underage possession or use, represent a common example. The key for counselors is to rule out any mental health concerns, including substance abuse, that might be contributing to the student's behavior. Usually this can be accomplished with a thorough interview or evaluation. For example, how much (if at all) has the student engaged in the behavior prior to getting in trouble? Is there any history of mental health-related problems? It is also important to assess the student's reaction to the infraction. For instance, does he or she accept responsibility for the behavior and display remorse, regret, or shame in reaction to the disciplinary charges?

Even with the best questioning, there will be cases in which it is difficult to make a clear determination of whether the behavior was primarily the result of immaturity or poor judgment as opposed to emotional impairment. Sometimes there can be a fine line between the two. However, assuming that there does not seem to be any clear evidence for disturbance in psychological functioning, students can probably be seen for just one or two mandatory sessions for evaluative purposes and then be allowed to pursue counseling voluntarily.

Disciplinary Infractions Associated With Emotional Disturbance

Students who are charged with a disciplinary infraction that is the result of or associated with some type of impairment in emotional or psychological functioning represent a somewhat more challenging situation. Although there may be evidence to suggest counseling would be beneficial, the question of whether counseling should be mandated is debatable.

An example is used to illustrate the quandary of this scenario. Imagine a female student who is found guilty of writing sexually demeaning comments and drawings on message boards and in bathroom stalls in her residence hall. If it is determined that this student has engaged in inappropriate behavior in the past and is known to have a history of emotional problems, then having her use counseling makes sense. The potential problems associated with trying to provide counseling to someone like this under conditions of coercion are addressed in the Counseling Implications section to follow. For now, suffice it to say that this remains a tough call to make. The situation could be dealt with simply as a disciplinary matter with counseling strongly recommended but not required. Thus, this could be used as an opportunity to persuade the student to enter (or reenter) counseling, and the student could use this as an opportunity to show that she is intent on addressing the behavior and returning to good standing at the school. However, if the student chooses not to pursue counseling, there is no negative consequence unless another infraction occurs.

Alternatively, such a situation could be viewed as a student behaving inappropriately due in part to emotional disturbance, with the expectation that the proper way to address the problematic behavior is through psychological counseling as opposed to purely disciplinary means. Requiring counseling could actually be a way to provide the student with a valuable support service that may help her learn to behave and express herself in more appropriate ways. This could even be conceived as a form of education within the larger overall mission of the institution. Students can only be required to meet with a counselor, however, and cannot be told how to conduct themselves in counseling. As a result, the ultimate success of counseling in such cases will vary considerably.

Suicide Risk

Another condition of mandated counseling involves students who pose concerns about risk of self-harm or suicide. This includes students who engage in self-injurious behavior (e.g., cutting), verbal suicidal threats, or suicidal behavior. Eating disorders may be viewed as a form of self-harm or even life-threatening behavior when students restrict their eating to the point that they are medically at risk. Typically, students who are hospitalized because of a suicide attempt are not permitted to return to campus until they provide evidence that they are ready to return. If and when they are allowed to resume their studies, there is usually an expectation or requirement that the students will use ongoing counseling.

With students who do not go as far as actually making a suicide attempt but display behavior that arouses concern for their safety or well-being, there is likely to be pressure placed on them to be in counseling. More and more schools may move in the direction of treating suicidal threats and behavior as violations of student conduct and subject to disciplinary sanctions. As long ago as 1984, the University of Illinois instituted a formal policy whereby students who threatened or attempted suicide were required to attend four sessions of counseling, and failure to comply with this policy could result in involuntary withdrawal from the university. The intent of the policy was to reduce the suicide rate among students, and data show that the rate of suicide has been significantly reduced since the policy was initiated (Sander, 2004).

Although the University of Illinois program provides evidence that mandated counseling may be effective in reducing the suicide rate on campus, concerns have been raised about the potential for the level of risk for self-harm to escalate as a result of mandating counseling (e.g., Stone & Lucas, 1994). For example, could a policy of treating suicidal threats and behavior as violations of student conduct inadvertently lower the probability of students seeking help? That is, might students fear negative consequences, such as having to withdraw from school, if they reveal suicidal thoughts or intentions? Perhaps so, but in terms of risk management, institutions need to find ways to ensure that students known to be at risk are evaluated and monitored as much as possible, and campus clinicians represent the most logical individuals to perform this task. Generally speaking, students considered at risk for suicide are expected to participate in mandated counseling until the treating clinician determines that the degree of risk has diminished.

Risk of Harm to Others

Similar to concerns about suicide risk, college officials also need to deal with students who are believed to be at risk for harm to others on the basis of threats or actual incidents of aggression perpetrated against others. In some of these cases, students may be automatically removed from campus. However, in other cases, the degree of risk may not be clear-cut.

As an example, consider a male student accused by another student, his former girlfriend, of stalking her. The female student files a report with campus police that her former boyfriend frequently appears at various places and events on campus that she attends, and she suspects him of stalking her. If evidence of stalking behavior is established, the college then has an obligation to take steps to prevent any foreseeable harm to the female student. For example, the male student might be allowed to remain on campus provided that he has no further contact with his ex-girlfriend. In such a case, mandated counseling may be imposed as a sanction. College officials must do everything within their power to ensure the safety of students, and mandating counseling for those students who pose a threat of harm is considered a reasonable response (Pollard, 1995).

Imagine the same scenario, but now the two students live on campus in close proximity, attend some of the same classes, and have several mutual friends. The charge of stalking may be harder to establish given how much their everyday lives overlap. This makes it more difficult to manage the potential for problems to occur. As noted earlier, if any evidence of stalking behavior can be established, then mandated counseling may be perceived by administrators as a risk management strategy for monitoring this potentially volatile situation.

As with clients deemed at risk for suicide, counselors are often called on to assess and work with students considered at risk for harm to others in order to monitor and minimize the degree of risk. In such cases, counselors must be aware of and explain to students the exceptions to confidentiality as stated in the *ACA Code of Ethics* (American Counseling Association [ACA], 2005), particularly Standard B.2.a, which addresses the need to protect clients and others from serious and foreseeable harm.

Counseling Implications

Client Motivation

Motivation to change is generally believed to be an important client characteristic for counseling to be effective. Self-determination theory (Deci & Ryan, 1985) posits that behavior is regulated by motivation, which may be either intrinsically or extrinsically driven. Intrinsically motivated behaviors are performed voluntarily and are not based on any rewards or external constraints, whereas extrinsically motivated behaviors tend to be engaged in for instrumental purposes (e.g., to receive a reward or avoid a punishment).

Applying this theory to counseling, most mandated clients would be conceptualized as extrinsically motivated (i.e., to avoid further punishment or negative consequences). People typically seek counseling because they are in distress and perceive a need to remedy problems in their lives. Under conditions of coercion, however, clients may not feel any need to change, and they may not even recognize a problem other than the fact that they got in trouble or aroused concern on campus. In other words, the connection between the student's behavior and the need for counseling is based primarily on the perceptions of others rather than self-perceptions.

For example, a student who is placed on disciplinary probation for public drunkenness and vandalism of college property may not necessarily view these behaviors as problematic, aside from the fact that they resulted in specific negative consequences at the college. Assuming the student takes the matter seriously, he or she will agree to whatever sanctions are imposed, such as paying fines and attending mandatory counseling sessions, in order to avoid any additional negative consequences and to remain in school. Being placed on disciplinary probation should at least reduce the likelihood that the student will engage in any further misconduct. Any counseling mandate imposed may not necessarily be effective in bringing about a change in the student's attitudes or behavior. However, for some students, getting in trouble at the college may be distressing enough to prompt some degree of introspection and perhaps openness to examining their choices and life decisions. Hence, it is conceivable that a student's motivational type may change from extrinsic to intrinsic once he or she is coerced into counseling.

If a client's motivation for counseling remains primarily extrinsic in nature, then the counselor might expect to obtain a limited amount of useful information from the client (Otani, 1989). Although many students coerced into counseling may not want to seem openly hostile or uncooperative, they may feel no need to be self-initiating or openly disclosing. This is understandable given the nature of mandatory counseling. Students are likely to be cautious and guarded about what and how much they share, perhaps fearing additional negative consequences if they reveal too much. Rather than limit how much they share, some coerced clients may find ways to manipulate the manner of communicating information with the counselor, such as abruptly changing topics (Otani, 1989).

A related concern has to do with the student's degree of honesty and propensity to withhold information. Even when a mandated client seems to share openly and disclose freely, it may just be an effort to tell the counselor what he or she thinks the counselor wants to hear. Students may be especially reluctant to reveal honestly about continuing to engage in the behavior that resulted in the mandated counseling in the first place. For example, a student on probation for an alcohol-related violation might be reluctant to talk about any subsequent use of alcohol.

Client Reluctance

All of the client behaviors discussed thus far—extrinsically based motivation, limited self-disclosure, and inhibitions about being completely open and honest—could be conceptualized as various symptoms of "reluctance." The term *reluctance* generally refers to those individuals who, if given the choice, would prefer not to be in counseling or talk about themselves (Ritchie, 1986). A related yet distinct concept is *resistance,* which is typically defined as an unwillingness to change (Otani, 1989; Ritchie, 1986).

Although client resistance is not that uncommon among those who seek help voluntarily, particularly when persuaded by others to seek counseling, it can be an especially salient issue with involuntary clients because they may see no reason to make any changes in their lives. As noted earlier, the reasons for being in counseling are externally imposed rather than self-imposed. As with voluntary clients who are encouraged by others to seek counseling, it is important to assess to what degree students acknowledge having concerns to address in counseling and, if so, how much they are willing to work on changing their behavior.

One factor that can be particularly important to assess is whether an involuntary client has had any previous counseling and how the individual experienced it. It might be especially problematic if the student has been coerced into counseling before. For example, some students may have had earlier experiences of being forced into counseling, often by their parents. If so, this earlier experience may have resulted in negative associations with counseling in general and coerced counseling in particular. This means that the earlier negative experience can get re-created. Therefore, it is essential to explore this aspect as much as possible and to allow the student an opportunity to share his or her feelings about the earlier experience as well as the current situation. Making a connection between the two experiences may help the student perceive the counselor as sensitive to the student's experience of being coerced into counseling.

Regardless of whether a student had an earlier experience of being coerced into counseling, it is generally good practice to explore the student's feelings about being mandated to counseling. This is a way for the counselor to acknowledge and work with, rather than against, the student's feelings of reluctance about being in counseling.

Other strategies for working with reluctant clients include the need to structure and clarify the purpose, expectations, length, and goals of counseling (Ritchie, 1986). It has also been recommended that clinicians refrain from asking too many questions when working with involuntary clients because clients may come to view the process of counseling as simply consisting of them answering counselors' questions (Brodsky & Lichtenstein, 1999). In addition, counselors should be careful not to be prematurely confrontational or to engage in power struggles with involuntary clients, either of which can damage the opportunity to develop a good working relationship (Ritchie, 1986).

When working with mandated clients, clinicians need to use techniques aimed at building rapport and establishing a sense of mutual trust. In addition to traditional techniques used by counselors with most any client for the purpose of building rapport (e.g., displaying empathy and support), involuntary clients may be especially responsive to counselors who acknowledge and show sensitivity to the experience of being coerced into counseling. It can also be important to give involuntary clients a sense of control and help them become active, rather than passive, participants in the process of counseling by encouraging them, for example, to establish goals for counseling.

Ethical Concerns

College clinicians need to be especially sensitive to the ethical concerns associated with doing mandated counseling (Hernandez & Fister, 2001; Ritchie, 1986), particularly those related to confidentiality and informed consent. The *ACA Code of Ethics* (ACA, 2005) provides guidance for ensuring informed consent in the counseling relationship but does not necessarily address the unique dilemmas of doing mandated counseling. It is vital that counselors be clear from the outset of counseling about what will and will not be kept confidential and inform mandated clients about what specific information is to be shared with others as part of the mandated-counseling contract (Larke, 1985). In some instances, verification of attendance is all that is requested, whereas, in other cases, there may be a request for the counselor to share his or her clinical impressions about the client's progress in counseling.

College clinicians are not ordinarily expected to report to the mandate source if the student continues to engage in the behavior that prompted the mandate because this would not allow for any trust in the counseling process. However, if the behavior involves some form of danger to self, such as excessive alcohol use or self-mutilation, then there may be an expectation that this would be reported to the mandate source. This represents a potential quandary for the counselor, who needs to maintain confidentiality to the fullest extent possible under the circumstances but at the same time may be pressured to report client behavior that is high-risk. For counseling to be effective, students need to feel safe enough to divulge about continuing to engage in behavior that prompted their forced entry into counseling.

Even though the client has not voluntarily chosen to be in counseling, the counseling should still be viewed as a collaborative effort in which the client is fully involved in the process. The counselor should therefore ensure that the client understands and agrees to all contact with others, and any potential dilemmas with confidentiality should be discussed with the client. For instance, a mutually agreed-on plan could be established with the client for handling client disclosures about dangerous or risky behavior. Although it may not be necessary to report such behavior to the mandate source, clients may be willing to allow communication between the clinician and other individuals, such as parents or other family members, in certain situations. In addition, the principles involved in responding to clients deemed to be at risk for harm to self or others are always in effect, regardless of whether clients are voluntary or mandated, and mandated clients need to understand the exceptions to confidentiality as stated in the *ACA Code of Ethics* (ACA, 2005).

In general, campus clinicians need to protect confidentiality while at the same time abiding by the limitations of confidentiality imposed by the mandated-counseling contract. Strein and Hershenson (1991) provided an example of how counselors should try to limit the amount and type of information they share with a mandate source. In the case of a student found guilty of vandalism in his or her residence hall, Strein and Hershenson stressed that it is not necessary to share any information not pertinent to share (e.g., underlying anger toward parents that may have contributed to the "acting out" behavior). Instead, the counselor should restrict the information shared to the specific situation that resulted in the mandate. In the case of vandalism, the counselor could share information about the student's commitment to a plan to live within the rules of the residence hall and could share the counselor's judgment about the student's ability to do so.

In some instances, counselors may need to educate mandate sources about the sensitive ethical issues involved with involuntary counseling. It may also be important to educate mandate sources about the nature of counseling and the need to protect confidentiality as much as possible, particularly when counseling is coerced. This education may be helpful in dispelling myths or unrealistic expectations for counseling with mandated clients (Larke, 1985).

Although there may be some variations from campus to campus, clinicians typically obtain a mandated client's consent to release confidential information on the basis of a request for this release from the mandate source. The procedure tends to be as follows: After a judicial hearing or administrative determination that a student has violated standards of the college code of conduct or displayed disruptive behavior on campus, the mandate source sends a letter to the student. This letter spells out the conditions and sanctions, which may include mandated counseling, that the student needs to agree to in order to remain enrolled. In certain cases, this letter may actually be a contract that the student is asked to sign. When counseling is mandated, the student is instructed to sign appropriate releases in order to allow information to be communicated between the counselor and the mandate source. Ideally, the nature of this communication should be specific (e.g., verification of attendance only). Counselors should receive a copy of the mandate letter or contract for their records and have a clear understanding of the letter or contract.

When the student mandated to counseling initiates contact with the counseling center, he or she needs to agree to and sign an informed-consent form and a release form consenting to release of confidential information. The informed-consent form can be the standard form used for all new clients. A standard release form can also be used, although it is worth considering the use of a form specifically designed for mandated clients. This form would not necessarily differ significantly from a standard release form but could clearly indicate that the release is for the purpose of meeting the requirements of a mandated-counseling contract. The release should be clear and explicit with regard to what information is to be shared and with whom. Students should receive a copy of the consent form for their own records and a copy of the release form if requested.

Counselor Reluctance

Finally, a clinical issue that warrants some discussion is the potential for clinicians to experience their own reluctance about seeing mandated clients. Just as students may be reluctant and resentful if coerced into counseling, counselors may experience resentment about being asked to work with involuntary clients (Kiracofe, 1993). Indeed, in a survey of college counselors, many respondents indicated that they preferred not to do mandated counseling (Stone & Lucas, 1994). Counselor resentment may stem, in part, from the perception of mandated counseling as a misuse of resources, particularly when there is a high demand for counseling from voluntary clients. Many counselors could probably attest to how frustrating it can be to do counseling with involuntary clients. Unfortunately, however, having reservations or feelings of resentment about seeing mandated clients is likely to result in negative countertransference and counterproductive counselor behavior. Therefore, counselors must find ways to manage such negative feelings if they are placed in a position of having to see students on an involuntary basis. Counselors may need to seek supervision or consultation with colleagues in managing mandated clients.

Campus Considerations

Although college clinicians may have significant concerns and reservations about doing mandated counseling, it is in their best interest to try to work in tandem with the school administration in an effort to provide a safe and healthy environment for students. As Francis (2000) appropriately noted, college counselors have a responsibility to the institution that supports their services. The challenge is for counselors and administrators to work together and come to an agreement about how to define and structure mandated counseling. This requires that counselors and administrators establish clear guidelines and policies regarding mandated counseling (Francis, 2000).

The potential for conflict between campus counselors and the institution may be quite high because of the delicate balance involved in maintaining the best interests of the individual student (client) versus the best interests of the institution. Clinicians tend to focus on the needs of their clients but also need to be aware of the impact that their clients' behavior has on the campus community. This is particularly true when the counselor is dealing with students who have been disruptive in some way within the campus environment. On the one hand, counselors may prefer to allow their clients to have some sense of autonomy in the treatment process, but, on the other hand, they need to ensure client safety and help manage client behavior that is disruptive to others.

It behooves college counselors to find ways to be responsive to administrative needs without compromising their ethics and clinical practices. For example, when a determination is made that a student's misconduct or disciplinary infraction is due, at least in part, to emotional or psychological problems, it might be preferable to agree to see the student for a mandated evaluation, and perhaps a mandatory follow-up session or two, with any additional sessions provided on a voluntary basis. This approach represents a conciliatory stance so that the counseling center does not refuse to provide mandated counseling (which may not sit well with administrators) but, at the same time, does not agree to do mandated counseling for a period of time deemed unreasonable. Mandating that the counseling occur off-campus may be an alternative way for administrators to respond, at least in some cases, which would avoid compromising limited counseling center resources.

Counseling centers might also consider denoting mandated interventions for students as forms of "assessment" or "education" as opposed to "counseling." Indeed, even some of the strongest critics of mandated counseling seem willing to offer mandated educational sessions (Gilbert & Sheiman, 1995), particularly for alcohol policy violations (Morgan & Cavendish, 1987).

Future Trends

College counselors are likely to be increasingly relied on by administrators to help in the institutional effort to manage disruptive students, manage risk and liability associated with suicidal and dangerous students, and contain or alleviate fears aroused within the campus community in response to emotionally disturbed students. Accordingly, the use of mandated counseling as an administrative response is likely to continue to grow.

However, counselors need not be the only professionals whom administrators rely on when dealing with problematic and emotionally troubled students who pose serious concerns within the campus environment. Many other campus professionals can be instrumental in this effort, including student health professionals, residential life staff, public safety officers, and disabilities specialists. Consultation and collaboration between these various services can be valuable in responding to students who display problematic behavior (Sharkin, 2006). In fact, many institutions have begun to establish case management teams or committees, consisting of representatives from different services, for the purpose of evaluating specific cases of problem behavior and making recommendations for an appropriate institutional response. This approach represents an ideal way to coordinate services and manage problematic student behavior.

Although mandated counseling is likely to continue to occur, involvement of other campus offices in managing problematic student behavior may at least lessen the burden that college counselors may currently feel when they agree to work with mandated clients. Such collaboration with other campus professionals will necessitate a certain degree of flexibility in order to work effectively within the constraints of confidentiality. Of course, this does not mean that counselors will no longer adhere to principles of confidentiality, but they will need to find ways to work within the system without alienating others simply for the sake of maintaining confidentiality. Clinicians can greatly benefit from the assistance of others when it comes to dealing with problematic students who arouse concern on campus; they should not have to carry the burden primarily on their own shoulders.

References

American Counseling Association. (2005). *ACA code of ethics*. Alexandria, VA: Author.

Brodsky, S. L., & Lichtenstein, B. (1999). Don't ask questions: A psychotherapeutic strategy for treatment of involuntary clients. *American Journal of Psychotherapy, 53,* 215–220.

Dannells, M., & Consolvo, C. (2000). Disciplinary counseling: Implications for policy and practice. *NASPA Journal, 38,* 44–57.

Deci, E. L., & Ryan, R. M. (1985). *Intrinsic motivation and self-determination in human behavior.* New York: Plenum Press.

Francis, P. C. (2000). Practicing ethically as a college counselor. In D. C. Davis & K. M. Humphrey (Eds.), *College counseling: Issues and strategies for a new millennium* (pp. 71–86). Alexandria, VA: American Counseling Association.

Francis, P. C. (2003). Developing ethical institutional policies and procedures for working with suicidal students on a college campus. *Journal of College Counseling, 6,* 114–123.

Gilbert, S. P. (1989). The juggling act of the college counseling center: A point of view. *The Counseling Psychologist, 17,* 477–489.

Gilbert, S. P., & Sheiman, J. A. (1995). Mandatory counseling of university students: An oxymoron? *Journal of College Student Psychotherapy, 9,* 3–21.

Hernandez, T. J., & Fister, D. L. (2001). Dealing with disruptive and emotional college students: A systems model. *Journal of College Counseling, 4,* 49–62.

Kiracofe, N. M. (1993). Changing demands on counseling centers: Problems and possibilities. *Journal of College Student Psychotherapy, 7,* 69–83.

Kitzrow, M. A. (2003). The mental health needs of today's college students: Challenges and recommendations. *NASPA Journal, 41,* 165–179.

Larke, J. (1985). Compulsory treatment: Some practical methods of treating the mandated client. *Psychotherapy: Theory, Practice, and Research, 22,* 262–268.

Morgan, E. J., & Cavendish, J. M. (1987). Medical, ethical, and legal issues in treating college student substance abusers. *Alcoholism Treatment Quarterly, 4,* 141–149.

Otani, A. (1989). Client resistance in counseling: Its theoretical rationale and taxonomic classification. *Journal of Counseling & Development, 67,* 458–461.

Pollard, J. W. (1995). Involuntary treatment: Counseling or consequence? *Journal of College Student Psychotherapy, 9,* 45–55.

Ritchie, M. H. (1986). Counseling the involuntary client. *Journal of Counseling & Development, 64,* 516–518.

Sander, E. (2004, October 15). Some colleges try zero-tolerance toward suicide attempts. *The Wall Street Journal, 244,* p. B1.

Schwitzer, A. M., Grogan, K., Kaddoura, K., & Ochoa, L. (1993). Effects of brief mandatory counseling on help-seeking and academic success among at-risk college students. *Journal of College Student Psychotherapy, 34,* 401–405.

Sharkin, B. S. (2006). *College students in distress: A resource guide for faculty, staff, and campus community.* Binghamton, NY: Haworth Press.

Stone, G. L., & Lucas, J. (1994). Disciplinary counseling in higher education: A neglected challenge. *Journal of Counseling & Development, 72,* 234–238.

Strein, W., & Hershenson, D. B. (1991). Confidentiality in nondyadic counseling situations. *Journal of Counseling & Development, 69,* 312–316.

12

Counseling Students Who Are Problem Drinkers: Screening, Assessment, and Intervention

Gary G. Gintner and Laura Hensley Choate

Introduction

Heavy alcohol use and its associated consequences continue to be a nationally recognized problem on college campuses (National Institute on Alcohol Abuse and Alcoholism [NIAAA], Alcoholism National Advisory Council, 2002). Despite heightened attention to this issue, recent surveys indicate that problem drinking persists at high levels (Core Institute, 2004; Johnston, O'Malley, & Bachman, 1998; Meilman, Cashin, McKillip, & Presley, 1998; Wechsler, Lee, Kuo, & Lee, 2000). Studies have consistently indicated a strong relationship between problem drinking and drinking-related problems, with the heaviest users incurring the most adverse consequences for themselves (e.g., missing class, charges of driving while intoxicated, fights, and unplanned or unprotected sexual activity) and others (e.g., sexual assault, unwanted sexual advances, and fights; Core Institute, 2004; Wechsler & Dowdall, 1995).

Because of the significance of these negative effects, the majority of colleges have implemented primary prevention programs during the past two decades (Wechsler, Kelley, & Weitzman, 2000). These programs generally entail alcohol education, environmental management (e.g., providing alcohol-free activities and living spaces and limiting alcohol advertisements), communication campaigns to alter student perceptions of campus drinking norms, and greater enforcement of college policy and drinking-related laws (O'Malley & Johnston, 2002; Wechsler et al., 2002). Although these "top-down" prevention programs have shown some success with moderate to light drinkers, they have not been effective with problem drinkers (Wechsler et al., 2002). These programs tend to be ineffective because problem drinkers do not view their alcohol use as problematic, nor do they report any intention to change their drinking-related behaviors anytime in the near future (Vik, Culbertson, & Sellers, 2000; Wechsler, Nelson, & Weitzman, 2000). Although there has been a recent call in the literature for more interventions targeted to the specific needs and motivational characteristics of problem drinkers, most campus resources remain dedicated to campuswide primary prevention programs (Weitzman, Nelson, Lee, & Wechsler, 2004; Werch, Pappas, & Castellon-Vogel, 1996).

In contrast, an alternative approach to primary prevention is to design and implement secondary prevention programs that are specifically targeted to students who are already experiencing drinking-related problems. Effective secondary prevention programs typically involve more direct approaches with students, including early identification of and brief interventions with problem drinkers (Clements, 1999; Gintner & Choate, 2003). Along these lines, promising approaches for problem drinkers involve two important components: (a) effective screening and assessment procedures and (b) brief interventions that are matched to students' personal goals and readiness to change. Although researchers have strongly advocated for the incorporation of alcohol screening into standard contacts with students (Foote, Wilkens, & Vavagiakis, 2004; Helmkamp et al., 2003; Larimer & Cronce, 2002) and for the provision of empirically supported brief interventions (Flemming, 2002; Helmkamp et al., 2003; Larimer & Cronce, 2002), campuses have dedicated little attention to these aspects of alcohol prevention and treatment.

Assessment Issues

Early identification of students who are problem drinkers is the first step in implementing effective assessment and treatment procedures. Unfortunately, the majority of current alcohol screening initiatives for problem drinkers are conducted in college student health centers, generally as part of medical history intake questions (Aertgeerts et al., 2000; Flemming, 2002; Foote et al., 2004; Helmkamp et al., 2003). Limiting alcohol screenings to health centers is problematic because only those students who seek help for medical problems will be screened. In addition, there is evidence that two thirds of health centers fail to conduct such screenings on a routine basis (Foote et al., 2004). College counseling centers, therefore, should take the lead in incorporating general alcohol screening questions as part of their standard intake sessions with all clients.

The Problem-Drinking Continuum

Prior to infusing screening efforts into their sessions with students, college counselors must have an understanding of problem drinking as a continuum that ranges from regular heavy use (e.g., frequent binge drinking [FBD]), to drinking that causes repeated adverse consequences (alcohol abuse), to compulsive use that leads to physical and psychosocial impairment (alcohol dependence; Institute of Medicine, 1990). Reports of FBD, defined as the consumption of five or more drinks for men (four or more drinks for women) per occasion, three or more times during a 2-week period, range from 25% to 40% of students (Reinert & Allen, 2002; Wechsler, Lee, et al., 2000). Those students particularly at risk for FBD include underage drinkers and first-year students (Clements, 1999; Helmkamp et al., 2003).

The two primary categories of disorders related to alcohol use are *alcohol abuse* and *alcohol dependence* (American Psychiatric Association [APA], 2000). To meet criteria for alcohol abuse, a client must have experienced at least one of the following during the past 12 months: (a) failure to fulfill role obligations (e.g., performs poorly on a test or misses class or work), (b) drinking in hazardous situations (e.g., drinking and driving or drinking while taking medications), (c) legal problems (e.g., underage drinking arrest, fighting, or sexual assault), or (d) interpersonal problems (e.g., conflicts with a significant other or friends). Approximately 10%–31% of college students meet criteria for alcohol abuse, with men showing higher rates of abuse than women (Aertgeerts et al., 2000; Clements, 1999; Knight et al., 2002).

Alcohol dependence constitutes a pattern of compulsive drinking frequently accompanied by physical changes, including tolerance and withdrawal (APA, 2000). A client must demonstrate three or more of the following symptoms in a 12-month period in order to meet *Diagnostic and Statistical Manual of Mental Disorders* (4th ed., text rev.; APA, 2000) criteria: (a) tolerance (e.g., needing more drinks to become intoxicated); (b) withdrawal (e.g., sweating, agitation, and insomnia after drinking is reduced or discontinued); (c) drinking larger amounts than intended; (d) a persistent desire or unsuccessful efforts to control drinking; (e) expenditure of significant time in obtaining alcohol, drinking alcohol, or recovering from its effects; (f) reduction of non-drinking-related social, school, or work activities; or (g) continued drinking despite physical (e.g., ulcers) or psychological (e.g., depression or interpersonal violence) consequences. College students with alcohol dependence are less likely to show symptoms of chronic long-term use such as withdrawal and medical problems because they are generally in the early stages of the disorder. Students who are most at risk for alcohol dependence include those who exhibit any of the following: (a) a high tolerance for alcohol, (b) a family history of alcoholism, (c) daily drinking, or (d) alcohol use to deal with stress or personal problems (Flemming, 2002). Rates for alcohol dependence in undergraduate samples have ranged from approximately 6% to 11% of students (Clements, 1999; Knight et al., 2002).

Screening and Assessment for Problem Drinkers

During intake interviews, college counselors should begin with basic rapport building, followed by questions to elicit information about functioning in important life areas (e.g., academic performance, relationships, and work). Because initial screening questions should be designed to minimize client defensiveness and encourage honesty (Flemming, 2002; Miller & Rollnick, 1991), the transition into conducting an alcohol screening can be made by using open-ended questions such as "It is not unusual for college students to drink alcohol. What's that like for you?" or "Drinking patterns often change when you come to college. How has that been for you?" Any affirmative answer about drinking can be followed by the screening questions listed below. To each response, it is useful to respond with a reflective statement of the student's answer prior to asking the next question.

Intake Screening Questions

The most widely used initial screening procedure is to ask questions related to consumption and associated problems. The following four questions can be used to determine frequency of alcohol use, quantity of consumption, extent of binge drinking, and adverse consequences (Flemming, 2002; Miller & Rollnick, 1991):

1. "How many days per week do you drink alcohol?" (frequency)
2. "On a typical day of drinking, how many drinks do you have?" (quantity)
3. "How many times per month do you drink five (four for females) or more drinks on a single occasion?" (extent of binge drinking)
4. "What are the good and not so good things about drinking?" (consequences)

It is important to note that of these four questions, the single most effective screen is to ask about binge drinking: "How many times in the past month have you had five or more drinks on a single occasion?" For example, Taj, Devera-Sales, and Vinson (1998) found that this question alone positively identified nearly three fourths of problem drinkers.

Screening and Assessment Instruments

The two most cited alcohol screening instruments used with college students (Aertgeerts et al., 2000; Flemming, 2002) are the CAGE (Ewing, 1984) and the Alcohol Use Disorders Identification Test (AUDIT; Barbor & Grant, 1989). CAGE is an acronym for the test's four questions:

- Have you ever felt that you needed to Cut down on your drinking?
- Have people Annoyed you by being critical of your drinking?
- Have you ever felt bad or Guilty about your drinking?
- Have you ever had a drink first thing in the morning to steady your nerves or to get rid of a hangover (Eye-opener)? (Ewing, 1984, p. 1906)

Both the CAGE and the AUDIT can be administered and scored quickly and easily. Despite being used widely in this population, however, the CAGE is not particularly sensitive with college students, incorrectly classifying more than half of problem drinkers (Aertgeerts et al., 2000). This occurs because the questions are designed to detect a serious and prolonged drinking history, which is rare in the majority of college students (Foote et al., 2004).

The AUDIT is a self-administered screening instrument created by the World Health Organization as a brief screening tool for early identification of alcohol use disorders and at-risk drinking in a diverse range of individuals (Barbor & Grant, 1989; Reinert & Allen, 2002). The AUDIT has been used extensively with college students and seems to be valid and reliable across racial/ethnic groups (Reinert & Allen, 2002; Volk, Steinbauer, Cantor, & Holzer, 1997). Unlike the CAGE, the AUDIT is well-suited to the college population because it includes questions that cover the continuum of drinking-related problems (Flemming, 2002; Helmkamp et al., 2003). The AUDIT consists of 10 questions that load in three conceptual domains: alcohol intake, alcohol dependence, and alcohol-related problems (Reinert & Allen, 2002). It can be administered in approximately 2 minutes and is easily scored by summing the numbers associated with the selected responses. Scores can range from 0 to 40, and scores of 8 or higher indicate a positive screen (Barbor & Grant, 1989). Later studies indicated that a score of 6 or higher is more sensitive for identifying problem drinking among females (Reinert & Allen, 2002).

Regardless of the screening method used, college counselors should consider clients to have a positive alcohol screening if any of the following are reported (Flemming, 2002; Reinert & Allen, 2002): (a) students have had two or more significant alcohol-related problems in the past year; (b) males have drunk five or more drinks (females four or more) on a single occasion in the past month; (c) signs of alcohol dependence (tolerance, withdrawal, etc.); or (d) scores of 6 to 8 or higher on the AUDIT, with the lower cutoff score more sensitive to identifying females who are problem drinkers. If the client's answers do indicate a positive screening, then the college counselor should consider conducting a more comprehensive alcohol assessment, including a detailed history of alcohol use:

- What substances is the client currently using?
- In a typical week, what is the extent of alcohol/other drug use?
- What types of adverse consequences have occurred as a result? What about social, legal, academic, work, or physical problems?
- At what age did drinking begin, and when was the first time the client was drunk? What has been the pattern of drinking since that time?
- Has anyone in the client's family had a drug or alcohol problem?
- Has the client had any treatment for drug or alcohol problems?

One commonly used assessment instrument that is particularly useful in identifying adverse consequences is the Rutgers Alcohol Problem Index (RAPI), a 23-item self-administered screening tool. Data suggest that the RAPI is appropriate for use in both clinical and nonclinical samples of adolescents and young adults (White & Labouvie, 1989).

In summary, the screening and assessment processes consist of four basic steps:

1. Ask how the client is doing in important life areas.
2. Ask the four questions related to alcohol consumption and associated problems. Administer the AUDIT if more information is needed.
3. Assess whether the responses indicate a positive screen.
4. Conduct a more comprehensive assessment for students with a positive screen.

If the comprehensive assessment supports the positive screen, the student is a candidate for a brief intervention. In the next section, these interventions are discussed as well as considerations for those students who may need more intensive treatment.

Counseling Implications

A number of different interventions have been tested with college students who show a pattern of problem drinking. Many of these interventions are based on the harm reduction model, which stands in stark contrast to traditional approaches to treating alcohol problems.

Harm Reduction

Traditional approaches for treating alcohol problems have largely relied on the disease model of alcoholism (Yalisove, 1998), which assumes that drinkers have an inevitable downhill course if treatment is not provided. Treatments tend to be intensive and long-term, with strong emphasis placed on abstinence goals and public acknowledgment of alcoholism. A number of studies, however, have suggested that the traditional model is a poor fit for college students because most "grow out of" their heavy drinking patterns (Larimer & Cronce, 2002) and are typically not willing to acknowledge alcohol problems (Knight et al., 2002; Vik et al., 2000). As a result, programs that emphasize abstinence and admission of alcohol problems as program entry criteria may actually dissuade many students from participating, especially those who most need the services (Gintner & Choate, 2003; Marlatt, 1996; Neighbors, Palmer, & Larimer, 2004).

Harm reduction (HR) has emerged as an alternative model for treating problem drinkers (Marlatt, 1996). Based on public health principles, it shifts the focus from simply drinking per se to reducing the harmful consequences of drinking that affect the drinker, significant others, and the community at large. With college students, HR focuses on how drinking affects critical life spheres such as academic performance, interpersonal relationships, health, life satisfaction, and legal standing. A basic premise is that any reduction in harm is a step in the right direction (Marlatt, 1996). HR advocates a stepped-care approach to treatment selection in which brief, low-intensive treatments are considered first (e.g., brief counseling). If these efforts are unsuccessful, they are followed by more protracted, intensive treatments (e.g., outpatient treatment or intensive outpatient treatment). Considering the fit of this model to the profile of student problem drinkers, it is not surprising that most of the empirically supported treatments discussed below are based on HR principles.

Interventions That Do Not Work

Education programs are the most common intervention used to reduce drinking on campus (Larimer & Cronce, 2002). Three forms of education have been evaluated: (a) knowledge-based programs that provide information about alcohol and alcohol-related harm, (b) values clarification programs that have students examine how drinking fits with their personal goals, and (c) normative information programs that have students compare personal drinking with that of the student population. These programs are typically offered as a class or a workshop. Evaluations of these types of programs have consistently shown no significant changes in alcohol consumption and alcohol-related harm, despite the fact that program participants show changes in knowledge, values, or personal norms (Flemming, 2002; Larimer & Cronce, 2002). Although various forms of education may be included as part of a multicomponent program (as is seen below), they seem to be insufficient on their own (NIAAA, Alcoholism National Advisory Council, 2002).

Programs That Work

Literature reviews (Larimer & Cronce, 2002) and governmental agency reports (Flemming, 2002; NIAAA, Alcoholism National Advisory Council, 2002) have identified a set of brief interventions that have demonstrated reductions in drinking and alcohol-related harm among college students who are problem drinkers. These include motivational enhancement interventions (e.g., Dimeff, Baer, Kivlahan, & Marlatt, 1999), alcohol skills training programs (e.g., Baer et al., 1992), and programs that include components of both (e.g., Flemming, 2002).

Motivational Enhancement

Students who are problem drinkers are often unmotivated to change. The stages-of-change model (Prochaska, DiClemente, & Norcross, 1992) has been used in the literature to assess students' readiness to change drinking habits (Vik et al., 2000). This model proposes that the change process entails a series of stages, each with different issues and therapeutic tasks. Clients in the precontemplation stage are unaware or unwilling to admit that there is a problem. Those clients in the contemplation stage recognize that a problem exists, but they are typically ambivalent about taking action for some reason. As ambivalence is resolved, clients move through the remaining stages of change: preparation, action, and maintenance. Therapeutically, motivational strategies are indicated for the precontemplation and contemplation stages, whereas more action-oriented interventions are better suited for the subsequent stages (Prochaska et al., 1992).

Studies indicate that most college students who are problem drinkers fit the profile of either precontemplators or contemplators (Helmkamp et al., 2003; Vik et al., 2000). Thus, strategies that increase problem recognition and motivation seem indicated for this population, especially in the early phases of counseling (Gintner & Choate, 2003).

Motivational interviewing (MI; Miller & Rollnick, 1991) was specifically developed to deal with clients in the precontemplation and contemplation stages. MI is best conceptualized as a set of interview strategies designed to involve students in the counseling process in a way that encourages them to find personally meaningful reasons to change. Five major strategies are used: (a) express empathy, (b) avoid argumentation, (c) roll with resistance, (d) create discrepancies, and (e) build self-efficacy.

Expressing empathy entails acknowledging the student's point of view and feelings through the use of various forms of reflective statements. For example, the following interchange illustrates *simple reflections* of what the student has just said as well as *double-sided reflections* that attempt to capture the upside and the downside of drinking:

> *Client:* After the final we all met at the bar to unwind. Wow was it a rough week.
> *Counselor:* So kicking back at the bar helped to take the edge off a tough week. (simple reflection)
> *Client:* You got it. We were there until two. I had to go to work at six and guess who wasn't on time. My boss can be such a pain when you're late.
> *Counselor:* So while going to the bar was fun, dealing with your boss wasn't. (double-sided reflection)

Rolling with resistance and *avoiding argumentation* are two key strategies to minimize resistance. A basic principle is that when individuals feel pressured, they may react by becoming more entrenched in their original position. Instead, MI advocates meeting resistance with reflection as a way of sidestepping an argument. Open-ended questions are used to elicit information about the problem so that it is the student who provides information about adverse consequences. The following dialogue illustrates these two principles with a hostile client:

> *Client:* This is a waste of time. You should be seeing Larry on our floor—now *he* can drink.
> *Counselor:* So being here makes no sense to you. (roll with resistance)
> *Client:* Of course not. Getting loaded one night doesn't make you an alcoholic.
> *Counselor:* You feel it's been blown out of proportion. Tell me about what happened. (avoid argumentation)

As a therapeutic alliance is established, the stage is set for using the last strategy, *creating discrepancies.* The idea is to point out discrepant pieces of information that the client has disclosed as a way of creating cognitive dissonance. The hope is that the client will resolve the discordance by rethinking the value of the drinking-related behavior. Discrepancies can be noted between past and current statements, between drinking and important life goals, and between the "good and not so good" things about drinking:

> *Counselor:* Earlier you said that the partying doesn't bother anyone, but from what you just said, it can really bother your girlfriend. Do I have that right? (noting discrepancies)
> *Client:* Yeah, it can really make her mad. She says that she gets embarrassed.
> *Counselor:* So there are not only good things about drinking but also some not so good things, like with your girlfriend.

Building self-efficacy becomes a more central strategy as clients begin to see that change may be in their own best interest. Students with enhanced self-efficacy are likely to feel that they can actually make the needed changes, once they have made the decision to act. Self-efficacy can be supported in a variety of ways (Gintner & Choate, 2003):

- Provide a small success experience (e.g., go one night without drinking).
- Reinforce any step in the right direction (e.g., "You only had two drinks last night. How did you do that?").
- Point out a past success experience (e.g., "Last fall you said you didn't drink . . .").
- Expose them to students like themselves who have moderated their drinking.

Studies that have used MI with college students have also included personalized feedback as a treatment component (Bosari & Carey, 2000; Marlatt et al., 1998). Assessment findings with regard to drinking, family history, and alcohol-related harm are presented to the client, who is then asked to respond to the findings. Drinking feedback is presented relative to typical college students, similar to the normative feedback discussed above. The counselor may introduce alcohol information on topics such as blood alcohol levels and tolerance as a way of helping students understand the relevance of the findings. Throughout this dialogue, MI principles are used to ensure that clients do not become overly defensive. Below is an example of how feedback about drinking levels is presented:

> *Counselor:* Well according to what you said last week, you typically drink about 30 drinks per week. What do you think is typical of other students?
> *Client:* I don't know, maybe about 20 drinks a week?
> *Counselor:* Actually, the average is about 6 drinks a week. What do you think about that?
> *Client:* No way! Most of my friends drink more than me.
> *Counselor:* Hard to believe. But you bring up a good point. Most people hang out with others who drink at similar levels.
> *Client:* I never thought of it that way.

This type of interchange is followed by a discussion about setting a goal to moderate drinking frequency, binge drinking, or drinking in high-risk situations. Studies that have tested motivational enhancement have frequently used a two-session model in which the first session consists of assessment and rapport building and the second session focuses on feedback and goal setting (Dimeff et al., 1999).

Alcohol Skills Training

Skills training approaches teach clients how to drink more responsibly and manage high-risk situations that can trigger binge drinking or drinking in risky situations. A variety of alcohol-specific skills are taught, including how to self-monitor weekly drinking, estimate blood alcohol levels (Dimeff et al., 1999), set drinking limits, pace drinking (e.g., by alternating alcohol and nonalcohol drinks or having no more than one drink an hour), and refuse drinks (Dimeff et al., 1999; Fromme, Marlatt, Baer, & Kivlahan, 1994). In addition, programs may include more general life skills such as meditation, exercise, and stress management (Larimer & Cronce, 2002). These programs are usually delivered in a group format of approximately six sessions (e.g., Fromme et al., 1994).

In these programs, students are initially asked to monitor their daily drinking, noting amount, place, time, persons present, and mood (Fromme et al., 1994). The students' self-monitoring is then used to identify situations in which drinking may be risky (e.g., drinking and driving) or excessive. During the session, coping plans for key situations are developed and rehearsed. An interesting finding in this area is that simply having students regularly monitor what they drink each day can, by itself, significantly reduce their drinking (Larimer & Cronce, 2002).

Although these programs show promise (Larimer & Cronce, 2002), it should be noted that they assume that clients are ready to change their drinking habits. Thus, these programs are best suited for motivated students or those who have already been provided motivational enhancement and are now ready to make changes. Integrated programs emphasize motivational enhancement strategies during early sessions and then include skills training components in subsequent sessions (e.g., Dimeff et al., 1999).

High-Risk Groups

High-risk groups within the student population include athletes, adult children of alcoholics (ACOAs), students who are mandated for university policy violations, Greek members, and first-year students (Dimeff et al., 1999; Flemming, 2002; Larimer & Cronce, 2002). It is surprising that only a handful of intervention studies have tested athletes, ACOAs, and mandated students. One study tested a multicomponent skills training intervention with athletes but did not find a significant effect for the program (Marcello, Danish, & Stolberg, 1989). Marlatt et al. (1998) found that the motivational enhancement interventions were comparably effective for ACOA and non-ACOA students. Finally, Flynn and Brown (1991) found that an alcohol education class was not effective with mandated students, but Fromme and Corbin (2004) found that a two-session multicomponent group intervention, similar to the integrated intervention discussed above, was equally effective for mandated and voluntary students.

Greek members have been shown to be among the heaviest drinking students on campus (Wechsler & Dowdall, 1995). Education, motivation enhancement, and alcohol skills training programs have been evaluated on this population (Larimer & Cronce, 2002). In general, both motivational enhancement and skill-based programs show promise, although the quality of studies in this area makes this conclusion tentative. The best designed study (Marlatt et al., 1998) in this area found that Greek members reduced their drinking significantly but still remained in the problem-drinking range.

A number of studies have yielded positive results with populations of first-year college students (Larimer & Cronce, 2002; Marlatt et al., 1998). Results indicate that both motivational enhancement and alcohol skills training are effective in reducing drinking and associated adverse consequences.

In summary, the interventions found to work with the general student population of problem drinkers seem to also be effective with these high-risk groups. This conclusion, however, is tempered for athletes, ACOAs, and mandated students because of the paucity of data available on these groups.

Indications and Contraindications for Brief Interventions

Brief interventions are most indicated for students whose drinking problems range from drinking in hazardous situations to meeting criteria for alcohol abuse (Flemming, 2002) or even mild alcohol dependence (Dimeff et al., 1999). If these interventions are not sufficient to change excessive or hazardous drinking, the counselor should consider a step up in intensity, such as more extended counseling with an alcohol specialist on campus or in the community. There is some evidence that those students who undergo a brief intervention are more likely to follow through on a referral for more intensive treatment than are those who have not participated in brief counseling (Dimeff et al., 1999; Larimer & Cronce, 2002; Marlatt, 1996).

Brief interventions, however, are not indicated for students who either show signs of moderate to severe dependence or have other psychological or drug problems. Signs of more serious dependence include symptoms of withdrawal, heavy daily drinking that has persisted for longer than 6 months, and medical or psychological problems that are associated with drinking. Significant psychological problems that would contraindicate these brief interventions include comorbid conditions such as serious depression, suicidality, bipolar disorder, or a history of psychotic episodes. Finally, drinking may be part of a more pervasive drug problem that needs to be evaluated by a substance abuse professional. Students with these types of conditions should be referred to appropriate campus or community-based agencies for evaluation and treatment.

Campus Considerations

Many colleges lack screening, intervention, and referral systems that are tailored to the needs of their particular campus. There are several issues to consider in the development of a comprehensive system.

The first area of consideration involves the development of procedures for screening and referral. It is important that screenings for problem drinkers take place at sites throughout the campus because most problem drinkers will not voluntarily present at the college counseling center for assistance in changing their drinking behaviors (Vik et al., 2000). Therefore, it is necessary for counselors to collaborate with other student affairs units in which there are professionals who regularly interact with problem drinkers in both academic and social realms. Counselors can encourage all student affairs professionals to conduct basic screenings during their standard contacts with students, using the questions outlined previously, and to refer those students who screen positive to the appropriate campus site (Foote et al., 2004).

Next, specific procedures for managing these types of referrals need to be determined. College counseling centers typically serve as the primary site for providing formal alcohol assessment and brief interventions such as motivational enhancement and alcohol skills training groups. At colleges with more specialized programs, however, professionals in wellness education or other areas of student health could be designated to provide such services. In addition, a system of off-campus referrals needs to be established for those students who require more intensive interventions.

A final area of consideration is adequate administrative and financial support for the implementation of these types of efforts. Administrators should play a key role in the development of policies and procedures necessary for maintaining a comprehensive screening, referral, and treatment system. Counselors can be instrumental in educating administrators regarding the time, cost-efficiency, and effectiveness of brief screenings and interventions.

Future Trends

Although effective assessment and intervention approaches have been identified, several challenges remain. First, training considerations for disseminating these approaches campuswide have largely been ignored. There is a need to examine effective and feasible ways of systematically making training available. All counseling center staff should be trained in the strategies and programs outlined in this chapter. In turn, counselors can take the lead in providing professional development opportunities for all student affairs staff and administrators regarding strategies for effective screening, advising, and referrals of problem drinkers. For example, at Louisiana State University, we implemented a workshop for staff covering such topics as (a) the scope of the alcohol problem on the campus; (b) the continuum of problem drinking; (c) screening, advising, and referral procedures; and (d) specific MI strategies. Modeling and student role-plays were used to help participants master the concepts and skills. The program emphasized how screening, referral, and treatment could be systematically coordinated within university channels.

A second challenge is addressing gaps in knowledge about treating problem drinkers. Effective treatments for high-risk groups need further development.

In addition, although there is evidence that treatments that are effective with males may not yield comparable results with female problem drinkers, little work has been done on tailoring treatments to gender differences (Fromme & Corbin, 2004; Larimer & Cronce, 2002). Finally, little attention has been paid to programs that bridge the gap from the college to community treatment. There is no information to our knowledge about rates of successful referral, retention, or program outcome for referred college students in the community.

Screening, assessment, and brief interventions have pivotal roles in the overall college response to curbing the drinking problem on college campuses. Current research indicates that identification and treatment of problem drinkers have a large payoff in terms of HR and enhanced academic performance for problem drinkers and those around them (Flemming, 2002; Larimer & Cronce, 2002). The key challenge in the future will be the systematic implementation of these programs across college campuses.

References

Aertgeerts, B., Buntinx, F., Bande-Knops, J., Vandermeulen, C., Roelants, M., Ansoms, S., et al. (2000). The value of CAGE, CUGE, and AUDIT in screening for alcohol abuse and dependence among college freshmen. *Alcoholism: Clinical and Experimental Research, 24,* 53–57.

American Psychiatric Association. (2000). *Diagnostic and statistical manual of mental disorders* (4th ed., text rev.). Washington, DC: Author.

Baer, J. S., Marlatt, G. A., Kivlahan, D. R., Fromme, K., Larimer, M. E., & Williams, E. (1992). An experimental test of three methods of alcohol risk reduction with young adults. *Journal of Consulting and Clinical Psychology, 60,* 974–979.

Barbor, T. F., & Grant, M. (1989). From clinical research to secondary prevention: International collaboration in the development of the Alcohol Use Disorders Identification Test (AUDIT). *American Health and Research World, 13,* 371–374.

Bosari, B., & Carey, K. B. (2000). Effects of brief motivational intervention with college student drinkers. *Journal of Consulting and Clinical Psychology, 68,* 728–733.

Clements, R. (1999). Prevalence of alcohol-use disorders and alcohol-related problems in a college student sample. *Journal of American College Health, 48,* 111–118.

Core Institute. (2004). *Core alcohol and drug survey results.* Retrieved March 7, 2005, from http://www.siu.edu/~coreinst/

Dimeff, L. A., Baer, J. S., Kivlahan, D. R., & Marlatt, G. A. (1999). *Brief Alcohol Screening and Intervention for College Students (BASICS): A harm reduction approach.* New York: Guilford Press.

Ewing, J. A. (1984). Detecting alcoholism. *Journal of the American Medical Association, 252,* 1905–1907.

Flemming, M. (2002). *Clinical protocols to reduce high risk drinking in college students: The college drinking prevention curriculum for health care providers.* Bethesda, MD: National Institute on Alcohol Abuse, Task Force on College Drinking.

Flynn, C. A., & Brown, W. E. (1991). The effects of a mandatory alcohol education program on college problem drinkers. *Journal of Alcohol Education, 37,* 15–24.

Foote, J., Wilkens, C., & Vavagiakis, P. (2004). A national survey of alcohol screening and referral in college health centers. *Journal of American College Health, 5,* 148–157.

Fromme, K., & Corbin, W. (2004). Prevention of heavy drinking and associated negative consequences among mandated and voluntary college students. *Journal of Consulting and Clinical Psychology, 72,* 1038–1049.

Fromme, K., Marlatt, G. A., Baer, J. S., & Kivlahan, D. R. (1994). The alcohol skills training program: A group intervention for young adult drinkers. *Journal of Substance Abuse Treatment, 11,* 143–154.

Gintner, G. G., & Choate, L. H. (2003). Stage-matched motivational interventions for college student binge drinkers. *Journal of College Counseling, 6,* 99–113.

Helmkamp, J. C., Hungerford, D. W., Williams, J. M., Manley, W. G., Furbee, P. M., Horn, K. A., et al. (2003). Screening and brief intervention for alcohol problems among college students treated in a university hospital emergency department. *Journal of American College Health, 52,* 7–16.

Institute of Medicine. (1990). *Broadening the base of treatment for alcohol problems.* Washington, DC: National Academy Press.

Johnston, L., O'Malley, P., & Bachman, J. (1998). *National survey results on drug use from the Monitoring the Future Study: 1975–1997* (NIH Publication No. 98-4346). Bethesda, MD: National Institutes of Health, National Institute on Drug Abuse.

Knight, J., Wechsler, H., Kuo, M., Seibring, M., Weitzman, E., & Schuckit, M. (2002). Alcohol abuse and dependence among U.S. college students. *Journal of Studies on Alcohol, 63,* 263–270.

Larimer, M., & Cronce, J. (2002). Identification, prevention and treatment: A review of individual-focused strategies to reduce problematic alcohol consumption by college students. *Journal of Studies on Alcohol, 63*(Suppl. 14), 148–163.

Marcello, R., Danish, S., & Stolberg, A. (1989). An evaluation of strategies developed to prevent substance abuse among student-athletes. *Sport Psychology, 3,* 196–211.

Marlatt, G. A. (1996). Harm reduction: Come as you are. *Addictive Behaviors, 21,* 779–788.

Marlatt, G. A., Baer, J. S., Kivlahan, D. R., Dimeff, L. A., Larimer, M. E., Quigley, L. A., et al. (1998). Screening and brief intervention for college student drinkers: Results from a 2-year follow-up assessment. *Journal of Consulting Psychology, 66,* 604–615.

Meilman, P., Cashin, J., McKillip, J., & Presley, C. (1998). Understanding the three national databases on collegiate alcohol and drug use. *Journal of American College Health, 46,* 159–162.

Miller, W. R., & Rollnick, S. (1991). *Motivational interviewing: Preparing people to change addictive behavior.* New York: Guilford Press.

National Institute on Alcohol Abuse and Alcoholism, Alcoholism National Advisory Council. (2002). *A call to action: Changing the culture of drinking at U.S. colleges* (NIH Publication No. 02-5010). Bethesda, MD: National Institutes of Health.

Neighbors, C., Palmer, R., & Larimer, M. (2004). Interest and participation in a college student alcohol intervention study as a function of typical drinking. *Journal of Studies on Alcohol, 65,* 736–740.

O'Malley, P. M., & Johnston, L. D. (2002). Epidemiology of alcohol and other drug use among American college students. *Journal of Studies on Alcohol, 14,* 23–39.

Prochaska, J., DiClemente, C., & Norcross, J. (1992). In search of how people change: Applications to addictive behaviors. *American Psychologist, 47,* 1102–1114.

Reinert, D. F., & Allen, J. P. (2002). The Alcohol Use Disorders Identification Test (AUDIT): A review of recent research. *Alcoholism: Clinical and Experimental Research, 26,* 272–279.

Taj, N., Devera-Sales, A., & Vinson, D. C. (1998). Screening for problem drinking: Does a single question work? *The Journal of Family Practice, 46,* 328–335.

Vik, P. W., Culbertson, K. A., & Sellers, K. (2000). Readiness to change drinking among heavy-drinking college students. *Journal of Studies on Alcohol, 6,* 674–680.

Volk, R. J., Steinbauer, J. R., Cantor, S. B., & Holzer, C. E. (1997). The Alcohol Use Disorders Identification Test (AUDIT) as a screen for at-risk drinking in primary care patients of different racial/ethnic backgrounds. *Addiction, 92,* 197–206.

Wechsler, H., & Dowdall, G. W. (1995). Correlates of college student binge drinking. *American Journal of Public Health, 85,* 921–926.

Wechsler, H., Kelley, K., & Weitzman, E. R. (2000). What colleges are doing about student binge drinking: A survey of college administrators. *Journal of American College Health, 48,* 219–226.

Wechsler, H., Lee, J. E., Kuo, M., & Lee, H. (2000). College binge drinking in the 1990s: A continuing problem: Results of the Harvard School of Public Health 1999 College Alcohol Study. *Journal of American College Health, 48,* 199–210.

Wechsler, H., Lee, J., Kuo, M., Seibring, M., Nelson, T., & Lee, H. (2002). Trends in college binge drinking during a period of increased prevention efforts. *Journal of American College Health, 50,* 203–217.

Wechsler, H., Nelson, T., & Weitzman, E. (2000). From knowledge to action: How Harvard's College Alcohol Study can help your campus design a campaign against student alcohol use. *Change, 32,* 38–43.

Weitzman, E. R., Nelson, T. F., Lee, H., & Wechsler, H. (2004). Reducing drinking and related harms in college: Evaluation of the "a matter of degree" program. *American Journal of Preventive Medicine, 27,* 187–196.

Werch, C., Pappas, D., & Castellon-Vogel, E. (1996). Drug use prevention efforts at colleges and universities in the United States. *Substance Abuse and Misuse, 31,* 65–80.

White, H. R., & Labouvie, E. W. (1989). Towards the assessment of adolescent problem drinking. *Journal of Studies on Alcohol, 50,* 30–37.

Yalisove, D. (1998). The origin and evolution of the disease concept of treatment. *Journal of Studies on Alcohol, 59,* 469–472.

13

Counseling for Success: Assisting Students in Academic Jeopardy

Brian Wlazelek and Kathleen Hartman

Introduction

The college experience offers many personal and social growth opportunities for students; however, the primary task remains academic. Students and parents bank on academic success and the completion of a degree program to open doors to a satisfying career and the many associated rewards. For this reason, real or threatened, academic failure represents a crisis in the life of a student, the ripples of which are felt in family and other significant relationships.

For college counselors, it is tempting to be most concerned with those crises that are life-threatening, such as suicide, chronic substance abuse, and serious eating disorders. These issues certainly require immediate and careful attention to ensure the safety of the student and to avoid disruption of the institution. Yet, academic failure also represents a crisis in the life of a student. Counselors, however, may not experience the same sense of urgency in responding to academic failure or the same power to intervene.

Unlike other crises in counseling, academic problems may creep up slowly and not be apparent until it is too late to intervene. Counselors need to look for and respond to academic problems as early as possible. Wlazelek and Coulter (1999) demonstrated the potential value of involving students in academic jeopardy in an academic counseling approach offered by counseling center staff. This type of counseling plays an important role in a well-rounded counseling program.

Academic failure has myriad causes and may itself be the cause of psychological, interpersonal, and financial consequences for students. The impact of academic failure extends beyond the direct effect on the life of an individual student to that of the educational institution itself. The effects of student academic failure touch a college in obvious ways, such as revenue loss and poor retention rates, and in more subtle ways, such as campus climate and faculty satisfaction.

Studies have revealed that almost 40% of the students who go to college leave before earning a degree (U.S. Department of Education, 2001) and that more than one third of these students leave in their first year (American College Testing Program, 1998). Although there are many reasons why students do not earn degrees, one is certainly academic failure.

Assessment Issues

When the risk of academic failure exists, counselors must treat it as an emergency in the life of a student. This means devoting time to a careful assessment of academic difficulties when other concerns may be of greater urgency to the student and of greater interest to the counselor. Although academic assessment does not take center stage when life-threatening clinical issues are present, ignoring academic performance in favor of psychological concerns leaves the student vulnerable to failure, which may compound other life difficulties and have long-lasting effects.

Intake Process

Although counselors develop their own format and outline for intake assessment, it is recommended that the intake process include an in-depth inquiry into academic performance along with some verification of performance whenever possible. It is also helpful for counselors to gather information about a student's academic performance before meeting the student so that questions about inconsistencies or patterns of performance can be addressed.

Exploration of academic performance should be more than asking, "How are your classes going?" It is important, for example, to understand the value that the student places on education and the college experience. For some students, college holds little personal meaning, and the students' efforts are understandable and consistent with their value structure.

Some students enter college reluctantly and at the urging of family members who see college as the best path to a lucrative and stable career. Studies have shown that parents are one of the most influential factors in students' decision to attend college (Elkins, Braxton, & James, 2000; Nieves & Hartman, 2001). Some students believe that they need a college degree in order to be happy or successful, but they would actually be happier pursuing a path that does not require a college degree. Other students view college as a way to extend adolescence or to delay entering the work world.

Turner, Husman, and Schallert (2002) focused on the importance of students' goals in working with students experiencing academic failure. Some students experiencing failure lack clear goals for their majors or careers. A lack of academic goals can result in a lack of motivation, which, in turn, can result in academic failure.

For students who have been pushed into college by family, or are looking for a way to extend their adolescence, setting clear goals may not be a pressing concern. Just experiencing the freedom of college life may be their only immediate goal. Not all students have the seriousness of purpose, goal directedness, or perseverance necessary to perform well academically.

Time Management

A recent survey suggests that only about 11% of full-time students spend the amount of time studying that faculty say is necessary in order to succeed in college (Hoover, 2004). Some students who were able to earn acceptable grades in high school with little or no effort are surprised and disappointed when they discover they cannot do the same in college. Students may be reluctant to acknowledge academic weaknesses or to accept that old habits no longer work.

Deficits in test-taking, time management, note-taking, memorization, and other academic skills may also be the basis for academic failure. As many as 30% of students who enter college are deficient in the reading, writing, and math skills that are needed at the college level (Fielstein & Bush, 1998). Students who do not have academic role models in their parents and may not have taken courses in high school in anticipation of entering college may be at particular risk for academic failure. Parents' level of education has been associated with academic persistence, as has completion of rigorous course work in high school (U.S. Department of Education, 2002; see also chapter 7 in this book, "From Blue Collar to Ivory Tower: Counseling First-Generation, Working-Class Students").

The counselor should also explore changes in the student's basic academic behavior. Have there been changes in study habits and the amount of time devoted to class preparation? As a result of the difficulties that led to seeking counseling, is the student approaching the current semester in a different manner than has resulted in success in the past? For example, prior to the current difficulties, a student may have worked ahead in certain areas or spread work out over the semester. Deviation from a student's past successful approach to a semester may not result in immediate problems but may lead to changes that compound over the semester and contribute to failure.

The possibilities of what can happen in the life of a student during any academic semester and affect academic performance are endless. Divorce, legal problems, illness, loss, military service, termination of employment, relationship breakups, and many other life events may result in a necessary reordering of life priorities and a shifting of focus and resources to address the life stressor that the student faces. Depending on the nature of the situational stressor and the demands of the semester, academic performance may suffer and add to the student's struggles. Whereas situational stressors resolve, academic transcripts are forever.

Profiles of students of the new millennium suggest that a larger percentage of students are working long hours or juggling family responsibilities while attending college than in the past. A national survey of college students revealed that 46% of full-time working students worked more than 25 hours per week, and nearly half of those students reported that they were working enough hours to negatively affect their academic achievement (King & Bannon, 2002). These students surveyed considered themselves primarily students, but work hours showed that their employee status often exceeded that of their student status.

Hey, Calderon, and Seabert (2003) found that working while in college adds more stress to some students' lives, interfering with school responsibilities. Such students who experience academic failure need to see the reality that working too many hours takes a toll on academic achievement and persistence. Schmid and Abell (2003) also found a correlation between students working full-time and the rate of nonreturn. Many students may believe they can "do it all," but when they fail, they may blame themselves without understanding that they can change their work or study patterns in order to improve academic performance. Working too many hours for lower wages can keep students from completing a degree that will provide them with a higher salary. What is more important can be a very difficult choice for students.

Also, the realities of child care, financial requirements, and relationship needs place students in the position of making difficult choices about the allocation of their time and effort. Mercer (1993) identified the above realities as barriers to persistence. Students with young children may interrupt or stop their studies, and the energy needed to balance school and family demands can hurt academic performance (Carney-Crompton & Tan, 2002). Students may see few options for change when facing academic struggles related to the competing demands for time in their lives, and the result could be not reaching their academic goals.

Still other students become too involved in sports, fraternities and sororities, student government, and other clubs and activities, spending more time on activities than on studying for class. Although all of these opportunities bring rewards for students (Shanette & Aries, 1999), both immediately and in their future careers, problems arise when academics become secondary.

Behavioral and Psychological Concerns

The counselor should also determine whether there have been any specific changes in the student's behavior. Has the student noticed changes in attention or concentration? Is class behavior different in terms of participation and relationships with faculty and peers? Is the student expending as much effort as necessary to master the information in courses? Is he or she prepared for classes and able to make use of lecture information? Has the student noticed any difference in his or her ability to memorize or organize information, especially in testing situations?

Students present with a wide range of difficulties, from attention-deficit/hyperactivity disorder and depression to personality disorders and psychosis. The symptoms and consequences of any of these problems may be associated with academic failure. Svanum and Zody (2001) noted, in their review of psychopathology and academic performance, that psychological difficulties may have an impact on college students primarily by affecting their productivity. In their own study, however, they did not find overall that students who met criteria for a *Diagnostic and Statistical Manual of Mental Disorders* (3rd ed., rev.; American Psychiatric Association, 1987) Axis I diagnosis were more likely to experience academic failure. They did note that the presence of certain disorders, such as substance abuse, was associated with lower grade point averages. At the same time, a diagnosis of anxiety disorders was associated with higher grade point averages. In their conclusion, Svanum and Zody asserted that the relationship between college academic performance and psychopathology is a complex one and that it may be more useful for students to attribute academic failure to factors over which they exert control, rather than internal psychiatric disorders.

Identifying Academic Strengths and Weaknesses

Finally, it is helpful for the counselor to ask the student about performance in each current class, rather than accepting a global impression of academic performance in a given semester. Feelings of shame may motivate a student to minimize or deny academic difficulties. Students may be fearful of failing or may be encouraged to withdraw from specific classes or the college because of difficulties. It is helpful to determine what information students are using to assess their current academic performance. Judgments based on a careful recording of graded assignments and course syllabi are likely to be more useful and reliable than impressions without evidence.

When academic failure is a risk, the counselor has a legitimate need to know a student's current and past academic performance as a means of determining the extent of the current struggles and the type of intervention necessary. In many cases, counselors have access to academic transcripts and midterm grades or progress reports, and students may be willing to share this information if it is viewed as necessary for assistance.

Students receive feedback about academic performance during a given semester in the form of graded assignments and, more formally, through midterm and final grades. It makes little sense to wait for a final course grade to deal with the issue of academic performance in the counseling relationship, but if students are not forthcoming about academic performance, this may be the only choice. Despite the many opportunities for feedback about performance, factors such as student disinterest, disorganization, distraction, and shame may stand in the way.

In addition to interviewing for areas of deficit and weakness, it is helpful for the counselor to inquire about the student's strengths and abilities. Students bring a history of learning experiences to the college setting and are often able to identify areas of academic strength on which interventions can be built. Students may be aware of ways in which they coped with prior academic difficulties that can be used to navigate current academic struggles. For example, the following assessment questions may be of value:

1. Are there classes in your current semester that are going better than others? What makes the difference?

2. When you think about times that you've struggled before in school, what helped you get through?
3. What is your greatest strength academically?
4. What do you notice about the times when you are most successful in courses?

Counseling Implications

Intervention

Motivation and Goal Setting

If students are in college for the wrong reasons, academic failure may very well follow, and students can benefit from counseling that focuses not on the failure alone but on what the students' real strengths and interests are, followed by realistic goal setting and honest discussion about what they really can do with their lives. Some students may never have been given permission to think outside of the college mind-set and enter the workplace or train for a profession that does not require going to college. Likewise, students who are in college at their families' urging benefit from understanding what their own goals are so that college becomes their choice.

Students need to come to the realization that a lack of goals and motivation may be at the root of poor academic performance. If so, they can begin the process of setting short-term goals, even if those goals entail leaving college for the workplace in order to gain more maturity or experience in terms of making decisions for their future.

Although some students may have the goal of getting a college degree, they may be unsure of a major or be in the wrong major, which could result in poor academic performance. Students who do not enjoy the classes they are in, or who see no relevance to a possible future, may not put in the time and effort to achieve success. Likewise, those students in a major for which they are not well-suited may be fighting a losing battle by remaining in a program when it is clear they are not able to handle the courses. For instance, students with low math ability who enroll as business majors may find themselves failing foundation courses in such areas as accounting and statistics. Students who do not have innate artistic ability but want to pursue a painting or design major are also at risk, not only for disappointment but also for failure. These students can benefit from work in goal setting and career assessment early in their college careers. Finding a good fit may make a significant difference in a student's self-esteem, perseverance, and academic performance.

Students who are getting their first taste of freedom may benefit from seeing the connection between their actions and their academic failure. Such students can learn to balance the enjoyable activities that come with freedom with their responsibilities as students. Especially for students who see success in college as an all-or-nothing proposition, the realization that a social life is possible while studying can be empowering. Learning to find the right balance is the key.

Some students do not have the academic skill sets necessary to succeed in college. These students need to come to this realization and avail themselves of support programs to make up for such deficits. Support programs such as tutoring, study skills courses, supplemental instruction, and remedial courses have been successful in improving academic performance (Congos, 1998; Lipsky & Ender, 1990).

Initiating Change

A factor that may be overlooked in working with students in academic jeopardy is the students' readiness for change and personal values, specifically the value placed on education. Many of the common recommendations and referrals for academic difficulties, such as tutoring and study skills development, may have limited success in the lives of students who have not made the decision to become actively involved in a change process or who do not value the college experience. Students may lack the self-awareness necessary to see the inconsistencies between their stated values and their actual behaviors. The decision to truly "become a student" may be fundamental to academic success because it carries with it the motivation required to engage in a process of change.

Considering stages of change and their influence in the process of change (Prochaska & Norcross, 2003), it is helpful to understand where students are in the change process when addressing academic failure. Students who fail to recognize that they have a problem (precontemplation stage) have counseling needs different from those who recognize their plight and are planning some sort of immediate action in response to the academic difficulty (preparation stage). For example, if academic failure is determined to be the result of skills deficits, active interventions such as tutoring and skills development may be most appropriate for students who acknowledge the problem and are ready to take action. Referring students to remedial academic services who are not willing to actively participate in a process of change may result in premature dropout or even a failure to follow through with recommendations.

Kelly (1996) noted that immediate student reactions to academic failure differ across the domains of affect, cognition, and behavior. In the affective realm, students tend to experience global, negative affective reactions, especially when academic outcomes run counter to expectations. In the cognitive arena, failure may be attributed to controllable or uncontrollable internal causes and stable or unstable external causes. Internal–controllable and external–unstable attributions of failure are characterized as most favorable in terms of future change. Kelly commented that, over time, affective reactions are more specific depending on student attributions.

Reporting the work of Arkin, Detchon, and Maruyama (1982), Kelly (1996) noted that attributing failure to internal–uncontrollable factors is related to greater feelings of shame. Similarly, over time, attributing academic failure to uncontrollable factors may result in lowered self-esteem and self-efficacy and reduced persistence as a behavioral consequence. In his discussion of theories of motivation, Seifert (2004) suggested that students with a greater sense of efficacy credit outcomes to their own abilities. These abilities are not fixed, such as "stupidity," but rather they are related to what the student learned or knew at a particular time. Attributions may be a fundamental area of exploration and intervention with students experiencing academic failure.

Treatment Planning

Developing a plan of treatment for students in academic jeopardy requires counselors to make some basic judgments following assessment. If academic problems are determined to be the result of psychological or situational difficulties, the focus is on academic adjustments that make it possible for the student to stay involved in treatment and again become fully engaged in his or her education. This may involve advocacy, policy interpretation, and referral. In these cases, the assumption is that students are interested and motivated to achieve academically but have been impaired by the symptoms or life situations with which they are dealing.

If the determination is made that psychological distress is the result of academic failure, it is valuable to explore attributions concerning the academic failure and the student's readiness to participate in the change process as noted previously. Aside from making appropriate academic referrals, it is important to address the basis of the failure and the emotional, cognitive, and behavioral effects of the failure, such as shame, diminished sense of efficacy, and discouragement. The counseling task with these students is encouraging realistic self-appraisal, addressing negative affect, correcting faulty attributions, and facilitating decision making in light of these academic experiences.

For most students, integrating academic failure into their self-perception is a difficult process that requires respect, sensitivity, and patience on the part of the counselor. Some students who are capable of success in a particular academic context will give up prematurely, and some students who are unlikely to succeed will persist. Respect for students' right to autonomy is central, balanced with the facts of performance.

In the midst of academic failure, students may lose sight of the resources they bring to their academic struggles. Counselors have the opportunity to identify student strengths and competencies and to explore ways they can best use those abilities. Exploring past academic successes, and using this information to construct a strategy for approaching current difficulties, provides a ready prescription for change. These student strengths may be specific academic skills or more general attitudes that facilitate engagement, encouragement, and persistence.

When situational difficulties are at the root of failure, counselors can play an important role in helping students realistically adjust the number of hours devoted to work, study, and relaxation in light of the situational stressors that are being faced and the workload of the semester. These considerations are the basis of a conversation with students about the realities of dealing with multiple life demands or temporary difficulties while attending college. Knowing the student's unique life situations will help in counseling the student toward the best possible balance among work, family/social, and academic demands.

Students can benefit from identifying long-term goals and planning the path that will best get them there.

Policies and Procedural Considerations

Although college counselors are an important resource for students experiencing academic failure, colleges differ widely in terms of what departments and personnel are delegated responsibility for this student population. Similarly, institutions differ in the rigidity of roles and the extent to which units isolate or cooperate with regard to students' needs. Given these differences, it is important for counselors to understand the expectations and limits of their role in working with students who have academic problems.

Wlazelek and Coulter (1999) demonstrated that intervention by counseling center personnel can be effective when working with students in academic jeopardy, although the intervention used was academic counseling, rather than personal counseling. Abelman and Molina (2001) found that, more than the content of the contact with students in academic jeopardy, the intrusiveness of the involvement was important in improving performance. Although more specifically an advising approach, intrusiveness referred to a process of actively reaching out to students experiencing academic failure and initiating personal contact. This is a process for which counselors are well-suited.

In some cases, the counseling focus will be limited to the psychological consequences or causes of academic failure. However, a clear advantage for students working with counselors in a college counseling center is the bridge that college counselors provide between the psychological needs of the students and the academic demands and culture of the institution. College counselors are uniquely positioned to psychologically assist students with academic struggles because of their knowledge of the academic context. To maximize this benefit to students, counselors must become familiar with academic policies and procedures that may be meaningful when helping students navigate academic struggles.

Academic policies vary greatly between institutions in terms of how helpful they are to students who are experiencing academic difficulties. For some, the presence of a psychological problem may become the basis of a request for an exception to a policy, such as academic dismissal. Counselors may also need to help students weigh options regarding dropping those courses that are most troublesome. Understanding the consequences of these decisions helps facilitate decision making. At times, it may be helpful or necessary to consult with the student's assigned advisor to gather information required to make an informed decision. It is also possible that decisions such as these are best made by the student's advisor, and counseling becomes the arena in which the student can process the emotional consequences of decisions that are made.

Counselors should understand the circumstances under which policy exceptions are granted for students when psychological problems or extenuating factors are present. Also, when possible academic adjustments are being explored, it is important to be aware of any academic, financial, and personal "costs" that may be associated with these adjustments.

When counselors examine academic options, it is useful to weigh other considerations, such as financial aid consequences, progress toward graduation, and timely completion of course sequences. Counselors should help students to determine whether and when it is best to take a semester off or to attend another institution. In light of that possible decision, counselors should know what the implications are if a student withdraws for a semester and the procedure for returning to the institution. In all cases, it is important to coordinate services with faculty or staff members who have a primary advising role for the student.

Support Services

If specific academic support is required in addition to personal counseling, it is important to be aware of academic resources on campus and how students access these services. This includes knowing the range and reputation of the various academic support services that are available on campus. Students may need assistance in sorting through the available options if a centralized intake and referral service is not available. It is helpful to establish some way to gather feedback about student participation in support programs and progress toward academic improvement. Students also benefit from self-monitoring, which requires knowledge of how to track performance in individual courses and to use resources such as progress reports, midterm grades, and meetings with individual faculty members.

Counselors may be able to verify and document psychological difficulties or extenuating circumstances with student permission and share this information with faculty in support of requests for accommodations or extra support. Counselors can also seek exceptions to policies on a student's behalf or refer a student to others on campus who can be advocates.

If students are referred off campus for services, counselors can function as a campus contact to address academic questions so that academic needs and success remain an element of treatment. Also, counselors can interpret academic policies and options to family members when students need help in discussing their academic situation.

Campus Considerations

It is important for counselors who work with students with academic difficulties to be aware of the campus climate and to stay up-to-date on what is happening on and off campus that could affect student success. Many concerns surface outside of the counselor's office that may affect a student's ability to do well academically, despite initial support from the counselor. These concerns may include (a) the occurrence of crime on and around campus; (b) the social atmosphere of the campus and the student's ability to avoid situations in which alcohol and other drugs are involved; (c) the student's involvement in sororities and fraternities; (d) the student's living environment, which may be rife with interpersonal conflicts, unhealthy living conditions, or lack of space to study freely and without interruption; (e) the student's difficulty with courses, professors, or advisors, which may cause him or her not to seek the extra help needed to do well in classes; and (f) financial problems, which can lead the student to give up or work instead of studying.

Counselors can work together with faculty, administration, and staff involved in all areas of campus life in order to understand what other issues students may be dealing with when they come in with academic difficulties. It is valuable to learn how students with academic difficulties are viewed by faculty and staff. Negative attitudes on the part of faculty and staff about academic struggles may prevent students from seeking help or acting on other recommendations offered in the counseling relationship.

Counselors can also consult with campus police to learn about crime statistics and prevention if safety is a factor that distracts students from focusing on academics. Counselors can work with staff in health and wellness facilities to understand the health issues that students face, including substance use, so that proper referrals can be made. This also may be true for counselors who work in colleges with a prominent Greek organization presence. Residence life staff may be a valuable resource for students with academic difficulties who may be experiencing problems with roommates or other conditions with their on-campus living that may be interfering with their studies.

Counselors can also advocate for students who face courses that have been historically difficult for students by helping to secure supplemental instructors or tutors for those courses. Furthermore, students can be referred to individual tutoring or to department chairs to improve advisor–advisee relationships.

Finally, given the potential impact that academic failure has on financial aid, staff members from the office of financial aid can be important allies in comprehensive planning with students in academic jeopardy. Financial aid staff can also meet with students whose financial situations have put undue strain on their study time so that these students can learn about financing alternatives, debt consolidation, or balancing school and jobs.

Counselors cannot work in a vacuum because students do not present the same problems or the same reasons for academic difficulty. Although the responsibility for academic success lies within the students, and the cause of difficulty may as well, the fact that the campus climate can play a role cannot be overlooked. When counselors create strong relationships with other offices and programs across campus, students are better served.

Future Trends

Current trends suggest that continuing to find the most successful strategies for helping students with academic difficulties succeed in college is an important endeavor for counselors, especially in light of the rewards that students reap from completing a degree. Statistics continue to support the economic value of a college degree over a lifetime, ensuring the attractiveness of a college education. According to a Census Bureau report, people with a 4-year degree earn about

$2.1 million over their lifetimes, whereas high school graduates earn about $1.6 million (Day & Newburger, 2002). Studies reveal other benefits as well. For example, college graduates tend to save more, gain more professional mobility, improve the quality of life for their families, and enjoy more leisure activities (Institute for Higher Education Policy, 1998).

Yet, although the value of a college education is positive, many students attend college who are neither prepared for nor able to complete college-level work. Recent trends show not only a stronger record of academic achievement among high school students than in the past but also less commitment to the work that college will require. For example, a survey revealed that whereas 45.7% of high school students earned A averages in 2002, only 33.4% studied 6 or more hours a week (Sax, 2003). When entering college, freshmen are increasingly optimistic about doing well in college, and the combination of optimism and decreased study may lead to unrealistic academic expectations (Sax, 2003). Thompson, Geren, and Ruth (2002) noted that students do not always know how to look at themselves as learners or how to set goals, apply strategies, or apply the self-regulation necessary for academic success. If a student does not do well, it is the counselor's role to look at how optimistic the student was and how realistic the expectations were and need to be. This is especially important because one third of all freshmen who enter a 4-year public college will drop out before the sophomore year (Thompson et al., 2002).

Factors beyond academic preparedness will continue to affect the academic success of college students and the work of counselors with students experiencing academic difficulty. Trends include an increase in college students with serious psychological problems and an increase in the number of students seeking counseling ("Flood of Students," 2003). Another reported trend is an increase in the number of students who expect to take jobs in order to pay for their education (Sax, 2003).

As these trends continue, the role of the counselor will take on greater importance. Although counselors may need to take on expanding roles, their ability to work with students in academic jeopardy can lead these same students to academic success.

References

Abelman, R., & Molina, A. (2001). Style over substance revisited: A longitudinal analysis of intrusive intervention. *NACADA Journal, 21,* 32–39.

American College Testing Program. (1998). *National college dropout and graduation rates, 1997.* Retrieved September 17, 2005, from http://act.org/news/releases/1998/04-01-98.html

American Psychiatric Association. (1987). *Diagnostic and statistical manual of mental disorders* (3rd ed., rev.). Washington, DC: Author.

Arkin, R. M., Detchon, S. S., & Maruyama, G. M. (1982). The role of attribution, affect, and cognitive inference in test anxiety. *Journal of Personality and Social Psychology, 43,* 1111–1124.

Carney-Crompton, S., & Tan, J. (2002). Support systems, psychological functioning, and academic performance of nontraditional female students. *Adult Education Quarterly, 52,* 140–154.

Congos, D. H. (1998). Inside supplemental instruction sessions: One model of what happens that improves grades and retention. *Research and Teaching in Developmental Education, 15,* 47–61.

Day, J. C., & Newburger, E. C. (2002). *The big payoff: Educational attainment and synthetic estimates of work-life earning* (Current Population Reports, Special Studies). Retrieved September 21, 2005, from the U.S. Department of Commerce Web site: http://census.gov/prod/2002pubs/p23-210.pdf

Elkins, S. A., Braxton, J. M., & James, G. W. (2000). Tinto's separation stage and its influence on first-semester college student persistence. *Research in Higher Education, 41,* 251–268.

Fielstein, L. L., & Bush, L. K. (1998). Remedial students' perceptions: Pre-college decision making, satisfaction with the freshman year, and self-perception of academic abilities. *Journal of the First-Year Experience, 10,* 41–55.

Flood of students with psychological problems. (2003, March 7). *Chronicle of Higher Education, 49,* 26.

Hey, W., Calderon, K. S., & Seabert, D. (2003). Student work issues: Implications for college transitions and retention. *Journal of College Orientation and Transition, 10,* 35–41.

Hoover, E. (2004, November 26). Students study less than expected, survey finds. *Chronicle of Higher Education, 51,* 14.

Institute for Higher Education Policy. (1998). *Reaping the benefits: Defining the public and private value of going to college. The New Millennium Project on Higher Education Costs, Pricing, and Productivity.* Washington, DC: Author.

Kelly, K. N. (1996). Causes, reactions, and consequences of academic probation: A theoretical model. *NACADA Journal, 16,* 28–34.

King, T., & Bannon, E. (2002). *At what cost? The price that working students pay for a college education.* Washington, DC: U.S. Public Interest Group (ERIC Document Reproduction Service No. ED470026).

Lipsky, S. A., & Ender, S. C. (1990). Impact of a study skills course on probationary students' academic performance. *Journal of the Freshmen Year Experience, 2,* 7–15.

Mercer, D. L. (1993). Older coeds: Predicting who will stay this time. *Journal of Research and Development in Education, 26,* 153–163.

Nieves, E., & Hartman, K. (2001). Significant events or persons influencing college decisions of conditionally-admitted and early-admitted freshmen. *Research & Teaching in Developmental Education, 18,* 5–13.

Prochaska, J. O., & Norcross, J. C. (2003). Comparative conclusions: Toward a transtheoretical therapy. In J. O. Prochaska & J. C. Norcross (Eds.), *Systems of psychotherapy: A transtheoretical analysis* (5th ed., pp. 519–535). Pacific Grove, CA: Brooks/Cole.

Sax, L. J. (2003). Our incoming students: What are they like? *About Campus, 8,* 15–20.

Schmid, C., & Abell, P. (2003). Demographic risk factors, study patterns, and campus involvement as related to student success among Guildford Community College students. *Community College Review, 31,* 1–16.

Seifert, T. L. (2004). Understanding student motivation. *Educational Research, 46,* 137–149.

Shanette, R., & Aries, E. (1999). The Division III student-athlete: Academic performance, campus involvement, and growth. *Journal of College Student Development, 40,* 211–218.

Svanum, S., & Zody, Z. B. (2001). Psychopathology and college grades. *Journal of Counseling Psychology, 48,* 72–76.

Thompson, B. R., Geren, P. R., & Ruth, P. (2002). Classroom strategies for identifying and helping college students at risk for academic failure. *College Student Journal, 36,* 398–402.

Turner, J. E., Husman, J., & Schallert, D. L. (2002). The importance of students' goals in their emotional experience of academic failure: Investigating the precursors and consequences of shame. *Educational Psychologist, 37,* 79–89.

U.S. Department of Education. (2001). *High school academic curriculum and the persistence path through college.* Washington, DC: U.S. Department of Education, National Center for Education Statistics.

U.S. Department of Education. (2002). *The condition of education 2002 in brief.* Washington, DC: U.S. Department of Education, National Center for Education Statistics.

Wlazelek, B., & Coulter, L. P. (1999). The role of counseling services for students in academic jeopardy: A preliminary study. *Journal of College Counseling, 2,* 33–41.

14

Counseling Students Who Are Grieving: Finding Meaning in Loss

Donna Knox

Introduction

A growing interest in death and dying in the academic community over the past few decades has lead to an abundance of research and literature dedicated to the subject of loss and grief. As Toth, Stockton, and Browne (2000) noted, "In its intensity and longevity loss is like no other emotional response to a life event" (p. 238). Little has been written, however, specifically addressing the unique needs of traditional-age college students experiencing loss—the needs of a population that does not fit neatly into the category of adolescent or adult. Moreover, the seriousness and prevalence of students facing the loss of family members and close friends have largely gone unrecognized in colleges (Balk, 2001).

Surveys have indicated that from 40% to 70% of traditional-age students will experience the death of someone close to them during their college years (Tyson-Rawson, 1996b). For many such students, this death will be their first significant loss. The lack of experience with grief, combined with the intensity of emotions it creates, can make it especially difficult for students to work through their grief, a process that can take months or years. Furthermore, students must often face the task of grieving alone, isolated by distance from family and friends, and within an environment that is rarely conducive to grieving (Janowiak, Mei-Tal, & Drapkin, 1995).

"There seems every reason to believe that bereaved college students are hidden grievers whose mourning is disenfranchised within the social environment of a university or college campus" (Balk et al., 1998, p. 5). College is not a place where bereaved students can easily share their grief. Peers who are inexperienced with bereavement seldom understand the intensity and duration of the grief process (Balk, 1997). Moreover, few students feel comfortable talking about death, especially when they are confronted with a "real person experiencing real grief" (Balk et al., 1998, p. 4). Grieving students have reported resentment about the pressure they feel to suppress their strong feelings of grief (Dodd, 1988) and about the frustration they feel at not being understood.

Many students who have experienced a close personal loss have also reported feeling that they had to "grow up fast," causing them to have a more serious, realistic view of life (Schaefer & Moos, 2001; Schwartzberg & Janoff-Bulman, 1991; Tyson-Rawson, 1996a). As these students come to terms with mortality, including their own, they may make adjustments in their value system. They may become more focused on responsibilities and less on their former social life, creating the perception that they have less in common with their peer group. Students who have lost a parent or caregiver may be faced for the first time with responsibility for their own welfare and sometimes that of other family members. Changing priorities may also create the dilemma of staying in school or going home, particularly if the death occurs during the semester. Students may feel a sense of obligation to be at home and yet are faced with the constant pressure to maintain academic priorities and productivity. For many students, the loss, changes, and pressures feel overwhelming.

Assessment Issues

The Grieving Process

Each loss and its meaning to the individual griever are unique based on multiple factors. These may include (a) the relationship and level of attachment of the griever to the deceased, (b) the manner in which the loved one died, (c) the suddenness of the death, (d) the lapse of time since the death, (e) the responses of the family culture to death and bereavement, (f) the gender of the griever, (g) the locus of control of the griever, and (h) the level of social support for the griever (Banyard & Cantor, 2004; Fleming & Balmer, 1996).

A common reaction immediately after the death of a loved one is shock and denial. This period of numbness and disbelief has the protective effects of preventing the griever from experiencing the full impact of the loss all at once (Wolfelt, 1992). Initially, a grieving student may present with feelings of confusion and disbelief about the death, sometimes describing the experience of feeling surreal or being in a fog. It is also commonly a period of hyperactivity during which the student tries to focus on arrangements and rituals or other tasks with the goal of just staying busy. It is not unusual, however, to find that the student's concentration and motivation fluctuate, making it difficult to accomplish even the most mundane tasks. This is a time when schoolwork is likely to suffer because daily tasks and responsibilities seem insignificant or mundane when compared with the experience of the death.

Even as the shock begins to dissipate, strong emotional reactions are common but generally not all-consuming. Stroebe and Schut (2001) used the term *oscillation* to refer to the dynamic regulatory process of alternating between coping with grief-related stressors and being completely distracted by grief. Students often express feelings of guilt because they have times of enjoyment and times when they do not think about the deceased. They need to be assured that this is a healthy and normal response. Moreover, the roller coaster of emotions causes confusion. Bereaved individuals often report that they will begin to feel as if they are coming to terms with their loss only to experience a fresh, overwhelming wave of sadness and grief. They also express concern that distressing emotions will continue to play a dominant and controlling role in their lives.

Some students struggle with grief because they feel they have been given the message by family members, other students, or society that their grief is not legitimate or significant or that there is some reason for shame (Doka, 2002; Sprang & McNeil, 1995). This is referred to as *disenfranchised grief* and may arise in situations such as (a) loss of an individual whose relationship with the mourner was not openly observed or recognized (e.g., loss of same-sex or co-habitant partners), (b) loss that some persons may not consider significant (e.g., loss of a pet or loss through abortion), (c) loss that may not be socially validated because the object of the loss is still physically alive (e.g., loss of "the person they knew" because of illness or trauma), or (d) loss that may not be socially acknowledged or supported because of the manner of death (e.g., death by suicide, drug overdose, or AIDS).

An issue that is typically given little consideration is that of secondary losses. Rando (1993) defined a *secondary loss* as "a physical or psychosocial loss that coincides with or develops as a consequence of the initial loss" (p. 20). The death of a loved one also brings with it the loss of the roles the deceased played in the student's life, such as a confidant, a support system, or a companion. The death of a parent may result in economic and life adjustments, such as the loss of financial support or the loss of a familiar home. Also lost is a future with that loved one. Students often express sadness that the deceased will no longer be there to share future milestones, such as seeing them graduate, get married, and have children. Secondary losses can be as significant as the death of the loved one (Rando, 1984) and must be acknowledged and respected as something to be mourned.

Loss History

The loss histories of all students should be assessed. Even if the loss is not recent, the student may be regrieving the loss because of developmental or environmental changes; anniversary dates of past loss; or more recent, sometimes seemingly less significant, losses.

As an individual grows and passes through developmental phases of late adolescence and early adulthood, he or she may revisit significant losses that occurred during childhood. The student may begin to process the experience of the death and the student's relationship with the deceased from a vantage point that was not possible earlier. Moreover, the life changes and losses that come with leaving home may make past losses more prominent. This process may precipitate a resurgence of grief (Oltjenbruns, 2001). The intensity of these grief reactions may be particularly upsetting and confusing to students who feel they should have come to terms with these past losses when they occurred.

Grieving Behaviors

One of the most important components in the assessment and facilitation of grief is to identify and reframe the client's symptoms as normal grieving. Many clients who come for counseling do so because the symptoms of their grief reaction are overwhelmingly acute or have included emotional experiences that are foreign to them, such as sensing or "seeing" the deceased. Clients often believe there is something wrong with them, and many fear they have completely lost or will lose their sanity or never survive the emotional intensity of their reaction.

Grief issues may not be the presenting complaint when these students seek counseling. They may instead complain of symptomatology, such as the inability to sleep, concentrate, and study (Hardison, Neimeyer, & Lichstein, 2005; Janowiak et al., 1995). If the death is not a recent experience, the student may not associate the symptoms as a grief reaction. A bereaved individual frequently will receive a diagnosis of depression, even when the reaction fits within normal limits of grief.

In his groundbreaking 1944 study, Lindemann concluded that the symptomatology of normal acute grief fell into five areas: somatic distress, preoccupation with the image of the deceased, guilt, hostile reactions, and loss of patterns of conduct. Worden (2002) expanded on this list, placing the extensive range of normal grief behaviors into four categories:

- *feelings,* such as sadness, anger, guilt, anxiety, loneliness, fatigue, help-lessness, numbness, fear, relief, irritability, apathy, vulnerability, abandonment, sense of freedom, yearning, and shock;
- *physical sensations,* such as hollowness in the stomach, tightness in the chest, difficulty with breathing, sensitivity to environmental stimuli, weakness, fatigue, sleep problems, change of appetite, hyperactivity, crying, sighing, and depersonalization;
- *cognitions,* such as disbelief, confusion, preoccupation, sensing the presence of the deceased loved one, and hallucinations; and
- *behaviors,* such as absentmindedness, slowed thinking, dreams of the deceased, avoidance of reminders of the loss, isolation, a need to tell and retell the story of the death, and aimless wandering.

Insomnia

A common and significant reaction to loss is insomnia. Hardison et al. (2005) found that 59% of the bereaved students in their survey reported problems with sleep subsequent to the death of their family member or friend. The effects of sleep deprivation can severely disrupt a student's ability to function on multiple levels, particularly if sleep difficulties are prolonged. It is often assumed that the greatest impact to sleep patterns occurs immediately following a loss. However, Hardison et al. found that students reported a significantly greater rate of insomnia during the period 7–12 months after the loss. Students who lost a loved one to a tragedy were significantly more likely to meet the criteria for insomnia than those whose loved one died from natural causes.

Complicated and Traumatic Grief

When the death is anticipated and "on the expected time line" (e.g., older grandparents), the duration of the grieving process is typically shorter than when the death is sudden, traumatic, or violent and "off the expected time line" (e.g., a peer or sibling). Because more than three quarters (77%) of deaths among adolescents are human-induced, from accidents, homicide, and suicide (Barrett, 1996), the death of a friend or loved one who is closer to the student's own age is more likely to be a traumatic death (Toth et al., 2000).

The specifics of the death—such as (a) a sudden or unexpected death, especially when the death was violent or traumatic; (b) death from a very lengthy illness; (c) the death of a child; or (d) the perception that the death could be avoided—can predispose an individual for a more complicated grief reaction (Rando, 1993). An angry, ambivalent, or highly dependent relationship with the deceased can also be a factor. The definition of *complicated mourning,* also referred to as abnormal, pathologic, or unresolved grief, is, at best, vague. Prigerson and Jacobs (2001) proposed the term *traumatic grief,* which more accurately describes the symptoms of traumatic separation and traumatic distress most frequently associated with a profound and prolonged reaction to death. Although there are no objective criteria to determine when mourning becomes complicated or traumatic (Rando, 1993), there are situations in which mourners seem to engage in maladaptive strategies to avoid the pain associated with their loss. These strategies, paradoxically, may serve to exacerbate and prolong their distress (Boelen, Kip, Voorsluijs, & Van den Bout, 2004). If the bereaved has a history of mental health problems or prior unaccommodated losses or perceives a lack of social support, adapting to the death of a loved one may be a more complicated process. Psychotherapeutic strategies are indicated for the facilitation of a complicated grief reaction.

Counseling Implications

Establishing Rapport

Questions are an important part of an initial consultation as a way of garnering information and stimulating disclosure. In working with a bereaved student, the counselor should be particularly aware of the purpose of these questions. Details about the student's relationship with the deceased or the manner of death may seem to be integral to an assessment. Asking these questions at the onset, however, may not be what is most beneficial to the student. Bereaved individuals often complain that, when others learn of the death, their first question is "How did it happen?" This question places these individuals in the forced situation of feeling that they need to explain the details of an experience they are struggling to understand themselves. This can be disconcerting if the death was by a less socially acceptable means, such as suicide or drug overdose. Clients may wish to share these specifics, but there may be other priorities that are more meaningful in early phases of the counseling relationship.

The "gift of presence" can be the counselor's most powerful intervention, providing students with a safe place to talk and cry (Rando, 1984). The telling and retelling of their own story helps the students to grasp the reality of their loss, as they attempt to make sense of the death. The fact that an emotional state is not always a rational state does not lessen its importance for expression. Rather than provide a treatment model, or even answers, the role of the counselor is to support the bereaved individuals. When asked, bereaved students stressed that a counselor's genuine, caring attitude and willingness to help were more important attributes than the counselor's specific actions and statements (Dodd, 1988; Range, Walston, & Pollard, 1992).

A counselor's primary goal in bereavement counseling should be to honor the individual's personal experience of grief. As Wolfelt (1992) stated, "I can only help people when I allow them to teach me about their unique journey" (p. vii). Allowing students to share their story from their own framework of culturally preestablished meanings for death and grief also teaches the counselor about the influence of culture on individuals' expressions of grief. In attempting to make sense of the death, individuals attempt to incorporate the loss into their own worldview, or fundamental and spiritual beliefs, about why death occurs (Davis, 2001). Previously held religious or spiritual beliefs may be brought into question, causing confusion regarding the individuals' identity. Death may challenge the individuals' concept of fairness and bring into awareness the fragility of life as well as the individuals' own mortality. The students need to confide and explore these thoughts in order to begin to regain their sense of self.

Understanding Grieving Time Lines

Students often ask, "How long will I feel this way?" It is difficult to place parameters on the longevity of grief or the duration of the varying dimensions of grief. It is logical to assume that, because no two losses are the same, the reaction to that loss will vary. "The lack of empirical definity regarding the duration of the grief response is most likely based on the number of endogenous variables (i.e., personality) influencing the individual's response to loss" (Sprang & McNeil, 1995, p. 10).

Western culture typically anticipates that the most intense emotional reaction to the death of a loved one should last only through the funeral, and the period granted to be away from school is very brief. The reported length of the grief process varies significantly in the literature, from a few months to 3 or more years (Schaefer & Moos 2001; Stevens, Pfost, & Wessels, 1987; Vickio, Cavanaugh, & Attig, 1990; Worden, 2002).

> Coming to an acceptance of the reality of the loss takes time because it involves not only an intellectual acceptance of the loss, but also an emotional one. . . . The individual may be intellectually aware of the finality of the loss long before the emotions allow full acceptance of the information as true. (Wolfelt, 1992, p. 29)

Today's students have generally been more sheltered from painful life experiences than previous generations and have come to expect a "quick fix" for the pain they do experience. It may be particularly hard for them to hear that there is no set formula or time line for grief, that it is an individual journey, and that it is work that cannot be indefinitely avoided if grief is to be resolved.

Although the question of how long grief will last cannot be given an accurate, quantitative answer, it is important to assure the student that this level of pain will not last forever and will diminish over time. Many college students, still retaining some of the egocentrism of adolescence, feel that their grief is so unique that no one could possibly feel as bad as they do and that their unparalleled suffering has no boundaries. These students can be offered the hope that they will eventually be able to get to the point where they can regain some control over their pain so that it no longer controls them.

"Moving on," "getting over it," "putting it behind you," and "seeking closure" are all phrases commonly associated with trauma counseling and frequently with bereavement counseling. Such terminology, however, should be challenged as placing unrealistic expectations on what it means to resolve grief and loss. "We don't believe that people 'get over' major losses, as implied in many stage models of grief. . . . Rather those losses become part of who we are" (Harvey, Carlson, Huff, & Green, 2001, p. 235).

Facilitating Loss Adaptations

The process of adapting to the loss of a loved one leaves indelible changes in the life of the bereaved individual. Silverman and Klass (1996) stated that "the bereaved . . . have to change their relationship to the deceased. It does not mean the relationship ends, though it changes in a decisive way" (p. xix). Rather than conceptualize death as the end of a relationship, it is more realistic to view it as developing a new and different relationship.

> Like a novel that loses a central character in the middle chapters, the life story disrupted by loss must be reorganized, rewritten, to find a new strand of continuity that bridges the past with the future in an indelible fashion. (Neimeyer, 2001, p. 263)

A common psychological issue that bereaved individuals face is giving meaning to the loss. Being able to attach positive meaning to the death enhances the process of adjusting to the loss and helps to reduce stress (Stroebe & Schut, 2001). Students often express that the death of a loved one helped them to define their values and to recognize what was important in their lives. Giving meaning to the death by creating memorials or becoming involved in a cause is seen as a way to honor the loved one's influence in the student's life.

Although the course of counseling should be primarily dictated by the needs of the student, the counselor's style will obviously have a significant impact on the counseling relationship. Confiding in another person provides the bereaved individual with the opportunity to make sense of the loss and begin to build a new identity from the changes he or she has experienced (Toth et al., 2000).

Intervention Tools

Intervention tools used in other modes of counseling can also provide ways of confiding and expressing thoughts and emotions, particularly those interventions that use creativity to encourage the expression of thoughts, feelings, and ideas. Journaling, letter writing, dance, and the fine arts can provide an outlet to move through the grief process. Inviting students to bring in something for counseling that reminds them of the deceased, such as a photograph, can help facilitate the telling of their story. A counselor can suggest these tools, but it is important that the client decides that this would be helpful. There are times when viewing a photograph or writing a letter will be too painful a task for the student. Assigning homework has the risk of having the counselor determine the course of the grief work, which could be counterproductive in the facilitation of grief.

Providing something tangible that the students can take with them to read can be helpful. Something as basic as a handout that lists common grief reactions can help to moderate some of the crisis reaction many students present with as they realize that the symptoms they find distressing are normal responses to grief. Although it is natural that a counselor will want to provide as much information as possible to moderate the clients' distress, this is generally not advisable, particularly with clients who are experiencing the shock of the death. Clients will typically not remember much of the first counseling sessions. This is not to say that information should not be given, but it should be anticipated that the information may not be absorbed or retained.

Support from the counselor may need to be provided for some of the most basic things, like reminding the student to eat regularly. Self-care is particularly important for a bereaved person. Students will often experience additional stress if they perceive that they have fallen behind with their responsibilities in school, and they will focus all of their time on keeping up with demands. The counselor should stress the importance to the students of taking care of themselves and encourage them to spend time doing things that will bring them comfort. The students should also be advised to be patient and compassionate with themselves as a way of facilitating the grieving process and helping to reduce their frustration with the symptoms that seem to be controlling them. Some students may benefit from maintaining a regular daily routine including exercise and time for relaxation.

Support Groups

Students may be particularly reluctant to share their feelings of grief if they fear, or their experience has proven, that others will not be sensitive to the importance of the deceased person or pet in their lives (Rando, 1993; Sharkin & Knox, 2003). These students may be less likely to seek support for their distress or be more likely to have other presenting issues when seeking counseling. Support groups can provide one of the most effective interventions for disenfranchised grief by providing a safe place to obtain recognition, understanding, and support (Worden, 2002). College campuses, however, may not have the resources or population to provide specialized support groups for disenfranchised mourners. These groups may be available in the community and are frequently advertised in local newspapers or on the Internet. Counselors can provide referrals and encourage students to use these resources.

With no robust research available on the efficacy of intervention strategies for the traditional-age college population, it is difficult to determine what services to offer students through college counseling centers. With demand for services in many counseling centers exceeding resources, and waiting lists for services becoming more common, bereavement support groups allow centers to offer services to a larger number of students. Students report that it can be comforting to talk with someone who shares their experience of loss. Knowing that they are not alone in their feelings can help to normalize the grief process. A support group also provides students with the opportunity to have time set aside to talk about their loss in an accepting environment.

Finding students willing to participate in a group format, however, can be particularly challenging with a young adult population. Janowiak et al. (1995) found that "even those students that did attend [group] screening interviews were highly ambivalent about participating in a group experience" (p. 62). Students expressed concern about showing emotions in front of others, or they had the sense that their grief was unique and would not be understood by their peers. There is some merit to these concerns. The vast differences in the manner and causes of loss experienced by college students dictate that groups be general in nature. This has the potential of creating an environment that causes "competitive grief" in which one student feels that his or her loss is more significant than another's loss (e.g., that the death of a parent is more traumatic than the death of a grandparent).

The efficacy of general bereavement groups with traditional-age college students is unknown. Most research has been done with specific populations of bereaved individuals, such as widows and widowers, those who have lost a sibling, or those who have lost a child. Instituting loss-specific groups, however, particularly on smaller campuses, may be difficult or impractical.

The decision to have a closed, structured group or an open, more traditional support group also needs to be addressed. The closed group has the advantage of continuity but excludes students who need support after the group has begun. An open group is available to all students when they may need it, but this can create a situation in which the participants change for each group, making it less likely that the group will be able to develop cohesion.

Campus Considerations

Student Advocacy

The manifestations of grief frequently impair the student's ability to function, both academically and socially, in the college environment. Normal grief reactions may create a situation in which concentrating on academics is difficult, and the student's grades, in turn, may suffer. Not being able to effectively continue to attend to predetermined goals may seem catastrophic to the student. Helping the student put academic pressures in realistic perspective can be a valuable intervention.

Counselors can help students understand their options, whether to request more time to complete work or withdraw from the semester. Counselors can also provide support by acting as a liaison between the student and professors as well as any other appropriate college personnel. A letter to a professor explaining the student's situation may be all that is needed. Furthermore, acting as a liaison between appropriate student services and departments, such as financial aid, and assisting the student with the requirements and details of taking a leave save the student from needing to repeat his or her story and situation multiple times.

There are times when being at home for a period of time after the death of a loved one is in the best interest of the student. It gives the student time to grieve with others who share his or her loss. Home can be a comfortable place to express the emotions of grief without the worry of being misunderstood. The family plays a crucial role in the grief process as individual members struggle to make sense of their loss and attach meaning to it by talking with each other (Nadeau, 2001).

The student may feel a sense of obligation to be at home. Developmentally, college students are involved in negotiating new, more adult relationships with their families (Tyson-Rawson, 1996b). The death of a family member can accelerate this process, and the student may feel the need to be at home to support and comfort other family members or take on roles formerly filled by the deceased.

Grieving students often have difficulty remaining in school and graduating (Balk & Vesta, 1998; Hardison et al., 2005). Balk (2001) argued that the prevalence of bereavement among college students should compel colleges to address this issue on their campuses:

> It would only seem rational for our universities to develop and implement effective interventions to assist bereaved students. The effects of bereavement place students at risk for doing poorly in their studies, and perhaps, of dropping out of school. If for no other reason than a university's interest to increase retention, graduation, and long-term alumni support, it makes sense for the university to engage systematically in efforts to assist bereaved students. (p. 73)

This chapter has focused on the role of counseling services for bereaved students. The majority of bereaved students, however, do not view their grief as a mental health problem (Balk, 2001). "It stands to reason, given the large numbers of students experiencing loss, that only a few will seek professional counseling" (Toth et al., 2000, p. 242). Therefore, alternatives to college counseling centers should be provided (Balk, 2001). To be most effective and reach the largest number of students, approaches to bereavement should be provided through both academic classes and student services. Academic classes on death, dying, and bereavement should be a part of the general curriculum and should not be reserved for those students majoring in humanities.

Education and Training

Educating the educators is also a critical step. Faculty members do not always provide allowance for the impact of grief on academic performance (Backels & Wheeler, 2001). The parameters of a "crisis period" are ambiguous and, therefore, most likely inconsistently defined within the academic community. At a minimum, faculty should be afforded the opportunity to learn about the impact of grief on the overall functioning and academic performance of students.

Student affairs professionals should initiate training and outreach programs that address the impact of loss and grief on students' capacity to fulfill social and academic tasks (Backels & Wheeler, 2001). Residence hall staff should be trained to understand and respond to grieving students, and campuswide education programs focused on grief and loss should be provided. Support groups and a resource area outside the counseling center environment may help to further reduce the implication that grief reactions are pathologic. Finally, all college staff interacting with students on an interpersonal level should be familiar with the broad scope of the grief reactions they may encounter.

Future Trends

Although new research is being presented regularly and interest in disenfranchised and complicated grief has grown in the literature, there is a paucity of information on counseling for the facilitation of the normal grief reaction. Information specifically targeting the college-age population is rare and has significant limitations. In addition, most research on bereavement in all adolescent age groups is culturally bound.

Western culture perpetuates many myths surrounding grief. For example, it sanctions a period, albeit brief, following the death in which the expression of emotions is expected. During this time, those who do not mourn are considered pathologic (Wortman & Silver, 2001). After the vague "normal" mourning period, thought by some to be as little as 2 weeks (Sprang & McNeil, 1995), outward expressions of grief may be looked on as synonymous with weakness. These myths do not show an appreciation for the tremendous diversity in how people react to loss and grief. Mourning, although often treated as such, does not look the same in all people. Future research should include a richer exploration of cultural variability in the understanding of loss and grief, which should in turn lead to further expansion of what is considered a "normal" reaction to grief.

A fundamental problem in the study of loss and grief is the lack of a universal language. The terms *grief, bereavement,* and *mourning* are often used interchangeably, and the literature subscribes to no set definitions. These terms need to be operationally and universally defined.

Confusion is caused by the lack of consistency regarding the primary concepts concerning loss and grief and by the inadequacy of research methodologies in the contemporary literature. As Neimeyer and Hogan (2001) noted, the human experience of bereavement, although often studied, has not been studied well, "owing in part to limitations in the most commonly used (scientific) methods adopted to study bereavement-related phenomena" (p. 89). In recent years there has been a proliferation of isolated, theoretically driven findings. Shaver and Tancredy (2001) pointed out that, although it is probable that most serious observations are valid, there is no framework into which all of these observations can be incorporated. Developing an integrative framework for loss and grief counseling can provide a foundation on which to develop an understanding of bereavement within individual populations, including traditional-age college students. This would greatly enhance the development of programs for the facilitation of loss and grief on college campuses.

References

Backels, K., & Wheeler, I. (2001). Faculty perceptions of mental health issues among college students. *Journal of College Student Development, 42,* 173–176.

Balk, D. E. (1997). Death, bereavement and college students: A descriptive analysis. *Mortality, 2,* 207–221.

Balk, D. E. (2001). College student bereavement, scholarship, and the university: A call for university engagement. *Death Studies, 25,* 67–85.

Balk, D. E., Lampe, S., Sharpe, B., Schwinn, S., Holen, K., Cook, L., et al. (1998). TAT results in a longitudinal study of bereaved college students. *Death Studies, 22,* 3–21.

Balk, D. E., & Vesta, L. C. (1998). Psychological development during four years of bereavement: A longitudinal case study. *Death Studies, 22,* 23–41.

Banyard, V. L., & Cantor, E. N. (2004). Adjustment to college among trauma survivors: An exploratory study of resilience. *Journal of College Student Development, 45,* 207–221.

Barrett, R. K. (1996). Adolescents, homicidal violence and death. In C. A. Corr & D. E. Balk (Eds.), *Handbook of adolescent death and bereavement* (pp. 42–84). New York: Springer Publishing Company.

Boelen, P. A., Kip, H. J., Voorsluijs, J. J., & Van den Bout, J. (2004). Irrational beliefs and basic assumptions in bereaved university students: A comparison study. *Journal of Rational–Emotive and Cognitive–Behavioral Therapy, 22,* 111–129.

Davis, D. G. (2001). The tormented and the transformed: Understanding responses to loss and trauma. In R. A. Neimeyer (Ed.), *Meaning reconstruction & the experience of loss* (pp. 137–155). Washington, DC: American Psychological Association.

Dodd, D. K. (1988). Responding to the bereaved: A student panel discussion. *Teaching of Psychology, 15,* 33–36.

Doka, K. J. (2002). Introduction. In K. J. Doka (Ed.), *Disenfranchised grief: New directions, challenges, and strategies for practice* (pp. 5–22). Champaign, IL: Research Press.

Fleming, S., & Balmer, L. (1996). Bereavement in adolescence. In C. A. Corr & D. E. Balk (Eds.), *Handbook of adolescent death and bereavement* (pp. 139–154). New York: Springer Publishing Company.

Hardison, H. G., Neimeyer, R. A., & Lichstein, K. L. (2005). Insomnia and complicated grief symptoms in bereaved college students. *Behavioral Sleep Medicine, 3,* 99–111.

Harvey, J. H., Carlson, H. R., Huff, T. M., & Green, M. A. (2001). Embracing their memory: The construction of accounts of loss and hope. In R. A. Neimeyer (Ed.), *Meaning reconstruction & the experience of loss* (pp. 231–243). Washington, DC: American Psychological Association.

Janowiak, S. M., Mei-Tal, R., & Drapkin, R. G. (1995). Living with loss: A group for bereaved college students. *Death Studies, 19,* 55–63.

Lindemann, E. (1944). Symptomatology and management of acute grief. *American Journal of Psychiatry, 101,* 141–148.

Nadeau, J. W. (2001). Family construction of meaning. In R. A. Neimeyer (Ed.), *Meaning reconstruction & the experience of loss* (pp. 95–111). Washington, DC: American Psychological Association.

Neimeyer, R. A. (2001). The language of loss: Grief therapy as a process of meaning reconstruction. In R. A. Neimeyer (Ed.), *Meaning reconstruction & the experience of loss* (pp. 261–292). Washington, DC: American Psychological Association.

Neimeyer, R. A., & Hogan, N. S. (2001). Quantitative or qualitative? Measurement issues in the study of grief. In M. S. Stroebe, R. O. Hansson, W. Stroebe, & H. Schut (Eds.), *Handbook of bereavement research* (pp. 89–118). Washington, DC: American Psychological Association.

Oltjenbruns, K. A. (2001). Developmental context of childhood: Grief and regrief phenomena. In M. S. Stroebe, R. O. Hansson, W. Stroebe, & H. Schut (Eds.), *Handbook of bereavement research* (pp. 169–218). Washington, DC: American Psychological Association.

Prigerson, H. G., & Jacobs, S. C. (2001). Traumatic grief as a distinct disorder: A rationale, consensus criteria, and a preliminary empirical test. In M. S. Stroebe, R. O. Hansson, W. Stroebe, & H. Schut (Eds.), *Handbook of bereavement research* (pp. 613–637). Washington, DC: American Psychological Association.

Rando, T. A. (1984). *Grief, dying and death: Clinical interventions for caregivers.* Champaign, IL: Research Press.

Rando, T. A. (1993). *Treatment of complicated mourning.* Champaign, IL: Research Press.

Range, L. M., Walston, A. S., & Pollard, P. M. (1992). Helpful and unhelpful comments after suicide, homicide, accident, or natural death. *Omega, 25,* 25–31.

Schaefer, J. A., & Moos, R. H. (2001). Bereavement experiences and personal growth. In M. S. Stroebe, R. O. Hansson, W. Stroebe, & H. Schut (Eds.), *Handbook of bereavement research* (pp. 145–167). Washington, DC: American Psychological Association.

Schwartzberg, S. S., & Janoff-Bulman, R. (1991). Grief and the search for meaning: Exploring the assumptive worlds of bereaved college students. *Journal of Social and Clinical Psychology, 10,* 270–288.

Sharkin, B. S., & Knox, D. (2003). Pet loss: Issues and implications for the psychologist. *Professional Psychology: Research and Practice, 34,* 414–421.

Shaver, P. R., & Tancredy, C. M. (2001). Emotion, attachment and bereavement: A conceptual commentary. In M. S. Stroebe, R. O. Hansson, W. Stroebe, & H. Schut (Eds.), *Handbook of bereavement research* (pp. 63–88). Washington, DC: American Psychological Association.

Silverman, P. R., & Klass, D. (1996). Preface. In D. Klass, P. R. Silverman, & S. L. Nickman (Eds.), *Continuing bonds: New understandings of grief* (pp. xvii–xx). Washington, DC: Taylor & Francis.

Sprang, G., & McNeil, J. (1995). *The many faces of bereavement: The nature and treatment of natural, traumatic, and stigmatized grief.* New York: Brunner/Mazel.

Stevens, M. J., Pfost, K. S., & Wessels, A. B. (1987). The relationship of purpose in life to coping strategies and time since the death of a significant other. *Journal of Counseling and Development, 65,* 424–426.

Stroebe, M. S., & Schut, H. (2001). Meaning making in the dual process model of coping with bereavement. In R. A. Neimeyer (Ed.), *Meaning reconstruction & the experience of loss* (pp. 55–73). Washington, DC: American Psychological Association.

Toth, P. L., Stockton, R., & Browne, F. (2000). College student grief and loss. In J. H. Harvey & E. D. Miller (Eds.), *Loss and trauma* (pp. 237–248). Philadelphia: Brunner-Routledge.

Tyson-Rawson, K. (1996a). Adolescent responses to the death of a parent. In C. A. Corr & D. E. Balk (Eds.), *Handbook of adolescent death and bereavement* (pp. 155–172). New York: Springer Publishing Company.

Tyson-Rawson, K. (1996b). Relationship and heritage: Manifestations of ongoing attachment following father death. In D. Klass, P. R. Silverman, & S. L. Nickman (Eds.), *Continuing bonds: New understandings of grief* (pp. 125–145). Washington, DC: Taylor & Francis.

Vickio, C. J., Cavanaugh, J. C., & Attig, T. W. (1990). Perceptions of grief among university students. *Death Studies, 14,* 231–240.

Wolfelt, A. D. (1992). *Understanding grief: Helping yourself heal.* Florence, KY: Accelerated Development.

Worden, J. W. (2002). *Grief counseling and grief therapy.* New York: Springer Publishing Company.

Wortman, C. B., & Silver, R. C. (2001). The myths of coping with loss revisited. In M. S. Stroebe, R. O. Hansson, W. Stroebe, & H. Schut (Eds.), *Handbook of bereavement research* (pp. 405–429). Washington, DC: American Psychological Association.

Section **IV**

Medical, Physical, and Severe Psychological Issues

Achieving Accessible Counseling for Students With Mobility Impairments

The chapter number "15" appears in a circle at the top.

Mark E. Beecher, Julie E. Preece,
and Norman L. Roberts

Introduction

When broadly defined, mobility impairments are among the most ubiquitous of all disorders. Most adults have experienced a trauma, strain, or sprain that affected their ability to walk, grasp, lift, or otherwise manage a range of routine daily activities. Such a mobility limitation, although momentarily a nuisance and inconvenience, provides a glimpse into the challenges that individuals with more significant and permanent mobility impairments may experience. One snowy day to a person temporarily using crutches for a broken foot can be quite enlightening, revealing the challenges of finding convenient parking, managing snow-piled curbs, and coping with slippery walkways, including those inside buildings. A sprained wrist wreaks havoc when one is trying to write a check at a crowded checkout counter. A sprained back may mean even the lightest lifting will be given a second thought. A once friendly environment becomes significantly less so.

With the assumption that many readers have a sense of the consequences of a mobility impairment, the focus of this chapter is on the provision of college counseling services to students who have permanent and significant, rather than temporary and moderately annoying, mobility impairments. For this chapter, mobility impairments refer to permanent disorders of the human muscular, skeletal, and/or neurological systems that significantly impair or limit an individual's ability to perform one or more of the basic daily living activities, such as walking, climbing stairs, lifting, opening doors, writing, grooming, or feeding oneself. Disorders excluded under this definition are those that limit an individual's ability to perform daily living activities primarily as a result of a psychological, intellectual, or visual disability.

Although we have developed a somewhat restrictive definition for this chapter, this cluster of mobility impairments still encompasses a diverse range of conditions, including (a) a spinal injury or a congenital disorder of the central nervous system that results in para- or quadriplegia; (b) a neurological disorder, such as multiple sclerosis, that impairs gait; (c) a chronic pain disorder that limits the range, duration, or extent of motion; or (d) an amputation that requires a prosthesis. The range of mobility impairments and their causes far exceeds these few examples. Furthermore, adding to the complexity of these conditions and their causes is the wide range of intraindividual variables, such as age, gender, education, ego strength, social support, and so forth.

Prevalence of Mobility Impairment

In a study by the National Center for Education Statistics, 9% of college students reported having a disability, and 29% of this group reported an orthopedic or mobility disability or difficulty that limited "one or more of the basic physical activities such as walking, climbing stairs, reaching, lifting or carrying" (Horn, Peter, & Rooney, 2002, p. 19). Mathematically, this suggests that approximately 2.6% of a student enrollment will report a mobility impairment. This may mean fewer than 50 students on small campuses but several hundred at larger colleges.

The count of students with mobility impairments may be somewhat larger than the 2.6% figure suggests. Fifteen percent of the college students in the National Center for Education Statistics study (Horn et al., 2002) reported health problems as the main limiting condition. The significance of the 15% figure is that the consequences of certain health problems, such as chronic pain, lupus, or fibromyalgia, may have a significant impact on an individual's mobility.

The prevalence of mobility-impaired students on college campuses may be directly linked to a variety of factors, but chief among them are changes in public policy and advances in medical treatments and technology. Public policy changes are highlighted by the specific legislation designed to create increased access to buildings and services available to people with disabilities, such as Section 504 of the Rehabilitation Act of 1973 and the Americans With Disabilities Act of 1990 (ADA). Medical treatments and technology have affected the survival rates, quality of life, and functioning of people with significant mobility impairments. Perhaps the most striking example is the improved outcome for individuals with spinal cord injuries. The last five decades have seen a gradual decline in the morbidity rates and an increase in survival for persons with spinal cord injuries with the development of modern emergency services, medications, antibiotics, and improved rehabilitation (Zeilig et al., 2000).

Our experience in working with persons with disabilities extends over 25 years. During this time, we have seen the continuous flow of changes that have increased the accessibility for people with mobility impairments. The early battles were about curb cuts, ramps, and accessible restrooms. In time, the focus has turned to more subtle, but still significant, obstacles to accessibility, including door designs and operation, hallway and office dimensions, elevator design, and emergency evacuation procedures.

Other changes have extended beyond architecture. Adaptations to computer operations have allowed individuals with even the most severe mobility impairments to access the computer's technological advantages. Without striking a key, people with severe impairments to fine motor dexterity or coordination can still dictate input to a computer. A variety of wheelchair modifications have allowed some students to be much more adept in their movements around campuses. Other electronic advances have allowed for significant independence.

Advances in medicine have increased the survival and quality of life for people with mobility impairments, and federal legislation has paved the way for equal access to higher education, including counseling services. It would seem clear, therefore, that with increasing numbers of students with mobility impairments on college campuses, professional development in understanding factors related to counseling students with mobility impairments, as well as other disabilities, would be a standard part of counselor graduate training. However, the data suggest that this training is not occurring.

Counselor Training

Few counselors have received training for understanding the needs of this population. Most counselors receive diversity training as part of their professional education and practical experience, but disability is generally not included or taken into account in this training (Leigh, Powers, Vash, & Nettles, 2004). A survey of graduates of counseling and clinical psychology programs found low levels of perceived competence in their abilities to provide services to people with physical challenges (Leigh et al., 2004). In addition, Gordon, Lewandowski, Murphy, and Dempsey (2002) noted that "most practicing psychologists received graduate training prior to the enactment of ADA law, so they may have limited familiarity with the law and its interpretation by the courts" (p. 358). Gordon et al. surveyed 147 clinicians about their knowledge of the ADA and its applications to practice. They found that there was great misunderstanding and disagreement among clinicians about the ADA and that most clinicians felt they needed additional training and understanding. Thus, most college counselors will likely struggle with inadequate preparation and training as they meet with students with mobility impairments.

This chapter is designed to provide practical guidelines that can help counselors fill their training gaps and feel more comfortable in counseling students with mobility impairments. The information and guidelines that follow should not be seen as a prescription for how to help every student with a mobility impairment. Instead, we intend to provide a context within which college counselors may address students' individual needs. We hope that readers recognize that the issues presented in this chapter may be neither unique nor universal to students with mobility impairments.

Assessment Issues

There is a wide range of causes and severity among students with mobility impairments, and each student responds differently to the experience. Many researchers have investigated possible reasons for differential reactions to mobility impairments and specifically to spinal cord injuries. Smith and Nicassio (1995) found that a person's age, behavioral choices, attitudes toward illness and health care providers, cognitive style, problem-solving approach, perception of health, locus of control, and use of social support can have a significant impact on how he or she reacts to a spinal cord injury. In addition, McCarthy (1999) suggested that spirituality has a significant impact.

Because of the many possible reactions to and experiences with a mobility impairment, it is important to assess not only what the impairment is but also how it affects multiple aspects of the student's life and how the student perceives and approaches the impairment. Though talking specifically about chronic pain, Turk and Okifuji (1999) suggested that understanding and appropriately treating patients requires an accurate assessment not only of the physical disorder but also of the "psychosocial, behavioural, and psychological factors—current mood (anxiety, depression, anger), interpretation of symptoms, expectations about the meanings of the symptoms, and responses to the patient's symptoms by others" (p. 1784). They further asserted that all of these elements interact to create the patient's subjective experience of the disorder.

Although talking again specifically about chronic pain, Turk and Okifuji (1999) suggested that physicians—and we would add college counselors—should consider the following three questions:

> The first question is what is the extent of the patient's disease or injury . . . ? The second question is what is the magnitude of the illness—i.e., to what extent is the patient suffering, disabled, and unable to enjoy activities? The final question is does the patient's behaviour during his or her interactions with the physician seem to reflect the nature and extent of the physical disease or injury, or is there evidence that symptoms are amplified for psychological or social reasons . . . ? (p. 1785)

On the basis of these three questions, we encourage the college counselor to consider and assess three domains of the mobility-impaired client: physical, functional, and emotional. The first domain and, to a great degree, the second domain are typically not within the scope of counselors' direct practice or evaluation, but failure to consider them creates a very narrow understanding of a client's universe. An inadequate understanding of a client's disability and the impact it has on daily functioning immediately impairs any in-depth understanding of the client's life and warps the counselor's access to an accurate empathic response. Without knowing and understanding the first two questions, the counselor has no, or very limited, access to the third question: What is the psychological impact of the disability for this particular client?

The college counselor who has a client with a spinal cord injury, or any other mobility impairment, may also want to consider the advice of Hayes and Potter

(1995). First, they cautioned the counselor to recognize that the person who has requested counseling services "may be well beyond initial reactions to their injuries (or impairments)" (Hayes & Potter, 1995, Preliminary Cautions section, para. 1). They recommended that the counselor assess the length of time the person has lived with the impairment and his or her level of expertise with the disability. Although there is no pure algebraic analog to dictate the effects of time and knowledge on adjustment to a disability, these two variables may contribute to assumptions the counselor has about the client's adjustment to the disability. Not all clients visiting a counselor's office will have freshly acquired disabilities.

Second, Hayes and Potter (1995) cautioned that

> not all problems are related to the disability. . . . For mental health counselors un-accustomed to working with clients with disabilities, there can be a tendency to see the client as his or her disability rather than as a person with a disability. (Preliminary Cautions section, para. 2)

As in any good practice, clinicians should avoid single-dimension thinking to recognize that the disability is not the person. As the old cliché suggests, the whole is greater than the sum of its parts. The disability is a critical feature that should not be ignored; it is a characteristic of the person similar to gender, age, or ethnicity. As such, the disability may be a critical or marginal aspect of the individual's presenting problem.

Counseling Implications

A mobility impairment has the potential to affect every aspect of a student's life. On the basis of our years of experience in working with students with mobility impairments, recent interviews with students, and the literature, we address four general areas of impact: physical, academic, social, and clinical.

Physical Impacts

It seems inherently obvious that having a mobility impairment would have a physical impact on a student's life. However, it is far from obvious how significant these impacts can be, because they may range from minor details in the counseling office to major obstacles off-campus. Single occasional stressors, even those that may be profound, may be well managed by individuals, but multiple continuous stressors have the potential, through their cumulative effect, to create substantial mental and physical problems.

Counselor's Office

As the beginning point in addressing the physical impact, counselors should be aware of the structure of their own office space and the degree to which the space is accessible to a student with a mobility impairment. There may be significant physical obstacles that will be exhausting or frustrating to students just in getting into counselors' offices. In evaluating the accessibility of his or her office space, the counselor may want to ask the following:

1. Can a student with a mobility impairment even get to my office? (If a student must climb stairs, manage a narrow hallway, or struggle to find nonexistent accessible parking close to the building, the student with the mobility impairment may not be able to access the office.)
2. Are there door-openers on my building's and suite's doors?
3. Is the receptionist's desk too high for a student in a wheelchair to be seen?
4. Are couches or other furniture in traffic areas positioned in such a way as to create narrow passages or to block access to my office door?
5. Is my office door of sufficient width to allow access by a student in a motorized wheelchair?
6. Is there enough room in my office for a wheelchair to turn around? (Figure 15.1 gives the dimensions required for a wheelchair to make a 180-degree turn.)
7. Are there accessible bathrooms nearby, not just in the building?

Each of these questions represents a potentially significant obstacle to a student having a positive counseling experience (and possibly to having any counseling experience at all). The less accessible or navigable the office space is, the greater the potential for the mobility-impaired client to experience frustration and to perceive the environment as minimally apathetic or ultimately hostile.

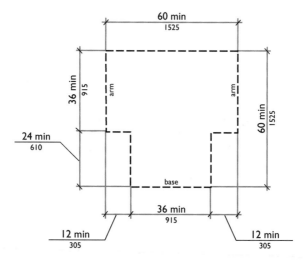

Figure 15.1

T-Shaped Turning Space

Note. From *ADA and ABA Accessibility Guidelines for Buildings and Facilities.* Retrieved March 22, 2006, from http://www.access-board.gov/ada-aba/final.htm#pgfId-1006182.

One may suspect that the client who must pass through "hostile territories" to access counseling has a diminished potential for successful counseling outcomes, if he or she returns for counseling at all.

Although there may be little college counselors can do to change the location of the counseling office, there is much they can do to create a welcoming and accessible environment in the counseling office itself. If students with mobility impairments must go through an exhausting range of obstacles, such as having to wait for counselors to clear a path into the office at the beginning of each session just to get into the counselors' office, it is unlikely they will feel welcomed or be ready to work on therapeutic issues. If students sense a safe, welcoming, and accommodating environment in the counselors' office, the original intent of the appointment, to pursue therapy, is not cluttered by avoidable resentment or alienation (Ward & Pointon, 2004).

Obstacles to Physical Mobility

Even if the counseling office is accessible, it is likely that a student with a mobility impairment faces countless obstacles to accessibility on the college campus. Common concerns include difficulties finding accessible parking that is close to buildings, insufficient time to get from one class to another, difficulties finding accessible housing, and problems using the cafeteria (e.g., they cannot hold a cafeteria tray). Even when a facility is said to be accessible, it may pose problems (e.g., "accessible" roll-in showers may be too narrow for many newer wheelchairs that are larger than the space provided). Although any one of these concerns may seem minor to a counselor, or even to the student with a mobility impairment, when added to all of the other "minor" obstacles encountered in a given day, it easily becomes frustrating and exhausting. The combination of obstacles may have an overlooked or unseen effect on a student's mental health. Students may feel a sense of fatigue that makes it very difficult, if not impossible, for them to fulfill the responsibilities of a college student or of a counseling client.

Off-campus, obstacles to mobility typically increase dramatically because disability laws do not apply to all privately owned enterprises. Many routine tasks of daily living, which are only mundane to a counselor, may be challenging, frustrating, or, in some instances, impossible for some students with mobility impairments to manage independently. Students may find themselves having to carefully plan routine transportation, grocery shopping, and even a social life. But again, it is not just the planning or the extra time that is necessarily the primary concern; it is the stress and anxiety that may be associated with just managing to live life as independently as possible. The cumulative effect of such obstacles may have a significant impact on therapeutic issues and should be considered by the counselor.

Academic Impacts

Similar to physical impacts, academic difficulties resulting from a mobility impairment may be easy for counselors to overlook or minimize, yet the additive effects may be significant. Consider the impact of the cluster and not just the single interruption.

Registering for classes is typically stressful for all students, but it can be especially frustrating for students with mobility impairments. They must carefully consider their needs and limitations in addition to the standard concerns their fellow classmates may have. The schedule must be properly structured to account for the time they need to prepare themselves in the morning, travel to campus, find appropriate parking, and move from one class to another. This simple list of concerns does not begin to address the unexpected interruptions that may arise, such as inclement weather or road construction. If fatigue is an issue, especially for those with mobility impairments due to a physical illness or those still recovering from accidents, considerations include limits to the number of classes and hours spent at school each day. For students in the final stages of their course work, the selection of course options becomes restricted, which may counter any ideal plans to create a feasible, realistic schedule for the students.

Student and Faculty Perceptions

Perceptions and reactions of other students and faculty may have a significant influence on a student's academic confidence and willingness to attend classes (Beilke & Yssel, 1999). Faculty may be patronizing or not take students with mobility impairments seriously. Faculty and other students may be so nervous or afraid of making a mistake or of offending that they ignore or avoid students with mobility impairments. If a student's mobility impairment is invisible, faculty or students may doubt that the student has a valid disability or may question the reasonableness of academic accommodations in an insulting or critical way (Beilke & Yssel, 1999). Research has suggested, however, that "the presence of students with disabilities in post-secondary education has also exposed the existence of faculty–student perceptual divides" (Beilke & Yssel, 1999, p. 368). This kind of hostile environment may weigh heavily on the student and make it difficult for him or her to feel confident academically and willing to request help when needed.

Similarly, the administrative climate of the college may communicate hostility or lack of understanding. If the campus is consistently inaccessible and little is done to make it accessible, the student may feel unwanted or unaccepted. Disability services providers may seem more like strict gatekeepers of services, rather than helpers. In the counseling office, what may seem like paranoia may actually be a reasonable response to a truly antagonistic environment.

Career Counseling Needs

Choosing a career and completing the requirements for such may be a source of discouragement or difficulty for students with mobility impairments. College counselors should be careful not to assume that certain careers are unattainable for students with mobility impairments. Young and Alfred (1994) found that work and activity were crucial elements to an individual's self-concept. Although some careers may be more difficult for these students, there are few careers that cannot be reached with the use of technology or other accommodations. However, helping faculty and administration to think creatively in order to help a student complete certain majors or requirements may involve considerable effort on the part of the student and the counselor. Barriers may not be limited to physical access only but may also extend to the attitudes of college personnel who need training in accommodating students with disabilities (Beilke & Yssel, 1999; Gibson, 2000; Vallandingham, 1997).

When career options are truly closed to students with mobility impairments, the students will likely feel frustration or anger at their loss of control and options. This may be particularly true for students who must alter career plans because of an impairment coming later in life (e.g., spinal cord injury). Students who are returning to college after experiencing a spinal cord injury may need assistance in locating different careers than they were originally pursuing.

Social Impacts

Social life is a major priority for most college students. This is no different for students with mobility impairments, and counselors should expect students with mobility impairments to raise social life as an issue. As with all of the areas discussed in this chapter, it is important not to assume that problems or issues are always related to the mobility impairment. However, in this section we address social issues that may be overlooked or not understood by counselors working with students with mobility impairments.

Family

Although family is often one of the greatest sources of support for students with mobility impairments, students may feel frustrated that they are so reliant on that support. They also may feel like a financial, emotional, and physical burden on their family. Padrone (1994) suggested that a disability affects the entire family. This is particularly true if the student's impairment is relatively recent and the student is used to being independent. Siblings may also have to adjust to the student's disability (Padrone, 1994) and may feel or express resentment that a majority of family resources is being directed toward the student. The siblings' resentment may result in the student feeling guilt, shame, or anger.

Social Inclusion and Isolation

Social inclusion is very important to most college students, and students with mobility impairments may feel a sense of isolation, loneliness, or abandonment if they are unable to participate in activities with friends or roommates. Physical issues, such as lack of bowel or bladder control, may be a source of embarrassment or shame that may lead a student to self-isolate or opt out of social activities (Hampton, 2004; Hendrick, 1981).

Transportation difficulties may be a major limiting factor. If students with mobility impairments do not have their own transportation, they may be limited to a certain mileage with a contract hire car (Ward & Pointon, 2004) or public transportation. In addition, friends' apartments may not be accessible, limiting the possibility of visiting or initiating contact with friends. Students who develop their mobility impairment later in life may feel particular isolation if they are unable to join friends in social activities they previously enjoyed (e.g., hiking, football, softball, or dancing; Boschen, 1996).

Students with invisible impairments, such as chronic pain, may push themselves beyond what will keep them healthy in order to participate in social activities. Preece (1994) found that students in a chronic pain and illness group repeatedly reported that they acted healthy and joined in social activities, even when it meant they would lose their health by staying up too late or by engaging in activities that were too physically demanding.

As in academic settings, peers of students with mobility impairments may be so nervous or afraid of making a mistake or of offending in social situations that they ignore or avoid students with mobility impairments. Alternatively, peers may be patronizing or condescending. Any of these reactions may create a sense of isolation or distance for these students.

Sexuality and Dating

Sexuality and dating are significant concerns for many students with mobility impairments, although they may shy away from these more personal issues (Ward & Pointon, 2004). It is beyond the scope of this chapter to discuss all that has been written about sexual counseling and rehabilitation for those with spinal cord injuries or mobility impairments, but we address some of the concerns that may arise for students.

Narum and Rodolfa (1984) reported results from surveys conducted by the Committee on Sexual Problems of the Disabled and the Sex and Disability Project that found that 50% of surveyed persons with spinal cord injuries expressed that they were currently experiencing sexual problems. More than 90% of those who responded expressed that they would desire and use sexual education and counseling if they were available. Farrow (1990) reported that possible client concerns include birth control methods, fertility, communication with partners, alternatives to sexual intercourse, and sexual identity and role definition.

Students with mobility impairments may be concerned about how to initiate physical contact (e.g., if quadriplegic, how to initiate a kiss) or how to communicate about sexuality. Farrow (1990) suggested the following:

> The essence of all relationships, and a necessary component in any mutually satisfying sexual relationship, is communication, which is especially important when one partner has a disability. Often partners of persons with spinal cord injuries are justifiably curious but are afraid of offending their partners by asking questions. If persons with spinal cord injuries can learn to be open and honest about their limitations and capabilities, subsequent problems and tensions resulting from unrealistic expectations and consequent disappointments might be alleviated. Communication between partners is vital. (Communication section, para. 1)

Westgren and Levi (1999) found that, instead of talking to their partners about their anxieties, women with disabilities rely, more than men do, on guesswork and assumptions in their sexual interactions. Farrow (1990) reported that men with disabilities tend to question their sex role because the majority of society believes that people with disabilities are supposed to be dependent and needy. Obviously, a major component of counseling about sexuality is about communication.

Clinical Impacts

It is initially important for the counselor to consider whether the counseling office and typical office procedures are accessible to students with mobility impairments. We have already discussed the physical office space, but it is also important to assure that students with mobility impairments are able to fill out intake forms and other paperwork. Counselors should train front desk staff on how to discreetly assist students who need help. If counselors use "homework" as a regular part of their counseling work, they may need to consider alternatives to activities that require manual dexterity. As discussed previously, thoughtfulness about these issues may mean the difference between students with mobility impairments feeling welcome and accepted or uninvited and excluded.

Counselor Comfort Issues

A counselor's comfort level in working with students with mobility impairments can have a major impact on the counseling environment. Beecher, Rabe, and Wilder (2004) provided a general reference for counseling students with disabilities, including general interaction guidelines and common themes that arise in the counseling environment. Although counselors should not assume that all issues are related to the mobility impairment, they should not be afraid to acknowledge and to ask questions about the disability. This is particularly important when working with students with invisible impairments.

Ward and Pointon (2004) suggested that it is most helpful when counselors acknowledge that there are differences between them and the students with disabilities but also emphasize that they are willing to try to bridge the gaps and accept those differences. Ward and Pointon further suggested that a supportive, yet challenging, atmosphere is productive. They made "an argument for treating clients with a disability in the same way as anyone else, as an individual, while holding in mind the awareness of their particular circumstances" (Ward & Pointon, 2004, As a client section, para. 10).

Common Presenting Issues

Although not unique to students with mobility impairments, there are some therapeutic issues that are common among these students that may be useful for counselors to understand because of the significant impact they may have on counseling efforts. These issues include locus of control/learned helplessness, sense of isolation/lack of belonging, and lack of validation.

Because students with mobility impairments typically fight constant obstacles and limited or denied options (e.g., few accessible housing options), they may feel they have little control over their lives and/or develop a sense of helplessness.

It is, therefore, important for counselors to recognize that this may be a theme in counseling. Numerous studies have shown that people are happier if they believe that they have a meaningful amount of control or choice over events in their lives (Bach, 1988; Langer & Rodin, 1976; Lefcourt, 1976; Rodin, 1976; Rodin & Langer, 1977; Schulz, 1976; Schulz & Hanusa, 1979; Shadish, Hickman, & Arrick, 1981). It may be that availability of choice and the opportunity to make a decision are actually more important to a person than the specific choice that is made. Boschen (1996) found that locus of control was correlated with life satisfaction in such a way that the more internal the orientation, the greater the satisfaction. Counselors can do much to help students develop a sense of control or self-efficacy and see options available to them.

As mentioned previously, students with mobility impairments may also feel a sense of isolation or lack of belonging. If they express loneliness in the counseling office, it is important for counselors to assess how much of that loneliness is due to physical impediments that prevent students from participating in activities with friends and roommates and how much is due to typical college student social concerns. Students with outwardly apparent disabilities may be left out of activities and conversations or be excluded from common physical touch (Beecher et al., 2004). Counselors can work with students with mobility impairments to find ways to participate in activities and to express their needs and desires to friends and roommates.

Lack of validation can have impacts on multiple levels. Students with apparent physical impairments may begin to doubt their validity as valuable human beings or to feel they lack social skills if they are continually excluded from activities (Beecher et al., 2004). Students with invisible impairments may feel lack of validation as they perceive themselves as different from their peers with and without impairments. There is also a high likelihood that they will feel invalidated as they seek help from faculty and peers who doubt the existence of their impairment or refuse to provide academic accommodations. By listening and earnestly striving to understand students' experience, counselors can do much to help students with mobility impairments to feel validated in the counseling office and to create an environment of openness and sharing.

Campus Considerations: Collaboration

The counselor can best meet the needs of students with mobility impairments by working in collaboration with other offices on campus. These offices collectively provide resources that can benefit both student and counselor. The counselor should be aware of the available resources and know to whom he or she can refer the student for each situation. Referrals are best facilitated when the counselor personally knows the staff of each office and can give the student the name of the contact person or, ideally, accompany the student to the office.

It is advisable for the counselor to develop a close working relationship with the staff of the disability services (DS) on campus. The DS staff members typically have the most expertise on campus about how to serve students with disabilities. They have responsibility for ensuring an accessible environment for these students, including physical campus and academic programs. It is also the job of the DS staff, along with the staff of the equal opportunity and legal counsel's offices, to educate and advise faculty and staff on disability issues. The counselor can consult the DS staff for help and advice on the needs of students with mobility impairments.

In addition, the counselor should become familiar with the local vocational rehabilitation (VR) office. VR staff can often provide significant assistance to students with mobility impairments. Each state's VR office has different laws, rules, and funding, but services may include financial aid, assistance in finding accessible housing, and equipment necessary to be successful in school (e.g., dictation software).

With the assistance and guidance of these other offices, the counselor can become an effective advocate for students struggling with various campus entities. The counselor, for example, can assist academic advisors and registrars in understanding that a student with a mobility impairment may need to schedule classes carefully to ensure enough time and energy to get between classes. Similarly, the counselor can help financial aid officers understand that a student's disability, because of specific physical limitations, may necessitate a reduced course load.

It is important to note that, although state, local, or university financial aid resources may have the latitude to allow a student to maintain scholarships, grants, and loans while taking a disability-justified reduced course load, most federal financial aid organizations, such as those administrating Pell grants, Stafford loans, and VR funds, will not allow this practice.

Future Trends

With new legislation and continued advancements in technology and medical treatment, colleges can expect to see increasing numbers of students with mobility impairments on their campuses (Brinkerhoff, Shaw, & McGuire, 1993; Henderson, 1999; Vogel, Leyser, Wyland, & Brulle, 1999) and at college counseling centers. It is important for counselors to maintain an attitude of continual learning and awareness about issues concerning students with mobility impairments as well as students with other disabilities. Counselors should remember, however, that a student's mobility impairment is likely secondary to other individual concerns the student may raise. The most helpful interventions a counselor may use will likely be those tailored to the individual rather than the disability. Often the success of counseling with students with mobility impairments, as with most students, will rely on the counselor's ability to create an open, respectful, and understanding relationship (Ward & Pointon, 2004). When in doubt about what is appropriate or what is best practice, ask the true expert, the student.

References

ADA and ABA Accessibility Guidelines for Buildings and Facilities. Retrieved March 22, 2006, from http://www.access-board.gov/ada-aba/final.htm#pgfId-1006182.

Americans With Disabilities Act of 1990, 42 U.S.C.A. § 12101 *et seq.* (West 1993).

Bach, C. A. (1988). The relationships among perceived control of activities of daily living, dependency and life satisfaction in quadriplegic adults (Doctoral dissertation, University of Texas at Austin, 1988). *Dissertation Abstracts International, 49,* 2563B.

Beecher, M. E., Rabe, R. A., & Wilder, L. K. (2004). Practical guidelines for counseling students with disabilities. *Journal of College Counseling, 7,* 83–89.

Beilke, J. R., & Yssel, N. (1999). The chilly climate for students with disabilities in higher education. *College Student Journal, 33,* 364–372.

Boschen, K. (1996). Correlates of life satisfaction, residential satisfaction, and locus of control among adults with spinal cord injuries. *Rehabilitation Counseling Bulletin, 39,* 230–244.

Brinkerhoff, L. C., Shaw, S., & McGuire, J. (1993). *Promoting postsecondary education for college students with learning disabilities: A handbook for practitioners.* Austin, TX: PRO-ED.

Farrow, J. (1990). Sexuality counseling with clients who have spinal cord injuries [Electronic version]. *Rehabilitation Counseling Bulletin, 33,* 251–260.

Gibson, J. M. (2000). Documentation of emotional and mental disabilities: The role of the counseling center. *Journal of College Counseling, 3,* 63–73.

Gordon, M., Lewandowski, L., Murphy, K., & Dempsey, K. (2002). ADA-based accommodations in higher education: A survey of clinicians about documentation requirements and diagnostic standards. *Journal of Learning Disabilities, 35,* 357–363.

Hampton, N. Z. (2004). Subjective well-being among people with spinal cord injuries: The role of self-efficacy, perceived social support, and perceived health. *Rehabilitation Counseling Bulletin, 48,* 31–37.

Hayes, R. L., & Potter, C. G. (1995). Counseling the client on wheels: A primer for mental health counselors new to spinal cord injury [Electronic version]. *Journal of Mental Health Counseling, 17,* 18–31.

Henderson, C. (1999). *College freshman with disabilities: A biennial statistical profile.* Washington, DC: American Council on Education.

Hendrick, S. S. (1981). Physical body losses. *Personnel and Guidance Journal, 59,* 355–359.

Horn, L., Peter, K., & Rooney, K. (2002). *Profile of undergraduates in U.S. postsecondary institutions: 1999–2000, NCES 2002.* Washington, DC: U.S. Department of Education, National Center for Education Statistics.

Langer, E. J., & Rodin, J. (1976). The effects of choice and enhanced personal responsibility for the aged: A field experiment in an institutional setting. *Journal of Personality and Social Psychology, 34,* 191–198.

Lefcourt, H. M. (1976). *Locus of control: Current trends in theory and research.* Hillsdale, NJ: Erlbaum.

Leigh, I., Powers, L., Vash, C., & Nettles, R. (2004). Survey of psychological services to clients with disabilities: The need for awareness. *Rehabilitation Psychology, 49,* 48–54.

McCarthy, H. (1999). Integrating spirituality into rehabilitation in a technocratic society. In R. P. Marinelli & A. E. Dell (Eds.), *The psychological and social impact of disability* (pp. 375–382). New York: Springer Publishing Company.

Narum, G. D., & Rodolfa, E. R. (1984). Sex therapy for the spinal cord injured client: Suggestions for professionals. *Professional Psychology: Research and Practice, 15,* 775–784.

Padrone, F. J. (1994). Psychotherapeutic issues with family members of persons with physical disabilities [Electronic version]. *American Journal of Psychotherapy, 48,* 195–208.

Preece, J. E. (1994). *An ethnographic study into the concerns and issues of participants attending a therapy group for individuals with chronic pain and/or illness.* Unpublished doctoral dissertation, Brigham Young University.

Rodin, J. (1976). Density, perceived control, and response to controllable and uncontrollable outcomes. *Journal of Experimental Social Psychology, 12,* 564–578.

Rodin, J., & Langer, E. J. (1977). Long-term effects of a control-relevant intervention with the institutionalized aged. *Journal of Personality and Social Psychology, 35,* 897–902.

Schulz, R. (1976). Effects of control and predictability on the physical and psychological well-being of the institutionalized aged. *Journal of Personality and Social Psychology, 33,* 563–573.

Schulz, R., & Hanusa, B. H. (1979). Environmental influences on the effectiveness of control and competence-enhancing interventions. In L. C. Perlmuter & R. A. Monty (Eds.), *Choice and perceived control* (pp. 315–337). Hillsdale, NJ: Erlbaum.

Section 504 of the Rehabilitation Act of 1973, as amended, 29 U.S.C. § 794.

Shadish, W. R., Hickman, D., & Arrick, M. C. (1981). Psychological problems of spinal cord injury patients: Emotional distress as a function of time and locus of control. *Journal of Consulting and Clinical Psychology, 49,* 297.

Smith, T. W, & Nicassio, P. M. (1995). Psychological practice: Clinical applications of the biopsychosocial model. In P. M. Nicassio & T. W. Smith (Eds.), *Managing chronic illness: A biopsychological perspective* (pp. 1–31). Washington, DC: American Psychological Association.

Turk, D.C., & Okifuji, A. (1999). Assessment of patients' reporting of pain: An integrated perceptive. *The Lancet, 353,* 1784–1788.

Vallandingham, D. (1997). Advising for the future: Advising students with disabilities. *NACADA Monograph Series, 5,* 79–81.

Vogel, S. A., Leyser, Y., Wyland, S., & Brulle, A. (1999). Students with learning disabilities in higher education: Faculty attitude and practices. *Learning Disabilities Research and Practice, 14,* 173–186.

Ward, R., & Pointon, C. (2004). Thoughts on therapy and disability [Electronic version]. *Counselling & Psychotherapy Journal, 15,* 18–20.

Westgren, N., & Levi, R. (1999). Sexuality after injury: Interviews with women after traumatic spinal cord injury. *Sexuality and Disability, 17,* 309–319.

Young, M. E., & Alfred, W. G. (1994). Vocational status of persons with spinal cord injury living in the community [Electronic version]. *Rehabilitation Counseling Bulletin, 37,* 229–243.

Zeilig, G., Dolev, M., Weingarden, H., Blumen, N., Shemesh, Y., & Ohry, A. (2000). Long-term morbidity and mortality after spinal cord injury: 50 years of follow-up. *Spinal Cord, 38,* 563–566.

16

Counseling Students Who Are Visually Impaired or Blind

D. Shane Koch

Introduction

The eye is an individual's "window on the world," and, as such, it is the organ primarily responsible for enabling individuals to access data outside of themselves (Panek, 2002). Although there are many different disorders and injuries that may lead to visual impairment and/or blindness (VIB), there are several types of disorders that are most often associated with vision loss.

Vision loss associated with visual functioning includes impairment of function associated with central vision, contrast sensitivity, visual field, binocular vision, color vision, and/or night vision (Falvo, 1999). Central vision is the process by which the eyes take a precise picture with the macula or central retina (Panek, 2002). The eyes' anatomy allows for the fine vision needed to perceive near and distant objects. Contrast sensitivity has to do with the ability to discern the difference between brightness and darkness and is useful for predicting reading capability, mobility performance, and overall functional capacity. Visual field is associated with an individual's peripheral or side vision. Binocular vision is the function associated with the ability to fix both eyes on a single object, generating a single image. Color vision is associated with an individual's ability to perceive certain hues of color. Finally, night vision, as one might assume, deals with when an individual is in a low-light environment (Corn & Koenig, 1996; Falvo, 1999; Panek, 2002).

Other disorders are associated with problems that occur within the visual system. The most common of these problems is the occurrence of cataracts. Cataracts produce clouding or opacity of the lens of the eye, which can significantly reduce vision. Another common problem is glaucoma, which occurs when an increase in intraocular pressure indirectly damages the optic nerve.

Severe visual impairments due to glaucoma can have a long period of onset, but irreversible damage often occurs before the individual is diagnosed with the disease. In addition, retinitis pigmentosa is a genetic condition that may cause loss of peripheral vision, night blindness, and loss of central acuity as the disease progresses. Retinitis pigmentosa is another disorder that has a long period of onset and slow progression (Falvo, 1999; Panek, 2002).

Finally, diabetic retinopathy is becoming more of an issue as diabetes becomes more common in the U.S. population (American Diabetes Association [ADA], 2005). There are three types of diabetic retinopathy, but, in each case, the capillaries and vessels of the retina are affected, and either lack of oxygen or hemorrhages may lead to severe visual impairments or blindness. Individuals who demonstrate poor glucose control or individuals who have been diabetic for extended periods are at risk for developing this disorder (ADA, 2005; Panek, 2002).

Persons with visual impairments share many of the same life experiences and concerns as other persons with disabilities. However, the history of rehabilitation services for this population differs from other disability groups. In many states, persons who are blind have their own rehabilitation service agencies and specialized programs (Moore, Huebner, & Maxson, 1997). Federal legislation has also been created specifically for persons who are blind, resulting in specialized programs, services, and legal protections for this population that do not exist for other persons with disabilities (Moore, Huebner, & Maxson, 1997; Rubin & Roessler, 2001). Furthermore, persons who are blind have historically received special consideration when considered for Social Security disability insurance (Social Security Administration, 2005). Because of this history of specialized legislation, intervention, and service delivery, a distinctive professional culture has grown up around this population, resulting in the development of a highly specialized professional language, disability-specific interventions, and disability-specific programming that affect every aspect of coordinating educational counseling services for students with VIB (Goodrich & Sowell, 1996; Moore, Huebner, & Maxson, 1997).

Assessment Issues

Visual Impairment

Although blindness certainly qualifies as "visual impairment," there are conditions that produce varying degrees of vision loss that may create substantial limitations for individuals with these disabilities. Professionals who work with individuals who experience "low vision" consider themselves to be a distinct discipline, and it is necessary to differentiate between low vision and blindness even though there is often not a clear definition of those who are *legally sighted* and those who are *legally blind* (Corn & Koenig, 1996). Corn and Koenig (1996) defined an individual with *low vision* as a person who has difficulty accomplishing visual tasks, even with prescribed corrective lenses, but who can enhance his or her ability to accomplish these tasks with the use of compensatory visual strategies, low vision and other devices, and environmental modifications. (p. 11)

There is significant variability among individuals who experience low vision, and the requirements of individual students can be diverse, ranging from a need for large-print type to a need for significant assistive technology in order to access materials in written form or via computerized resources.

Blindness

Although there is still considerable variation among individuals who are legally blind, *legal blindness* is defined in the United States as central visual acuity of 20/200 or less in the better eye or a residual field of 20 degrees or less in the better eye (Panek, 2002). Despite this specific definition, however, many individual states have created their own definitions of blindness. These states maintain registries of the individuals they have categorized as legally blind in order to determine incidence and prevalence of the disability, allocate resources to potential consumers, and maintain long-term records regarding programmatic eligibility. If students are not on the registry, it is unlikely that they will be able to receive services, and, therefore, they may not be able to obtain the resources necessary to attend college.

There remains considerable discrepancy between medical definitions of blindness (which generally rely on the need for medical services) and definitions used by rehabilitation professionals that rely on determining the impact of the disability on an individual's ability to perform work and daily living activities (Dickerson, Smith, & Moore, 1997; Falvo, 1999). Although the legal definitions are typically more relevant to the issue of determining eligibility, the rehabilitation assessment models are more useful in clinical and educational settings to determine the actual impact of the disability on a student's daily life.

Rehabilitation Model for VIB

The foundation of the rehabilitation model for VIB is the functional capacity assessment (Smart, 2001). Using this model, rehabilitation counselors seek to identify an individual's strengths, limitations, and interests in order to establish a baseline on which to create an individual rehabilitation plan. Typically, this plan focuses on employment, but it also touches nearly every aspect of an individual's life, accomplishing the general goal of enhancing the individual's independence and participation in his or her community (Rubin & Roessler, 2001). Ongoing assessment and monitoring are stressed, due to the ever-changing, ever-evolving nature of the individual's disability experience (Rubin & Roessler, 2001).

Finally, counselors should be aware that medical and rehabilitation management and assessment sometimes become the focus of the lives of students with

VIB, rather than a means of assuring that they are able to be independent and functional individuals. Medical and rehabilitation interventions may distract students from their academic life and overshadow their vocational and educational goals (Graves & McCaa, 1997). Furthermore, students may perceive themselves only in the context of their disabling condition, rather than as human beings who are uniquely able to contribute to the life of their communities (Smart, 2001).

Counseling Implications

Congenital Onset

Individuals who experience disability from birth will have many shared experiences that influence formation of their attitudes, beliefs, and values. Persons who experience congenital disorders will have never established an identity that did not include the disability. Consequently, the disability will have had an effect on many aspects of their educational, social, and family life (Smart, 2001).

When a child is born with a disability, the perceptions of family members about the disability and about their own roles with the child have a tremendous impact on the child's development and self-concept (Smart, 2001). For example, if family members become overprotective of the child or overemphasize the negative impact of the disability, they may exaggerate the functional limitations because of a misperception of the impact of the disability. Students may arrive at college with a fundamental belief that they are flawed or incapable because of their familial experience.

If the family feels moral guilt about the disability, this can also significantly affect the student's self-concept (Falvo, 1999; Smart, 2001). In some families, individuals may still operate out of a biblical framework that interprets the disability as the result of a moral failing or demonic possession (Rubin & Roessler, 2001). I have counseled college advisees with disabilities whose families believed that, if they just "prayed hard enough," the disability would be removed.

Students with VIB may have radically different childhood experiences than those children who do not have VIB. Many of the conditions leading to VIB require consistent medical monitoring and interventions. As a result, these students may have grown up in the medical environment and had significantly more interactions with adults than the typical student (Smart, 2001). These atypical childhood experiences may result in the development of attitudes, beliefs, and values that are quite different from those of other students. Counselors should not expect any stereotypical response to these experiences from the students, but counselors should look for ways in which these experiences have shaped the students' identities.

Finally, young persons who grew up with VIB will necessarily have had educational experiences that are unique to this population. Special educators, rehabilitation teachers, orientation and mobility instructors, and other rehabilitation professionals are likely to have been directly involved in facilitating the educational process. In addition, there will have been designated case management teams with specific plans in place to serve the students' needs while they were in the public school system (Rubin & Roessler, 2001). Students entering the college environment must assume new roles and responsibilities in establishing relationships with campus disability services, and they may require additional support from counselors who can ease their fears and frustrations regarding accessing college services.

The adaption to new social roles can be particularly difficult for students who grew up in nontraditional educational settings or experienced isolation because of their disability. Both Smart (2001) and Falvo (1999) suggested that one of the most challenging aspects of congenital disabilities is developing effective socialization skills. Knowing that it is difficult for students without disabilities to make this transition, counselors should expect that students with VIB may need support in this area. The counselor may wish to consult with rehabilitation specialists who have worked with this population to discuss strategies that are effective in developing the new skills necessary during the transition to the college environment.

Acquired Disability

Although students who have acquired their disabilities later in life may experience many of the same challenges as individuals with congenital disabilities, several issues are specific to acquired disabilities. First, these students may need to form a new identity that takes into account the disabling condition. Smart (2001) suggested that individuals with disabilities need to begin to "subordinate the physical"; that is, they must begin to value physical attributes less than they may have valued them in the past. Adaption to the disability may mean adjusting to having a different appearance or a different manner of interaction with the community.

Smart (2001) also suggested that students with disabilities benefit from developing *asset values* as opposed to *comparison values*. This coping strategy involves focusing on individual strengths rather than identifying weaknesses or dissimilarities that may lead to individual isolation or feelings of anxiety.

Panek (2002) emphasized the extreme emotional impact that occurs because of the onset of blindness or visual loss. Individual response to the disability is dependent on the coping skills the individual may have developed prior to the disability. Many individuals may not possess the necessary resources to adjust or adapt to the disability without extended counseling interventions. This is particularly true when individuals are experiencing other coexisting disabilities that may have already negatively affected their coping skills, such as substance abuse or mental illness (Koch, Nelipovich, & Sneed, 2002).

Panek (2002) noted that disability effects are not isolated. The VIB impairments affect other areas of an individual's life, including physical integrity, personal mobility, ability to perceive nonverbal communications, and ability to adjust to diverse environments. Counselors can benefit from collaborating with rehabilitation professionals to assess the student's overall adjustment to these psychological issues in cases of late-onset VIB disabilities (Falvo, 1999). Although students who have congenital onset of these disabilities may have had access to significant resources to help them adjust to the functional limitations caused by the VIB, adult-onset individuals may not have had access to those resources or may still be in the process of making these adjustments when they enter the college environment.

Adjustment to VIB

As with any disability, adjustment to VIB must occur across multiple dimensions. Students who experience VIB must address biomedical, psychological, and social challenges if they are to adjust successfully to their disability.

Medical needs and the student's health maintenance are the first priority. It is critical that students receive appropriate medical services that can help to stabilize the progression of VIB, if possible, and minimize any additional negative consequences that may arise because of underlying medical conditions. This necessitates dedication of time and resources to self-care and may prove to be a significant demand depending on the type of medical concerns that the student is experiencing. Students who have other priorities in college settings may be reluctant or resistant to maintain or establish appropriate health regimens. In addition, they may be unaware of financial and professional resources that are available to them in this new environment, and they may avoid services because of a real or perceived lack of support from the college service structure.

Several psychological adjustments must take place in order for individuals to respond positively to VIB disabilities. Smart (2001) suggested that there are three categories of *good* responses to disability: behavioral, cognitive, and affective. Behaviorally, individuals must master the skills necessary to (a) achieve independence (i.e., orientation and mobility, activities of daily living, and specific occupational/educational skills), (b) comply with medical management routines, (c) interact in social environments, and (d) actively return to work/school. Cognitively, individuals must be able to respond to the disability by redefining their reality, rather than avoiding or denying it. Affectively, they must explore how they feel about their disability and discover ways to deal with negative emotions that arise in response to their disability.

Social challenges may significantly impede students' ability to adapt to a disability. Persons with VIB face overt and covert discrimination that takes several different forms. Moore, Graves, and Patterson (1997) and Hahn (1988a) discussed some of the common stereotypes associated with disabilities and suggested that it may be these stereotypes, rather than the actual physical disability, that constitute the real disability. Moore, Graves, and Patterson reviewed commonly held misperceptions, including (a) people who are blind are being punished because of sin, (b) people who are blind have extraordinary compensatory sensory powers, (c) people who are blind are not intelligent, and (d) people who are blind also have other diminished sensory powers.

Moore, Graves, and Patterson (1997) also noted that generalized fears about disability among the general population cause anxiety toward persons with disabilities and reluctance to interact with these individuals, thereby resulting in the social exclusion and isolation of these individuals. Hahn (1988b) coined the term *aesthetic anxiety* to describe the fears that arise when nondisabled individuals encounter persons who are disabled (physically different). Thus, when a student experiences VIB disabilities, there is more to adjustment than just managing the physical and psychological complications. The most serious challenge may be the inability to enter into the academic community as a respected and valued member of that community.

Adaption

The terms *adjustment* and *adaption* appear alone and together in this chapter as components of the individual response to disability. Despite the fact that these terms are related, some disability theorists suggest that adaption has special meaning and value and should be the goal for individuals who experience disability.

Livneh (1986) described adaption as a gradual process whereby an individual creates a new identity over time. Although Livneh addressed positive adaption, the process of identity transformation can be either positive or negative. Smart (2001) articulated that successful adaption to the disability requires that individuals (a) understand and accept their reality and the implications of their disability, (b) establish new values and goals that do not conflict with the disability, and (c) explore and use their strengths and abilities.

Smart's (2001) definition of adaption, and the implications inherent in actualizing one's full potential, echoes the work of another disability theorist, Carolyn Vash, who described the possibility for individual transcendence of disability. Vash (1981) suggested that true adaption occurs when the individual transcends the disability and sees it as an opportunity for growth and learning.

Negative Compensatory Strategies

Alternatively, students with VIB can transform their identity by developing and using negative compensatory strategies. When individuals respond in this fashion, extremely negative outcomes can occur. These individuals will likely fail to actualize their potential and will not be as likely to succeed in competitive academic environments.

Smart (2001) discussed negative compensatory strategies in the form of seeking *secondary gains,* such as (a) financial compensation, (b) pity, (c) negative attention, (d) freedom from evaluation and competition, and (e) free time. In all of these cases, she suggested, seeking secondary gains becomes a sort of avoidance/self-protection strategy that results in the individual's inability to participate actively and independently in his or her family and community. All of these strategies tend to foster unnecessary dependence on others, feelings of helplessness, shame, low self-esteem, immaturity, and extreme external locus of control.

Finally, in terms of negative cognitive strategies, several maladaptive responses can occur. Examples include unrealistic or "magical thinking," blaming, self-pity, hypersensitivity to criticism, passivity, emotional liability, and resignation (Livneh & Antonak, 1997). When interacting with students who have VIB, counselors may observe these behaviors and choose either to intervene directly or to refer students for specialized counseling services that can assist them in becoming more positively focused.

Coexisting Disabilities

Several years ago, I received a grant focused on assisting individuals with VIB to access alcohol and other drug abuse (AODA) resources. When a colleague approached me to ask what I was working on during the summer, I responded by describing the project. The colleague then stated, "Wow, you mean people who are blind use drugs?" This incident accurately reflects much of the research on professional awareness about coexisting disabilities (AODA co-occurring with other disabling conditions; Koch, 2005).

Koch, Shearer, and Nelipovich (2004) reported that many persons with VIB struggle with coexisting AODA disorders, but this struggle goes unrecognized by professionals who lack awareness, knowledge, and skills about VIB. Furthermore, individuals with VIB are typically unable to access AODA services because the AODA providers lack awareness about VIB. This is unfortunate, because persons who have VIB experience significantly higher rates of substance abuse disorders than the general population (Nelipovich, Wergin, & Kossick, 1998).

Counselors need to be aware that many persons with VIB experience significant substance use disorders, and these disorders can impede progress in educational and rehabilitation programs. These students may have experienced AODA disorders before their disability, and the AODA may have contributed to the onset of VIB, or the students may experience AODA disorders as a negative coping strategy occurring after the onset of the disability.

Campus Considerations

Collaboration and Coordination of Services

College counselors may wish to consult with specialists who have worked with the population with VIB to discuss strategies that are effective in working with these students. Corn and Koenig (1996) provided examples of what a potential team of collaborators might look like for a student experiencing VIB. Eye care providers might include optometrists, ophthalmologists, and clinical low-vision specialists. Rehabilitation specialists might include rehabilitation teachers, rehabilitation counselors, and orientation and mobility specialists. Other allied health personnel who would be valuable team members might include speech and language specialists, occupational therapists, physical therapists, and transition coordinators.

Rehabilitation teachers are professionals who work with individuals who are newly blind or visually impaired. They focus on helping persons with VIB disabilities learn how to overcome their physical challenges, with the goal of learning the knowledge and skills necessary to independently perform activities of daily living, such as home management, personal management, communication and education, leisure activity, and home orientation skills (Moore, Graves, & Patterson, 1997). Rehabilitation teachers are often employed in regional or local offices of a state agency, by community rehabilitation programs, or in residential training programs.

Orientation and mobility specialists are professionals who teach the skills necessary for persons with VIB disabilities to become independent travelers, such as the use of electronic aids, a long cane, or sighted (human) guides (Moore, Graves, & Patterson, 1997). Orientation and mobility instructors do not teach individuals how to use dog guides. Individuals who wish to learn to travel using dog guides enroll at specialized dog guide schools where they learn to use this resource.

Many states have specialized residential programs designed to help individuals with new VIB adjust or adapt to their new life situations. These facilities usually have rehabilitation counselors, other health care specialists, and all of the blindness-specific professionals on staff. The residential programs can be extremely valuable resources for college counselors.

Assistive Technology

Students with VIB disabilities need access to assistive and informational technologies if they are to be successful in their educational programs. Counselors should work closely with on-campus experts to facilitate effective student access to these resources. Some examples of VIB-related technology include large monitors, screen-enlarging software (built into Windows), voice output, and character recognition software. One of the most popular programs is Job Access With Speech. This program produces voice output that allows Windows users to manage their files, access the Internet, read e-mail, and perform other computer-related tasks. The Kurzweil products are also popular tools that enable users to scan documents, convert them to text, and then read them back (Scherer, 2004).

Scherer (2004) created a comprehensive list of devices that are potentially useful for persons with VIB, including a portable cassette recorder, large-print materials, a handheld magnifier, a Braille note taker, a Braille typewriter, an adapted keyboard, and an alternate mouse/pointer, as well as the adaptive computer hardware and software systems previously mentioned. One mistaken belief of persons who do not work with VIB is that all persons with VIB read Braille. The fact is that most individuals with VIB do not use Braille at all.

Future Trends

The American Federation for the Blind (2005) has reported that there are 10 million people with VIB in the United States, but this number is expected to increase because of changing demographics and emerging health concerns

(Panek, 2002; Prevent Blindness America & National Eye Institute, 2002). College counselors can therefore expect to encounter an increase in the number of students with VIB.

Changing demographics will exacerbate the challenges of serving persons with VIB. As the general U.S. population ages, VIB disabilities will increase as a public health issue (American Public Health Association, 2004; Panek, 2002; Prevent Blindness America & National Eye Institute, 2002). Although these disabilities can occur to persons across the life span, they tend to increase with age as well as with onset of other disabling conditions (American Federation for the Blind, 2005; Falvo, 1999). Thus, with the continuing increase in older "returning" students at American colleges (Marques & Luna, 2005), college counselors will necessarily be assisting more students with VIB.

In addition, the United States has been experiencing a dramatic increase in the number of citizens diagnosed with diabetes. The ADA (2005) reported that 18.2 million Americans have diabetes. Given the direct correlation between diabetes and retinopathy (Falvo, 1999; Hornichter, 2002), counselors may expect that the increase in diabetes will produce an increase in diabetic-related visual impairments and blindness. This is particularly alarming because many of the new cases of diabetes are among younger Americans (ADA, 2005), again suggesting that the number of individuals experiencing VIB disabilities will be increasing among college populations.

A more positive trend is the expanding availability of low-cost assistive technology. Scherer (2004) commented that the realities of new technology are what have made inclusion of persons with disabilities in education possible. VIB professionals, particularly those professionals in residential programs and state agency offices who are dedicated to serving this single population, are valuable resources in identifying and accessing appropriate hardware devices and software programs that can greatly support students with disabilities. Consequently, although the population of persons with VIB may be increasing, the technological resources to support them are increasing as well, making it much easier for them to participate fully in educational programs.

References

American Diabetes Association. (2005). *All about diabetes*. Retrieved April 1, 2005, from http://www.diabetes.org/about-diabetes.jsp

American Federation for the Blind. (2005). *Blindness statistics*. Retrieved April 1, 2005, from http://www.afb.org/Section.asp?SectionID=15#num

American Public Health Association. (2004). Vision loss: An increasing health problem. *Nation's Health, 34*, 14.

Corn, A. L., & Koenig, A. J. (1996). Perspectives on low vision. In A. L. Corn & A. J. Koenig (Eds.), *Foundations of low vision: Clinical and functional perspectives* (pp. 3–25). New York: AFB Press.

Dickerson, L. R., Smith, P. B., & Moore, J. E. (1997). An overview of blindness and visual impairment. In J. E. Moore, W. H. Graves, & J. B. Patterson (Eds.), *Foundations of rehabilitation counseling with persons who are blind or visually impaired* (pp. 3–24). New York: AFB Press.

Falvo, D. (1999). *Medical and psychosocial aspects of chronic illness and disability* (2nd ed.). Gaithersburg, MD: Aspen.

Goodrich, G. L., & Sowell, V. M. (1996). Low vision: A history in progress. In A. L. Corn & A. J. Koenig (Eds.), *Foundations of low vision: Clinical and functional perspectives* (pp. 399–404). New York: AFB Press.

Graves, W. H., & McCaa, C. (1997). Medical assessment. In J. E. Moore, W. H. Graves, & J. B. Patterson (Eds.), *Foundations of rehabilitation counseling with persons who are blind or visually impaired* (pp. 107–128). New York: AFB Press.

Hahn, H. (1988a). Can disability be beautiful? *Social Policy, 18,* 26–32.

Hahn, H. (1988b). The politics of physical differences: Disability and discrimination. *Journal of Social Issues, 44,* 39–47.

Hornichter, R. D. (2002). Diabetes mellitus. In M. G. Brodwin, F. Tellez, & S. K. Brodwin (Eds.), *Medical, psychosocial, and vocational aspects of disability* (2nd ed., pp. 213–225). Athens, GA: Elliot & Fitzpatrick.

Koch, D. S. (2005, July). *Substance abuse and disability: Opening the doors to treatment for persons with coexisting disabilities.* Paper presented at the 29th Annual Meeting of the National Association of Alcoholism and Drug Abuse Counselors/31st Annual State Conference of the Texas Association of Addiction Professionals, Corpus Christi, TX.

Koch, D. S., Nelipovich, M., & Sneed, Z. (2002). Alcohol and other drug abuse as coexisting disabilities: Considerations for counselors serving individuals who are blind or visually impaired. *RE:View, 33,* 151–160.

Koch, D. S., Shearer, B., & Nelipovich, M. (2004). Service delivery for persons with blindness and visual impairment as coexisting disabilities: Implications for addiction science education. *Journal of Teaching in the Addictions, 3,* 21–48.

Livneh, H. (1986). A unified approach to existing models of adaption to disability: A model of adaption. *Journal of Applied Rehabilitation Counseling, 17,* 5–16.

Livneh, H., & Antonak, R. F. (1997). *Psychosocial adaption to chronic illness and disability.* Gaithersburg, MD: Aspen.

Marques, J. F., & Luna, R. (2005). Advising adult learners: The practice of peer partisanship. *Recruitment & Retention in Higher Education, 19,* 5–6.

Moore, J. E., Graves, W. H., & Patterson, J. B. (Eds.). (1997). *Foundations of rehabilitation counseling with persons who are blind or visually impaired.* New York: AFB Press.

Moore, J. E., Huebner, K. M., & Maxson, J. H. (1997). Service systems and resources. In J. E. Moore, W. H. Graves, & J. B. Patterson (Eds.), *Foundations of rehabilitation counseling with persons who are blind or visually impaired* (pp. 225–256). New York: AFB Press.

Nelipovich, M., Wergin, C., & Kossick, R. (1998). The MARCO model: Making substance abuse services accessible. *Journal of Visual Impairment & Blindness, 92,* 567–569.

Panek, W. C. (2002). Visual disabilities. In M. G. Brodwin, F. Tellez, & S. K. Brodwin (Eds.), *Medical, psychosocial, and vocational aspects of disability* (2nd ed., pp. 157–171). Athens, GA: Elliot & Fitzpatrick.

Prevent Blindness America & National Eye Institute. (2002). *Vision problems in the U.S.: Prevalence of adult vision impairment and age-related eye disease in America.* Chicago: Author.

Rubin, S. E., & Roessler, R. T. (2001). *Foundations of the vocational rehabilitation process* (5th ed.). Austin, TX: PRO-ED.

Scherer, M. J. (2004). *Connecting to learn: Educational and assistive technology for people with disabilities.* Washington, DC: American Psychological Association.

Smart, J. (2001). *Disability, society, and the individual.* Gaithersburg, MD: Aspen.

Social Security Administration. (2005). *If you are blind or have low vision—how we can help.* Retrieved April 10, 2005, from http://www.socialsecurity.gov/pubs/10052.html

Vash, C. L. (1981). *The psychology of disability.* New York: Springer Publishing Company.

Counseling Students Who Are Deaf

Kendra L. Smith and Lauri L. Rush

Introduction

The National Center for Health Statistics (2002) estimated that 6.7% of the general population ages 18 to 44 years have a hearing loss. Of people over the age of 18, almost 14 million people with a hearing loss have at least some college education. These statistics indicate that almost every college counselor will have some opportunity to work with students who are hard-of-hearing or deaf. According to Steinberg (1991), working with deaf clients may be the ultimate challenge for mental health professionals, requiring them to examine their preconceived ideas about the relationship between thought and language. This chapter explores the unique experience of working with deaf students in a college counseling center. It is our goal to demystify working with deaf clients and to help college counselors feel better prepared to provide appropriate services to deaf clients.

Attitudes toward deaf individuals are roughly divided into two groups: the medical/pathological model and the cultural/linguistic model (Porter, 1999). Although there is much historical emphasis on the medical/pathological model, the cultural/linguistic model is considered more culturally considerate and therapeutically appropriate when one is working in a counseling setting. Deaf individuals comprise a heterogeneous group on at least four levels: audiological condition, educational setting and achievement, sociocultural characteristics and behaviors, and communication abilities and preferences (Sussman & Brauer, 1999). Reflecting this, the following sections address audiological condition and cultural identity, educational experience and psychosocial development, and communication abilities and preferences.

Audiological Condition and Cultural Identity

Audiologically, hearing loss can range from mild to profound. Depending on the type of loss (i.e., conductive or sensorineural), hearing may be amplified through use of various types of equipment, including hearing aids and cochlear implants, with varying degrees of success. Many people, whether born deaf or having lost their hearing later, are acculturated to hearing society, and their first language is a spoken language. They may identify as deaf, hard-of-hearing, hearing impaired, or even hearing. A large number of deaf persons, however, are acculturated to the visual–spatial language and society of the *Deaf community*, or what is otherwise called *Deaf culture* (Lane, 1992). We primarily focus on this group in this chapter. We use lowercase *deaf* in this chapter when referring to the audiological condition of not hearing and uppercase *Deaf* when specifically referring to those deaf persons who belong to Deaf culture.

Deaf Culture

Culturally Deaf persons, like members of other cultural minorities, share a common language (i.e., a natural sign language), history, arts, beliefs, mores, behavior patterns, and social institutions. For members of Deaf culture, the degree of hearing loss is not relevant to their identity, and they do not see themselves as "broken" hearing people. The acculturation process of Deaf persons need not happen at an early age. Because of choices made early on by others in the individuals' lives, many Deaf people join the Deaf community after childhood. The hearing outsider may not be able to distinguish between a person who is deaf and one who is Deaf. Thus, it is important for the college counselor to be open to the difference and permit the student to express his or her identification. It is also important for the counselor to have an understanding of the cultural norms of the Deaf community in order to effectively evaluate and treat Deaf clients.

It is important at this juncture to take a brief look at how psychological literature has historically described deaf persons. Unfortunately, much of that literature involves negative stereotypes, determined by misperceptions and the paternalistic posture of hearing clinicians. Harlan Lane (1992), a professor of psychology and linguistics at Northeastern University, reviewed psychology journals and textbooks from the 1920s to the 1990s for their descriptions of deaf people. What he found were scores of negative traits assigned to deaf individuals (e.g., hedonistic, easily frustrated, impulsive, rigid, and lacking initiative). On closer examination, Lane found that the tests being administered to determine these attributions were far from objective and were often not valid or reliable when used with deaf persons.

Clinicians traditionally see deaf persons through comparison with the hearing norm and consider them deviant or deficient. Many of the goals of psychology and education for deaf individuals, therefore, are intended to remedy the deficiencies (Paul & Jackson, 1993). Added to this is the general societal perspective that being "other" than the majority is not desirable, which leads people to consider deafness to be a very heavy and sad burden. Although some deaf people experience these feelings about themselves, members of the Deaf community, as noted above, do not see themselves as disabled or handicapped but instead as members of a rich cultural minority.

Educational Experience and Psychosocial Development

With regard to educational setting, there are a number of possible experiences that deaf students may have encountered prior to entering college. These include being taught in self-contained deaf classes in mainstream public schools, being fully mainstreamed into hearing classrooms (with or without interpreters), or attending residential schools specifically for Deaf children (either as day or residential students). They may or may not have also participated in early intervention programs for Deaf children and their parents. For ages birth to 5 years, these programs are typically designed to provide parents with education about raising a deaf child and exposing the child to preliteracy skills, accessible communication, and socialization opportunities. The deaf student may have experienced one or a combination of these settings.

The client's educational background is important to understand in terms of his or her educational achievement and psychosocial development. For example, many deaf students who were fully mainstreamed were socially isolated from their peers because of barriers in communication. Conversely, residential students may have been separated from their families for long periods while they attended school, and this separation may have affected their psychosocial development. In addition to educational background, counselors should give consideration to the diverse ethnic and racial backgrounds of deaf persons.

Communication Abilities and Preferences

American Sign Language

The final category of heterogeneity is communication abilities and preferences. As already noted, Deaf people have in common the use of a natural sign language. Natural sign languages are not universal; each country has its own naturally developed sign language. American Sign Language (ASL) is the language of Deaf people in the United States and parts of Canada.[1] ASL is recognized as a distinct language with its own highly complex linguistic features and is not a manual form of English. Not all deaf people use ASL though, and many may have been exposed to a variety of communication modes during their primary and secondary educations. Deaf college students may use one or a combination of ASL, spoken English (including speech reading), or artificial systems purportedly designed to code English (such as Seeing Essential English, Signing Exact English, or Cued Speech). Deaf college students, particularly those for whom English is not their first language, will have varying degrees of achievement in written English. Once again, these differences can be confusing to the college counselor. It is best to allow the client to determine which communication mode is preferable for the counseling and assessment environment.

As Williams and Abeles (2004) noted, "given that communication is critical for all aspects of the therapeutic process, the paramount issue that arises in working with deaf clients is the language barrier" (p. 644). Communication alone can

---

[1]Langue des Signes Québécoise is the language used in French-speaking areas of Canada.

make or break the therapeutic relationship and determine the validity and reliability of assessment. Therefore, it is critical that effective communication be established between the counselor and the client. Counselors unaccustomed to working with Deaf clients often assume that Deaf persons are as comfortable communicating in English as the counselors are. This assumption may hold true for those audiologically deaf persons who do not know a natural sign language. Such clients may want to use a combination of spoken English and speech reading. This is often an imprecise process though, given that only 26%–40% of English words can actually be distinguished on the lips (Porter, 1999).

For most deaf persons, spoken English is not an accessible means of communication. Expecting deaf persons to use written or typed English, particularly to communicate emotionally charged material or for more than very brief exchanges (e.g., scheduling an appointment), is far from optimal and can be a lengthy and arduous process for both the counselor and the client. In addition, surveys have shown that Deaf persons are more willing to see a counselor when sign language is the primary form of communication (Williams & Abeles, 2004). Because the majority of college counselors do not know ASL, the question arises as to the best way to serve Deaf clients.

It is our opinion that if there are mental health professionals available in the local community who are either Deaf or hearing and proficient in ASL, then the Deaf client should be referred to one of these professionals for counseling or assessment. Such professionals are in short supply, however, and thus the second best option is to procure the services of an interpreter. It is important to point out that the interpreter is there to provide assistance to the counselor as well as the student and should not be seen as a service solely for the benefit of the student. After all, the counselor is probably more handicapped by the language barrier than the student because most deaf people are exposed to frequent interactions that require communicative flexibility.

Interpreter Services

Once the decision has been made to obtain the services of an interpreter, there are a few considerations to be kept in mind. First, the interpreter should be qualified. Not everyone who knows sign language is qualified to interpret. According to the Americans With Disabilities Act of 1990 (ADA), a *qualified interpreter* is one who is able to interpret effectively, accurately, and impartially, both receptively and expressively, using any necessary specialized vocabulary. In mental health settings, this usually eliminates friends or relatives of the Deaf person. Using nationally or state-certified interpreters will ensure the highest quality of interpretation.

Second, familiarity with the process and specialized language of assessment or counseling is important, although most interpreters do not receive formal training in this milieu. The counselor and the interpreter may want to meet in advance of the client meeting so that the counselor can explain the use of specialized vocabulary, and the interpreter can prepare the counselor in the proper ways of using an interpreter (e.g., optimal seating arrangements, proper eye contact, and directly addressing the client). The most effective working alliance between counselor and interpreter occurs when the expertise of both is acknowledged; that is, the counselor is the expert in therapeutic and assessment issues, and the interpreter is the expert in communication issues (Williams & Abeles, 2004).

It is important for the counselor to keep in mind that the interpreter is involved in the process of making communication effective. The interpreter's job is not to answer questions the counselor has about Deaf persons in general or the client in particular. These questions are best asked of the client. An additional consideration in using an interpreter is that the Deaf community is small and the number of qualified interpreters is even smaller. This means that the client and the interpreter may know each other from encounters outside of the counseling center. Sign language interpreters have a code of ethics similar to that of mental health professionals that requires strict confidentiality. Even so, given the likelihood that the client will know the interpreter, it is best for the client to have input into the selection of the interpreter when possible. The scarcity of interpreters will also mean that more time may be necessary to coordinate the schedules of the interpreter, the counselor, and the client.

Culturally Specific Behaviors

Culturally specific behaviors are an important subcategory of communication. For Deaf persons, these include eye contact, nonverbal communication, personal use of space, and attention-getting behaviors. It is not uncommon for hearing Americans to feel uncomfortable with sustained eye contact, yet Deaf Americans rely on eye contact to establish a communicative connection. When using an interpreter, the Deaf client's eye gaze will be directed at the interpreter when the counselor is speaking. When the Deaf client signs, he or she will maintain eye contact with the counselor. The counselor, in return, should become comfortable in maintaining that contact for longer periods of time than customary because failure to return eye contact is considered evasive or even hostile in the Deaf community (Glickman, 1996).

ASL, being a visual–spatial language, relies on facial expressions to indicate many grammatical features. For example, yes–no questions are marked by raising the eyebrows, an expression that may be interpreted by those unfamiliar with ASL as surprise or doubt. There are instances in which clinicians have misunderstood these grammatical markers, leading to misdiagnosis. In addition, Deaf people may be more attuned to the counselor's body language because of their extensive experience in having to search for additional cues in less-than-ideal communication exchanges.

Personal space is another language-related issue for Deaf persons. The physical distance between two Deaf people may be reduced to ensure privacy of a conversation or to signal intimacy. Adequate space is necessary for full visibility of the signing space, but Deaf people often reduce or expand this space to fit the situation (i.e., the greater the distance between the persons communicating, the larger the signing space).

Unlike their hearing peers, Deaf students may also use touch (e.g., tapping the shoulder) to get the attention of the person with whom they want to speak. Waving, tapping the table, and flicking the lights are other ways of getting another's attention.

Assessment Issues

Considerations for the Clinician

The historical literature regarding the clinical assessment of deaf individuals in the mental health system is fraught with horrific stories of misdiagnoses and mistreatment by professionals who were unqualified to provide assessment or treatment of deaf individuals (DeVinney, 2003; Orr, DeMatteo, Heller, Lee, & Nguyen, 1987; Vernon & Daigle-King, 1999). If a clinician is asked to conduct a psychological assessment with a Deaf client, but the clinician is unfamiliar with ASL and Deaf culture, our recommendation is simple: Refer the client to a trained clinician who can communicate directly with the client. Psychological assessment with Deaf individuals is an extremely complex process (Kachman, 1999). Specialized training is required even for those fluent in ASL. The clinician must understand that many assessment tools are not appropriate for Deaf individuals, and most tests do not have norms for Deaf persons.

The uninformed clinician may decide to give a Deaf student a written psychological test, such as the Minnesota Multiphasic Personality Inventory, in order to avoid using an interpreter. However, it is critical to remember that English is a second language for many Deaf students, and, therefore, the reading levels may not be appropriate for the client. In addition, the questions themselves may be culturally biased and inappropriate for this population.

The mental health clinician should also be trained and experienced with the clinical population with whom he or she is working. A school psychologist, for example, fluent in ASL and familiar with testing protocol of Deaf children may not be trained and knowledgeable about the college population.

Working through an interpreter not only is less than ideal but also can affect the validity and reliability of the assessment and lead to misinterpretation and misdiagnosis. If a clinician is unable to refer the Deaf person to a qualified, signing professional, and the use of an interpreter is required, great caution should be taken in choosing an interpreter with expertise in mental health assessment. Something as simple as determining orientation to time, place, and person can be distorted with a simple misinterpretation.

One of the authors (Lauri L. Rush) recalls during her internship year being asked to interpret for an emergency admission of a Deaf patient in the psychiatric unit until the certified interpreter arrived. Because she was new to the area and unfamiliar with the regional signs, she misinterpreted the regional sign for "September," saying "fall" instead. This gave the psychiatrist who was conducting the mental status examination the impression that the patient did not know which month it was and was, therefore, disoriented to time. If something this simple can be misinterpreted by an unqualified interpreter, imagine what could happen when administering a Rorschach or an intelligence test for which the subtleties of language and interpretation could dramatically alter the outcome of the assessment.

Diagnostic Considerations

There is a risk of erroneously assuming a causal relationship between deafness and mental illness (Pollard, 1998). In general, the incidence of mental illness in the Deaf community mirrors that in the hearing population (Gulati, 2003; Pollard, 1998). However, the incidence of neurological impairments, such as learning disabilities and attention-deficit disorders, is higher in subgroups of Deaf individuals when the etiology of the deafness also causes neurological impairments (e.g., meningitis or rubella; Hardy-Braz, Sporn, Yetman, & Brice, 1999; Pollard, 1998). A clinician evaluating a Deaf student would need to consider these facts when assigning a diagnosis.

Whether the diagnostic process involves a clinical interview with a mental status examination or a full psychological assessment, the mental health provider should be knowledgeable about deafness from audiological, developmental, educational, vocational, legal, social, and cultural perspectives (Pollard, 1996). Moreover, the clinician must have an understanding of the impact of deafness on the administration and interpretation of various methods of evaluation. As a case in point, a mental status exam with a Deaf client is an area vulnerable to misinterpretations when conducted by a clinician unfamiliar with the nuances of ASL and Deaf culture (Evans & Elliott, 1987; Steinberg, 1991). Great caution should be taken when making inferences about insight, mood, affect, use of language, judgment, and thought processes. One of the risks is that clinicians who are unfamiliar with ASL and Deaf culture may misinterpret the grammatical facial expressions of Deaf clients when assessing a client's mood.

It is difficult, even through an interpreter, to assess a client's rate of speech or signs when one is unfamiliar with the typical use of the language. For example, Deaf people's signing can vary depending on their psychological state. Signing can be rapid, pressured, and emotionally slurred (Evans & Elliott, 1987). When using an interpreter, it may be difficult to determine a client's thought processes because the clinician would have to factor in misinterpretation by the interpreter and difference in the use of language. Even for clinicians experienced in this field, there are often struggles when evaluating the thought processes of a deaf person from another country or one who is a new signer. It is a challenge to factor out language deficits and/or cognitive deficits from thought disorders.

An interesting question that clinicians often ask when learning about the field of mental health with deaf individuals is whether deaf individuals have auditory hallucinations. A clinician may mistakenly avoid asking this question of a client, feeling that it may be ridiculous to ask a deaf person if he or she "hears voices." Although the question may need to be rephrased in the interview, it is interesting to note that deaf psychotic clients do often report "hearing voices" (Gulati, 2003; Pollard, 1998).

Initial Clinical Interview

In preparing for an initial clinical interview with a college student, most college counseling centers use some type of client information form. At the Gallaudet University Mental Health Center, our forms look very similar to those of other colleges. However, some unique questions are included to provide the clinician with a better sense of the Deaf individual's family and educational background, development, and experiences. For example, we ask students how they identify themselves (Deaf, hard-of-hearing, late-deafened, deaf/visual impaired, or hearing). The answer to this question not only gives information about a student's hearing status but also gives the clinician information about the student's cultural affiliation with the Deaf community. We also ask students to identify their preferred communication methods and how they communicate with family members. In addition, we ask about the hearing status of their parents. Ninety percent of deaf individuals are born to hearing families (Harvey, 1989).

Generally, the developmental experience of Deaf children born into Deaf families differs immensely from that of Deaf children from hearing families. Research has demonstrated that Deaf children from Deaf families tend to have more positive self-esteem, greater self-confidence, better academic achievement, and lower rates of depression than Deaf children from hearing families (Evans & Elliott, 1987; Glickman, 1996; Schlesinger & Meadow, 1972). This difference can be explained by early language exposure; effective communication; social training; and a positive, accepting parental attitude about the deaf child. Hearing parents who have deaf children often experience grief reactions. Further, most hearing parents never become fluent in sign language, thus limiting their ability for effective communication with their child. This has extensive implications on the psychological development of these deaf children.

Our Client Information Form also asks for information about the etiology and age of onset of the student's hearing loss. Etiology can provide information about other potential disabilities and developmental factors, such as childhood illnesses or injury. The age of onset of hearing loss can provide additional information about the adjustment for the individual and family.

Not only do the educational experiences of Deaf individuals vary greatly from those of hearing individuals, but there is also great variability within the Deaf community in terms of their educational backgrounds and experiences. Therefore, our information form also asks questions about the type of primary and secondary school programs the Deaf student attended. The clinician should be aware of the type of educational programs the client attended and the psychological and educational impact of those programs on the individual.

After gathering this background information on paper, the clinician can, during the clinical interview, clarify the meaning of these data for the psychological development and characteristics of the Deaf student. Otherwise, the clinical interview with a Deaf student would be similar to an interview with a hearing student. The clinician should discuss presenting problem, along with obtaining information about family and personal history, while keeping in mind the factors unique to the Deaf student.

It is important to recognize and remember the vast similarities of Deaf and hearing students. Although there are unique developmental, familial, social, and educational factors in the experience of Deaf individuals that must be considered in a clinical assessment, many presenting problems and psychological troubles Deaf students face are the same as those of their hearing counterparts. The clinician must be culturally aware and focus on the individual, his or her deafness, and his or her culture, as well as the relationship of these factors (Rush, 1991). However, a clinician unfamiliar with this population may run the risk of viewing the Deaf individual's problems as resulting from the deafness and miss other important clinical information.

Throughout many years of working in a Deaf university, we often hear the question "How do your students at Gallaudet University differ from the students at other universities?" The answer is that, in essence, they are not different. They use a different language and affiliate with a different cultural environment, but they struggle with the same challenges that other college students face, such as homesickness, peer pressure, drug and alcohol abuse, acquaintance rape, academic pressure, relationship problems, eating disorders, grief, depression, anxiety, attention problems, personality disorders, and so forth. The range of challenges for Deaf college students mirrors that of hearing college students. There are also psychologically healthy Deaf students who are very successful and happy.

Counseling Implications

Common Presenting Issues

Deaf students are likely to enter counseling with the same concerns and problems as hearing students. These include normal developmental needs and crises such as identity development, values clarification, sexuality and intimacy, relationship endings, and parental divorce, as well as time and stress management, addictive behaviors, and career uncertainty. Also, like their hearing counterparts, a proportionate number of Deaf students will have more severe emotional, psychological, and developmental problems on entering college. Although the presenting issues may be no different than those of their hearing peers, there are factors in the life experiences of deaf people that are important to consider during treatment.

Identity Development

Self-concept develops within the context of language development and the general socialization process (Williams & Abeles, 2004). Depending on decisions made by important figures in the deaf student's life at an early age, including educational placement and the use of assistive technology or speech therapy, the deaf college student may have developed a negative sense of self. As noted previously, the medical view of deafness is focused on deficits in functioning. Physicians, audiologists, teachers, and parents are usually referring to the malfunctioning of the "broken" ear, but the deaf person may internalize this message to mean that the individual is broken, inferior, or sick (Williams & Abeles, 2004). Communicative isolation from family and peers will also confound the socialization process.

In addition, deaf clients who have adopted the disability identity may see themselves as incapable of change (Williams & Abeles, 2004). This presents a challenge to the therapy process, which is based on transition and change. Helping clients to recognize and appreciate their strengths will support their ability to be open to a new, healthier identity and behaviors. Deaf persons brought up within Deaf culture are less likely to feel isolated and more likely to have developed a positive sense of self, viewing themselves as members of a cultural and linguistic minority, instead of focusing on having deficiencies. Societal pressures are strong, however, and even students who identify as members of Deaf culture may have internalized negative messages.

Discrimination

In addition to issues of self-concept, Deaf people have historically experienced discrimination in educational settings, employment opportunities, and social interactions (William & Abeles, 2004). As with any cultural minority, the experiences of repeated discrimination and oppression can lead to anger, suspicion, and mistrust—all concerns that the Deaf college student may need to address in counseling.

Isolation

Isolation is a frequent concern for deaf students, particularly those who are fully mainstreamed and whose parents are hearing. The counselor does not want to recreate this isolation in the therapy process and must work to ensure that the client feels respected and included in the work. Selecting a method for communication that is comfortable for the client is one of the easiest ways to avoid isolation.

Interpreters

If an interpreter is used to aid communication, the dynamics of the usually dyadic relationship will change, including the transference process and development of an alliance (Harvey, 1989). These are not insurmountable obstacles, but the counselor needs to be aware of the changed dynamics. Skilled interpreters will help to minimize the process interference by sitting to the side and slightly behind the counselor and using direct forms of address (e.g., "I want to know" instead of "He wants to know"; Porter, 1999).

The counselor should also be aware that the interpreter may be subject to similar kinds of countertransference reactions as the counselor. It may be important for the counselor to assist the interpreter in figuring out how to deal with these reactions. Some counselors meet with the interpreter following the client session; however, caution should be exercised in using this approach. The counselor cannot become the interpreter's counselor, and this extrasession meeting may result in disruption of the therapeutic alliance with the client, contributing to the client's confusion about the respective roles of the counselor and the interpreter (Harvey, 1989). Because the therapeutic relationship requires stability and consistency, and because dynamics develop over time, it is recommended that the same interpreter be used throughout treatment.

Confidentiality

Counselors are generally aware of the rights of clients regarding confidentiality, but working with the Deaf student may pose a challenge. Because the Deaf community is very small, it is highly likely that Deaf students on a campus will know and socialize with each other. This is of relevance to maintaining the privacy of the individual in counseling but also to the incidental information the counselor may be privy to in the course of his or her everyday work. Counselors on small campuses may have already experienced one client knowing and talking about another client within the counseling session. With multiple Deaf clients, regardless of the campus size, this is almost unavoidable. Faculty and administrators will also often talk about "that deaf student," making it easy to identify the client through the sheer lack of numbers. The counselor will find a need to decide how to integrate this externally gained incidental information into his or her work with the Deaf client.

Campus Considerations

Programs and Services

The type of college that Deaf students attend has a significant impact on their college experience. The experience of Deaf college students varies not only by their personal history and situation but also by the number of other Deaf students in the college, by their sense of belonging, and by their access to accommodations such as interpreters, real-time captioners, and note-takers.

Quigley, Jenne, and Phillips (1968) reported that higher education for Deaf persons was traditionally provided by Gallaudet College. Gallaudet University,[2] established in 1864, is the world's only university in which all programs and services are specifically designed to accommodate Deaf and hard-of-hearing students. The university serves approximately 1,800 students and is sometimes referred to as the "Deaf Mecca." Gallaudet students come from various educational backgrounds into this environment, which is generally a culturally Deaf environment. Classes are conducted in ASL, and 40% of the faculty and staff are Deaf or hard-of-hearing. In addition to the traditional challenges of new college students, some students at Gallaudet who come from mainstreamed educational experiences initially struggle to adjust to the new culture. Students from resi-

---

[2]Gallaudet College became a university in 1986.

dential schools for the Deaf often have an easier adjustment. The university has a mental health center, which serves the mental health needs of Gallaudet students and the Deaf community. The center also provides training for graduate students and professionals in mental health.

Another college with a mission to serve deaf students is the National Technical Institute for the Deaf (NTID), the world's first and largest technological college for students who are Deaf or hard-of-hearing. It is one of the colleges within the Rochester Institute of Technology and has approximately 1,200 Deaf and hard-of-hearing students (NTID, n.d.). Because of the large number of Deaf students at Gallaudet University and NTID, there tends to be a firmer sense of belonging for the students, and accommodations and support services are easily accessible.

Other colleges provide services to deaf students on their campuses that range from providing interpreters to providing more extensive programs (e.g., tutoring, classes in ASL, and deaf clubs) specifically designed for Deaf students. For example, 200 Deaf and hard-of-hearing students attend California State University, Northridge. The campus houses the National Center on Deafness, which was established in 1972. In addition to classroom accommodations for Deaf students, there are Deaf clubs, Deaf intramural teams, and sororities/fraternities that recruit Deaf members (California State University, Northridge, 2005).

Accommodations

Since the passage of the ADA, many more Deaf students have entered "hearing" colleges and have been provided with accommodations such as sign language interpreters, real-time captioners, note-takers, and other technological equipment. This has increased the options and opportunities for Deaf individuals not only in education but also in employment and other aspects of Deaf individuals' lives. Deaf students now have the option of selecting a college on the basis of the institution's reputation, offered majors, costs, and location, instead of determining which colleges will simply provide them with interpreters. Thus, many more students are opting to attend college closer to home.

It should be noted that many deaf students qualify for financial support from state vocational rehabilitation services. In the past, the vocational rehabilitation counselors would often immediately send Deaf students to Gallaudet University or NTID. With the implementation of the ADA, vocational rehabilitation counselors are sometimes encouraging, or even requiring, students to attend local colleges to reduce costs.

Although the ADA has provided many more options for deaf college students, the danger of mainstreaming is social isolation. Sign language interpreters may work well in the classroom setting, but communication is not accessible to these students in the dormitories, student center, library, sports teams, campus organizations, and parties. These cocurricular activities contribute greatly to the college student's educational experience. The deaf student without access to these activities may miss this aspect of learning.

As previously described, a counseling center may require the services of an interpreter when accommodating Deaf students. Yet, the Deaf student may not want the office of disabled student services or the interpreting office to be informed that he or she has requested counseling. The student may also be uncomfortable using the same interpreter in a counseling setting whom he or she uses in class. If the student does request an interpreter or other accommodations, the counseling center staff would be wise to first consult with the student on interpreter preferences and even consider having the student sign a consent form to release information if the student's name will be released to another office. This process can be delicate and complicated because the ethical principles of confidentiality and dual relationships may collide. The welfare of the client should always take precedence.

Procuring the services of an off-campus interpreting agency may be an option for the counseling center. If the student agrees to involve the office that coordinates support services for disabled students, the counseling center should take advantage of the expertise of the staff members in that office in obtaining the services of a qualified interpreter. Different colleges fund the interpreters in various ways, and the counseling center should clarify the payment for interpreters on their campus. Service providers unfamiliar with the process of providing interpreters are often surprised at the costs of interpreting services. Another alternative is to pay for the Deaf client to receive services by a signing clinician off-campus. The costs may be similar to paying for an interpreter and may better serve the client's needs.

The counseling center should also consider the needs of Deaf students in their prevention and outreach programs. Interpreters should be offered and provided to students for counseling center workshops and other programs such as National Depression Screening Day.

As counseling centers consider how to meet the needs of Deaf students, they may want to consider seeking out additional resources such as the PEPNet Resource Center (PRC; www.pepnet.org). PRC is an extremely helpful and informative site that provides materials, training, and information to postsecondary programs serving Deaf and hard-of-hearing students. PRC products include a variety of topics that may be helpful to counselors working with deaf clients: (a) hiring an interpreter, (b) serving Deaf students who have cochlear implants, (c) helping students who are late-deafened, (d) understanding Deaf culture, and (e) providing counseling services for students who are deaf. They also sponsor annual conferences and online training programs.

Future Trends

One of the challenges faced by all college counseling centers is keeping abreast of the constantly evolving issues of campus life, from being aware of the latest fads to understanding the newest legal developments in parent notification for suicidal clients. Continuing to identify and address the changing trends is critical to providing quality services to all students. Some of these trends are unique to Deaf college students. For example, as of May 2003, 77% of states and the District of Columbia had enacted some form of newborn hearing screening legislation (Deafness Research Foundation, 2005). The early identification of deaf infants has already begun to affect the current generation of children who will soon be enrolling in college. With early identification comes the adaptation of more effective parenting skills, increased access to appropriate language input during the peak time for language learning, and myriad other potential improvements for the lives of deaf children. This will inevitably have an impact on the issues that Deaf college students bring to counseling.

Several events in recent years have led hearing people in the United States to become more aware of Deaf culture and ASL, including the passage of the ADA, the Deaf President Now protest at Gallaudet University in 1988, and the recognition of ASL for foreign language credit in many schools throughout the country. As this awareness and exposure continue to grow, Deaf people will experience greater accessibility to social, educational, and employment opportunities with hearing people.

In addition, cochlear implants and other assistive listening technology continue to be introduced and refined. It remains unclear what impact this advancing technology will have on the provision of counseling services to future generations of Deaf college students.

Videophones are another recent addition to the Deaf experience. Recent advances in technology have made it possible for sign language to be clearly understood across high-speed Internet lines. Not only will the resulting increase in accessible communication alter the social, educational, and employment experiences of Deaf individuals, but college counselors may soon face the need to consider the provision of counseling services via videophone. The American Psychological Association and the American Counseling Association have already begun developing standards for how the use of the Internet will best be adapted for use in the counseling and assessment environment.

Increasing numbers of college students are also exploring distance learning through the Internet. For a Deaf person, the Internet often acts as the great equalizer. That is, a person's hearing status is invisible on the Internet, and communication often becomes more readily accessible, without the use of an interpreter.

The future holds many exciting changes for college counselors, some of which may present unique challenges. Counselors need to continue to remain current in their knowledge about the changing field. This is by no means different for counselors working with Deaf college students.

References

Americans With Disabilities Act of 1990, 42 U.S.C.A. § 12101 *et seq.* (West 1993). Retrieved April 14, 2005, from http://www.sba.gov/ada/adaact.txt
California State University, Northridge. (2005). *National Center on Deafness.* Retrieved April 14, 2005, from http://ncod.csun.edu/

Deafness Research Foundation. (2005). *Early detection and intervention*. Retrieved April 15, 2005, from http://www.drf.org/WCHH/Hearing_Loss/early_detection.htm

DeVinney, J. (2003). Prologue: My story. In N. S. Glickman & S. Gulati (Eds.), *Mental health care of deaf people: A culturally affirmative approach* (pp. xxi–xxxvi). Mahwah, NJ: Erlbaum.

Evans, J. W., & Elliott, H. (1987). The mental status examination. In H. Elliott, L. Glass, & J. W. Evans (Eds.), *Mental health assessment of deaf clients* (pp. 83–92). Boston: Little, Brown.

Glickman, N. S. (1996). What is culturally affirmative psychotherapy? In N. S. Glickman & M. A. Harvey (Eds.), *Culturally affirmative psychotherapy with deaf persons* (pp. 1–55). Mahwah, NJ: Erlbaum.

Gulati, S. (2003). Psychiatric care of culturally deaf people. In N. S. Glickman & S. Gulati (Eds.), *Mental health care of deaf people: A culturally affirmative approach* (pp. 33–108). Mahwah, NJ: Erlbaum.

Hardy-Braz, S., Sporn, M., Yetman, M., & Brice, P. J. (1999). Socio-emotional development and self-regulatory processes in children who are deaf or hard of hearing. In H. Markowicz & C. Berdichevsky (Eds.), *Bridging the gap between research and practice* (pp. 93–104). Washington, DC: Gallaudet University.

Harvey, M. A. (1989). *Psychotherapy with deaf and hard-of-hearing persons: A systemic model.* Hillsdale, NJ: Erlbaum.

Kachman, W. (1999). Identifying learning disabilities in deaf or hard of hearing college students. In H. Markowicz & C. Berdichevsky (Eds.), *Bridging the gap between research and practice* (pp. 35–46). Washington, DC: Gallaudet University.

Lane, H. (1992). *The mask of benevolence.* New York: Knopf.

National Center for Health Statistics. (2002). *National Health Interview Survey 2002.* Retrieved April 13, 2005, from http://www.cdc.gov/nchs/fastats/disable.htm

National Technical Institute for the Deaf. (n.d.). *About NTID.* Retrieved April 14, 2005, from http://www.ntid.rit.edu/index.php

Orr, F. C., DeMatteo, A., Heller, B., Lee, M., & Nguyen, M. (1987). Psychological assessment. In H. Elliott, L. Glass, & J. W. Evans (Eds.), *Mental health assessment of deaf clients* (pp. 93–106). Boston: Little, Brown.

Paul, P., & Jackson, D. (1993). *Toward a psychology of deafness.* Boston: Allyn & Bacon.

Pollard, R. Q. (1996). Professional psychology and deaf people: The emergence of a discipline. *American Psychologist, 51,* 389–396.

Pollard, R. Q. (1998). Psychopathology. In M. Marschark & M. D. Clark (Eds.), *Psychological perspectives on deafness* (Vol. 2, pp. 171–198). Mahwah, NJ: Erlbaum.

Porter, A. (1999). Sign-language interpretation in psychotherapy with deaf patients. *American Journal of Psychotherapy, 53,* 163–176.

Quigley, S. P., Jenne, W. C., & Phillips, S. B. (1968). *Deaf students in colleges and universities.* Washington, DC: Alexander Graham Bell Association for the Deaf.

Rush, L. L. (1991). Counseling style and effectiveness ratings: An examination of deaf student perceptions. *Dissertation Abstracts International, 52*(7-B), 3914. (UMI No. 9128070)

Schlesinger, H. S., & Meadow, K. P. (1972). *Sound and sign: Childhood deafness and mental health.* Berkeley: University of California Press.

Steinberg, A. (1991). Issues in providing mental health services to hearing-impaired persons. *Hospital and Community Psychiatry, 42,* 380–389.

Sussman, A., & Brauer, B. (1999). *On being a psychotherapist with deaf clients.* Unpublished manuscript.

Vernon, M., & Daigle-King, B. (1999). Historical overview of inpatient care of mental patients who are deaf. *American Annals of the Deaf, 144,* 51–61.

Williams, C. R., & Abeles, N. (2004). Issues and implications of deaf culture in therapy. *Professional Psychology: Research and Practice, 35,* 643–648.

18
Counseling Students With Chronic, Progressive, or Life-Threatening Medical Conditions

Laurane S. McGlynn

Introduction

Since the latter half of the 20th century, the incidence of chronic medical conditions has grown dramatically. It is estimated that more than 90 million Americans live with chronic illnesses (Centers for Disease Control and Prevention, 2004), which comprise a spectrum of diseases including cancer and HIV/AIDS. Disease progression can be chronic, progressive, or life-threatening. With the advances of medical science, the symptoms of chronic medical conditions, such as diabetes, muscular dystrophy, gastrointestinal disorders, and epilepsy, can be controlled.

With the increasing incidence of medical diagnoses among young adults, the demand for psychological services is increasing, and the role of the counselor in college settings is changing. Counseling has evolved from its earliest roots, when it provided assessment, advice, and guidance, to developing a flexible plan that can accommodate the restrictions and challenges resulting from chronic medical illness. Counselors assist students in formulating strategies and soliciting resources that can help manage their disease. A collaborative approach to the management and treatment of students with chronic medical conditions requires the involvement of numerous campus professionals.

Assessment Issues

The assessment process provides an opportunity to understand the phenomenology of the client. A comprehensive evaluation of students with chronic medical conditions includes an assessment of the biological, psychological, and social processes that influence health and illness. The clinical interview assesses the direct and indirect influences of these factors on the student's overall functioning. Assessment requires gathering information from several domains, including the client's medical history, family and social support systems, level of cognitive functioning, behavioral patterns, coping style, and personality traits.

During the initial clinical encounter, there is an advantage to beginning the interview with those topics that are of immediate importance for the client (Parker, 1995). Identifying the physical demands, psychosocial sequelae, personality changes, and protracted psychological distress can help determine the most appropriate approach to treatment. In addition, the counselor should become familiar with the side effects of medication and treatment procedures that can interfere with and inhibit the student's ability to cope with the illness.

Focusing on these concerns elicits the client's participation and investment in treatment (Parker, 1995). Personality traits and coping styles play an important role in the client's ability to adapt to the challenges of chronic illness. Similarly, behavioral mechanisms can contribute positively or negatively to the course of disease. In addition, treatment procedures, activity level, self-care behaviors, impact of illness, and academic concerns should be discussed. The client's religious or cultural beliefs are also contributing factors when a treatment plan is being developed.

Understanding the biological, cognitive, affective, social, behavioral, and developmental components of illness is essential to the assessment process. These elements affect memory, learning ability, health behavior, processing of information, emotions, and motivation for treatment and provide a framework for therapy. An analysis of this information provides an overview of moderating variables that influence health outcomes when considered within the context and nature of the disease. Evaluating this information provides an understanding of the client's resources and identifies where they need support.

Counseling Implications

Taking care of oneself when ill, even in the most stable and supportive environment, can be a burden. Living with a chronic or life-threatening illness for a student, especially when family support is unavailable, can be a lonely, self-defining experience. It gives rise to existential, as well as practical, concerns. The ability to cope varies depending on the severity of the illness in terms of its threat to life and impact on functioning. Some students reach out to connect more deeply in an effort to solicit support, whereas others isolate themselves, unable to secure the services they need. Counseling encourages connection to a support system and information regarding available services and resources that can accommodate the student's special needs.

Consequences of chronic medical conditions include chronic pain, fatigue, unpredictable symptom flare-up, and emotional distress. Common responses to these disturbances include depression, anxiety, a feeling of being burdened, a sense of loss and grief, a shift in body image, social discomfort, increased stress, and decreased psychological functioning. Clients can also experience feelings of despair, resentment, hopelessness, helplessness, and isolation (Livneh & Antonak, 2005).

Some clients with chronic medical conditions cope by minimizing or denying the seriousness of their condition. These defenses help protect against threatening emotions such as anger, guilt, and hostility. Although denial can be adaptive during the initial phase of diagnosis in preventing depression and anxiety, the long-term effect can be counterproductive and potentially life-threatening.

Feelings and reactions that have been repressed, denied, or minimized can be triggered when the client enters therapy. Loneliness, helplessness, apprehension, and despair are frequently reported (Livneh & Antonak, 2005). Although depression is a common response to chronic illness, it can reach clinical significance when symptoms persist, increase in severity, or interrupt the student's ability to function effectively.

Students with chronic medical illness may face an increase in the frequency and severity of stressful situations (Falvo, 1999). The extent, type, and timing of incapacitation are all factors in the level of stress. In addition, stress levels can be exacerbated by constant daily threats to independence, autonomy, and fulfillment of academic and social roles; the unpredictability of future plans and goals; and fear of deterioration of physical health and death (Parker, 1995).

Communication with a counselor is essential to assist these students in moderating the ongoing stress of negotiating medical and academic demands while attempting to maintain autonomy and independence. Prolonged stress results in a disturbance in psychological, behavioral, and social equilibrium (Livneh & Antonak, 2005). Inability to adapt to chronic illness creates feelings of anxiety, depression, psychogenic pain, chronic fatigue, social withdrawal, and cognitive distortions (Livneh & Antonak, 1997).

Guilt and anger are common responses to the negative feelings that develop from coping with chronic medical illness. Many people experience a sense of personal failure. Self-blame produces reactions of internalized anger and external hostility. Students may feel they must assume sole responsibility for the success or failure of their health or academic performance. If symptoms worsen, bitterness and self-loathing can impede progress in therapy. Even when lifestyle or personal choices have contributed to the illness, forgiveness and acceptance help students cope.

Fear is the most common response to serious illness (McDaniel, Hepworth, & Doherty, 1999). The goal of therapy is not to alleviate fear but to find the courage to face the fear, the illness, and the treatment. An important goal in therapy is to encourage students to share their fears with the counselor. The counselor becomes an active listener, gathering information and providing support as the student navigates the psychosocial and physical demands created by the illness. Establishing a boundary between the illness and the individual prevents the relationship from being solely defined in terms of illness or disability (Wood, 1995).

Loss is another common theme for students coping with illness. Loss can take the form of loss of control, abilities, relationships, and freedom. Death is viewed as the ultimate loss. However, loss can also inspire students to appreciate life's gifts. Students find healing in discovering meaning in their lives through relationships or newly defined priorities and goals. Students who are pursuing their degrees despite their illnesses attempt to find personal identity beyond their medical diagnoses.

Attitudes Toward Medically Ill Clients

There are a variety of attitudes toward clients who are medically ill. Counselors encounter clients who elicit strong emotional responses within them, but they are trained to separate their emotions from the clinical encounter. Nevertheless, working with clients with physical illness presents a threat to the counselor's physical vulnerabilities and triggers concerns over death and dying (Belar & Geisser, 1995).

Anxiety is a common countertransference reaction when one is counseling a medically ill client. The counselor's comfort level is challenged when discussing issues of death and disease. The ability to talk openly about the fear and anxiety surrounding death is essential because it can be a common and recurrent theme in therapy. For individuals who are chronically ill, the awareness of death is always present. Facing the possibility of death can be a self-defining moment for clients who are ill, motivating them to make personal changes that can heal relationships in their lives and allowing them to define goals and set priorities. Many clients who are ill struggle to find meaning and purpose in their lives. An existential shift, however, can occur during therapy, through which a renewed appreciation for life emerges.

Although it is important to discuss feelings of loss, the task of therapy is also to focus on living fully. Creating a community of support on campus for students with chronic medical conditions is a key factor in their academic success. Adjustment to student life requires the ability to adapt to the emotional, physical, and environmental demands of academia. To facilitate this process, counselors can use therapeutic approaches that employ cognitive–behavioral, psychodynamic, and biopsychosocial models.

Integrating these approaches within a campus environment requires a collaborative approach to treatment. Including faculty and staff from student health services, disability services, public safety, housing and residential life, college counseling, food services, and academic affairs provides a community of resources to offer students. Issues related to confidentiality, however, can arise when one is working with a multidisciplinary approach. A discussion with clients regarding the information that can be released to other professionals involved in their care is required.

Therapeutic Interventions

There are numerous approaches that have been applied in the treatment of clients with chronic illness. Experts in the field of health psychology, however, recommend cognitive–behavioral therapy (CBT), application of the biopsychosocial model of treatment, and psychodynamic approaches (Livneh & Antonak, 2005; Nicassio, Meyerowitz, & Kerns, 2004; Smith & Nicassio, 1995; Turk & Solovey, 1995). Counselors develop strategies based on clinical observation, client-reported symptoms, medical history, stage of illness, and psychosocial stressors (Livneh & Antonak, 1997).

Cognitive–Behavioral Therapy

Providing a universal definition of illness is challenging. One individual may perceive it to be somatic symptoms such as a headache or back pain, whereas others may classify it in terms of a diagnosed medical illness that requires medication or surgery. The manner in which individuals interpret and respond to their symptoms is determined by their concept of illness (Turk & Solovey, 1995). The cognitive–behavioral approach to treatment of medical illness addresses the connection between interpretation of events and the behavioral and emotional responses that result. The focus of treatment is to identify, evaluate, and challenge the maladaptive thinking of individuals regarding their illness.

Turk and Solovey (1995) discussed the process of chronic illness from a cognitive–behavioral perspective. In the initial stage following diagnosis, the counselor assists the client in examining their interpretation of the consequences of the illness and its symptoms. The next phase involves the help-seeking stage, which includes gathering information about the illness and treatment approaches and seeking medical advice. Once the initial crisis of the diagnosis subsides, emotional distress surfaces, and illness behavior is established. It is during the establishment of the individual's responses to his or her illness that CBT is effective (Turk & Solovey, 1995).

Panic and fear are common responses to medical illness. CBT is aimed at mediating panic symptoms and easing muscle tension, thereby reducing the level of pain and anxiety experienced by the client. When the etiology of the symptoms is unclear, it can be difficult for the client to discern whether they are related to the illness or whether they are a physiological response to anxiety.

CBT is designed to reconceptualize symptoms in a way that minimizes the client's emotional suffering (Turk & Solovey, 1995). The focus of treatment is to structure the client's illness schema in a manner that decreases maladaptive thoughts and feelings that can contribute to symptom exacerbation and increased suffering. The aim of CBT is to reduce stress, improve physical functioning, reduce symptoms, and regulate inappropriate use of medical care (Turk & Solovey, 1995).

There is a reconceptualization of treatment from a medical model to a cognitively based approach. Physical symptoms that may once have been overwhelming are now viewed as manageable. Clients are encouraged to regulate their cognitions, affect, and behavior. Caution is exercised in communicating to clients that they caused their illness. Clarification that emphasizes the distinction between the disease and the accompanying physical symptoms, and the client's cognitive, affective, and behavioral responses to the illness, is essential.

Some of the psychophysiological interventions used in CBT include meditation techniques, autogenic training, relaxation techniques, guided imagery, controlled breathing, and biofeedback. Other CBT techniques include cognitive restructuring, problem-solving training, distraction skills training, and communication skills training. These techniques are designed to improve the mood of clients, modify their perception of their illness, and provide them with the skills necessary to improve their cognitive processes and problem-solving skills (Turk & Solovey, 1995).

An alternative form of CBT has been developed at the Centre for Addiction and Mental Health in Toronto, Ontario, Canada. The program, mindfulness-based cognitive therapy (MBCT), integrates CBT with components of a mindfulness-based stress reduction program created by Kabat-Zinn (1990). The program was developed to reduce relapse in depressed patients, but, in recent years, its use has expanded to include individuals with anxiety disorder, cancer, chronic pain, and medical illness.

Unlike CBT, MBCT does not emphasize changing the content of thoughts. Rather, the focus is on awareness of, and changing the relationship to, unwanted thoughts, feelings, and bodily sensations (Ma & Teasdale, 2004). Individuals with chronic medical illness struggle with the turmoil they feel in their bodies in the form of somatic complaints. MBCT works to uncover the nature of pain. This process of discovery allows the counselor to help clients examine what kinds of thoughts and beliefs are at the root of these feelings.

The aim of MBCT is to manage symptoms by integrating mindfulness with cognitive therapy. The component of CBT that is incorporated into MBCT is the notion that faulty thinking leads to emotional and behavioral disturbances—that negative thoughts can trigger the onset of bodily sensations. MBCT works to clear the clutter of negative thoughts and achieve clarity through meditation. Meditation and mindfulness-based activities minimize the tendency to catastrophize and ruminate over negative thoughts. Studies have examined the incidence of increased immune response to viruses and disease in clients who practice meditation (University of Massachusetts Medical Center, 2004). Meditation promotes the relaxation response, which reduces stress (Benson, Beary, & Carol, 1974).

Mindfulness-based interventions acknowledge and accept the association between thoughts, feelings, and physiological responses in the body (Kabat-Zinn, 1990). Mindfulness-based stress reduction (MBSR) is a client-centered treatment modality that works with the individual's own stress, illness, challenges, and demands of daily living (Krasner, 2004). Studies have explored the use of MBSR with patients with chronic pain and cancer (Kabat-Zinn, 1982; Kabat-Zinn, Lipworth, Burney, & Sellers, 1986; Tacon, Caldera, & Ronagham, 2004).

The goal of MBSR is a self-affirming paradigm that teaches clients skills that they can proactively apply in their lives once the training has ended. MBSR teaches clients to "center" by becoming mindful. The program includes daily formal mindfulness-based practices such as meditation, mindfulness yoga, and the body scan. There are also informal practices used in everyday living such as conscious eating, walking meditation, and awareness of breath and thoughts. Through these practices, clients develop the capacity to accept whatever challenges arise in the present moment.

There are MBSR training programs throughout the country. Most hospitals can provide information on the location of local programs. Training programs are available within a treatment group for patients and a wellness group for people interested in learning the techniques. There are also workshops and training programs available throughout the country.

A Biopsychosocial Perspective

The biopsychosocial model emphasizes the reciprocal interactions of biological, psychological, and social processes on the etiology and experience of illness and treatment of disease (McDaniel, Belar, Schroeder, Hargrove, & Freeman, 2002). It reconceptualizes illness from a medical model that reflects only biological malfunctions to an integrative model that also includes psychological and social factors (Smith & Nicassio, 1995). The biopsychosocial model has been adopted as the dominant conceptual framework for the application of health psychology interventions (Nicassio et al., 2004). These interventions are aimed at (a) cognitive restructuring; (b) restoring a sense of self-concept; (c) symptom management; (d) creating meaning from suffering; (e) identifying coping strategies; and (f) developing social, academic, and personal goals (Smith & Nicassio, 1995).

The biopsychosocial model can be helpful in guiding clinical decision making (Smith & Nicassio, 1995). Evaluating the link between biological, psychological, and social factors helps clarify their direct or indirect influence on health outcomes. Conducting a functional analysis helps evaluate the relationship between psychosocial factors and health outcomes. The functional analysis examines patterns of associations between environmental events and health outcomes (Smith & Nicassio, 1995). For example, if students experience increased stress at school or work, their pain levels may increase. Identifying these reciprocal relationships helps develop treatment strategies to mediate the psychosocial influences that cause functional difficulties. Assessing the conditions that affect the client's functioning is a key to treatment planning.

Applying the biopsychosocial model to a college population requires an evaluation of the interrelationship between academic demands, social support, psychological functioning, and physiological responses in the body. The biopsychosocial model, conceptualized from an educational systems perspective, allows the educational institution to be the interactive focal point interconnected with three evolving components: the illness, the individual, and the college. The individual is seen as part of a larger, interconnected system. The responsivity of the system shapes the adaptive response of the individual to the demands of school.

According to this model, the college is seen as a resource. It emphasizes the fit between the demands of the illness and the support and services offered by the college. The student is encouraged to adopt a unified approach to the illness:

our challenge versus your problem. The student becomes empowered as the college is used as a support system that can share the burdens and responsibilities of the physical and psychosocial demands of the illness. Social support and integration provide a sense of community and identification with a larger system that can meet emotional, academic, and material needs.

Psychodynamic Approaches

Psychodynamic strategies focus on issues of loss, grief, mourning, and suffering (Livneh & Antonak, 2005) in a three-phase approach. In the initial phase of treatment, clients are encouraged to express their feelings of loss and grief. Through this process of emotional healing, they move into the second stage, to find personal meaning for their illness. When clients have reached a level of acceptance, they are able to work in the third phase, to attain a sense of mastery over their lives. The sense of control found in the third phase lifts the clients' burden of being immobilized and controlled by their illness.

Campus Considerations

When young adults enter college, they are faced with issues of separation and differentiation from their family. There is a shift from dependence to self-management. During this transition they must assume responsibility for management of their medical needs. This developmental stage is often the first experience with independence for a young adult. Although complete autonomy can be appealing, interdependence within a support system can ease the transition.

The developmental tasks and stressors associated with adjustment to college life are compounded for students with chronic medical illness. They face difficulties with campus accessibility developing a social support network, negotiating educational accommodations, coping with limited resources, along with reconciling negative faculty and peer attitudes surrounding medical illness. Social isolation and adjustment to college life are common problems reported by students with chronic illness. Perceived social support is particularly important to psychological adjustment to college.

Students with chronic medical conditions enter higher education to realize their potential, find meaning for their life, develop an independent lifestyle, solidify plans for their future, and acquire the skills and knowledge necessary to enhance their employment opportunities. Students with chronic medical conditions require assistance in meeting these goals. They need access to services such as transportation, equipment provision, and health services. These students also require assistance with the transition to residence life, information about the availability of financial aid and campus disability services, and resources to meet special dietary needs.

The availability of these services, and the success in obtaining them, can either exacerbate or ameliorate health issues. Poor diet, reduced activity level, increases in stress level, smoking, and alcohol and drug abuse can ensue if students feel discouraged, displaced, or unsupported. Students with a history of emotional or sexual abuse or alcohol or drug abuse experience increased difficulty in coping. Alcohol or drug abuse alters the students' cognitive ability to make decisions related to treatment adherence, which further compromises their health. Counseling is essential to support the students while they are negotiating the physical challenges and academic demands of college life.

Chronically ill students live in a world filled with challenges. They must be vigilant regarding their physical needs and negotiate their place in a world where they experience the dichotomy of being invisible at times or conversely receiving negative or overreactive social responses. The discomfort of peers can result in rejection of the student. In a college setting, social status may be negatively affected because of a lack of ability to adapt to the college environment. The social stigma associated with medical illness can prevent the development of peer relationships that provide support and interaction.

Peer and teacher reactions to high incidences of absenteeism from classes are another source of concern. Chronic illness has a direct impact on academic functioning. The manner in which the college system responds to the students can either enhance or hinder their functioning. Coordinating services, campus professionals, and administrators and integrating the students with their psychosocial surroundings are key functions of therapy.

Overresponsiveness can result in undermining the students' ability to develop the skills necessary for self-efficacy and control. Loss of control is a common source of psychological distress in chronic illness. Individuals who believe they have control over the course of their illness respond remarkably differently than those who perceive that external sources affect the outcome. Internal locus of control allows for the development of self-efficacy and adaptive behaviors. External locus of control results in reliance on other professionals and systems and a loss of personal control over decision-making and disease processes.

The client's passivity can directly affect his or her health behaviors and ability to seek out medical treatment. Cultural, religious, racial, and ethnic beliefs can also contribute to the client's beliefs about illness and death. Investigating alternative solutions and offering choices reduces the sense of loss of control. Identifying and anticipating future challenges allows the client to develop a plan of action.

Future Trends

Current trends in the health care system emphasize collaboration between medical and behavioral health care providers (Levant, 2005). There is a shift toward the biopsychosocial model of treatment. The American Psychological Association has established the Health Care for the Whole Person Task Force to provide a statement to the government supporting a collaborative, integrative, multidisciplinary approach to health care (Levant, 2005). This initiative aims to illustrate the importance of the biopsychosocial model as a behavioral-health intervention that can ease the nation's public health problems. This project seeks to remove the boundaries between physical and mental health that exist within communities, schools, and health care settings. It offers an approach to treatment that is directed toward the whole person, not merely the presenting symptoms or the illness.

The field of health psychology encourages clinicians to design interventions that move beyond generic approaches and target individual differences such as illness duration, cultural background, age, gender, and dispositional variables (Nicassio et al., 2004). It is imperative for counselors to avoid the assumption of homogeneity in clients with medical illness. Each client presents with his or her own cluster of symptoms, and, thus, various clients may respond differently to similar interventions.

The efficacy of psychological treatment of individuals with medical illness has been well documented. Although research has targeted special populations such as women, the elderly, minorities, and children, outcome research is needed on interventions with college students. Advances in research with college populations would provide more relevant, clinically effective interventions that maximize health benefits and treatment effectiveness.

With the enactment of the Americans With Disabilities Act of 1990 and the Individuals With Disabilities Education Improvement Act of 2004, increased numbers of individuals with chronic medical illness and disabilities are entering higher education. Counselors can play an active role in supporting students by advocating for accommodations (e.g., permission to audio- or videotape lectures, provision of note-taking services and books on tape, extended testing time, and alternative assignments or extensions) when health-related issues prevent students from being physically present in the classroom. As more people with medical conditions choose to enter college, administrators and campus professionals must increase their understanding of the challenges faced by these students.

Counselors are faced with the task of supporting students in their quest to live productive, fulfilling, and meaningful lives. Counselors offer students choices, opportunities, and possibilities. With the advances in medical science, life expectancy and treatment options have improved substantially. Medical interventions can treat the disease, but therapy can heal beyond a physical level.

The mind and body are intimately connected. Thoughts that arise in the mind, sensations that are felt in the body, and behaviors that serve to alleviate fear and suffering all contribute to the experience of disease. An essential element of being healthy is the ability to find the freedom to navigate around the demands of the illness. Individuals who strive to set goals, and seek support to find alternate ways to achieve them, can move beyond their diagnosis and live fully.

References

Americans With Disabilities Act of 1990, 42 U.S.C.A. § 12101 *et seq.* (West 1993). Retrieved May 15, 2005, from http://www.sba.gov/ada/adaact.txt

Belar, C. D., & Geisser, M. E. (1995). Roles of clinical health psychologists in the management of chronic illness. In P. M. Nicassio & T. W. Smith (Eds.), *Managing chronic illness: A biopsychosocial perspective* (pp. 33–57). Washington, DC: American Psychological Association.

Benson, H., Beary, J. F., & Carol, M. P. (1974). The relaxation response. *Psychiatry, 37,* 37–46.

Centers for Disease Control and Prevention. (2004). *Chronic disease overview.* Retrieved July 9, 2006, from http://www.cdc.gov/nccdphp/overview.htm

Falvo, D. (1999). *Medical and psychosocial aspects of chronic illness and disability* (2nd ed.). Gaithersburg, MD: Aspen.

Individuals With Disabilities Education Improvement Act of 2004, Pub. L. No. 108-446, 118 Stat. 2647 (2004). Retrieved September 23, 2005, from http://www.ed.gov/policy/speced/guid/idea/idea2004.html

Kabat-Zinn, J. (1982). An outpatient program in behavioral medicine for chronic pain patients based on the practice of mindfulness meditation: Theoretical consideration and preliminary results. *General Hospital Psychiatry, 4,* 33–47.

Kabat-Zinn, J. (1990). *Full catastrophe living: The program of the Stress Reduction Clinic at the University of Massachusetts Medical Center.* New York: Dell.

Kabat-Zinn, J., Lipworth, L., Burney, R., & Sellers, W. (1986). Four-year follow-up of a meditation-based program for the self-regulation of chronic pain: Treatment outcomes and compliance. *Clinical Journal of Pain, 2,* 159–173.

Krasner, M. (2004). Mindfulness-based interventions: Coming of age? *Families, Systems & Health, 22,* 207–212.

Levant, R. F. (2005, May). Health care for the whole person. *Monitor on Psychology, 36,* 5.

Livneh, H., & Antonak, R. F. (1997). *Psychosocial adaptation to chronic illness and disability.* Gaithersburg, MD: Aspen.

Livneh, H., & Antonak, R. F. (2005). Psychosocial adaptation to chronic illness and disability: A primer for counselors. *Journal of Counseling & Development, 83,* 12–20.

Ma, S. H., & Teasdale, J. D. (2004). Mindfulness-based cognitive therapy for depression. *Journal of Consulting and Clinical Psychology, 72,* 31–40.

McDaniel, S. H., Belar, C. D., Schroeder, C., Hargrove, D. S., & Freeman, E. L. (2002). A training curriculum for professional psychologists in primary care. *Professional Psychology: Research and Practice, 33,* 65–72.

McDaniel, S. H., Hepworth, J., & Doherty, W. J. (1999). The shared emotional themes of illness. *Journal of Family Psychotherapy, 10,* 1–8.

Nicassio, P. M., Meyerowitz, B. E., & Kerns, R. D. (2004). The future of health psychology interventions. *Health Psychology, 23,* 132–137.

Parker, J. C. (1995). Stress management. In P. M. Nicassio & T. W. Smith (Eds.), *Managing chronic illness: A biopsychosocial perspective* (pp. 285–312). Washington, DC: American Psychological Association.

Smith, T. W., & Nicassio, P. M. (1995). Psychological practice: Clinical application of the biopsychosocial model. In P. M. Nicassio & T. W. Smith (Eds.), *Managing chronic illness: A biopsychosocial perspective* (pp. 1–31). Washington, DC: American Psychological Association.

Tacon, A. M., Caldera, Y. M., & Ronagham, C. (2004). Mindfulness-based stress reduction in women with breast cancer. *Families, Systems & Health, 22,* 193–203.

Turk, D. C., & Solovey, P. (1995). Cognitive–behavioral treatment of illness behavior. In P. M. Nicassio & T. W. Smith (Eds.), *Managing chronic illness: A biopsychosocial perspective* (pp. 245–284). Washington, DC: American Psychological Association.

University of Massachusetts Medical Center. (2004). *Center for mindfulness: Major research findings.* Retrieved June 5, 2004, from http://www.umassed.edu

Wood, B. L. (1995). A developmental biopsychosocial approach to the treatment of chronic illness in children and adolescents. In R. H. Mikesell, D. D. Lusterman, & S. H. McDaniel (Eds.), *Integrating family therapy: Handbook of family psychology and systems theory* (pp. 437–455). Washington, DC: American Psychological Association.

19

The Hidden Disabilities:
Counseling Students With
Learning Disabilities

Joyce Williams Bergin and James J. Bergin

Introduction

Learning disabilities can manifest themselves across the life span. Typically identified in elementary school, learning disabilities negatively affect academic learning. However, learning disabilities can affect social skills development as well. The definition of learning disabilities most often used to identify the disability first appeared in Public Law 94-142, the Education for All Handicapped Children Act of 1975:

> The term "specific learning disability" means those children who have a disorder in one or more of the basic psychological processes involved in understanding or in using language, spoken or written, which disorder may manifest itself in imperfect ability to listen, think, speak, read, write, spell, or to do mathematical calculations. The term includes such conditions as perceptual handicaps, brain injury, minimal brain dysfunction, dyslexia, and developmental aphasia. The term does not include a learning problem that is primarily the result of visual, hearing, or motor handicaps, of mental retardation, of emotional disturbance, or of environmental, cultural, or economic disadvantage. (U.S. Department of Education, 1977)

In 1997, the National Joint Committee on Learning Disabilities published a definition that expanded the federal definition:

> Learning disabilities is a general term that refers to a heterogeneous group of disorders manifested by significant difficulties in the acquisition and use of listening, speaking, reading, writing, reasoning, or mathematical abilities. These disorders are intrinsic to the individual, are presumed to be due to central nervous system dysfunction, and may occur across the life span. Problems in self-regulatory behaviors, social perception, and social interaction may exist with learning disabilities but do not by themselves constitute a learning disability. Although a learning disability may occur

concomitantly with other disabilities (for example, sensory impairment, mental retardation, or serious emotional disturbance) or with extrinsic influences (such as cultural differences or insufficient/inappropriate instruction), it would not be a result of those conditions or influences. (p. 29)

Both of these definitions attempt to describe the typical manifestations of problems that affect approximately 6% of the school-age population in the United States (U.S. Department of Education, 2002). The number of individuals being identified has increased steadily since the implementation of the federal definition in 1975. The term *learning disabilities* represents a heterogeneous group of disorders with no consistent profile of characteristics. Lerner (2005) pointed out common elements, however, among the many definitions of the disorder that have arisen from the fields of education, medicine, and psychology over the history of the development of learning disabilities as a field of study: evidence of central nervous system dysfunction, psychological processing deficits, difficulty in academic and learning tasks, and a discrepancy between aptitude and achievement. The definitions exclude other causes, such as sensory loss, lack of schooling, or intellectual disability.

Because this group of disorders represents what is often termed a *hidden disability* (i.e., a disability that is not evident in the physical appearance of the individual), the person with learning disabilities may be viewed by nondisabled peers as unintelligent or unmotivated. Despite more than 30 years of research supporting the existence of learning disabilities, including current brain research involving spectrography and functional magnetic resonance imaging (Galaburda, 2005), the field continues to be controversial (Elksnin et al., 2001; Fiedorowicz, 1999; Weintraub, 2005). Individuals with learning disabilities face a twofold problem: (a) their innate deficits that can disrupt academic learning and social development and (b) a tendency on the part of those whom they encounter to dismiss their disabilities as nonexistent.

Assessment Issues

Learning disabilities are intrinsic to the individual. Because they exist across the life span, young adults continue to face a number of challenges as they move into postsecondary education. Section 504 of the Rehabilitation Act of 1973 (Section 504) and the Americans With Disabilities Act of 1990 (ADA) have provided support for young adults to enter postsecondary educational institutions and to receive necessary accommodations during their educational experiences (Thomas, 2000). During the decade 1990 through 2000, the percentage of college freshmen entering 4-year institutions who reported having learning disabilities increased from 1.4% to 2.4% (Henderson, 2001). Today, greater numbers of students with learning disabilities are electing to pursue a college education.

Henderson (2001) found in 1988 that only 16.1% of full-time learning disabled freshmen attending 4-year institutions identified themselves as having learning disabilities. In 2000, the percentage rose to 40.4%. More male students than female students identified themselves as having learning disabilities. When compared with other freshmen reporting disabilities, those who identified themselves as having learning disabilities were the most likely to have the following characteristics: (a) to be from White/Caucasian families; (b) to be 19 years of age or older; (c) to be from families whose annual income exceeded $100,000; (d) to have parents who were college graduates; (e) to have received C or D averages in high school; (f) to expect that they will require remedial work or special tutoring in English, reading, and mathematics; (g) to consider majoring in arts and sciences while being the least likely to express interest in the professional fields; (h) to rank themselves lowest in mathematics ability, intellectual self-confidence, academic ability, and writing ability; and (i) to value special programs offered by colleges (Henderson, 2001).

When individuals with learning disabilities enter institutions of higher education, they confront a series of complex interactions with staff and faculty. They must be able to navigate the advisement process, schedule appropriate classes, advocate for accommodations, compensate for their disabilities, and meet other challenges unique to the college experience. Reiff, Hatzes, Bramel, and Gibbon (2001) found that college students with learning disabilities reported experiencing a greater degree of stress than their nondisabled peers. Their study also found that college students with learning disabilities demonstrated lower scores on measures of adaptability than their nondisabled peers, thereby indicating less ability to "cope with environmental demands and to size up and deal with problematic situations" (Reiff et al., 2001, p. 75).

Although most young adults with learning disabilities who enter college are quite capable of succeeding academically, other problems common to their disabilities can disrupt their educational careers. Typical problems that carry over from childhood include impulsiveness, poor judgment, disorganization, lack of social perception, self-esteem issues, difficulty making and keeping friends, immaturity (Bender, 1998; Osmon, 1982), and language difficulties, especially in the area of pragmatics (Bergin & Bergin, 2004).

The majority of individuals with learning disabilities have underlying language difficulties. Dysfunctions in phonology and morphology result in reading and spelling problems. Difficulties in semantics and pragmatics result in deficits in spoken language and social discourse. Pragmatics deals with the manner in which humans use language to get their needs met.

Often individuals with learning disabilities have difficulty formulating questions, especially those that keep a conversation going. Some individuals may use malapropisms, whereas others have disnomia—an inability to recall a desired word while speaking—leading to circumlocution. In some cases, individuals with underlying, as opposed to obvious, language deficits may be unable to understand jokes, double entendre, and other verbal subtleties. These language problems may interfere with the social interactions required during self-advocacy, establishing social relationships with peers, and maintaining necessary working relationships with college faculty and staff (Bergin & Bergin, 2004).

Under Section 504 and the ADA, college students with learning disabilities are eligible for reasonable accommodations as well as auxiliary aids and services. Students may be provided with accommodations or services, such as extended time for taking tests, equipment, specialized software programs, individuals to read textbooks aloud to them, individuals to take class notes, use of tape recorders to tape class lectures, and test environments modified to reduce distractions. Despite the various kinds of accommodations or auxiliary services provided, the individuals who receive them are held to the same academic standards as their nondisabled peers (Wells & Hanebrink, 1997).

Counseling Implications

According to Fenton, Newberry, McManus, Korabik, and Evans (2000), students with learning disabilities who achieve success in college are those who not only receive suitable accommodations and support but also have a clear understanding of their specific learning disabilities, develop compensatory strategies to manage their time and achievement, and are able to advocate effectively for themselves in meeting the academic and social challenges of college life. Professional counselors are uniquely qualified to support the success of these students and can foster their development by providing them with the direct services of individual and group counseling, group guidance/advisement, and mentoring/peer-helping interventions and support programs. The goals of these services are (a) to promote the academic achievement and retention of each student, (b) to aid the students' integration with the mainstream college student population, (c) to ensure the students' use of all of the learning disabilities resources and the accommodations to which the students are entitled, and (d) to provide the students with appropriate social support outside of the classroom.

Specific counseling and guidance interventions and activities should focus on developing the individual student's sense of self-worth and psychological well-being. Counseling should also enhance the students' knowledge of their personal learning disabilities; their legal rights for accommodations; and their skills in self-advocacy, career planning, and social competence. These issues are addressed below with suggestions for the counselor.

Self-Worth

Self-worth is frequently a counseling issue for students with learning disabilities (DeBecker, 1993). Learning disabled students often harbor feelings of anxiety about their attempts to achieve success and believe that their disabilities stigmatize them as being inadequate in comparison to their peers. Counseling, therefore, needs to focus on the self-efficacy of these students, enhancing their sense of belonging and normalcy in relationship to peers, promoting their development of independence through skill acquisition, and helping them accept and understand their specific learning disabilities. Many learning disabled students have had painful experiences in both academic and social settings that have led to low self-efficacy and to feelings of being "dumb" (Harrison, 2003). They need to have a strong therapeutic alliance with a counselor who knows and appreciates the struggles of having a learning disability (Sicoli, 1986).

The strength of this alliance is critical for individual counseling with learning disabled students who are in academic crisis (Allard, Dodd, & Peralez, 1987). In this scenario, the student may be experiencing feelings of helplessness with regard to his or her impending academic failure. The bond of trust between the counselor and the client not only reduces anxiety and restores self-worth but also provides an avenue to uncover the previous stages of the problem.

For example, the student may have started the semester with an academically devalued self-concept. To hide this fact from others, the student may have engaged in avoidance behavior, "hiding out" in the classroom and failing to participate in learning activities that involved direct interaction with peers and the instructor. As examinations or required student presentations drew closer during the semester, however, avoidance games became futile, and the student experienced feelings of being trapped. Hence, having nowhere to turn and doubting the adequacy of his or her own academic abilities, the student became overwhelmed with panic and feelings of helplessness. Exploring this chain of events with the student, the counselor helps the student to understand how passivity creates problems (Roffman, Herzog, & Wershba-Gershon, 1994) and sets the stage for exploring more proactive and assertive approaches to academic achievement.

Additional suggestions for using the individual counseling relationship to support self-worth and reduce anxiety include

- helping the student to interpret his or her test data in order to increase self-knowledge of individual strengths and learning style (Aune & Ness, 1991);
- motivating the student to develop a goal-directed orientation to academic achievement, with the understanding that determination and hard work are key factors to attaining success (Hicks-Coolick & Kurtz, 1997);
- assisting the student to "mourn" for the abilities he or she lacks and to appreciate those abilities the student does have (Sicoli, 1986);
- challenging the student's inaccurate self-perceptions through reality testing and helping the student overcome resistance to discussing the learning disability (Yuan, 1994; Brinckerhoff, 1994, underscored the importance of overcoming this resistance by stating, "If students choose not to make a disclosure, then they cannot expect faculty members to anticipate needs or to make accommodations retroactively"; p. 231); and
- exploring the student's experiences as a learning disabled individual and helping the student express ideas and feelings regarding those experiences (Goss, 2001, recommended the use of metaphors in facilitating this exploration).

Counselors also can use group counseling interventions to foster self-worth. Students with learning disabilities need the opportunity to participate in group process as well as informal discussion groups (Strichart & Mangrum, 1985). Learning disabled individuals often have delays in their psychosocial development and may tend to remain dependent on others rather than developing academic autonomy and mature interpersonal relationships (Costello & English, 2001). In addition, they are ambivalent about self-disclosure in an integrated setting and may not be willing to risk further stigmatization by their nondisabled peers (Eisenman & Tascione, 2002). Therefore, group counseling designed specifically for students with learning disabilities can be a powerful asset to these students.

The counseling group can be used to help individuals overcome feelings of shame, doubt, inferiority/incompetence, and isolation. The group also provides peer support to members as they attempt to assert themselves as autonomous, competent individuals with clear personal identities and goals. Through group member disclosure, members can gain a better understanding of the nature of learning disabilities and of their own specific disabilities. The group can engage in problem-solving activities and develop coping strategies for members to practice within the group setting prior to attempting them in the academic and social environment of the campus. The supportive nature of the group itself serves as a positive reinforcement for group members in their efforts to transfer their newly acquired skills to campus life. It is therefore recommended that the counselor use group counseling when conducting stress inoculation training with learning disabled students (Sicoli, 1986).

Knowledge and Skills

Learning disabled students need accurate information about learning disabilities so that they can evaluate the misconceptions that other persons hold regarding disabilities and respond to the discrimination that they may encounter in society (Eisenman & Tascione, 2002). These students also need to be fully aware of their specific rights to accommodations under the law and how to access those accommodations. In particular, the students need to have a clear understanding of their own diagnostic reports so that they can articulate their specific learning disabilities in plain language (Aune & Ness, 1991).

The counselor can help these students obtain this knowledge and guide them in acquiring the accommodations to which they are entitled. Small- and large-group guidance activities are particularly well-suited to these tasks because they center on dissemination of facts and exchange of opinions and concerns while simultaneously encouraging individuals to personalize the information under discussion. Thus, the student can acquire relevant data and be exposed to a variety of viewpoints that may help in understanding his or her own disabilities and rights. Recommendations for counselors conducting guidance groups include (a) emphasizing the need for the learning disabled students to know themselves, (b) suggesting that they get to know their instructors and use the teacher–student relationship in order to personalize instruction, and (c) encouraging them to seek out independent study classes as a means of individualizing their education (Mooney & Cole, 2000).

In these group guidance sessions, it is important that the counselor point out the differences between students' rights under the Individuals With Disabilities Education Act (IDEA; 1997) and their rights under Section 504 and the ADA (Brinckerhoff, 1994; Simon, 2001). Under the IDEA, public school personnel have the major responsibility for guaranteeing these accommodations. Under Section 504 and the ADA, however, students must advocate for themselves. Thus, in order to prevent discrimination and secure the accommodations allowed by law, learning disabled college students must actively advocate for their rights.

Yuan (1994) suggested that information and guidance activities for learning disabled students could be packaged into a college credit course on understanding learning disabilities, which would promote self-understanding and self-advocacy through self-assessment. Brinckerhoff (1994) recommended self-advocacy seminars that provide information about the nature of learning disabilities and legal rights and teach self-advocacy through role-playing strategies.

Methods of teaching self-advocacy skills to learning disabled students usually include role-play and may include direct instruction (Merchant & Gajar, 1997). Given the reluctance of many learning disabled students to be assertive in academic and/or social situations, however, it is recommended that the counselor use group counseling procedures rather than, or in addition to, group guidance when teaching self-advocacy skills. Group counseling provides a safer, more supportive environment for trying out new skills and affords the student the opportunity to receive peer encouragement in overcoming anxieties about acting assertively.

The following is a list of suggested self-advocacy support groups that the counselor can use in designing the group counseling activities:

1. The "Lead Group" (Pocock, Lambros, Algozzine, Wood, & Martin, 2002) is designed to develop student ownership of the educational process and to develop leadership among learning disabled students.
2. Durlak, Ernest, and Bursuck's (1994) seven-step procedure for direct instruction in self-advocacy emphasizes the use of role-play techniques.
3. The "I-PLAN" (Van Reusen, Deshler, & Schumaker, 1989) includes the steps to Inventory personal strengths and areas of improvement, Provide information, Listen and respond, Ask questions, and Name your goals.
4. The "Self-Directed I.E.P." (Martin, Marshall, Maxson, & Jerman, 1996) emphasizes personal planning.
5. The "Choice-Maker Self-Determination Curriculum Series" (Martin & Marshall, 1995) also focuses on personal planning.
6. "Steps to Self-Determination" (Field & Hoffman, 1996) and "Next S.T.E.P." (Halpern et al., 1997) provide systematic procedures for teaching decision making and assertive behavior.

7. The "O.P.E.N." program (Webb, 2000) includes recommendations for teaching high school learning disabled students specific plans and techniques for transition to college.

In addition, the counselor may wish to use group counseling to address issues in the areas of communication skills, social interaction skills, and career development. Learning disabled students need to enhance their skills in listening and writing and to develop strategies for effectively using these skills during classroom instruction. Note-taking, essay writing, and listening for comprehension are essential. Harrison (2003) described peer writing workshops that have been productive in enhancing these skills and also recommended the use of literature circles.

Communication includes various subcomponents, such as negotiation, persuasion, compromise, and body language (Test, Fowler, Wood, Brewer, & Eddy, 2005) Acquiring facility in these personal interaction skills can help students assert themselves, especially in terms of knowing how and when to seek assistance from teachers (Skinner & Schenck, 1992). Results from Roffman et al.'s (1994) social skills training intervention program also supported this contention. These skills are important for the students in career settings as well as interpersonal settings.

Finally, group counseling can be used to provide career services to learning disabled students. Because of delays in their career development, these students need support in assessing ability, acquiring work experiences, and discussing their learning disabilities with their employers. They may also need help in "processing" their real work experiences (e.g., internships or job shadowing) in order to understand them (Michaels & Barr, 2002). The needs of learning disabled employees, therefore, require counselors to teach self-management skills in addition to self-advocacy skills. The implication for counselors is to take an ecological approach to the group members, designing the group procedures to prepare the students for independent living as well as employment (Yuan, 1994).

It is suggested that the counselor take advantage of other career services provided on-campus to supplement the group procedures with real work experiences and transition activities. Programs that provide career development information, job placement, and training activities to address transition from college to work are especially helpful in complementing the knowledge, skills, and experiences acquired in the counseling group sessions. An example of a program that emphasizes experienced-based career preparation and includes both job placement and follow-up on the career maturity of the student can be found in the work of Rosenthal (1989).

Campus Considerations

On many college campuses, the primary source of continuous support for students with learning disabilities is the student disability resource center. These centers typically are designed to provide an equal educational opportunity to qualified students with disabilities, to protect the academic freedom of faculty members, to assure college compliance with disability legislation, and to protect the academic integrity of the college. In addressing these purposes, disability resource center staff members not only directly provide a variety of services and accommodations to the students but also advocate for students' needs with the faculty and administration.

Counselors, by virtue of their knowledge and skills in consultation, can also be powerful advocates for students. In collaboration with disability resource center staff, counselors can consult with faculty and administration to promote understanding of the needs of learning disabled students, to remove systemic barriers that hinder their educational opportunity, and to develop policies and procedures that enhance their success in school and transition to employment following graduation.

Consultation With Faculty

According to Field (1996), there is a definitive need to develop programs of preparation for all personnel serving the learning disabled student so that they understand and encourage the student to engage in self-determination. College faculty members, in particular, are among the personnel who need to be well-informed about the nature of learning disabilities. Instructors need to understand that these students experience learning as a "reflective activity" and that they need time to process the information being presented in class (Harrison, 2003). Faculty also need to be informed about the laws (e.g., Section 504 and the ADA) affecting the rights of disabled students. Scott, Wells, and Hanebrink (1997) recommended that this information be included in the faculty handbook and be part of new faculty orientation.

In addition, it is recommended that counselors and disability resource center staff establish mentoring programs as an outreach project to new faculty to reinforce this orientation. Beyond promoting faculty understanding of learning disabilities, mentoring programs can teach faculty alternative ways of assessing learning disabled students' progress. The programs can also guide faculty members in their role as academic advisers to help learning disabled students plan their courses of study, balance their course loads, and choose their professors (Sicoli, 1986).

Consultation with faculty and mentoring programs can also be helpful in clarifying the issue of faculty rights versus student accommodations. Some professors view accommodations as an unfair advantage, as unnecessary, or as too labor-intensive (Lehmann, Davies, & Laurin, 2000). They may view accommodations as "watering down" the course or as an excuse for the student to "get out of" work. In some cases, professors may believe that accommodations are suggestions, not requirements, because of their ignorance of the law or ignorance of how to make appropriate accommodations (Norton, 1997). Faculty need to know that they are partners in the accommodations process and that accommodations that violate the academic integrity of the course are not granted. Although the civil rights of students are not negotiable, the determination of reasonable accommodations is negotiable.

Consultation With Administration

To create a campus environment where learning disabled students can compete fairly, consultation with administration should focus on the removal of systemic barriers (especially physical and time constraints) and on the development of facilities and programs that provide social support and academic assistance to these students. Administrative support of the student disability services center and advocacy with faculty toward providing accommodations to learning disabled students are necessary first steps. There is also a need, however, to develop programs of family support for learning disabled students that facilitate the shift from traditional roles of parent and child. Such programs should encourage self-advocacy on the part of the students and support their transition to self-determination (Field, 1996).

In addition, administrators can reward faculty for conducting research in self-advocacy (Algozzine, Browder, Karvonen, Test, & Wood, 2001) and for including statements on course syllabi that invite students to meet with the instructor to discuss any academic accommodations to which they are entitled. Administrators, especially deans, should consider allowing learning disabled students to take substitute courses for those required of all students or to take required classes at a community or junior college, where the courses may be taught in a more basic fashion and with a smaller class size (Sicoli, 1986).

Finally, administrators can support learning disabled students by providing career counseling services to them as well as a follow-up service for their job placement after graduation. The focus of business and industry is on qualified individuals, not on training employees and meeting accommodations of individuals with disabilities (Michaels & Barr, 2002). Therefore, the college must engage in career counseling (Brown, 2000) and in outreach to business and industry to help learning disabled students make a better transition to employment and to assess and support their career maturity and satisfaction (Rosenthal, 1989).

Consultation With Public Schools

Several authors (Durlak et al., 1994; Lock & Layton, 2001; McGuire, Hall, & Litt, 1991; Merchant & Gajar, 1997; Skinner & Schenck, 1992) have called for postsecondary and high school service providers to collaborate in preparing learning disabled students for college. They have called for a multisystem approach to empower students during the transition to college, including (a) individual counseling, (b) student self-advocacy group counseling, (c) family transition planning support, and (d) close working relationships among the various school and college personnel. On the basis of the results of their 1997 study, Hicks-Coolick and Kurtz contended that this multisystem collaboration had the positive effects of helping learning disabled students identify their individual strengths and weaknesses and develop their self-advocacy skills in problem solving and assertiveness. Such an approach can also serve to help students develop transition strategies and self-advocacy plans (Lock & Layton, 2001). Students can use the written plan as an advance organizer to guide them during discussions with their professors regarding their strengths, weaknesses, and required accommodations.

Collaboration with public school personnel might also include providing high school students with an orientation to the student disability services on the college campus. Orientation would allow the college personnel the opportunity to underscore the importance of self-advocacy skills, training in the use of learning strategies, and competence in the process of writing in order for learning disabled students to succeed in college (McGuire et al., 1991).

Future Trends

Current trends indicate that more students with learning disabilities are choosing to enter college, and there is little reason to expect that this trend will change in the foreseeable future (Weintraub, 2005). The increase of students with learning disabilities in college populations will necessitate continued and, perhaps, broader support services. These services need to be more comprehensive than, but also more fully integrated into, the services that are typically provided for all students, such as counseling, career counseling and placement, and academic advisement. Counselors will be required to broaden their spheres of influence across campuses and collaborate more fully with the staffs of disability services centers in order to advocate effectively for the increasing numbers of students with learning disabilities.

Research with college students with learning disabilities conducted by Bergin and Bergin (2005) revealed that participants ranked the following as necessary for improving the kinds of support and assistance offered to students with learning disabilities:

- support personnel who have been educated to understand what having a learning disability means;
- counseling designed to help students better understand their specific disabilities before they leave college and embark on a career;
- advisory services to help students review course schedules they have selected to ensure that they will not be "overloaded" by study demands;
- counseling or advisory services that help students secure career information necessary to decide on career opportunities;
- advisory services to help students understand the "hidden curriculum" of the campus, such as how to use the Writing Center, which librarian is particularly helpful, or which professors understand learning disabilities;
- advice, provided on an as-needed basis, on how to organize time to balance study and other activities; and
- support groups made up of students with similar disabilities who can meet regularly to share their frustrations and successes.

Students with learning disabilities who enter college are held to the same academic standards as their nondisabled peers. Their success depends on receiving the supports and accommodations that guarantee the equal access afforded them by federal law. Counselors, working in harmony with other college personnel, can help students with learning disabilities receive the supports, services, and accommodations they require.

References

Algozzine, B., Browder, D., Karvonen, M., Test, D., & Wood, W. (2001). Effects of interventions to promote self-determination for individuals with disabilities. *Review of Educational Research, 71*, 219–277.

Allard, W., Dodd, J., & Peralez, E. (1987). Keeping LD students in college. *Academic Therapy, 22*, 359–365.

Americans With Disabilities Act of 1990, 42 U.S.C.A. § 12101 *et seq.* (West 1993).

Aune, E., & Ness, J. (1991). *Tools for transition: Preparing students with learning disabilities for post secondary education.* Circle Pines, MN: American Guidance Service.

Bender, W. (1998). *Learning disabilities: Characteristics, identification, and teaching strategies* (3rd ed.). Boston: Allyn & Bacon.

Bergin, J. W., & Bergin, J. J. (2004). The forgotten student. *ASCA School Counselor, 41*, 38–41.

Bergin, J. W., & Bergin, J. J. (2005). [Support systems and personal strengths of students with disabilities who succeed in college or university]. Unpublished raw data.

Brinckerhoff, L. (1994). Developing effective self-advocacy skills in college-bound students with learning disabilities. *Intervention in School and Clinic, 29*, 229–237.

Brown, D. (2000). *Learning a living: A guide to planning your career and finding a job for people with learning disabilities, attention deficit disorder, and dyslexia.* Bethesda, MD: Woodbine House.

Costello, J., & English, R. (2001). The psychological development of college students with and without learning disabilities. *Journal of Postsecondary Education and Disability, 15*, 16–27.

DeBecker, S. (1993). *The college bound L.D. student: Let's bury the myths. Opinion paper.* Carbondale: Southern Illinois University. (ERIC Document Reproduction Service No. ED356612)

Durlak, C., Ernest, R., & Bursuck, W. (1994). Preparing high school students with learning disabilities for the transition to postsecondary education: Teaching the skills of self-determination. *Journal of Learning Disabilities, 27*, 51–59.

Eisenman, L., & Tascione, L. (2002). "How come nobody told me?" Fostering self-realization through a high school English curriculum. *Learning Disabilities Research and Practice, 17*, 35–46.

Elksnin, L., Bryant, D., Gartland, D., King-Sears, M., Rosenberg, M., Scanlon, D., et al. (2001). LD summit: Important issues for the field of learning disabilities. *Learning Disabilities Quarterly, 24*, 297–305.

Fenton, S., Newberry, J., McManus, K., Korabik, K., & Evans, M. (2000). Evaluating the learning opportunities program: Some challenges and lessons learned [Special issue]. *Canadian Journal of Program Evaluation, 15*, 163–174.

Fiedorowicz, C. (1999). *Neurobiological bases of learning disabilities: An overview* (Second Canadian Forum Proceedings Report, Canadian Child Care Federation Symposium, pp. 64–67). Retrieved April 8, 2005, from http://www.cfc_efc.ca/cccf

Field, S. (1996). Self-determination instructional strategies for youth with learning disabilities. *Journal of Learning Disabilities, 29*, 40–52.

Field, S., & Hoffman, A. (1996). *Steps to self-determination.* Austin, TX: PRO-ED.

Galaburda, A. (2005). Neurology of learning disabilities: What will the future bring? The answer comes from the successes of the recent past. *Learning Disabilities Quarterly, 28*, 107–109.

Goss, D. (2001). Chasing the rabbit: Metaphors used by adult learners to describe their learning disabilities. *Adult Learning, 12*, 8–9.

Halpern, A., Herr, C., Wolf, N., Doren, B., Johnson, M., & Lawson, J. (1997). *The Next S.T.E.P.: Student transition and educational planning.* Austin, TX: PRO-ED.

Harrison, S. (2003). Creating a successful environment for postsecondary students with learning disabilities: Policy and practice. *Journal of College Reading and Learning, 33*, 131–145.

Henderson, C. (2001). *College freshmen with disabilities: A biennial statistical profile.* Washington, DC: American Council on Education.

Hicks-Coolick, A., & Kurtz, P. (1997). Preparing students with learning disabilities for success in postsecondary education: Needs and services. *Social Work in Education, 97*, 31–43.

Individuals With Disabilities Education Act (IDEA), 20 U.S.C. § 1401 *et seq.* (1997).

Lehmann, J., Davies, P., & Laurin, K. (2000). Listening to student voices about postsecondary education. *Teaching Exceptional Children, 32*, 60–65.

Lerner, J. (2005). *Learning disabilities and related disorders: Characteristics and teaching strategies* (10th ed.). New York: Houghton Mifflin.

Lock, R., & Layton, C. (2001). Succeeding in postsecondary education through self-advocacy. *Exceptional Children, 34*, 66–71.

Martin, J., & Marshall, L. (1995). ChoiceMaker: A comprehensive self-determination transition program. *Intervention in School and Clinic, 30*, 147–156.

Martin, J., Marshall, L., Maxson, L., & Jerman, P. (1996). *Self-directed I.E.P.* Longmont, CO: Sopris West.

McGuire, J., Hall, D., & Litt, A. (1991). A field-based study of the direct service needs of college students with learning disabilities. *Journal of College Student Development, 32*, 101–108.

Merchant, D., & Gajar, A. (1997). A review of the literature on self-advocacy components in transition programs for students with learning disabilities. *Journal of Vocational Rehabilitation, 8*, 223–231.

Michaels, C., & Barr, V. (2002). Best practices in career development programs for post secondary students with learning disabilities: A ten-year follow-up. *Career Planning and Adult Development Journal, 18*, 61–79.

Mooney, L., & Cole, D. (2000). *Learning outside the lines.* New York: Fireside Books/Simon & Schuster.

National Joint Committee on Learning Disabilities. (1997). Operationalizing the NJCLD definition for ongoing assessment in schools. *Perspectives: The International Dyslexia Association, 23*, 29–33.

Norton, S. (1997). Examination of accommodations for community college students with learning disabilities: How are they viewed by faculty and students? *Community College Journal of Research and Practice, 21*, 57–69.

Osmon, B. (1982). *No one to play with: The social side of learning disabilities.* Novato, CA: Academic Therapy.

Pocock, A., Lambros, S., Algozzine, B., Wood, W., & Martin, J. (2002). Successful strategies for promoting self-advocacy among students with LD: The Lead Group. *Intervention in School and Clinic, 37*, 209–216.

Reiff, H., Hatzes, N., Bramel, M., & Gibbon, J. (2001). The relation of LD and gender with emotional intelligence in college students. *Journal of Learning Disabilities, 34*, 66–78.

Roffman, A., Herzog, J., & Wershba-Gershon, P. (1994). Helping young adults understand their learning disabilities. *Journal of Learning Disabilities, 27*, 413–419.

Rosenthal, I. (1989). Model transition programs for learning disabled high school and college students. *Rehabilitation Counseling Bulletin, 33*, 54–66.

Scott, S., Wells, S., & Hanebrink, S. (Eds.). (1997). *Educating college students with disabilities: What academic and fieldwork educators need to know.* Bethesda, MD: American Occupational Therapy Association.

Section 504 of the Rehabilitation Act of 1973, as amended, 29 U.S.C. § 794.

Sicoli, M. (1986). Counseling strategies for college students with learning disabilities. *Journal of Reading, Writing, and Learning Disabilities International, 2*, 291–293.

Simon, J. (2001). Legal issues in serving postsecondary students with disabilities. *Topics in Language Disorders, 21*, 1–16.

Skinner, M., & Schenck, S. (1992). Counseling the college bound student with a learning disability. *School Counselor, 39*, 369–376.

Strichart, S., & Mangrum, C. (1985). Selecting a college for the LD student. *Academic Therapy, 2,* 75–79.

Test, D., Fowler, C., Wood, W., Brewer, D., & Eddy, S. (2005). A conceptual framework of self-advocacy for students with disabilities. *Remedial and Special Education, 26,* 43–54.

Thomas, S. (2000). College students and disability law. *The Journal of Special Education, 33,* 248–257.

U.S. Department of Education. (1977). *Assistance to states for education of handicapped children: Procedures for evaluating specific learning disabilities.* 42 Fed. Reg. 65082-65085 (August 23, 1977).

U.S. Department of Education. (2002). *To assure the free appropriate public education of all children with disabilities* (24th Annual Report to Congress on the Implementation of the Individuals With Disabilities Education Act). Washington, DC: U.S. Government Printing Office.

Van Reusen, A., Deshler, D., & Schumaker, J. (1989). Effects of a student participation strategy in facilitating the involvement of adolescents with learning disabilities in the individualized education program planning process. *Learning Disabilities, 1,* 23–34.

Webb, K. (2000). *Transition to postsecondary education: Strategies for students with disabilities.* Austin, TX: PRO-ED.

Weintraub, F. (2005). The evolution of LD policy and future challenges. *Learning Disabilities Quarterly, 28,* 97–99.

Wells, S., & Hanebrink, S. (1997). Auxiliary aids, adjustments, and reasonable accommodations. In S. Scott, S. Wells, & S. Hanebrink (Eds.), *Educating college students with disabilities: What academic and fieldwork educators need to know* (pp. 37–51). Bethesda, MD: American Occupational Therapy Association.

Yuan, F. (1994). Moving toward self-acceptance: A course for students with learning disabilities. *Intervention in School and Clinic, 29,* 301–309.

Counseling Students With Autism and Asperger's Syndrome: A Primer for Success as a Social Being and a Student

Scott Browning and Patricia Miron

Introduction

An increase in early identification, services, and treatment for individuals with an autism spectrum disorder has led to an apparent increase in the number of these individuals attending institutions of higher learning (Farrell, 2004). For many years, the prevalence of autism spectrum disorders had been estimated at 4 or 5 per 10,000 births (Wing, 1976), but current estimates range from 2 to 6 per 1,000 individuals (Strock, 2004).

Autism, first reported by Leo Kanner in 1943, is a diagnostic category that first appeared in the third edition of the *Diagnostic and Statistical Manual of Mental Disorders* (*DSM–III*; American Psychiatric Association [APA], 1980). At that time, many higher functioning individuals with autism did not meet the diagnostic criteria (Mesibov, 2001). Asperger's syndrome was first reported by Hans Asperger in 1944 (Wing, 1998) and was first included in the fourth edition of the *DSM* (*DSM–IV*; APA, 1994) under the general heading of pervasive developmental syndromes.

According to the fourth edition, text revision of the *DSM* (*DSM–IV–TR*; APA, 2000), the diagnostic criteria for an autism spectrum disorder are based on behavioral symptoms and involve three core characteristics: "1) qualitative impairment in social interaction, 2) significant impairment in social, occupational and verbal and nonverbal communication, and 3) restricted repetitive and stereotyped patterns of behavior and interests" (p. 80). The behavioral symptoms

273

involved in the diagnosis of any of the autism spectrum disorders can range from mild to severe. Individuals with high-functioning autism and Asperger's syndrome are considered to be at the mild end of the spectrum, and it is these individuals who may attend college.

The *DSM–IV* (APA, 1994) attempted to delineate Asperger's syndrome as a separate condition from autism. Asperger's syndrome includes (a) qualitative impairment in social interaction; (b) restricted repetitive and stereotyped patterns of behavior, interests, and activities; (c) clinically significant impairment in social, occupation, or other important areas of functioning; and (d) no significant delay in language, cognitive development, self-help skills, adaptive behavior, and curiosity about the environment. Asperger's syndrome is differentiated from autism by the lack of qualitative impairment in communication and the lack of delays in multiple areas.

There are many difficulties in attempting to distinguish Asperger's syndrome from high-functioning autism. Although early language and cognitive function are reportedly not delayed in individuals with Asperger's syndrome, this lack is often based on retrospective reports (Frith, 2004). In comparing the clinical symptoms, Eisenmajer et al. (1996) found that as individuals with high-functioning autism and Asperger's syndrome aged, there were fewer differences in communication impairments, and they increasingly came to resemble each other. Macintosh and Dissanayake (2004) also reviewed empirical evidence for the similarities and differences between individuals with high-functioning autism and Asperger's syndrome and found very few qualitative differences, particularly as the individuals aged. Outcome studies by Howlin (2003) and Szatmari et al. (2000) similarly found that older individuals with high-functioning autism and Asperger's syndrome share many features and that it is often difficult to tell them apart. As Frith (2004) stated, "At present, the label 'high-functioning autism' is much used and is often interchangeable with Asperger Syndrome" (p. 675). For this chapter, the terms *high-functioning autism* and *Asperger's syndrome* are collectively referred to as *Asperger's*.

Assessment Issues

Students with Asperger's may seek assistance in the counseling center for issues related to anxiety, depression, or difficulties adapting to the social demands of the college environment. It is also possible that a student with Asperger's has not been previously diagnosed. Therefore, it is important to understand some of the subtle characteristics of these individuals. Troubles may be evident in the areas of language, cognition, socialization, and responses to sensory stimuli. Sensory processing difficulties may include being hyper- or hyposensitive to tactile, auditory, vestibular, proprioceptive, visual, or olfactory sensory information (Ayres, 1972; Bogdashina, 2003; Strock, 2004).

The process of assessing an individual with Asperger's is best considered as involving two primary orientations: the psychometric assessment and the clinical interview. Combining a standardized assessment with a specific clinical interview provides the best determination of what is necessary to be helpful to the student.

Psychometric Assessment

The recommended psychometric assessment is the Autism Quotient (AQ), created by Baron-Cohen, Wheelwright, Skinner, Martin, and Clubley (2001; refer to the cited article to obtain the complete instrument and the scoring key). Many of the questions within the 50-item AQ serve as an important catalyst for discussion. Although there are a number of instruments that assess for autism spectrum disorders and Asperger's syndrome, we have found the AQ to be the most useful for diagnostic screening and educated discussion. This screening tool can highlight particular areas in which intervention can ease the transition to college.

To illustrate use of the AQ, let us look at Paul, a 19-year-old freshman who meets the diagnostic criteria for Asperger's. He is friendly but very wary of engaging in conversation because he is afraid that he might bore his listener. He is aware that many people in the past have told him that they are interested in hearing about his area of interest only for a short period of time and then they want to be invited to give their opinion on the topic. Paul believes that there is little point in speaking about Impressionist art if he cannot fully explore the topics and cover many painters and their art. Therefore, even though his opinions on art are often well worth hearing, many people begin to become bored if Paul has not prepared them for his discussion.

In this case, the AQ served as a good springboard for discussion on this topic with Paul. One of the items, "I know how to tell if someone listening to me is getting bored," motivated Paul to inquire as to how one would notice such a thing. Not only did Paul feel uncertain as to how to determine whether others were bored, but he also assumed that others were just tolerating his discussion, regardless of topic. He frequently apologized for going on at too great a length. In fact, Paul's tendency to apologize became a behavior that had to be addressed. Even though he had become more aware of standard rules of conversation, his apologies were often entirely unnecessary and would become as disruptive to a conversation as his previous loquaciousness had been.

The Clinical Interview

The second step in completing a comprehensive assessment is to conduct a clinical interview, preferably as an intake to lead into ongoing therapeutic support throughout the school year. The primary goal of such a clinical assessment is to accept the student exactly as he or she is.

Establishing an Authentic Relationship

A key factor in becoming an important person to an individual with Asperger's is the creation of an authentic relationship. Although this may seem to represent a minimal standard for a counselor to achieve, creating such a relationship is critical for providing a genuine resource to those using the college counseling center. In a sense, the formation of such a relationship is the first step in assessing the student's capacity to form a bond with another person. The counselor should begin the process with the very important tools of sincere interest and patience, determining whether the student can be put at ease, learning about his or her interests, and beginning to recognize any interpersonal patterns that are likely to poorly serve this student in forming relationships with other students or faculty.

For example, let us look at Susan, a 21-year-old student with Asperger's and an anxiety disorder. When meeting Susan, the therapist recognizes that the conversation is greatly lengthened by Susan's style of repeating all points that are made and then giving examples. Although the counselor is aware of this pattern from the first meeting, it would not be useful to approach this interpersonal style as a goal for change too early in the relationship building.

The question of what to expect when meeting an individual with Asperger's is difficult to answer. In large part this is due to the range of styles and related behaviors associated with these neurologically based disorders. There are a few overarching similarities that can be expected, such as literal mindedness, social awkwardness, and inconsistencies of skills. However, beyond a general outline, individuals with Asperger's express their symptoms of the disorders in a variety of manners.

Although problems with language may not be apparent in the ability of individuals with Asperger's to talk about topics of interest, difficulties may be present in their ability to express feelings or engage in conversation about topics if they have no interest in them. These individuals may demonstrate trouble initiating a conversation or switching topics, and they may make irrelevant comments or interrupt others when speaking. Difficulties may also be evident in understanding the complexities of language, including the use of social language, and in understanding words with multiple meanings.

Individuals with Asperger's generally experience mild frustration in understanding social nuances and in determining the intent of others—what has been referred to by Baron-Cohen (1995) as "theory of mind." These individuals may seem self-centered because of difficulties in inferring what others are thinking or feeling on the basis of facial expressions, nonverbal gestures, or tone of voice.

Cognitively, individuals with Asperger's may experience mild struggles with flexibility, problem solving, attention, organizational skills, and abstract thought. Thinking through the complexities of problems may be challenging because thinking tends to be rigid. These individuals may experience difficulty adapting to change or failure and may have trouble understanding that others view an issue differently from their view.

Individuals with Asperger's may also be challenged in processing multiple sensory stimuli. These individuals may overreact to some stimuli and be underreactive to other stimuli. Common sensory processing difficulties are seen in relationship to touch and sound. However, problems may also exist in the areas of taste, smell, or proprioception.

The First Session and Beyond

Because of the distinct ways in which students with Asperger's process information and form social contacts, it is often helpful for the counselor to be very calm in an initial session with these students. The introductory session should be geared to find the strengths of the individual, identifying areas of interest that are relevant to the creation of a social network or may be useful in academic pursuits. The counselor's office should be a tranquil and welcoming place, and the clinical stance should emphasize sincere interest and patience to reduce social anxiety. The counselor should be aware that the standard emphasis on problem solving is often off-putting and may not feel supportive to many individuals with Asperger's. In addition, the classic stance taught to most counselors to keep good eye-to-eye contact may make these students feel uncomfortable and increase their anxiety. The alternative is not to be distracted and seemingly uninterested, but rather for the counselor to shift his or her gaze away at times to determine what style of interaction seems to increase the student's comfort.

As the assessment continues, the counselor will want to inquire about the individual's high school experience. A great deal can be learned about particular challenges and successful coping from hearing how high school was structured and how past obstacles were overcome. If there are some useful suggestions garnered from the high school experience, they should be judged to determine whether the same solution might apply in the college setting. It is certainly possible that some of the past solutions had been determined through an individualized education plan, and although colleges do not follow this model, the use of accommodations is always available by law. However, accommodations that relate specifically to learning disabilities must be accompanied by a formal psychoeducational evaluation that clearly establishes the need for particular accommodations. Therefore, if the student with Asperger's begins to comment on accommodations that might be desired (e.g., longer test-taking time or a quiet room), the counselor must determine whether the proper documentation exists. If it does not, the necessary evaluation must be initiated, either through the college, if possible, or through an outside evaluator (see chapter 19 in this book, "The Hidden Disabilities: Counseling Students With Learning Disabilities").

Other past behaviors and accommodations should also be explored. In particular, it is useful to determine whether the students have consistent routines in which they engage. For example, let us look at James, a 20-year-old student with high-functioning autism who attends a community college. James is compelled to stand up twice an hour and turn a full circle. Although this behavior may seem somewhat unusual to fellow students and the professor, James can greatly lessen the effect by letting people know that he feels a compulsion to so act, and others need not interpret it as requiring any response. Sometimes just acknowledging a behavior is less captivating than allowing it to remain mysterious. It should be understood that, although James's behavior may lose some of its peculiarity by being explained, it may still be annoying to those around him. The task of alerting others to the nature of the autism spectrum may fall to the counselor, who may be required to provide information to the classmates so that they can become more informed of the involuntary nature of James's actions. Even with involuntary behavior, however, some modification is often possible.

In a sense, the clinical assessment of an individual with Asperger's is tapping into the counselor's own ability to determine what styles and behaviors were easy to relate to and which were more difficult. This information is not shared initially with the client because to do so would put the client on the defensive, but it helps the counselor to set a baseline and continue to assist the client in forming relationships with other students, college staff, and professors.

Although an emphasis on problem solving and specific techniques will certainly be of use with this population, the initial session is really about forming a relationship. In doing so, the student with Asperger's must feel that he or she is understood. Often an individual with Asperger's perceives that there is something about an interaction that is difficult for the other person, and that awareness of the frustration of the other person increases the anxiety of the individual with Asperger's. Therefore, the success of an initial meeting of a counselor with a client with Asperger's is based on the formation of the relationship, not necessarily on the problems solved.

Counseling Implications

As previously noted, the creation of an authentic relationship remains the most important task of the counselor with an individual with Asperger's. However, in addition to that crucial task, there are a variety of topics that must, on most occasions, be discussed and supported through the counseling relationship.

Developing a Treatment Plan

Using the relationship that has been established, the counselor should begin to talk openly with the client about his or her preferences for support. By having this dialogue, the counselor facilitates the client's ability to learn to be his or her own advocate. The counselor should determine whether the relationship will be primarily that of a coach or a therapist or both. The college counselor can assist the student in a manner that engages most of the typical counseling stances: empathy, cognitive reshaping, comprehensive understanding, and clinical interventions based on theoretical grounds. In contrast, the counselor may be far more helpful as one who, in essence, writes for the client a primer of succeeding as a social being and a student. Complicating this conceivable spectrum of services is the fact that neither the counselor nor the student will be clear as to the best approach. There are occasions when the clinical role must be emphasized because there are, in fact, clinical issues that exist in tandem with the neurological uniqueness.

Because of the neurological uniqueness of Asperger's, the student's capacity to engage in the clinical process will vary. The reason that this is problematic is that, in most cases, the role of counselor is usually that of a therapist. Although some clients use both individual and group treatment at college counseling centers, most predominantly use one format. With this population, therefore, the counselor often wrestles with the balance of services and may become personally unsure whether his or her efforts are useful, asking, "Should I keep pushing the educative part of my counseling, or does the client need me to back off and really understand his/her experience?" Yet, if the treatment becomes very clinically therapeutic, the counselor's concern may become, even if the therapy is quite good, "Am I becoming more comfortable in the client's worldview but not helping him/her to connect with people on campus?"

With all clients, the ratio of time spent in a therapeutic mode is offset by activities that are educational. When one is working with individuals with Asperger's, the treatment plan should be clearly articulated, and the creation and ongoing evolution of the treatment plan should be accomplished in a collegial manner. Prince-Hughes (2002) pointed out that "many autistic people say that written English is their first language, and spoken English their second" (p. 7). Working with a client who is very literal, but who is also challenged by some of the nuances of language and relational dynamics, pushes the counselor to write out the treatment agenda and remain open to adjusting it when necessary.

Just because a student is an individual with Asperger's does not mean that his or her treatment will be predetermined. However, some of the tasks of adjusting to college life are uniform enough that it is possible to outline some of the primary issues that should be addressed in counseling. The first and most important issue is the attribution of interpersonal problems.

Let us return to the case of Paul. He is convinced that he is socially incapable of being enjoyable company to anyone outside of his immediate family. He believes that outside people will not find him interesting and that it is "impossible to come up with the opening sentence to interest others." The first step for the counselor in this situation, and in most clinical cases, is to determine "To what does the client attribute the continuation of this difficulty?"

Because of Paul's anxiety and genuine desire not to be boring, he would so rapidly assume that the other person was trying to exit the conversation that he would begin to apologize about his topic before the other person had even had a chance to decide whether it was interesting. Paul needed to understand that his belief that he was invariably uninteresting, and therefore that he must apologize, was a much greater factor in ending conversations than was the topic being discussed. Paul had to learn to reframe his belief to "I need to watch other people to see if they are nodding and seem interested before I assume they are bored." By making this shift alone, Paul was able to extend the length of numerous contacts with acquaintances as well as determine potential friends.

A second emphasis that is commonly useful with this population is to assist the student in learning how to disclose information in such a manner that the listener is aware of the requested response. If information is disclosed in a profoundly brusque manner, the listener may perceive a challenge, rather than an invitation to dialogue. A counselor can approach this topic through the use of social stories and comic book scripts (Gray, 1994). As part of this process, the client will often benefit greatly from an introductory tutorial on human emotional expression, most often exhibited through tone of voice, facial expressions, and body language.

Social stories are individualized short stories that "describe a situation, skill, or concept in terms of relevant social cues, perspectives and common responses"

(Gray, 1994). The social story affirms what the individual already does well and contains the additional information needed for successful interaction. *Comic strip conversations* (Gray, 1994) are drawings of people engaged in a conversation that serve to help the individual identify the emotional content and motivation behind what was said. During a conversation in which there is a quick exchange of information, individuals with an autism spectrum disorder may need additional processing time to understand the less salient cues. Comic strip conversations are often used following an unsuccessful interaction.

The importance of teaching practical skills to individuals with Asperger's cannot be overemphasized. It often begins with a review of a theory of mind to assist the student in becoming a researcher of his or her own style and with an investigation as to how others seem to form interpersonal relationships. In providing this guidance, three levels of intervention can be integrated into the student's treatment that can improve his or her approach to interacting with others: (a) teaching practical skills, such as conversation skills, classroom decorum, roommate conflicts, and interacting with the opposite sex; (b) creating scholarly interest groups, or workshops, that emphasize an intellectual exchange on narrow areas of knowledge; and (c) establishing a program of intermediated social contact in which student assistants interact as mentor/peer counselors and as social coaches.

Teaching Practical Skills

The first level of intervention, teaching practical skills, uses the active group/teaching format to elucidate the survival skills of college life. The group also functions as a supportive environment to learn coping strategies and interaction skills and as a way to meet others with the same concerns. Although teaching skills to facilitate adjustment to the academic and social challenges of college life is important, it is also critical to encourage the client's own problem solving. Problem-solving skills allow students with Asperger's to learn not only how to cope with a given situation but also how to generalize these coping strategies to other situations and facilitate their ability to advocate for themselves.

Early group topics may include (a) adjusting to living away from home, (b) living with a roommate and potential conflicts, (c) navigating the residence hall or the cafeteria, and (d) managing time. A focus on building a repertoire of interactional skills and managing social situations should also be a priority, including how to expand and elaborate on a range of topics that are initiated by others; how to begin and end a conversation; and how to negotiate, persuade, and disagree through verbal means. Difficulties with predicting behavior and making inferences may also be present, and exploration of social situations in which these skills are required will help participants understand the motivation of others. In addition, it is vital to facilitate an increase in awareness and teach rules regarding nonverbal communication, such as the use and meaning of eye contact and eye gaze patterns and the conveyance of messages through tone of voice, facial expression, and hand gestures.

There are many additional topics that could be covered in these sessions, and further reading in the area of social skills development should be recommended to this group of individuals. Role-playing various situations related to the topic of discussion can easily be incorporated into these sessions, increasing the possibility of generalization to situations outside of the group. A discussion of how and when these skills have been practiced outside of the group may also facilitate the individual's ability to generalize the skills learned.

Creating Scholarly Interest Groups

The second level of intervention involves the creation of scholarly interest groups in the form of a workshop series open to anyone on campus. Three or four short lectures would be presented per workshop on topics of particular interest. Anyone on campus would be invited to present and attend, and those individuals with Asperger's would be strongly encouraged to share their particular interests with a wider community. The advantage of the workshops is that they provide a healthy intellectual environment for all students on campus and provide a unique forum to students to learn and to generate social contact.

Establishing Intermediated Social Contact

The third level of intervention, establishing intermediated social contact, involves a learning laboratory in which social discourse is investigated in the presence of trained mentors who serve as both coaches and models. This type of intervention also facilitates further learning of material that was primarily taught in a didactic fashion in the first style of intervention. The idea, as discussed by Shore (2003), is to assist people in learning about social interaction by using a role-play format and video playback as a method of closely analyzing the interactions, offering feedback, and moving toward more successful models. The student mentors are involved as volunteers; as students who are interested in the population and willing to provide this service as practical training; or, potentially, as paid student assistants. Role-plays, including situations such as meeting with a professor to request accommodations or dealing with a conflict with a roommate, are videotaped. Following the role-play, the participants review the video.

The video may need to be reviewed several times to increase the individual's ability to understand all of the nuances of his or her behavior, the other person's behavior, and the effect that they had on each other. For example, the first time the video is watched, the focus may be on nonverbal behavior (e.g., eye contact, facial expression, tone of voice, and interpersonal distance). Following the first viewing, the individual verbalizes what he or she saw. The second time through the video, the focus may be on the other person's nonverbal behavior.

Each review of the video is leading the individual to (a) understand the reasons behind the other person's behavior, (b) understand any misunderstandings that occurred in the interaction, (c) attempt to understand the unwritten rules that were implicit in the interaction, (d) learn what information he or she is missing when interacting with others, and (e) understand the emotional states of the other person. Use of this framework will help these individuals develop an understanding of what works and what does not work in social situations and learn to problem solve alternative solutions. Encouraging the individual to practice these skills outside of the laboratory furthers the individual's ability to generalize the skill and to actively engage in problem solving in social situations.

Campus Considerations

Some college administrations are dedicated to making the campus a welcoming environment for students with special needs and understand that individuals with Asperger's need assistance with the social life and academic pressures of college. In these colleges, it is probable that the counseling center staff have the blessing of the administration to advocate for the needs of students with Asperger's and to assist faculty, staff, and students in understanding some of the variety of issues present with these individuals. Although many individuals with Asperger's have attended college without specific support, the dropout rate of such individuals has been greatly increased by misunderstandings and resolvable problems. More colleges, however, are becoming aware of the fact that assisting these students to succeed is both humane and good business.

Assessing how one can assist a student to succeed does not mean that it is the college's job to guarantee that everyone succeeds. Success would not be so worthy a goal if it were assured, but to assist anyone to use his or her mind to the fullest capacity possible is a gift to all involved.

The college can greatly assist a student with Asperger's to succeed. The college should make it clear in its literature that people who have neurological syndromes or nonverbal learning disorders are welcome and that there are staff and professors familiar with the conditions. In addition, the school should offer an in-depth orientation that is directly geared for an individual with Asperger's. A component of this orientation would be a tour to show the student all of the important areas in the college to be aware of, such as the cafeteria, library, meeting place for clubs, bulletin boards, faculty offices, and dorms. Also, some of the basic practices in place to assist these students in dealing with the practical realities should be emphasized. It is particularly unfair for a student to be discouraged about the college experience by obstacles that can be overcome.

One tremendously important support that the college can and should offer this population of students is a quiet space that is available 24 hours a day. This need only be a room that can be accessed by a code so that it will be used only by those students who need a safe place to retire to if the pressures become too great in class, around campus, or in the dorm.

Ideally, the students who need a quiet dorm should be afforded the opportunity of having such a living space; however, many campuses do not have such a place. Even without a quiet dorm, an individual with Asperger's should be offered a quiet hall and a mellow roommate.

If students with Asperger's arrive on campus without laptop computers, they should be assisted in obtaining them. Some colleges will have loaner machines, whereas other colleges will have a recommendation for the students and their families. In either case, the students should be encouraged to have personal laptop computers because they are essential in facilitating the students' ability to communicate freely with professors and to access online resources such as "Blackboard." A crowded computer center would, more than likely, result in overstimulation. The college can offer additional assistance by downloading a daily schedule to the students' computers that would facilitate increased organization.

Colleges can also assist these students by encouraging those who can to be tutors. Because students with Asperger's often have excellent academic skills in one area, they are frequently interested in imparting that knowledge to others through a tutoring center. The great advantage is that, while these students may be receiving tutoring in a subject in which they have a weakness, they are also providing help in an area in which they are highly skilled. One preeminent authority on autism, Shore (2003), noted the importance for these students of being tutors. The tutor–student relationship, unlike many other relationships, has the possibility of growing within a very structured setting where typical social niceties are not necessary.

Ideally, colleges will help graduates of their programs succeed in the workplace by forming links with jobs that have hospitable environments for those individuals with Asperger's. The relationship that was established with the counselor, which emphasized successful integration into the college community and facilitated self-advocacy, should allow these individuals to generalize the skills learned to the world at large.

Finally, it is critical that colleges educate their faculty and staff in order to understand students with Asperger's. Without a good practice guide, faculty frequently do not understand how Asperger's affects the students' ability to learn and their style of interaction, nor do they understand what hurdles these students have to overcome.

Future Trends

The only institution of higher learning noted for having a completely integrated program designed to support students with an autism spectrum disorder is Marshall University in Huntington, West Virginia. The West Virginia Autism Training Center at Marshall University provides many of the programs discussed in this chapter and more to support students. It is a model of how colleges can fully support students with these needs while maintaining academic standards (see www.marshall.edu/coe/atc).

There are some private centers supporting students with Asperger's, serving a selection of colleges that form an informal consortium. Although rare, these facilities are beginning to be used in a few regions of the country. An example of such a private support center is the Brevard Center in Melbourne, Florida, where any student who is willing to pay an extra fee can receive first-rate coaching and support services (see www.brevardcenter.org).

Although no one program can guarantee that a student with unique social and academic needs will succeed in college, programs designed specifically to address the needs of students with Asperger's should make the graduation rate of these students significantly higher. It is hoped that the future trend will be that every college has services that are truly supportive of students who have an autism spectrum disorder. Each counseling center can begin to make a difference so that no student leaves college simply because fellow students and faculty misunderstood his or her style of interaction or approach to learning. Higher education should be, and can be, better than that.

References

American Psychiatric Association. (1980). *Diagnostic and statistical manual of mental disorders* (3rd ed.). Washington, DC: Author.

American Psychiatric Association. (1994). *Diagnostic and statistical manual of mental disorders* (4th ed.). Washington, DC: Author.

American Psychiatric Association. (2000). *Diagnostic and statistical manual of mental disorders* (4th ed., text rev.). Washington, DC: Author.

Ayres, A. J. (1972). *Sensory integration and learning syndromes.* Los Angeles: Western Psychological Services.

Baron-Cohen, S. (1995). *Mindblindness: An essay on autism and theory of mind.* Cambridge, MA: MIT Press.

Baron-Cohen, S., Wheelwright, S., Skinner, R., Martin, J., & Clubley, E. (2001). The autism-spectrum quotient (AQ): Evidence from Asperger syndrome/high-functioning autism, males and females, scientists and mathematicians. *Journal of Autism and Developmental Disorder, 31,* 5–17.

Bogdashina, O. (2003). *Sensory perceptual issues in autism: Different sensory experiences, different perceptual worlds.* Philadelphia: Jessica Kingsley.

Eisenmajer, R., Prior, M., Leekam, S., Wing, L., Gould, J., Welham, M., et al. (1996). Comparison of clinical symptoms in autism and Asperger's syndrome. *Journal of the American Academy of Child and Adolescent Psychiatry, 35,* 1523–1531.

Farrell, E. F. (2004, October 8). Asperger's confounds colleges. *Chronicle of Higher Education, 51,* A35–A36.

Frith, U. (2004). Emanuel Miller lecture: Confusions and controversies about Asperger syndrome. *Journal of Child Psychology and Psychiatry, 45,* 672–686.

Gray, C. (1994). *Comic book conversations.* Arlington, TX: Future Horizons.

Howlin, P. (2003). Outcome in high functioning adults with autism with and without early language delays: Implications for the differentiation between autism and Asperger syndrome. *Journal of Autism and Developmental Syndromes, 33,* 3–13.

Kanner, L. (1943). Autistic disturbances of affective contact. *Nervous Child, 2,* 217–250.

Macintosh, K. E., & Dissanayake, C. (2004). Annotation: The similarities and differences between autistic syndrome and Asperger's syndrome: A review of the empirical evidence. *Journal of Child Psychology and Psychiatry, 45,* 421–434.

Mesibov, G. B. (2001). *Understanding Asperger syndrome and high functioning autism.* Hingham, MA: Kluwer Academic.

Prince-Hughes, D. (2002). *Aquamarine blue 5.* Columbus: Ohio University Press.

Shore, S. (2003). Beyond the wall: Personal experiences with autism and Asperger syndrome. Shawnee Mission, KS: Autism Asperger Publishing.

Strock, M. (2004). *Autism spectrum syndromes (pervasive developmental syndrome;* NIH Publication No. NIH 04-5511). Bethesda, MD: National Institute of Mental Health.

Szatmari, P., Bryson, S. E., Streiner, D., Wilson, F., Archer, L., & Ryerse, C. (2000). Two-year outcome of preschool children with autism or Asperger's syndrome. *American Journal of Psychiatry, 157,* 1980–1987.

Wing, L. (1976). *Early childhood autism: Clinical, educational and social aspects* (2nd ed.). Oxford, England: Pergamon Press.

Wing, L. (1998). The history of Asperger syndrome. In E. Schopler, G. B. Mesibov, & L. J. Kunce (Eds.), *Asperger syndrome or high-functioning autism?* (pp. 11–27). New York: Plenum Press.

21

When Psychopathology Challenges Education: Counseling Students With Severe Psychiatric Disorders

Joseph A. Lippincott

Introduction

Students with severe psychiatric disorders often pose a daunting challenge for college counselors. The term *psychiatric* has been chosen in describing the condition of this population because these are students who experience severe psychopathology, often receive psychotropic medications, and may require inpatient psychiatric hospitalization. The diagnostic categories comprising these students include, but are not limited to, schizophrenia and other psychotic disorders, personality disorders (particularly borderline phenomena with flagrant acting-out episodes), and bipolar disorder with severe symptomatology (American Psychiatric Association, 2000). The acuteness and complexity of the symptoms, behaviors, and histories presented by these students demand appreciably more time and attention from college counselors than almost any other population and require a high level of professional competence. As Gilbert (1992) observed, "When confronted with severe pathology, some clinicians, I fear, are either naïve about the magnitude of the task or grandiose about their abilities to accomplish it in a university outpatient setting" (p. 699).

The typical age of onset of many severe psychiatric disorders is late adolescence and young adulthood (e.g., Becker, Martin, Wajeeh, Ward, & Shern, 2002; Collins & Mowbray, 2005). Those students who arrive at college with existing psychiatric histories often experience recurring decompensatory episodes throughout their college careers (Sher, Wood, & Gotham, 1996). The result may be disruptive or disturbing behavior, potentially affecting numerous people on the college campus, including roommates, classmates, faculty, and staff (Kitzrow, 2003).

Improvements in psychotropic medications and psychiatric rehabilitation methods are enabling more individuals with severe psychiatric disorders to pursue college education and, ultimately, more rewarding careers (Collins & Mowbray, 2005). Although data in the 1990s indicated that more than 80% of students with psychiatric disorders dropped out of college without a degree (Collins & Mowbray, 2005), there is reason for optimism that increasing numbers of these students will graduate. College counseling centers can play an important role in making this happen by maintaining counselors who possess the skills to assess and diagnose severe psychiatric disorders in students; the judgment to determine appropriate referrals; and the experience to manage decompensatory episodes, including the resulting impact on the students, their families, and the campus community.

Assessment Issues

Counselors may first encounter a student with severe psychiatric disorders when he or she is experiencing prepsychotic phenomena or even a full-blown psychotic episode. Some of these students will have a history of symptoms and subsequent treatment. Those students who have not had previous treatment are likely to be scared and at a loss to understand what is happening to them.

Assessment Interview

A detailed assessment interview is vital. Counselors need to develop an understanding of what the student is experiencing, including specific thoughts (e.g., "I think people are talking about me"), and precipitating events or relationship issues (e.g., the student remained awake for 48 hours cramming for an exam and then developed hypomanic symptoms). A student having a manic episode, for example, may report exhilaration or enjoyment, or a student with persecutory delusions may report distress or fear. Counselors should also assess personal and family histories, particularly because many of these students will have close relatives who have experienced symptoms or have been diagnosed. The most important overall aspect is to join with and engage the student regarding his or her experiences and to provide a safe "holding environment." The therapeutic bond with its inherent support, trust, and comfort will allow the student to get through the episode with the least possible negative consequences.

In work with clients with severe psychiatric disorders, the term *assessment* is often used in its most clinical, literal sense. There is a certain level of mutual inclusivity between assessments in psychology and psychiatry. Typically psychological assessments are a combination of clinical interviews and psychometric tests and, to a lesser extent, projective tests, whereas psychiatric diagnoses fall into the realm of the *Diagnostic and Statistical Manual of Mental Disorders* (4th ed., text rev.; American Psychiatric Association, 2000) and structured clinical interviews. College counselors who work with clients with severe psychiatric distress should have a working familiarity with these various forms of assessment and diagnosis.

It may at times prove difficult to establish a confident diagnosis, often due to a lack of information about premorbid behavior, ambiguous data, or not meeting specific clinical criteria. In such cases, consultation with colleagues or other knowledgeable professionals is advised. Obtaining as detailed a personal history as possible is also important. Often, however, even when a diagnosis seems clear-cut, treatment considerations present a quandary.

Referrals

Major considerations in offering treatment to students with severe pathology are the counseling center's philosophy and policy regarding treatment length and referrals and the composition and expertise of counseling center staff and consultants. Stone and Archer (1990) adopted a strategic planning perspective for counseling centers in the 1990s and strongly advised that clients with severe pathology be referred to the community for treatment, believing that their treatment needs are inherently long-term (i.e., greater than the 10 or 15 sessions in a typical semester). Referral plans need to include follow-up strategies and attempts to ensure minimal interruption of services (Herlihy & Corey, 2005).

Even if a student is being treated off-campus, he or she may appear at the counseling center when intense symptoms reoccur. In such cases, brief intervention models are helpful in dealing with the student's acute distress and planning for further clinical follow-up. Brief therapy is also often used as a supportive adjunct for students as they are transitioned into a longer term treatment modality. However, brief therapy as the sole mode of treatment for clients with severe pathology is generally contraindicated (Gilbert, 1992; Lacour & Carter, 2002; May, 1992). Therefore, unless a college counseling center has adequate resources, including psychiatric coverage and crisis intervention capabilities, long-term treatment in the community is generally advised.

A study of decision-making influences for referrals among 42 college counseling centers reported that the five primary reasons to refer were (a) whether the client requested referral, (b) the severity of client issues, (c) the length of therapy required, (d) the staff's ability to meet the client's needs, and (e) the limitations posed by staff expertise (Lawe, Penick, Raskin, & Raymond, 1999). The authors also reported a mean referral rate of 15.8% among centers.

A review of the literature regarding referral decisions in college counseling confirms that making a referral involves numerous factors, not the least of which is the length of time involved in the referral process itself (Lacour & Carter, 2002). A prudent approach to this dilemma may be to offer several supportive, preparatory sessions aimed at transitioning the client to a community-based clinician offering long-term treatment options and appropriate resources. Such a transition may be particularly difficult for clients with severe personality disorders who already experience fragile senses of self and object constancy (Gilbert, 1992). An ideal, and hence not always practical, scenario would be for the college counselor to introduce the client to the community counselor in a shared session.

Several other factors also influence the decision to refer. As discussed, the treatment focus and philosophy of the center is perhaps the primary consideration regarding ability to provide treatment. Ethical considerations include the provision of a standard of care for all students, dependent in large part on the center's human and economic resources. Gilbert (1992) noted that it is unwise ethically, as well as risky legally, to "attempt to carry out a treatment mission with inadequate resources" (p. 698). Gilbert added that the duty of referral should be carried out through the use of selective treatment criteria and that the process should not be considered abandonment of the client.

Although the literature often recommends off-campus referrals, this need not always occur. On some campuses, especially in rural areas, referral options are scant or nonexistent. Other centers may self-evaluate and choose to provide longer term treatment. There needs to be communication and agreement among counseling center staff and college administrators regarding the mission, scope of services, and overall resources involved in these decision-making processes (Gilbert, 1992; May, 1992). The need for "high level administrative support" cannot be overemphasized in order for counseling center staff to be able to meet the needs of students with severe pathology (Hoffman & Mastrianni, 1989, p. 19).

Counseling Implications

Students presenting with acute psychiatric symptomatology require immediate intervention strategies. Safety issues are paramount, and counselors must assess the potential for harm to the student and others. Often, the counselor's most effective and therapeutic initial intervention is to offer the student a sense of calm and confidence. Individuals who are experiencing severe psychiatric distress are often frightened and bewildered. The student needs to "borrow" ego strength from the counselor while the student's own ego remains temporarily disintegrated. This contact between counselor and student can potentially form the basis for a rewarding, ongoing therapeutic relationship. As the student becomes a client, a sense of trust is formed that, ideally, will encourage the student to seek counseling services at the initial onset of symptom reoccurrence.

A student who is decompensating will benefit greatly from a calm counselor who is able to provide a sense of control during what feels to the student like an uncontrollable life event. The counselor should proceed to develop a decision tree and initiate an action plan based on presenting symptoms and other circumstances and, when practical, in consultation with colleagues. Decisions may include contacting a parent or significant other and arranging transportation to a psychiatrist's office or hospital emergency room for evaluation and subsequent treatment. Counseling centers should have well-planned policies and procedures in place regarding psychiatric evaluations and means of transport.

In an ideal scenario, signed consents are obtained from the student so that treatment information can be mutually shared between the counseling center and other involved agencies or institutions. In addition, formal consents to notify professors (without providing overly detailed information) are helpful to coordinate academic assignments, temporary leaves of absence, incomplete grades, and so forth.

Collaboration

College counselors are often comfortable taking a fairly autonomous counseling approach with their clients. Clients exhibiting more severe pathology are best treated with a consultative or team approach. A review of psychiatric disability services among 275 colleges stressed the importance of collaboration of counseling center staff and psychiatrists, community mental health providers, disability coordinators, individual faculty, and family members (Collins & Mowbray, 2005).

Collaboration with the prescribing source of psychotropic medications is essential for counselors working with these students. The prescribing source ideally is a psychiatrist or psychiatric nurse specialist, although it is not uncommon for family practice physicians to prescribe. Counselors should encourage clients to seek knowledge about, and gain a sense of comfort and confidence in, their adjunctive medication therapy, regardless of the prescribing source. Family members and significant others are also often eager to learn about medication issues.

Psychotropic medications can be a mysterious and even negative issue for counselors (Stone & Archer, 1990). For example, counselors with humanistic and psychoanalytic backgrounds may feel that psychotropic medications impede clients from examining and working through emotional conflicts. These counselors are urged to explore their own feelings and potential biases regarding medications. For clients with severe pathology, medications often provide symptom relief while enhancing their abilities to remain matriculated in college (Weiss, Bilder, & Fleischacker, 2002).

In addition to collaboration with outpatient prescribing professionals, counselors are advised to maintain working relationships with one or more inpatient psychiatric facilities. Familiarity with a facility's admission guidelines, treatment protocols, and aftercare (discharge) planning practices is important in forming a mutually beneficial working alliance. Counseling center staff should also review and regularly revise their in-house hospitalization protocols, including transportation and release-of-information issues.

Crisis Intervention

Family involvement and intervention is advisable in the case of students with severe pathology. Counselors often provide support, consultation, and referral for family members, particularly during crises and periods of client decompensation. When an initial diagnosis is made, involved family members can be invited in for psychoeducational purposes, to allay anxiety, and to explore strategies and contingency plans. It becomes particularly important when working with family members to enlist a team approach, including appropriate on- and off-campus professionals. In their popular press book, *College of the Overwhelmed:*

The Campus Mental Health Crisis and What You Can Do About It, Kadison and DiGeronimo (2004) urged parents to be aware and involved and to actively seek counseling center collaboration and support.

Crisis intervention plans and services are important elements in the provision of care for severely pathological students, even when community referrals are already in place. Staff, students, and faculty often respond to crisis episodes with anxiety or alarm, and counseling center services are immediately sought. The manner in which crises are mediated varies among centers. The ability to handle psychiatric emergencies that are, by definition, unscheduled and unpredictable is an important function of counseling centers. A fortunate few centers have emergency psychiatric care as part of a larger clinic or hospital. For all centers, 24-hour crisis service procedures for both on and off campus need to be identified, tested, and ultimately implemented. Campus health centers, however, vary widely in their policies regarding treating psychiatric crises, and comprehensive crisis intervention systems are often complicated by economic and staffing restrictions (Cornish, Riva, Henderson, Kominars, & McIntosh, 2000).

Crises may at times be averted through early psychoeducation and prophylactic treatment. Students who are experiencing an initial onset of symptoms can be understandably frightened. Their notions and stigma of "mental illness" may have been influenced by media characterizations and misinformation. Students who have experienced a previous "breakdown" episode may expect a similar, or worse, course of events to unfold.

Counselors can explore client anxieties while simultaneously assessing present symptoms and sharing possible outcomes with the client. This process is best conceptualized in terms of goal or treatment planning. Potential decisions such as when to initiate or reassess medications, involve family members, modify academic course loads, or seek more intensive treatment options can be explored with the client in a manner that is simultaneously preventive and anticipatory.

On larger campuses, there often exist a sizable number of students with severe pathology. The use of supportive group counseling can serve as a therapeutic adjunct to individual counseling and medication. Students are often able to discuss effective coping strategies, learn about resources, and gain confidence in navigating campus life through group support (Cornish et al., 2000). In addition to on-campus supports, organizations providing information, support, and referral include the National Alliance for the Mentally Ill (www.nami.org) and the National Mental Health Association (www.nmha.org).

To meet the needs of students with severe pathology, it is wise for all counseling center staff to develop familiarity with the diagnosis and treatment of severe psychopathology. A consideration in hiring new staff members should be their comfort and confidence with this population. A working knowledge of psychotropic medications and community resources and a willingness and ability to engage in crisis intervention by each counseling staff member will serve to provide equitable and integrated care. In addition, engagement by each member in ongoing professional training and development in these areas is a key element in providing a robust standard of care for students with severe psychiatric disorders.

Campus Considerations

Almost every campus office and department is affected at one time or another by students with severe psychiatric disorders. Faculty members, librarians, secretaries, athletic personnel, custodial staff, and others often interact with and seek to refer students who seem in obvious need of counseling intervention. In rare instances, there are episodes of student behavior (e.g., stark manic episodes or acute psychosis) to which members of the campus community respond with alarm or panic. In the aftermath of such events, counselors may be called on to meet with or "debrief" those involved. Although confidentiality issues do not allow discussions about salient issues regarding the particular student, those students, faculty, and staff who witnessed and were affected by the event can be provided the opportunity to share and express their concerns and reactions. Such interventions can be particularly helpful for the roommates, housemates, or dormmates of the particular student. In addition, students exhibiting disruptive behaviors may face disciplinary sanctions (Amada, 1995; see chapter 11 in this book, "Against Their Will? Counseling Mandated Students"), which can lead them to seek counseling services.

Disability offices are more frequently becoming campus points of contact for students with severe pathology because of these students' inclusion under the Americans With Disabilities Act of 1990. On many campuses, however, disability offices have not been able to adequately assist these students because they have not been staffed with individuals sufficiently knowledgeable about psychiatric disabilities (Collins & Mowbray, 2005). There is a need for a working relationship between disabilities offices and counseling centers, and counselors can often provide the needed knowledge about psychiatric disabilities to the disability services staff.

Students with severe psychiatric disabilities may also be able to benefit from a relatively new psychosocial rehabilitation model called *supported education* (SEd), which is designed to help students with psychiatric disabilities achieve postsecondary education goals:

> The program theory behind SEd is to engage students in the program through support and reassurance; to provide opportunities to develop a new, positive identity as student in contrast to the stigmatized role of psychiatric patient; and to enable students to take control of their disability, their environment and their futures through knowledge and skill practice. (Mowbray et al., 2005, p. 10)

In these programs, students identified with psychiatric disabilities typically attend classes with other students while receiving support and clinical services on campus, from the disabilities office or counseling center, or off campus, from outpatient professionals. There are more than 100 SEd programs in the United States and Canada, based in a number of different settings including college campuses. Although there has been insufficient research to date to determine the extent to which students involved in SEd programs obtain their college degrees, the increasing data provide strong evidence that SEd programs are well used and successful (Mowbray et al., 2005). Mowbray, Brown, Furlong-

Norman, and Sullivan-Soydan's (2002) book, *Supported Education and Psychiatric Rehabilitation: Models and Methods,* is highly recommended for college counselors.

It should be noted that, in the not-too-distant past, students exhibiting psychiatric symptomatology were routinely dismissed from college (Archer & Cooper, 1998; Becker et al., 2002). An attitudinal survey of faculty and students at a large university reported that more than 50% of faculty did not feel comfortable around students exhibiting signs of mental illness, and a minority of faculty and students predicted fear and personal safety issues in similar situations (Becker et al., 2002). Numerous other studies have shown an inverse relationship between endorsing psychiatric stigma and contact with persons with severe pathology (Corrigan et al., 2001). Outreach efforts by college counseling centers should include increasing the awareness and decreasing the stigma about students with severe psychiatric disorders among other students, staff, and faculty. In this way, counselors could "enrich the institutional environment because other students, staff, and faculty would have a real-life experience in humanitarian ethical issues" (Archer & Cooper, 1998, p. 109).

Future Trends

There is a need for more research regarding the incidence and prevalence, as well as specific treatment issues, of college students exhibiting severe psychiatric disorders. An initial step is to develop shared operational definitions of what constitutes severe pathology (Sharkin, 1997). More research is also warranted concerning clinical and programming issues (Stone, 1992), psychopharmacology (Weiss et al., 2002), and community resources for students with severe psychiatric disorders (Lacour & Carter, 2002). Furthermore, there exists a need to explore affiliative, collaborative relationships among counseling centers, inpatient and outpatient community service providers, and private practitioners.

College counselors should become familiar with supported education and other psychosocial rehabilitation programs. In addition, as more students with severe pathology enter colleges, there seems to be a growing need for case managers—persons to assist in the coordination of on- and off-campus services for these students. Although case management is a familiar concept in community mental and physical health settings, few colleges formally use case management approaches. On a less formal basis, however, many college counselors actually provide ad hoc case management for some of their clients.

Case management has traditionally been one of the domains of social work, and it should not be surprising that mental health settings contain the largest percentage of social workers (Mowbray et al., 2005). Case managers typically work closely with clinicians to coordinate care, explore eligibility for various benefits and services, directly provide information to the client, and coordinate referrals. Referral follow-up and compliance is an acute issue for students with severe pathology and one for which research is sparse (Lawe et al., 1999). Counselors are morally and ethically, if not legally, responsible for the continuation of care of their clients via referrals, yet referrals often pose the largest cracks through which these clients fall.

At least one center has created a "referral expediter" role in which a portion of one staff member's time is spent gathering general community referral information and specifically following up on individual student referrals into the community (Lacour & Carter, 2002). A somewhat similar system is in place in the United Kingdom in which "guidance workers" maintain links between university counselors and community mental health care providers (James, 2002). Although challenging from a financial and personnel standpoint, employment of professional counselors, social workers, or psychiatric nurses as case managers in college counseling centers may be an idea worth serious consideration.

References

Amada, G. (1995). The disruptive college student: Some thoughts and considerations. *Journal of American College Health, 43,* 62–67.

American Psychiatric Association. (2000). *Diagnostic and statistical manual of mental disorders* (4th ed., text rev.). Washington, DC: Author.

Americans With Disabilities Act of 1990, 42 U.S.C.A. § 12101 *et seq.* (West 1993). Retrieved August 4, 2005, from http://www.sba.gov/ada/adaact.text

Archer, J., & Cooper, S. (1998). *Counseling and mental health services on campus: A handbook of contemporary practices and challenges.* San Francisco: Jossey-Bass.

Becker, M., Martin, L., Wajeeh, E., Ward, J., & Shern, D. (2002). Students with mental illness in a university setting: Faculty and student attitudes, beliefs, and experiences. *Psychiatric Rehabilitation Journal, 25,* 359–368.

Collins, M. E., & Mowbray, C. T. (2005). Higher education and psychiatric disabilities: National survey of campus disability services. *American Journal of Orthopsychiatry, 75,* 304–315.

Cornish, J. A. E., Riva, M. T., Henderson, M. C., Kominars, K. D., & McIntosh, S. (2000). Perceived distress in university counseling center clients across a six-year period. *Journal of College Student Development, 41,* 104–109.

Corrigan, P. W., River, L. P., Lundin, R. K., Penn, D. L., Waskowski. K. U., Campion, J., et al. (2001). Three strategies for changing attributions about severe mental illness. *Schizophrenia Bulletin, 27,* 187–195.

Gilbert, S. P. (1992). Ethical issues in the treatment of severe psychopathology in university and college counseling students. *Journal of Counseling and Development, 70,* 695–699.

Herlihy, B., & Corey, G. (Eds.). (2005). *ACA ethical standards casebook* (6th ed.). Alexandria, VA: American Counseling Association.

Hoffman, F. L., & Mastrianni, X. (1989). The mentally ill student on campus: Theory and practice. *Journal of American College Health, 38,* 15–20.

James, K. (2002). A model of supportive services in further education. In N. Stanley & J. Manthorpe (Eds.), *Students' mental health needs: Problems and responses* (pp. 191–206). London: Jessica Kingsley.

Kadison, R., & DiGeronimo, T. F. (2004). *College of the overwhelmed: The campus mental health crisis and what you can do about it.* San Francisco: Jossey-Bass.

Kitzrow, M. A. (2003). The mental health needs of today's college students: Challenges and recommendations. *National Association of Student Personnel Administrators, 41,* 167–181.

Lacour, M. A. M., & Carter, E. F. (2002). Challenges in referral decisions in college counseling. *Journal of College Student Psychotherapy, 17,* 39–52.

Lawe, C. F., Penick, J. M., Raskin, J. D., & Raymond, V. V. (1999). Influences on decisions to refer at university counseling centers. *Journal of College Student Psychotherapy, 14,* 59–68.

May, R. (1992). Severe psychopathology in counseling centers: Reaction to Gilbert. *Journal of Counseling & Development, 70,* 702–703.

Mowbray, C. T., Brown, K. S., Furlong-Norman, K., & Sullivan-Soydan, A. S. (Eds.). (2002). *Supported education and psychiatric rehabilitation: Models and methods.* Linthicum, MD: International Association of Psychiatric Rehabilitation Services.

Mowbray, C. T., Collins, M. E., Bellamy, C. D., Megivern, D. A., Bybee, D., & Szilivagyi, S. (2005). Supported education for adults with psychiatric disabilities: An innovation for social work and psychosocial rehabilitation. *Social Work, 50,* 7–20.

Sharkin, B. S. (1997). Increasing severity of presenting problems in college counseling centers: A closer look. *Journal of Counseling & Development, 75,* 275–281.

Sher, K. J., Wood, P. K., & Gotham, H. J. (1996). The course of psychological distress in college: A prospective high-risk study. *Journal of College Student Development, 37,* 42–51.

Stone, G. L. (1992). A "good stuff" reaction. *Journal of Counseling & Development, 70,* 700–701.

Stone, G. L., & Archer, J. (1990). College and university counseling centers in the 1990s: Challenges and limits. *The Counseling Psychologist, 18,* 539–607.

Weiss, E. M., Bilder, R. M., & Fleischacker, W. W. (2002). The effects of second-generation antipsychotics on cognitive functioning and psychosocial outcome in schizophrenia. *Psychopharmacology, 162,* 11–17.

22

Self-Injurious Behavior: Counseling Students Who Self-Injure

Victoria E. Kress, Heather Trepal,
Aaron Petuch, and Stacey Ilko-Hancock

Introduction

As college counselors report an increase in students presenting with self-injurious behaviors (SIBs), the topic of college student self-injury has received increased attention (in the professional literature, on college counseling center electronic mailing lists, at conferences, etc.; White, Trepal-Wollenzier, & Nolan, 2002). There has been limited research in the area of SIB in college students because of several factors (White et al., 2002). The paucity of research on the issue of self-injury has contributed to a lack of consistency in terms of diagnosing, treating, recognizing warning signs, reporting self-injurers, and identifying appropriate referrals. In this chapter, general information about self-injury is provided, along with strategies and considerations for college counselors who work with students who self-injure.

Overview of Self-Injury

SIB refers to purposeful damage to one's own body tissue, in the absence of suicidal intent, and can range from stereotypic skin rubbing to more severe actions such as burning one's skin or head banging (Nock & Prinstein, 2004). In order to effectively understand SIB, it is important to clarify the difference between self-injury and suicidal ideation. Researchers and writers (e.g., Doctors, 1981; Firestone & Seiden, 1990; Graff & Mallin, 1967; Grunebaum & Klerman, 1967; Gustafson, 1991; Lee, 1987; Pao, 1969; Rosen, Walsh, & Rode, 1990; Schwartz, Cohen, Hoffman, & Meeks, 1989; Sonneborn & Vanstraelen, 1992) have asserted that SIB is not an intent to take one's life; it is separate from suicidal acts and gestures in how the client views the event, the proposed function of the behavior, and the associated features.

Self-injury can, therefore, be defined as an intentional act with the aim to do harm to the body without any intention to die (Simeon & Favazza, 2001; Yarura-Tobias, Neziroglu, & Kaplan, 1995). Specific methods include scratching, branding, cutting, self-hitting, burning, and biting (Pattison & Kahan, 1983). There are numerous ways in which college students self-injure. Self-cutting, however, is the most prevalent method used by women, the dominant help-seeking population on college campuses (Briere & Gil, 1998; S. Ross & Heath, 2002; Taiminen, Kallio-Soulainen, Nokso-Koivisto, Kaljonen, & Helenius, 1998).

According to Briere and Gil (1998), estimates of SIB range from 1% to 4% of the general population. Studies have confirmed that adolescence is a risky period for self-injury and that 14%–39% of adolescents engage in SIB (Lloyd, 1998; S. Ross & Heath, 2002). Furthermore, individuals are most likely to begin self-cutting behaviors in adolescence and young adulthood between 13 and 23 years of age (Favazza & Conterio, 1988; A. R. Gardner & Gardner, 1975; Suyemoto & MacDonald, 1995). Although there is a common conception that most people who self-injure are female, the data are inconclusive. More research is needed to distinguish the differing rates and types of self-injury among males and females (White et al., 2002).

Self-Injury and College Students: Why People Engage in SIB and Who Is at Risk

There are a variety of reasons for engaging in SIB. Nock and Prinstein (2004) proposed that self-injury serves as a form of autonomic reinforcement (i.e., emotion regulation) and/or is a means of obtaining social reinforcement (e.g., gaining support from others). Other research has indicated that people may self-injure in order to diminish dissociation, depersonalization, and derealization and to relieve feelings of emptiness and numbness (Dallam, 1997; Simeon & Favazza, 2001). Many self-injurers acknowledge that self-harm helps them gain a sense of control over their lives and emotional experiences.

Biological theories have also been proposed in explaining the reasons why people self-injure. It has been suggested that people have genetic predispositions or chemical imbalances or that they experience rushes of endorphins when self-injuring, which may explain why they repeatedly engage in this behavior (Dallam, 1997; Pies & Popli, 1995; Simeon et al., 1992).

According to Deiter, Nicholls, and Pearlman (2000), childhood sexual abuse and family violence are two of the best predictors of self-injury. Individuals who engage in SIB are more likely to come from families in which divorce, neglect, or parental deprivation was evident (Carroll, Schaffer, Spensley, & Abramowitz, 1980; Friedman, Glasser, Laufer, Laufer, & Wohl, 1972; Graff & Mallin, 1967; Grunebaum & Klerman, 1967; Leibenluft, Gardner, & Cowdry, 1987; Pao, 1969; Pattison & Kahan, 1983; Rosen et al., 1990; Rosenthal, Rinzler, Wallsh, & Klausner, 1972; C. A. Simpson & Porter, 1981; M. A. Simpson, 1975).

Because individuals subjected to abuse or violence often experience constant emotional dysregulation, they may not develop the skills to standardize intense emotional experiences. Such individuals may resort to self-injury in an attempt to regulate strong emotions (Levenkron, 1998).

According to Fong (2003), individuals with a lack of impulse control may be more likely to engage in self-injury. Fong stated that self-injury shares two qualities with impulse control disorders (e.g., gambling or stealing): (a) an inability to resist impulses or urges to engage in a particular act or behavior and (b) an increase in autonomic nervous system activity before the act that is followed by a release of pleasure or satisfaction after the act. In addition, Fong noted that impulsive self-injurers may feel a need to act, instead of using alternative coping methods, when social pressures demand immediate decisions.

Many questions arise when one considers self-injury as it relates to college students:

- Can SIB begin in college?
- Can college stress be a trigger of SIB?
- Could self-injury just be a reactive, harmless, short-lived phase that some college students go through?

Because there are numerous variables directly and indirectly affecting college students, questions like these have no definitive answer. For example, factors that are directly related to SIB include (a) traumatic stressors, (b) watching others engage in self-injury (e.g., in the media or friends), (c) depression, and (d) anxiety. As previously mentioned, additional factors, such as genetic predispositions, temperament, and other personality-related traits, may play roles in the development of SIB (Dallam, 1997; Pies & Popli, 1995; Simeon et al., 1992).

Normal college stressors may also contribute to the development and maintenance of self-injury. When an individual departs for college for the first time, myriad challenges and stressors are unleashed. Students must begin to deal with residence hall life, separation from and/or meeting romantic partners, difficult classes, and financial aid, among a host of other dilemmas.

Assessment Issues

People who self-injure are varied and unique, with different histories, stories, and experiences. People who self-injure report a variety of reasons for injuring, and the self-injury serves many different functions. Some people initially begin self-injuring for one reason and then find that they develop additional reasons to self-injure. Some people begin to self-injure using one method but over time injure using different or multiple methods. To combine all people who self-injure into one diagnostic category, or to state that all people injure for one reason, is overly simplistic.

The first step to understanding a client's self-injury dynamics is the completion of a thorough assessment of the client's SIBs (Kress, Costin, & Drouhard, 2005). The following are important issues to consider when a client discloses self-injury: (a) age of onset of the self-injury; (b) path of the behavior (i.e., has it been consistent or has it increased or decreased in occurrence?); (c) current frequency of SIB; (d) change in SIBs over time; (e) medical complications (e.g., stitches, surgeries, infections, or corrective operations); (f) types of tools used to self-injure; (g) emotional state when injuring; (h) antecedents leading to the self-injury; (i) immediate and more long-term aftermath of injuring; and (j) recent life experiences, past traumatic events, and current life stressors that may be relevant to comprehending the student's context and situation (Simeon & Favazza, 2001). In addition, the counselor should assess whether the student takes proper care of wounds, whether the student shares self-injury apparatuses with other individuals or uses unclean or rusty tools, and whether individuals who associate with the student know about the self-injury. Furthermore, it is important to assess the function and meaning of the SIB as perceived by the individual client (White et al., 2002). Finally, a process that involves the assessment of both suicide and self-injury will help the counselor decide whether the student is in imminent danger and whether there are any additional risk management issues.

During the assessment process, some counselors prefer to use a more detailed and structured approach. Nock and Prinstein (2004) asserted that many therapists use a functional approach to self-injury that classifies and treats behaviors according to the functional processes that create and sustain them (i.e., antecedent and consequent contextual issues). Other counselors prefer a syndromal approach that focuses on the categorization and treatment of behaviors according to their topographical characteristics (i.e., associated signs and symptoms; Nock & Prinstein, 2004). In either case, these counselors prefer to use physical or mental checklists in which they check off associated behaviors and emotions and evaluate whether the student meets the criteria for a specific disorder.

It is important to assess for additional mental health-related issues. Many students who engage in SIB also exhibit symptoms associated with other potentially serious diagnoses (e.g., depression or anxiety). Prescribed assessment procedures must be implemented in order to rule out comorbidity.

The most common psychiatric disorders associated with self-injury include (a) major depression, (b) minor depression, (c) dissociative identity disorder (formally known as multiple personality disorder), (d) obsessive–compulsive disorder, (e) alcoholism and other disorders with substance abuse, (f) eating disorders, (g) schizophrenia, (h) anxiety disorders, (i) adjustment disorders, and (j) numerous personality disorders (Brittlebank et al., 1990; Darche, 1990; Dulit, Fyer, Leon, Brodsky, & Frances, 1994; Favazza, DeRosear, & Conterio, 1989; Garrison et al., 1993; Ghaziuddin, Tsai, Naylor, & Ghaziuddin, 1992; Graff & Mallin, 1967; Gustafson, 1991; Herpertz, 1995; Himber, 1994; Langbehn & Pfohl 1993; Novotny, 1972; Offer & Barglow, 1960; Pao, 1969; Rosenthal et al., 1972; Schwartz et al., 1989; Scott & Powell, 1993; C. A. Simpson & Porter, 1981; M. A. Simpson, 1975; Sonneborn & Vanstraelen, 1992; Suyemoto & MacDonald, 1995).

Self-injury has also been associated with more severe pathology, signifying that self-injury is a marker for especially severe personality disorder (e.g., Dulit et al., 1994; Simeon et al., 1992; Soloff, Lis, Kelly, Cornelius, & Ulrich, 1994).

Furthermore, SIB has sometimes been correlated with a diagnosis of borderline personality disorder (D. L. Gardner & Cowdry, 1985; Kernberg, 1988; Langbehn & Pfohl, 1993; Leibenluft et al., 1987; Offer & Barglow, 1960; Walsh & Rosen, 1988).

It has been argued that consistent self-injury is an impulse control disorder similar to eating disorders. Although many self-injurers are diagnosed with personality disorders, the symptoms that fulfill a personality disorder often subside once the self-injury stops, leading to a further intricacy of the bias many have toward believing that people who self-injure must have personality disorder diagnoses (Suyemoto, 1998). Moreover, there is a broad argument for the autonomy of deliberate self-harm as a diagnosis, including itemizing the characteristic symptoms, course, frequency, population, predisposing factors, and differential diagnosis criteria of deliberate self-harm (Kahan & Pattison, 1984).

Counseling Implications

When a student who self-injures seeks treatment, the counselor must first establish a therapeutic relationship by demonstrating empathy, understanding, and positive regard. According to White et al. (2002), the principal goal for the counselor is to create a secure, structured counseling environment, exemplified by consistency and respect for the student's dignity.

After a thorough assessment is conducted and a therapeutic relationship is established, the counselor and the client may develop a succinct and specific list of goals on which to work during the treatment process. The developed goals will be a function of a number of factors: (a) the counselor's style and theoretical orientation, (b) the session limits of the counseling center, (c) the client's stated goals and counseling expectations (e.g., the client's desire, through counseling, to stop self-injuring), and (d) the client's strengths and resources as well as challenges (e.g., psychopathology).

Depending on these factors, examples of counseling goals might include (a) increasing self-esteem, (b) increasing positive interpersonal relationships and social skills, (c) reinforcing incompatible behaviors with self-injuring, (d) finding alternative avenues to obtain the positive feelings that are associated with SIB, and (e) understanding the underlying meanings of self-injury.

Therapeutic Treatment Options

Some college counselors elect cognitive–behavioral therapy (CBT) as the treatment of choice when dealing with students who self-injure. Cognitive–behavioral approaches focus on eliminating cognitive distortions, addressing automatic thoughts, and altering patterns of thinking by using a plethora of interventions: homework assignments, journaling, cognitive rehearsal, modeling, systematic desensitization, and conditioning. In one study, the use of CBT with clients who self-injured increased their positive thinking about the future and decreased their depression and suicidal thoughts (Macleod, Tata, & Evans, 1998). In a study conducted by Leyshon (2005), however, clients were assigned to either a CBT group or a "treatment-as-usual" group. In the 12 months of the study, Leyshon found that 39% of those clients in the CBT group, compared with 46% of the clients in the treatment-as-usual group, reduced self-harm behaviors. Leyshon noted that in order to increase the efficacy of CBT, other approaches should be implemented simultaneously.

Some researchers (e.g., van der Sande, Buskens, Allart, van der Graf, & van Engeland, 1997) have indicated that problem-solving therapy is effective in decreasing SIB. A derivative of problem-solving therapy, problem-solving skills training (PSST) is effective in reducing symptoms associated with SIB (Salkovskis, Atha, & Storer, 1990). Specifically, PSST reduces hopelessness, helps the client look at dilemmas from different perspectives, and helps the client generate new alternative solutions (Raj, Kumaraiah, & Bhide, 2001). Raj et al. also asserted that PSST helps clients change their perception of the problem, handle related negative cognitive factors, decrease suicidal thoughts, and gain motivation to change future situations. O'Connell (1998) stated that brief solution-focused therapy teaches problem-solving techniques in a closely knit relationship that places the client in a central role.

Dialectical behavior therapy (DBT) has received attention as a helpful approach to managing SIB in persons with borderline personality disorder dynamics. This therapy includes both behavioral and psychoanalytic techniques and was originally developed for treating borderline personality disorders (Linehan, 1993a, 1993b). Like other therapeutic models, DBT places the therapeutic relationship as the most important variable and focuses on (a) the validation of the client, (b) the etiological significance of the client having experienced an "invalidating environment" in childhood, and (c) the confrontation of resistances. DBT has been shown to be successful for clients who engage in multiple self-harm episodes but was not significant in reducing symptoms at 1-year follow-up (Linehan, Armstrong, Suarez, Allmon, & Heard, 1991). In another study (Raj et al., 2001), DBT was given for 1 year to clients also diagnosed with borderline personality disorder and addressed the SIB symptom of "feelings of hopelessness." Raj et al. found that DBT did not lead to improvements in hopelessness. Thus, it is likely that clients with SIB who are diagnosed with borderline personality disorder will need more intensive and prolonged treatment in order to decrease associated SIB symptoms.

Psychodynamic approaches have also been used with people who self-injure. The chief purpose of this therapy is the development of insight into the meaning that underlies behavior (Suyemoto, 1998). Psychodynamic approaches focus on the resolution of transference through a just relationship, and both the counselor and the client are equally involved in the process.

Some clinicians advocate using brief interpersonal psychodynamic therapy, reporting treatment gains and client satisfaction (Guthrie, Kapur, & Mackway-Jones, 2001). Allen (1995) warned, however, that clinicians must be aware of the deleterious effects of conducting such therapy, including lack of structure or focus in dynamic or analytic therapies and the confrontational stance. Because people who self-injure may have trouble enduring ambiguity about interpersonal expectations, Allen contended that a therapy this unstructured may increase the likelihood that they will feel overwhelmed.

According to Fong (2003), SIB is multidimensional, and many doctors prescribe antidepressants (e.g., selective serotonin reuptake inhibitors [SSRIs]), atypical antipsychotics (e.g., olanzapine and clozapine), mood stabilizers (e.g., lithium, divalproex, and topiramate), anxiolytics (e.g., benzodiazepines, lorazepam, and clonazepam), and opiate antagonists (e.g., naltrexone and nalmefene). Fong asserted that SSRIs are an appropriate first-line treatment for self-injury because of their general safety profile, their effectiveness in treating mood reactivity, and self-injurers' known deficits in serotonergic neurotransmission.

Whether a counselor is fulfilling the consultant role, giving a workshop on SIB, or treating a student who self-injures, countertransference reactions and attempts to control the individual must be eliminated. White et al. (2002) indicated that it is important that counselors monitor their personal reactions to disclosures of self-injury and make decisions based on student-reported experiences and intentions, rather than on transference reactions such as fear or a desire to control the person's SIB. Attempts to control the person's SIB can be especially obvious or apparent when one is dealing with SIB for the first time. Prior to working with a self-injurer, counselors unconsciously rely on preconceived notions concerning the likely reasons for self-injury, lifestyle of the individual, possible comorbidity, and prognosis. Deiter and Pearlman (1998) found that evading power struggles, looking at self-injury as a coping mechanism, monitoring personal reactions, and maintaining consultation and supervision can help in ensuring that counselors strive for objectivity when working with people who self-injure.

Campus Considerations

College counselors should consider a number of factors related to the larger campus community when dealing with self-injurious students. For example, college mental health and resident life staff should be made aware of the possibility of contagion, a situation in which two or more people influence each other's self-injury (Rosen & Walsh, 1989; R. R. Ross & McKay, 1979; Taiminen et al., 1998; Walsh & Rosen, 1985). Imitation seems to play a role in people who already self-injure or are at an increased risk for SIB, and college counselors must take into account the role of propinquity and close intimate connections between residents so as to fully maximize prevention initiatives (White et al., 2002).

Colleges often have mandatory withdrawal policies for students who initiate suicide attempts (White et al., 2002), and many individuals at these institutions believe that self-injury is synonymous with suicide attempts. Counselors should serve as advocates of self-injurious students by educating departments such as student life, judicial affairs, career services, and academic services about SIB (White et al., 2002). Education can provide a means of preventing the stereotypes that are often associated with self-injury, helping staff to understand the

dynamics of SIB and the fact that students who self-injure are generally not suicidal or at risk of harming others.

Counselors can serve effectively as consultants to student affairs staff. Many
staff members prefer direct contact with a counselor instead of obtaining information from Web sites and pamphlets. This face-to-face contact provides a
blanket of security, and advice seekers will be more likely to fulfill their implicit
obligation to help students who self-injure. Counselors can also assist student
affairs staff by providing information as to what the staff should do if a student
discloses that a roommate, teammate, and so forth is self-injuring. The presence
of self-injuring students can be very disturbing and disruptive to the people
around them, and it is often these people who approach staff seeking advice on
helping the students who are self-injuring.

Counselors can teach the campus community how to approach students who
may be self-injuring and how to make effective referrals for such students (White
et al., 2002). They can also be helpful in providing interventions to groups of students who may be living with a person who self-injures. In addition, counselors
might consider providing a seminar or workshop on the topic of how to deal with
a friend who self-injures, or they might provide handouts on such topics.

Some colleges offer workshops and seminars that are open to the public for
professionals who deal or potentially deal with the SIB population. In addition, college counseling centers often provide information via Internet Web
sites and offer SIB question-and-answer sheets to students as a means of educating people on campus (Davis & Humphrey, 2000; Komives & Woodard,
1996). Furthermore, many counseling centers help in guiding students, faculty,
and staff by directing them to the numerous professional Web sites that address self-injury (Prasad & Owens, 2001).

Another option to address the issue of SIB on campuses is support groups.
Some campuses offer groups in which individuals who self-injure can meet one
another and share experiences. The groups are usually led by a licensed mental
health professional. Unlike individual counseling, students can empathize with
others and offer suggestions for managing SIB. As students decrease SIBs, new
members replace the former members in the group. It is important to periodically assess the function of the group, knowing that self-injury discussions can serve
as triggers for some individuals. These students should be referred for individual
counseling to better meet their needs. Some students may also opt to join Internet
support groups or use Internet discussion boards as a means of support.

Finally, some colleges offer a variety of pamphlets on SIB for display in their
counseling centers, medical offices, and nursing departments. The brochures,
like the Web-based resources, offer referral information, treatment options, dos
and don'ts, and support information.

Future Trends

Despite the increased publicity about SIB, many college counselors have not
worked with clients who self-injure, and the behavior patterns unique to SIB

present unique challenges to effective counseling practice (White et al., 2002). This chapter discussed several dimensions of self-injury, including etiology, clinical counseling considerations, and recommendations for addressing SIB on college campuses. There is a need, as with all clients, for a careful and thorough assessment and evaluation of the client's SIB, including the age of onset, course, function, and purpose of the behavior, as well as client historical issues. A suicide assessment is also warranted. After a consideration of potential risks, a plan of service or referral should be conducted. If the client continues in counseling, there are a number of treatment options. Finally, if needed, a college counselor should be prepared to provide residence life staff and roommates with self-injury education and information.

References

Allen, C. (1995). Helping with deliberate self-harm: Some practical guidelines. *Journal of Mental Health, 4,* 243–250.

Briere, J., & Gil, E. (1998). Self-mutilation in clinical and general population samples: Prevalence, correlates and functions. *American Journal of Orthopsychiatry, 68,* 609–620.

Brittlebank, A. D., Cole, A., Hassanyeh, F., Kenny, M., Simpson, D., & Scott, K. (1990). Hostility, hopelessness and deliberate self-harm: A prospective follow-up study. *Acta Psychiatrica Scandinavica, 81,* 280–283.

Carroll, J., Schaffer, C., Spensley, J., & Abramowitz, S. I. (1980). Family experiences in self-mutilating patients. *American Journal of Psychiatry, 137,* 852–853.

Dallam, S. J. (1997). The identification and management of self-mutilating patients in primary care. *The Nurse Practitioner, 22,* 151–164.

Darche, M. A. (1990). Psychological factors differentiating self-mutilating and non-self-mutilating adolescent inpatient females. *The Psychiatric Hospital, 21,* 31–35.

Davis, D. C., & Humphrey, K. M. (Eds.). (2000). *College counseling: Issues and strategies for a new millennium.* Alexandria, VA: American Counseling Association.

Deiter, P. J., Nicholls, S. S., & Pearlman, L. A. (2000). Self-injury and self-capacities: Assisting an individual in crisis. *Journal of Clinical Psychology, 56,* 1173–1191.

Deiter, P. J., & Pearlman, L. A. (1998). Responding to self-injurious behavior. In P. M. Kleespies (Ed.), *Emergencies in mental health practice: Evaluation and management* (pp. 235–257). New York: Guilford Press.

Doctors, S. (1981). The symptom of delicate self-cutting in adolescent females: A developmental view. In S. C. Feinstein, J. G. Looney, A. Z. Schwartzberg, & A. D. Sorosky (Eds.), *Adolescent psychiatry* (Vol. 9, pp. 443–460). Chicago: University of Chicago Press.

Dulit, R. A., Fyer, M. R., Leon, A. C., Brodsky, B. S., & Frances, A. J. (1994). Clinical correlates of self-mutilation in borderline personality disorder. *American Journal of Psychiatry, 151,* 1305–1311.

Favazza, A. R., & Conterio, K. (1988). The plight of chronic self-mutilators. *Community Mental Health Journal, 24,* 22–30.

Favazza, A. R., DeRosear, L., & Conterio, K. (1989). Self-mutilation and eating disorders. *Suicide and Life-Threatening Behavior, 19,* 352–361.

Firestone, R. W., & Seiden, R. H. (1990). Suicide and the continuum of self-destructive behavior. *Journal of American College Health, 38,* 207–213.

Fong, T. (2003). Self-mutilation: Impulsive traits suggest new drug therapies. *Current Psychiatry, 2*(2), 144–152.

Friedman, M., Glasser, M., Laufer, E., Laufer, M., & Wohl, M. (1972). Attempted suicide and self-mutilation in adolescence: Some observations from a psychoanalytic research project. *British Journal of Psychoanalysis, 53,* 179–183.

Gardner, A. R., & Gardner, A. J. (1975). Self-mutilation, obsessionality and narcissism. *British Journal of Psychiatry, 127,* 127–132.

Gardner, D. L., & Cowdry, R. W. (1985). Suicidal and parasuicidal behavior in borderline personality disorder. *Psychiatric Clinics of North America, 8,* 359–403.

Garrison, C. Z., Addy, C. L., McKeown, R. E., Cuffe, S. P., Jackson, K. L., & Waller, J. L. (1993). Nonsuicidal physically self-damaging acts in adolescents. *Journal of Child and Family Services, 2,* 339–352.

Ghaziuddin, M., Tsai, L., Naylor, M., & Ghaziuddin, N. (1992). Mood disorder in a group of self-cutting adolescents. *Acta Paedopsychiatrica, 55,* 103–105.

Graff, H., & Mallin, R. (1967). The syndrome of the wrist cutter. *American Journal of Psychiatry, 124,* 74–80.

Grunebaum, H. U., & Klerman, G. L. (1967). Wrist slashing. *American Journal of Psychiatry, 124,* 527–534.

Gustafson, M. S. (1991). *A comparison of the childhood histories of self-mutilating and non-self-mutilating psychiatric patients.* Unpublished master's thesis, University of Massachusetts at Amherst.

Guthrie, E., Kapur, N., & Mackway-Jones, K. (2001). Randomized control trial of brief psychological intervention after deliberate self poisoning. *British Medical Journal, 323,* 135–138.

Herpertz, S. (1995). Self-injurious behavior: Psychopathological and nosological characteristics in subtypes of self-injurers. *Acta Psychiatrica Scandinavica, 91,* 57–68.

Himber, J. (1994). Blood rituals: Self-cutting in female psychiatric inpatients. *Psychotherapy, 31,* 620–631.

Kahan, J., & Pattison, E. M. (1984). Proposal for a distinctive diagnosis: The deliberate self-harm syndrome. *Suicide and Life-Threatening Behavior, 14,* 17–35.

Kernberg, O. F. (1988). Clinical dimensions of masochism. In R. A. Glick & D. I. Myers (Eds.), *Masochism: Current psychoanalytic perspectives* (pp. 61–80). Hillsdale, NJ: Analytic Press.

Komives, S. R., & Woodard, D. B. (Eds.). (1996). *Student services: A handbook for the profession* (3rd ed.). San Francisco: Jossey-Bass.

Kress, V. E., Costin, A., & Drouhard, N. (2005). *Students who self-injure: School counselor ethical and legal considerations.* Manuscript submitted for publication.

Langbehn, D. R., & Pfohl, B. (1993). Clinical correlates of self-mutilation among psychiatric inpatients. *Annals of Clinical Psychiatry, 5,* 45–51.

Lee, D. E. (1987). The self-deception of the self-destructive. *Perceptual and Motor Skills, 65,* 975–989.

Leibenluft, E., Gardner, D. L., & Cowdry, R. W. (1987). The inner experience of the borderline self-mutilator. *Journal of Personality Disorders, 1,* 317–324.

Levenkron, S. (1998). *Cutting: Understanding & overcoming self-mutilation.* New York: Norton.

Leyshon, S. (2005). Deliberate self-harm. *Primary Health Care, 15*(3), 8.

Linehan, M. M. (1993a). *Cognitive–behavioral treatment of borderline personality disorder.* New York: Guilford Press.

Linehan, M. M. (1993b). *Skills training manual for treating borderline personality disorder.* New York: Guilford Press.

Linehan, M. M., Armstrong, H. E., Suarez, A., Allmon, D., & Heard, H. L. (1991). Cognitive–behavioral treatment of chronically parasuicidal borderline patients. *Archives of General Psychiatry, 48,* 1060–1064.

Lloyd, E. E. (1998). Self-mutilation in a community sample of adolescents. *Dissertation Abstracts International, 58,* 5127. (UMI No. 04194217)

Macleod, A. K., Tata, P., & Evans, K. (1998). Recovery of positive thinking within a high-risk parasuicide group: Results from a pilot randomized controlled trial. *British Journal of Clinical Psychology, 37,* 371–379.

Nock, M. K., & Prinstein, M. J. (2004). A functional approach to the assessment of self-mutilative behavior. *Journal of Consulting and Clinical Psychology, 72,* 885–890.

Novotny, P. (1972). Self-cutting. *Bulletin of the Menninger Clinic, 36,* 505–514.

O'Connell, B. (1998). *Solution-focused therapy.* London: Sage.

Offer, D., & Barglow, P. (1960). Adolescent and young adult self-mutilation incidents in a general psychiatric hospital. *Archives of General Psychiatry, 3,* 194–204.

Pao, P. N. (1969). The syndrome of delicate self-cutting. *British Journal of Medical Psychology, 42,* 195–206.

Pattison, E. M., & Kahan, J. (1983). The deliberate self-harm syndrome. *American Journal of Psychiatry, 140,* 867–872.

Pies, R. W., & Popli, A. P. (1995). Self-injurious behavior: Pathophysiology and implications for treatment. *Journal of Clinical Psychiatry, 56,* 580–588.

Prasad, V., & Owens, D. (2001). Using the Internet as a source of self-help for people who self-harm. *Psychiatric Bulletin, 25,* 222–225.

Raj, M. A. J., Kumaraiah, V., & Bhide, A. V. (2001). Cognitive–behavioral intervention in deliberate self-harm. *Acta Psychiatrica Scandinavica, 104,* 340–345.

Rosen, P. M., & Walsh B. W. (1989). Patterns of contagion in self-mutilation epidemics. *American Journal of Psychiatry, 146,* 656–658.

Rosen, P. M., Walsh, B. W., & Rode, S. A. (1990). Interpersonal loss and self-mutilation. *Suicide and Life-Threatening Behavior, 20,* 177–184.

Rosenthal, R. J., Rinzler, C., Wallsh, R., & Klausner, E. (1972). Wrist cutting syndrome: The meaning of a gesture. *American Journal of Psychiatry, 128,* 47–52.

Ross, R. R., & McKay, H. B. (1979). *Self-mutilation.* Lexington, MA: Heath.

Ross, S., & Heath, N. (2002). A study of the frequency of self-mutilation in a community sample of adolescents. *Journal of Youth and Adolescence, 31,* 67–77.

Salkovskis, P. M., Atha, C., & Storer, D. (1990). Cognitive–behavioral problem solving in the treatment of patients who repeatedly attempt suicide: A controlled study. *British Journal of Psychiatry, 157,* 871–876.

Schwartz, R. H., Cohen, P., Hoffman, N. G., & Meeks, J. E. (1989). Self harm behaviors (carving) in female adolescent drug abusers. *Clinical Pediatrics, 28,* 340–346.

Scott, S. W., & Powell, J. C. (1993). Brief report: Adolescent self-mutilation in a rural area. *Journal of Adolescence, 16,* 101–105.

Simeon, D., & Favazza, A. R. (2001). Self-injurious behaviors: Phenomenology and assessment. In D. Simeon & E. Hollander (Eds.), *Self-injurious behaviors: Assessment and treatment* (pp. 1–28). Washington, DC: American Psychiatric Press.

Simeon, D., Stanley, B., Frances, A., Mann, J. J., Winchel, R., & Stanley, M. (1992). Self-mutilation in personality disorders: Psychological and biological correlates. *American Journal of Psychiatry, 149,* 221–226.

Simpson, C. A., & Porter, G. L. (1981). Self-mutilation in children and adolescents. *Bulletin of the Menninger Clinic, 45,* 428–438.

Simpson, M. A. (1975). The phenomenology of self-mutilation in a general hospital setting. *Canadian Psychiatric Association Journal, 20,* 429–434.

Soloff, P. H., Lis, J. A., Kelly, T., Cornelius, J., & Ulrich, R. (1994). Self-mutilation and suicidal behavior in borderline personality disorder. *Journal of Personality Disorders, 8,* 257–267.

Sonneborn, C. K., & Vanstraelen, P. M. (1992). A retrospective study of self-inflicted burns. *General Hospital Psychiatry, 14,* 404–407.

Suyemoto, K. L. (1998). The functions of self-mutilation. *Clinical Psychology Review, 18,* 531–554.

Suyemoto, K. L., & MacDonald, M. L. (1995). Self-cutting in female adolescents. *Psychotherapy, 32,* 162–171.

Taiminen, T. J., Kallio-Soulainen, K., Nokso-Koivisto, H., Kaljonen, S., & Helenius, H. (1998). Contagion of deliberate self-harm among adolescent inpatients. *Journal of the American Academy of Child and Adolescent Psychiatry, 37,* 211–217.

van der Sande, R., Buskens, E., Allart, E., van der Graf, Y., & van Engeland, H. (1997). Psychosocial intervention following suicide attempt: A systematic review of treatment interventions. *Acta Psychiatrica Scandinavica, 96,* 43–50.

Walsh, B. W., & Rosen, P. (1985). Self-mutilation and contagion: An empirical test. *American Journal of Psychiatry, 142,* 119–120.

Walsh, B. W., & Rosen, P. M. (1988). *Self-mutilation: Theory, research, and treatment.* New York: Guilford Press.

White, V. E., Trepal-Wollenzier, H., & Nolan, J. (2002). College students and self-injury: Intervention strategies for counselors. *Journal of College Counseling, 5,* 105–113.

Yarura-Tobias, J. A., Neziroglu, F. A., & Kaplan, S. (1995). Self-mutilation, anorexia, and dysmenorrhea in obsessive compulsive disorder. *International Journal of Eating Disorders, 17,* 33–38.

Index

Alcohol Use Disorders Identification Test (AUDIT), 160–61
Alfred, W. G., 210
Allen, C., 302–3
American Academy of Obstetricians and Gynecologists, 118
American Association of Community Colleges, 3
American Counseling Association (ACA)
  Code of Ethics, 25, 27, 148, 150, 151
  Internet use standards for deaf persons, 244
  and religious and spiritual issues, 44
American Federation for the Blind, 227
American Psychiatric Association, 40
American Psychological Association (APA)
  ethical principles and student athletes, 25, 27
  Health Care for the Whole Person Task Force, 255–56
  Internet use standards for deaf persons, 244
  and religious/spiritual issues, 44, 45
American Sign Language (ASL), 233–34, 235, 236, 237, 241
Americans With Disabilities Act of 1990, 204, 205, 234, 242, 256, 260, 262, 265, 293
Ancis, J. R., 53, 55
anger
  medical illness and, 249
  students with military backgrounds and, 15–16
anxiety, medical illness and, 250
anxiety management therapy (AMT), for sexual assault victim, 135–36
Applied Sport Psychology: Personal Growth to Peak Performance (Williams), 25
Archer, J., 289
Arkin, R. M., 179
Armsworth, M. W., 133
Asperger, Hans, 273
Asperger's syndrome. See autism and Asperger's syndrome
assessment for problem drinkers, 159–60, 162
  intake screening questions, 160
  screening and assessment instruments, 160–61
Association for the Advancement of Applied Sport Psychology, 33

Association of Spiritual, Ethical, and Religious Values in Counseling, 38, 41
athletic injuries, students recovering from, 23
athletics. See student athletes
autism and Asperger's syndrome, 273–74
  assessment issues, 274–78
  campus considerations, 282–83
  clinical interview, 275–78
  counseling implications, 278–82
  creating scholarly interest groups, 281
  developing a treatment plan, 278–82
  establishing intermediated social contact, 281–82
  future trends, 283–84
  psychometric assessment, 275
  teaching practical skills, 280–81
Autism Quotient (AQ), 275

B

Balk, D. E., 196
Baron-Cohen, S., 275, 276
battering, 117
Bechhofer, L., 121
Beck Depression Inventory, 92
Beecher, M. E., 213
Beidel, D. C., 8–9
Bennett, J. M., 68
Bennett, M. J., 65, 70
bereavement. See grieving students, counseling
Berenson, A. B., 122
Bergin, J. J., 269
Bergin, J. W., 269
Berkel, L. A., 101, 121
Berry, J. W., 16
binocular vision, 219
blindness. See visually impaired or blind students
Bockting, W. O., 52
Boschen, K., 214
Bramel, M., 261
Brandon Teena Story, The (film), 51
Brevard Center, 283
Brewer, B. W., 25
brief interventions
  for adult learners, 104–5
  for drinking problems, 167
  for psychiatric disorders, 289

Briere, J., 298
Brinckerhoff, L., 265
Brown, K. S., 293–94
Brown, W. E., 166
Browne, F., 187
Bryant, R. A., 134–35
Bullis, R. K., 42
Burkhart, B. R., 132–33
Burnett, J. W., 133

CAGE (alcohol screening test), 160–61
Calderon, K. S., 176
California State University, Northridge, 242
cataracts, 219
Center for Working-Class Studies, Youngstown State University, 96–97
Centers for Disease Control and Prevention (CDC), 120
central vision, 219
Centre for Addiction and Mental Health, Ontario, 252
Chickering, A. W., 79–80
Christ, C. P., 42
Christopher, R., 96
chronic medical conditions, 247
    assessment issues, 247–48
    attitudes toward medically ill clients, 250
    biopsychosocial perspective, 253–54
    campus considerations, 254–55
    cognitive-behavioral therapy, 251–53
    counseling implications, 248–50
    future trends, 255–56
    psychodynamic approaches, 254
    therapeutic interventions, 250–54
Clubley, E., 275
cognitive-behavior therapy counseling
    for adult learners, 103–4
    for chronic medical conditions, 251–53
    for self-injurious behavior, 301–2
    for sexual assault victims, 134–35, 136
cognitive processing therapy (CPT), 136
cognitive restructuring, 136
College of the Overwhelmed: The Campus Mental Health Crisis and What You Can Do About It (Kadison and DiGeronimo), 291–92

color vision, 219
combat-related PTSD, 8–9
comic strip conversations, 280
Committee on Sexual Problems of the Disabled and the Sex and Disability Project, 212
competitive grief, 195
complicated mourning, 191
confidentiality
    deaf students and, 241
    student athletes and, 27–28
Constantine, M. G., 49
contrast sensitivity, 219
Cook, D. A., 42
Corbin, W., 166
Corn, A. L., 220–21, 226
Cottrell, A. B., 72, 73
Coulter, L. P., 173, 181
Council for Accreditation of Counseling and Related Educational Programs (CACREP), 45
courtship violence, 117
cultural competence counseling, 107–9
cultural identity
    audiological hearing loss and, 231–32
    cultural identity development, 65
culture
    adult learners and cultural customs, 109
    culturally specific behaviors for deaf persons, 235–36
culture shock, and reentry culture shock, 65–68, 72

D

Darwin, Charles, 40
dating violence. See relationship violence
deaf students, counseling, 231
    accommodations, 242–43
    American Sign Language, 233–34
    assessment issues, 236–39
    audiological condition and cultural identity, 231–32
    campus considerations, 241–43
    communication abilities and preferences, 233–36
    confidentiality, 241
    considerations for the clinician, 236–37
    counseling implications, 239–41
    culturally specific behaviors, 235–36

G

Gallaudet University, 238–39, 241–42, 244
gay and lesbian students
"safe zone" for, 44
student athletes, 23
gay, lesbian, and transgender (GLBT) students, 52–53, 55
gender-based counseling, 106–7
gender dysphoria, 50
gender identity. *See* transgender students, counseling
gender role egalitarianism, violence against women and, 121
Geren, P. R., 184
Gestalt empty chair technique, 42
Gibbon, J., 261
Gil, E., 298
Gilbert, S. P., 287, 290
glaucoma, 219–20
Gordon, M., 205
Gould, D., 25
Granfield, R., 94
Graves, W. H., 224–25
Gregory, E., 100
grieving students, counseling, 187–88
assessment issues, 188–91
campus considerations, 195–97
complicated and traumatic grief, 191
counseling implications, 191–95
education and training, 197
establishing rapport, 191–93
facilitating loss adaptations, 193–95
future trends, 197–98
grieving behaviors, 190–91
the grieving process, 188–90
insomnia, 190–91
intervention tools, 194
loss history, 189–90
student advocacy, 195–96
support groups, 194–95
understanding grieving time lines, 192–93
Grohol, J., 110
group therapy, for relationship violence, 123
groups, support, 101–2, 107
bereavement, 194–95
guilt, medical illness and, 249
Gulf War syndrome, 10
Gullahorn, J. E., 66, 67
Gullahorn, J. T., 66, 67

H

Hadley, S. M., 123
Hahn, H., 224, 225
Hahn, Thich Nhat, 42
Handbook of Sport Psychology (Singer, Hausenblas, and Janelle), 25
Hanebrink, S., 267
Hardison, H. G., 190–91
harm
mandated students and risk of harm to others, 147–48
problem drinkers and harm reduction, 162–63
Harrison, S., 266
Harry Benjamin International Gender Dysphoria Association, 51–52
Hatzes, N., 261
Hausenblas, H., 25
Hayes, R. L., 206–7
Heflin, A. H., 133
Henderson, C., 260–61
Hershenson, D. B., 151
Hertel, J. B., 96
Hey, W., 176
Hicks-Coolick, A., 268
hidden disability, 260
high-functioning autism. *See* autism and Asperger's syndrome
Hogan, N. S., 197–98
homophobia, 23
Hotaling, G. T., 118, 120
House of Representatives Subcommittee on Education, Training, Employment and Housing on Veterans' Affairs, U.S., 3
Howard, D. E., 118–19
Howlin, P., 274
Humphrey, J. A., 129
Husman, J., 174

I

identity issues
deaf students and identity development, 239–40
gender-based counseling, 106–7
military service and loss of identity, 13–14
in multicultural counseling, 108
for multiracial students, 80–84
third-culture students and, 65

working-class students. *See* first-
generation students, counseling
World Health Organization (WHO), 161
World War I, 8, 17
World War II, 8, 17
Wright, K., 50

Young, M. E., 210
Yuan, F., 265

Zamarripa, M., 100
Zody, Z. B., 176–77